Dwellings of the Philosophers

AND HERMETIC SYMBOLISM IN RELATIONSHIP WITH
SACRED ART AND THE ESOTERISM OF GRAND WORK

VOLUMES ONE AND TWO

Fulcanelli

Rouen – Mansion of Bourgtheroulde (16th Century)
Salamander in frontispiece

Dwellings of the Philosophers

© and translation 2018-2021 by Daniel Bernardo

2021 EDITION

SOJOURNER BOOKS
https://sojournerbooks.com

Translated from:
Les Demeures Philosophales -1929/30

ISBN: 978-0-9916709-9-4

Table of Contents

SECOND VOLUME

Preface

This is the second and last book written by the mysterious Fulcanelli, published in 1929-30 in France, as two volumes in a short-run edition. This translation follows faithfully that edition.[1]

It is believed that Fulcanelli was able to discover the philosopher's stone shortly before 1930, and it is thought that this discovery had much to do with his disappearance.

Although many speculate that Fulcanelli may have been the artist Julien Champagne, or Eugene Canseliet (who wrote several introductions to Dwellings of the Philosophers), no one knows for sure who Fulcanelli was.

Dwellings of the Philosophers is a fundamental work for alchemy scholars. It is a general treatise on alchemy, enriched by many explanations and comments on the main traditional authors texts. Also, analyzing the hermetic symbolism applied to civil constructions, Fulcanelli sheds light on many alchemical riddles.

This book analyses in depth the architectural elements and motifs of different buildings, from a modest house built in the 16th century in Lisieux (a small Norman town), the Dampierre Castle, the Holyrood Palace in Edinburgh, and several other chosen examples.

Fulcanelli clearly explains, at the beginning of his work (in History and Monument), that carvings and statues offer a truer message than the always distorted written accounts. He said: "It will therefore be explained why we prefer to see the Middle Ages, as the Gothic buildings reveal to us, rather than believing the description of historians".

Likewise, Fulcanelli offers much information about the operations and procedures of the alchemical work, analyzing and unveiling the allegories used by many writers of hermetic art to veil the knowledge from those who are not deserving of it.

---

1   The introduction written by Eugene Canseliet is excluded from this edition, because, although the text of Fulcanelli is in the Public Domain, the introductions is not.

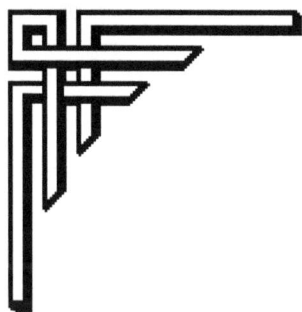

FIRST
VOLUME

Book I

I

History and Monument

Paradoxical in its manifestations, disconcerting in its signs, the Middle Ages offers to the sagacity of its admirers the resolution of a singular contradiction. How to reconcile the irreconcilable? How to harmonize the testimony of historical facts with that of medieval art works?

The chroniclers portray this unhappy epoch in the darkest colors. These are, for several centuries, only invasions, wars, famines, epidemics. And yet the monuments –faithful and sincere witnesses of these nebulous times– bear no trace of such scourges. On the contrary, they seem to have been built in the enthusiasm of a powerful inspiration of ideal and faith, by a people happy to live, in a flourishing and highly organized society.

Must we doubt the veracity of the historical narratives, the authenticity of the events they report and believe, with the wisdom of the nations, that happy people have no history? Unless, without completely refuting the entire history, we prefer to discover, in a relative absence of incidents, the justification of medieval obscurity.

Anyway, what remains undeniable is that all the Gothic buildings without exception reflect a serenity, an expansiveness, an unparalleled nobility. If we examine closely the expression of statuary in particular, we will quickly be edified by the peaceful character, the pure tranquility that emanates from these figures. All are calm and smiling, pleasant and good-natured. Lapidary humanity, silent and good company. Women are overweight, which indicates, in their models, the excellence of a rich and substantial diet. The children are chubby, full, happy. Priests, deacons, Capuchins, brother suppliers, clerics and singers sport a jovial face or the pleasing silhouette of their bellied dignity. Their interpreters –these wonderful and modest image cutters–, do not deceive us and cannot be wrong. They take their types from everyday life, among the people who are move around them and in the midst of which they live themselves. Many of these figures, picked at random from the alley, from the tavern or school, from the sacristy or from the studio, are perhaps altogether marked or overdone, but in the picturesque note, with the concern of character, cheerful sense, broad form. Grotesque, if you like, but joyfully grotesque and full of teaching. Satires of people who love to laugh, drink, sing and enjoy life. Masterpieces of a realistic school, deeply human and confident of its mastery, conscious of its means, ignoring however what is pain, misery, oppression or slavery. This is so true, that you may have a good search, interrogate the ogival statues, you will never discover a figure of Christ whose expression reveals real suffering. You will recognize with us that the *latomi*[1] gave themselves enormous trouble to endow their crucified with a serious physiognomy without always succeeding. The best, scarcely emaciated, have closed eyelids and seem to rest. On our cathedrals, the scenes of the last Judgment show demons grimacing, counterfeit, monstrous, more comical than terrible; as for the damned, cursed anesthetized, they cook slowly, in their pot, without useless regret or real pain.

These free, virile and healthy images prove to the point that the artists of the Middle Ages did not know the depressing spectacle of human miseries. If the people had suffered, if the masses had groaned in misfortune, the monuments would have remembered them. Now, we know that art, that superior expression of civilized humanity, can develop freely only in favor of a stable and secure peace. Like science, art can not exert its genius in the atmosphere of troubled societies. All the high manifestations of human thought are there; revolutions, wars, upheavals are fatal to them. They demand the security of order and concord, in order to grow, to flourish and to grow. For such strong reasons we are bound to accept only with circumspection the medieval events reported by history. And we confess that the affirmation of a "series of calamities, disasters, ruins accumulated during one hundred and forty-six years" seems really excessive. This is an inexplicable anomaly, since it is precisely during this unfortunate Hundred Years War, which extends from the year 1337 to the year 1453, that the richest buildings of our flamboyant style were built. It is the culminating point, the culmination of form and boldness, the marvelous phase in which the spirit, divine flame, imposes its signature on the latest creations of Gothic thought. It is the time of completion of the great basilicas; but we also raise other important monuments, collegiate or abbey, religious architecture: the abbeys of Solesmes, Cluny, Saint-Riquier, the Chartreuse of Dijon, Saint-Wulfran d'Abbeville, Saint-Etienne de Beauvais, etc. From the Hospice de Beaune to the Palais de Justice in Rouen and the Compiègne Town Hall, remarkable civil buildings emerge from the ground; from the hotels built everywhere by Jacques Coeur, to the belfries of the free cities, Bethune, Douai, Dunkerque, etc. In our big cities, the narrow streets dig their narrow beds under the conglomeration of corbelled gables, turrets and balconies, houses of carved wood, houses of stone with delicately decorated facades. And everywhere, under the guaranty of corporations, trades are developing; everywhere the companions compete with skill; everywhere emulation multiplies masterpieces. The University trains brilliant students, and his fame extends over the old world; famous doctors and illustrious scholars spread and propagate the benefits of science and philosophy; the Spagyrists amass, in the silence of the laboratory, the materials which will later serve as a basis for our chemistry; great Adepts give the hermetic truth a new impetus ... What ardor spread in all branches of human activity! And what richness, what fertility, what powerful faith, what confidence in the future is reflected in this desire to build, to create, to seek and discover in the middle of an invasion, in this miserable country of France subjected to foreign domination, and knowing all the horrors of an interminable war!

In truth, we do not understand ...

It will therefore be explained why we prefer to see the Middle Ages, as the Gothic buildings reveal to us, rather than believing the description of historians.

---

1   Stonemason.

It is easy to fabricate texts and documents, old charters with hot patinas, parchments and seals of archaic appearance, even some sumptuous book of hours, annotated in its margins, beautifully illuminated padlocks, borders and miniatures. Montmartre delivers to whoever desires it, and according to the offered price, the unknown Rembrandt or the authentic Teniers. A skilful craftsman of the district of the Halles fashion, with a verve, a dizzying mastery, of small Egyptian divinities of gold and massive bronze, marvels of imitation that are disputed by some antique dealers. Who does not remember the infamous Tiara of Saïtaphernès ... Falsification, counterfeiting are as old as the world, and history, having horror of the chronological void, sometimes had to call them to its aid. A very learned Jesuit of the seventeenth century, Father Jean Hardouin did not hesitate to denounce as apocryphal a number of Greek and Roman coins and medals, minted during the Renaissance period, buried in order to "fill" large historical gaps. Anatole de Montaiglon tells us that Jacques de Bie published, in 1639, a folio volume with plates and entitled: *The Families of France*, illustrated by the monuments of ancient and modern medals, "which", he says, "contains more invented medals than real".[2] Let us agree that, in order to provide History with the documentation it lacked, Jacques de Bie used a faster and cheaper method, which was denounced by Father Hardouin. Victor Hugo, citing the four Histoires de France the most famous around 1830, –those of Dupleix, Mézeray, Vély and father Daniel–, said that the author, "Jesuit famous for his descriptions of battles, has made in twenty years a story which has no other merit than erudition, and in which the Count de Boulainvilliers found scarcely ten thousand errors"[3]. It is known that Caligula erected in the year 40, near Boulogne-sur-Mer, the tower of Odre "to deceive the future generations on an alleged raid of Caligula in Great Britain".[4] Converted into a lighthouse (*turris ardens*) by one of his successors, the Tower of Odre collapsed in 1645.

Which historian will furnish us with the reason –superficial or profound– invoked by the sovereigns of England to justify the quality and the title of kings of France which they preserved until the eighteenth century? And yet, the English currency of this period still bears the imprint of such pretense.[5]

Formerly, on the school benches, we were taught that the first French king was named Pharamond, and the year 420 was set as the date of his accession. Today, the royal genealogy begins at Clodion the Hairy, because it was recognized that his father, Pharamond, had never reigned. But, in those distant times of the fifth century, are we certain of the authenticity of the documents relating to the acts and actions of Clodion? Will not these be challenged someday, before being relegated to the realm of legends and fables?

---

2   Anatole de Montaiglon. Preface by the *Curiosites of Paris*, reprinted from the original edition of 1716. Paris, 1883.

3   Victor Hugo, *Littérature et Philosophie mêlées* (Literature and Philosophy mingled). Paris, Furne, 1841, p. 31.

4   Anthyme Saint-Paul.

5   According to English historians, the kings of England bore the title of kings of France until 1453. Perhaps they sought to justify it by the possession of Calais, which they lost in 1558. They continued however until to the Revolution to claim the quality of French sovereigns. Jusserand says of Henry VIII, appointed Defender of the Faith by Pope Leo XI, in 1521, that "This voluntary and unscrupulous prince felt that what was good to take was good to keep; it was a reasoning he had applied to the kingdom of England himself, and as a result of which he had dispossessed, imprisoned and killed his cousin Richard VI". All English monarchs practiced this principle, because all professed the selfish axiom: *What I like, I keep it,* and act accordingly.

For Huysmans, History is "the most solemn of lies and the most childlike of lures...". "Events," he says, "are, for a talented man, only a springboard of ideas and style, since all are becoming divided or aggravated, according to the needs of a cause, or according to the temperament of the writer who handles them. As for the documents that support them, it's worse, because none of them are irreducible, and all are revisable. If they are not apocryphal, others, no less certain, unearth themselves later who oppose them, until they themselves are demonetized by the exhumation of no less secure archives".[6]

The tombs of historical figures are also sources of controversial information. We have seen it more than once.[7] The inhabitants of Bergamo experienced, in 1922, such an unpleasant surprise. Could they believe that their local celebrity, this fiery condottiere Bartholomeo Coleoni who filled, in the fifteenth century, the Italian annals of his bellicose whims, was only a legendary shadow? Now, on a doubt of the king, visiting Bergamo, the municipality moved the mausoleum adorned with the famous equestrian statue, to open the tomb, and all the assistants noticed with amazement that it was empty ... In France, at least, one does not push offhandedness so far. Authentic or not, our burials contain bones. Amédée de Ponthieu recounts that the sarcophagus of François Myron, Parisian architect of 1604, was found during the demolitions of the house bearing the number 13 of the rue d'Arcole, building erected on the foundations of the Sainte-Marine church, in which he had been buried. "The lead coffin," writes the author, "has the shape of a compressed ellipse ... The epitaph was erased. When we lifted the lid of the coffin, we only found a skeleton surrounded by a blackish soot, mixed with dust ... A singular thing, we did not discover the insignia of its charge, neither his sword, his ring, etc., nor even traces of his coat of arms ... However, the commission of the Beaux-Arts, by the mouths of its experts, declared that it was indeed the great Parisian lord, and these illustrious relics were descended into the vaults of Notre-Dame".[8] A testimony of similar value is reported by Fernand Bournon in his book Paris-Atlas. "We will only speak for the sake of remembrance," he says, "of the house on the flower quay, where it bears the numbers 9-11, and that an inscription, without the shadow of authenticity or even verisimilitude, indicates like the old habitation of Heloise and Abelard in 1118, rebuilt in 1849. Such statements engraved on marble are a challenge to common sense". Let us hasten to recognize that, in his historical deformations, Father Loriquet displays much less boldness!

Let us here allow ourselves a digression intended to clarify and define our thought. It is a very tenacious prejudice which, for a long time, attributed the paternity of the wheelbarrow to the scientist Pascal. And although the falsity of this attribution has now been demonstrated, the fact remains that the great majority of the people persist in believing it to be well founded. Ask a schoolboy, he will answer you that this practical vehicle, known to all, owes its design to the illustrious physicist. Among the mischievous, boisterous and often distracted from the small world of education, it is above all to this realization claimed that Pascal's name is a must for young people intelligence. Many primaries, indeed, ignorant of what were Descartes, Michelangelo, Denis Papin or Torricelli, will not hesitate for a second about Pascal. It would

---

6   JK Huysmans, *Là-bas* (Over there). Paris, Plon, 1891. ch. II.

7   That lovers of historical memories will take the trouble, for their edification, to claim at the town hall of Dourdan (Seine-et-Oise) an extract of the register of civil status, with indication of the folio, the act of death of Rustam-Pasha (Roustan), Mameluck of Napoleon I. Roustan died at Dourdan in 1845, aged fifty-five.

8   Amédée de Ponthieu, *Légendes du Vieux-Paris* (Legends of Old Paris), Paris, Bachelin-Deflorenne, 1867.

be interesting to know why our children, between so many admirable discoveries whose daily application they have before their eyes, know rather Pascal and his wheelbarrow, than the men of genius to whom we owe the steam, the electric battery, the beet sugar, and the stearic candle. Is it because the wheelbarrow touches them more closely, interests them more, is more familiar to them? Perhaps. Be that as it may, the vulgar error propagated by the elementary history books could easily be unmasked: it was enough to flip through a few illuminated manuscripts of the thirteenth and fourteenth centuries, several of which represent medieval farmers using the wheelbarrow.[9] And even, without undertaking such delicate research, a glance at the monuments would have made it possible to restore the truth. Among the motifs decorating an archivolt of the north porch of the cathedral of Beauvais, for example, a rustic old fifteenth century is represented pushing its wheelbarrow, a wheelbarrow model similar to those we currently use (Plate I).

BEAUVAIS - Saint-Pierre Cathedral
Archivolte du Porche Nord - The man pushing a wheelbarrow - Plate I

---

9   Cf. National Library, mss. 2090, 2091 and 2092, French collection. These three volumes origi-nally formed a single work, which was offered in 1317 to King Philip the Long by Gilles de Pontoise, Abbot of Saint-Denis. These illuminations and miniatures are reproduced in black in the work of Henry Martin, entitled *Légende de Saint-Denis* (Legend of Saint-Denis). Paris, Champion, 1908.

The same utensil can also be seen on agricultural scenes forming the subject of two carved misericords, from the stalls of Saint-Lucien Abbey, near Beauvais (1492-1500).[10] Moreover, if the truth forces us to deny Pascal the benefit of a very old invention, several centuries before his birth, it cannot diminish in any way the greatness and power of his genius. The immortal author of *Thoughts*, the calculation of probabilities, the inventor of the hydraulic press, the calculating machine, etc., forces our admiration with superior works and discoveries of a scope other than that of the wheelbarrow. But what is important to identify, what matters only to us, is that, in the search for the truth, it is better to call upon the edifice rather than historical documents, sometimes incomplete, often biased, almost always subject to questioning.

It is to a parallel conclusion reached by Andre Geiger, when, struck by the inexplicable homage rendered by Hadrian to the statue of Nero, he does justice to the unjust accusations made against this emperor and against Tiberius. Like us, he refuses any claim to historical reports, falsified by design, concerning these so-called human monsters, and does not hesitate to write: "I rely more on monuments and logic than on stories".

If, as we have said, the rigging of a text, the writing of a column requires only a little skill and know-how, on the other hand it is impossible to build a cathedral. Let us therefore address the buildings, they will provide us with more serious, better indications. There, at least, we will see our characters "depicting alive", fixed on the stone or on the wood, with their real physiognomy, their dress and their gestures, whether they appear in sacred scenes or compose profane subjects. We will contact them and will soon love them. Sometimes we will question the harvester of the thirteenth century, who sharpens his scythe at the gate of Paris, sometimes the apothecary of the fifteenth, who, in the stalls of Amiens, pounding no one knows what drugs in his wooden mortar. His neighbor, the drunkard with a flowery nose, is not unknown to us; we remembers having met this happy drunkard several times, at the chance of our peregrinations. Would it not be our man who cried, in full "Mystery", before the spectacle of the miracle of Jesus at the Marriage of Cana:

"If I could do what he does,
All the Sea of Galilee
Will be converted [today] into wine;
And never would earth have
A drop of water, nothing would rain
From the sky but wine".

And this beggar, escaped from the Court of Miracles, with no other stigma of distress than his rags and his lice, we also recognize him. It is the one whom the Companions of the Passion introduce at the feet of Christ, and who, pitifully, recites this soliloquy:

"I look at my rags
To see if any money's been thrown in there;
I have heard of you: give it to him!
There is not a penny, not even half of it....
A poor man has no friends.

In spite of all that has been written, we must, whether we like it or not, accustom ourselves to the truth that at the beginning of the Middle Ages society was already rising to

---

10 These stalls, kept at the Cluny Museum, are marked B. 399 and B. 414.

the highest degree of civilization and splendor. John of Salisbury, who visited Paris in 1176, expresses on this subject, in his *Polycration*, the most sincere enthusiasm. "When I saw," said he, "the abundance of subsistence, the gayety of the people, the good behavior of the clergy, the majesty and glory of the whole Church, the various occupations of men admitted to the study of philosophy it seemed to me to see that ladder of Jacob, whose ridge reached the sky and where the angels ascended and descended. I was forced to admit that truly, the Lord was in this place and I did not know it. This passage of a poet also came back to my mind: 'Blessed is he to whom this place is assigned for exile!'."[11]

---

11 Parisius cum viderem victualium copiam, lætitiam populi, reverentiam cleri, et totus ecclesiæ majestatem et gloriam, et variam occupationes philosophantium, admiratus velut illam scalam Jacob, cujus summitas cœlum tangebat, eratque via ascendentium et descendentium angelorum, coactus sum profiteri quod sere Dominus est in loco ipso, et ego nesciebam. Illud quoque poeticum ad mentem rediit : felix exilium cui locus iste datur!

II

Middle Age and Renaissance

No one is arguing today, about the high value of medieval works. But who will ever be able to explain the strange scorn of which they were victims until the nineteenth century? Who will tell us why, since the Renaissance, the elite of artists, scholars and thinkers made it a point of honor to affect the utmost indifference to the bold creations of a misunderstood era, so original and magnificently expressive of French genius? What could be the profound cause of the change of opinion, then of banishment, of exclusion, which weighed so long on Gothic art? Should we incriminate ignorance, caprice, the perversion of taste? We do not know. A French writer, Charles de Remusat, thinks he found the first reason for this unjust disdain in the absence of literature, which does not leave to surprise. "The Renaissance," he assures us, "despised the Middle Ages, because true French literature, that which succeeded it, has effaced the last traces of it. And yet medieval France offers a striking spectacle. His genius was remarkable and severe. It took pleasure in serious meditations, in deep research; it exposed, in a language without grace and without brilliance, sublime truths and subtle hypotheses. It produced a singularly philosophical literature. No doubt this literature has exercised the human spirit more than it has served it. In vain have men of the first order successively illustrated it; for the modern generations, their works are considered null and void. They had the wit and ideas, but not the talent to speak well in a language that was not borrowed. Scott Érigène recalls in certain moments Plato; Philosophic liberty has scarcely been carried beyond him, and he boldly rises in this region of the clouds where the truth shines only by lightning; he thought for himself in the ninth century. Saint Anselm is an original metaphysician whose scholarly idealism regenerates vulgar beliefs, and he conceived and realized the audacious thought of directly reaching the notion of divinity. It is the theologian of pure reason. Saint Bernard is sometimes brilliant and ingenious, sometimes grave and pathetic. Mystical like Fenelon, he resembles an active and popular Bossuet, who dominates the century by the word and commands kings instead of praising and serving them. His sad rival, his noble victim, Abelard, In the exhibition of dialectical science, an unknown rigor and a relative lucidity, which testify a nervous and flexible mind, made to understand everything and to explain everything. It is a great propagator of ideas. Heloise has forced a dry and pedantic tongue to render the delicacies of an elite intelligence, the sorrows of the most proud and most tender soul, the transports of a desperate passion. John of Salisbury is a clairvoyant critic to whom the human mind makes spectacle and who describes it in its progress, in its movements, in its returns, with premature truth and impartiality. He seems to have guessed this talent of our time, this art of putting intellectual society before you to judge it ... Saint Thomas, embracing at once all the philosophy of his time, has at times preceded that of ours; he has bound all human science in a perpetual syllogism and has rethought it all through continuous reasoning, thus realizing the union of a vast mind and a logical mind. Gerson, finally, Gerson, a theologian whom sentiment disputes with deduction, who understood and neglected philosophy, knew how to submit reason without humiliating it, to captivate hearts without offending the spirits, finally to imitate the God who is made to believe in himself, making love. All these men, and I do not name all their equals, were great and their works admirable. To be admired, to preserve a constant influence on posterior literature, what did they miss? It is neither science, nor thought, nor genius; I'm afraid it's just one thing, the style.

"French literature does not come from them. It does not claim its authority, it does not adorn itself with their names; she has done nothing but erase them".[1]

From which we can conclude that, if the Middle Ages shared the spirit, the Renaissance took pleasure in imprisoning us in the letter ...

What Charles de Remusat says is very judicious, at least as far as the first medieval period, the period when intellectuality appears subject to Byzantine influence, and still imbued with Romanesque doctrines. A century later, the same reasoning loses much of its value; For example, one cannot dispute that the works in the epic of the Round Table have a certain charm that cannot be detached from an already more refined style. Thibaut, Count of Champagne, in his Songs of the King of Navarre, Guillaume de Lorris and Jehan Clopinel, authors of the Roman de la Rose, all our troubadours and troubadours of the thirteenth and fourteenth centuries, without having the proud genius of the philosophical scholars, their ancestors, know how to use their language well and often express themselves with the grace and suppleness which characterize the literature of our days.

We do not see why the Renaissance judged harshly the Middle Ages and took note of its alleged literary deficiency to proscribe and reject it to the chaos of nascent civilizations, barely out of barbarism.

As for us, we believe that medieval thought reveals itself as being of scientific essence and of no other. Art and literature are for her only the humble servants of traditional science. Their express mission is to symbolically translate the truths that the Middle Ages received from antiquity and of which it remained the faithful depositary. Subject to the purely allegorical expression, held under the imperative will of the same parable which subtracts from the layman the Christian mystery, art and literature show an obvious discomfort and display some stiffness; but the strength and simplicity of their execution still contribute to endow them with an unquestionable originality. Admittedly, the observer will never find the image of Christ, as portrayed by the Romans, where Jesus, in the center of the mystical almond, appears surrounded by the four evangelical animals. It is enough for us that his divinity is underlined by his own emblems and thus announces itself revealing of a secret teaching. We admire the Gothic masterpieces for their nobility and the boldness of their expression; if they do not have the delicate perfection of form, they possess in the highest degree the initiatory power of a learned and transcendent philosophy. They are serious and austere productions, not of light

---

1   Charles de Remusat, *Critiques et Études littéraires* (Critics and Literary Studies).

motives, graceful, pleasing, like those which art, from the Renaissance, was pleased to lavish upon us. But while the latter aspire only to flatter the eye or charm the senses, the artistic and literary works of the Middle Ages are supported by a superior, real and concrete thought, the cornerstone of an immutable science, indestructible base of Religion. If we were to define these two tendencies, one deep, the other superficial, we would say that Gothic art is entirely in the learned majesty of its buildings and the Renaissance in the pleasant finery of its dwellings.

The medieval colossus did not collapse all at once in the decline of the fifteenth century. In many places his genius has long resisted the imposition of new directives. We see the agony extend to the middle of the next century and find, in some buildings of this time, the philosophical impulse, the depth of wisdom that generated, for three centuries, so many imperishable works. Also, without taking into account their more recent edification, we will stop on these works of less importance, but of similar meaning, with the hope of recognizing the secret idea, symbolically expressed, of their authors.

It is these refuges of ancient esotericism, these asylums of traditional science, which have become extremely rare today, that, without taking into account their allocation or their usefulness, we classify in hermetic iconology, among the artistic guardians of the high philosophical truths.

Do we want an example? Here is the beautiful tympanum[2] which decorated, in the distant twelfth century, the entrance door of an old Reims house (Plate II).

REIMS - LAPIDAIRE MUSEUM
Tympanum of a 12th century house - Plate II

---

2 This tympanum is preserved in the Lapidary Museum of Reims, established in the premises of the civil hospital (former abbey of St. Remi, Simon Street). It was discovered around 1857, during the construction of the prison, in the foundations of the house known as the Christianity of Reims, located on the Place du Parvis, and bearing the inscription: Fides, Spes, Caritas. This house belonged to the chapter.

The subject, which is very transparent, would be easy to describe. Under a large archway, inscribing two other twin arcades, a teacher instruct his disciple and points to him, on the pages of an open book, the passage he comments. Below, a young and vigorous athlete strangles a monstrous animal, perhaps a dragon, of which only its head and neck are visible. He stands next to two young people tightly entwined. Science thus appears as the dominator of Force and Love, opposing the superiority of the spirit to the physical manifestations of power and feeling.

How can one admit that a construction signed by such a thought has not belonged to some unknown philosopher? Why should we refuse to this bas-relief the credit of a symbolic conception emanating from a cultivated brain, from an educated man asserting his taste for study and preaching the example? We would be certainly mistaken, to exclude this dwelling, with its characteristic frontispiece, from the number of emblematic works which we propose to study under the general title of *Dwellings of the Philosophers*.

III
Medieval Alchemy

Of all the sciences cultivated in the Middle Ages, certainly none was more fashionable and was as highly regarded as alchemical science. This is the name under which the Arabs hid the sacred or sacerdotal Art they had inherited from the Egyptians and which the medieval West was to welcome later with so much enthusiasm.

Many controversies have arisen over the various etymologies attributed to the word alchemy. Pierre-Jean Fabre, in his *Abrégé des Secrets chymiques*[1] recalls the name of Cham, son of Noah, who would have been the first alchemical artisan, and he writes it as *alchamie*. The anonymous author of a curious manuscript thinks that "the word alchemy is derived from *als*, which means salt in Greek, and from *chymie*, which means fusion; and so it is well said, because the salt which is so admirable is usurped".[2] But if salt is said to be ἅλς in the Greek language, χειμεία, put for χυμεία, alchemy, has no other meaning than that of the juice or secretion. Others discover its origin in the first denomination of the land of Egypt, homeland of Sacred Art, Kymie or Chemi. Napoleon Landais notes no difference between the two words *chemistry* and *alchemy*; he only adds that the prefix *al* can not be confused with the Arabic article and simply means a wonderful virtue. Those who support the opposite thesis by using the article *al* and the substantive *chemistry*, intend to designate the chemistry par excellence or hyperchemistry of modern occultists. If we were to bring into this debate our personal opinion, we would say that the phonetic cabal recognizes a close relationship between the Greek words Χειμεία, Χυμεία and Χεῦμα, which indicates what flows, stream, run down, and especially marks the molten metal, the fusion itself, as well as any work made of molten metal. This would be a brief and succinct definition of alchemy as a metallurgical technique.[3] But we

---

1   Summary of Chemical Secrets.

2   *L'Interruption du Sommeil cabalistique ou le Dévoilement des Tableaux de l'Antiquité* (The Interruption of Cabalistic Sleep or the Unveiling of the Tables of Antiquity)... Mss. with figures of the eighteenth century, libr. Arsenal, No. 2520 (175 SAF). - National Library, former French collection, No. 670 (71235), 17th century. - Library Sainte-Geneviève, No. 2267, Treaty II, XVIIIth century.

3   Would this definition be better suited to *archimie* or *voarchadumie*, part of the science which teaches the transmutation of metals into each other, than to alchemy proper.

know, on the other hand, that the name and the thing are based on the permutation of form by light, fire or spirit; that is, at least, the true meaning indicated by the language of the Birds.

Born in the East, home of mystery and wonder, alchemical science has spread in the West by three great paths of penetration: Byzantine, Mediterranean and Hispanic. It was mainly the result of Arab conquests. This curious, studious people, eager for philosophy and culture, a civilizing people par excellence, form the hyphen, the chain that connects Eastern antiquity to the Western Middle Ages. It plays, in fact, in the history of human progress, a role comparable to that exercised by the Phoenician merchants between Egypt and Assyria. The Arabs, educators of the Greeks and Persians, transmitted to Europe the science of Egypt and Babylon, augmented by their own acquisitions, across the European continent (the Byzantine Road) and around the eighth century AD. On the other hand, the Arab influence exerted its action in our countries at the return of the expeditions of Palestine (Mediterranean Road), and it is the Crusaders of the twelfth century which imported most of the ancient knowledge. Finally, closer to us, at the dawn of the thirteenth century, new elements of civilization, science and art, from the eighth century of northern Africa, spread in Spain (Hispanic Road) and are increasing the first contributions of the Greco-Byzantine source of learning.

At first timid and hesitant, alchemy slowly wakes up and soon becomes stronger. It tends to impose itself, and in this way, this exotic science, transplanted into our soil, gets acclimated to it wonderfully, develops with so much vigor that we see it soon blossom into an exuberant flowering. Its extension, its progress are prodigious. It was barely cultivated, and only in the shadow of monastic cells, in the twelfth century; in the 14th century, it spread everywhere, radiating on all social classes where it shines most brightly. Each country offers to this mysterious science a nursery of fervent disciples, and every condition hastens to sacrifice it. Noblesse and high bourgeoisie do it. Scholars, monks, princes, prelates profess it; even tradesmen and small craftsmen, goldsmiths, gentlemen glassmakers, enamellers, apothecaries not feel the irresistible desire to handle the retorte. And if nobody professed it openly –the royal authority chases the puffers[4] and the popes fulminate against them–[5], no one failed to study it clandestinely. The company of philosophers, real or alleged, was avidly sought. Philosophers undertook long journeys, with the intention of increasing their baggage of knowledge, or they wrote between them, from country to country, from kingdom to kingdom encrypted messages. The manuscripts of the great Adepts, those of the Panapolitan Zozime, Ostanes, Synesius,were disputed; copies of Geber, Rhazes, Artephius. The books of Morien, of Mary the Prophetess, the fragments of Hermes were negotiated at high prices. The fever seized the intellectuals and, with the fraternities, the lodges, the initiatic centers, the puffers grew and multiplied. Few families escaped the pernicious attraction of the golden chimera; very few were those who do not count within their bosom some practicing alchemist, some hunter of the impossible. The imagination was given free rein. The *L'Auri sacra fames* ruined the noble, despaired the commoner, starved anyone who lets himself be caught and benefited only the charlatan. "Abbots, bishops, doctors, solitaries," wrote Lenglet-Dufresnoy, "all made an occupation of them; it was the madness of that time, and it is known that each century

---

4   Puffer is a derogative nickname for a pretended alchemist who is preoccupied with transmuting base metals into gold.

5   Cf. the bull *Spondent Pariter,* launched against the alchemists by Pope John XXII, in 1317, who, however, had written his very singular *Ars transmutatoria metallorum.*

has one of its own; but unfortunately it has prevailed longer than the others and is not even completely gone".[6]

With what passion, what spirit, what hopes, that cursed science envelops the Gothic cities, asleep under the stars! Subterranean and secret fermentation, which, at night, throngs the deep cellars with strange pulsations, exhales from the vents in intermittent flashes, rises in sulphurous volutes at the summit of the gables!

After the famous name of Artephius (around 1130), the fame of the masters who succeed him consecrates the hermetic reality and stimulates the ardor of the postulants to the Adeptate. In the thirteenth century, there was the illustrious English monk Roger Bacon, whom his followers nicknamed *Doctor admirabilis* (1214-1292), and whose enormous reputation became universal; in we found France Alain de l'Isle, doctor of Paris and monk of Cîteaux (died around 1298); Christophe le Parisien (around 1260) and master Arnaud de Villeneuve (1245-1310), while Thomas Aquinas –*Doctor angelicus*–, (1225) and the monk Ferrari (1280) shine in Italy.

The fourteenth century saw the emergence of a whole host of artists. Raymon Llull –Doctor illuminatus–, Spanish Franciscan monk (1235-1315); Jean Daustin, English philosopher; Jean Cremer, Abbot of Westminster; Richard, nicknamed Robert the Englishman, author of *Correctum alchymiae* (around 1330); the Italian Pierre Bon of Lombardy; the French Pope John XXII (1244-1317); William of Paris, instigator of the hermetic bas-reliefs of the porch of Notre-Dame, Jehan de Mehun, known as Clopinel, one of the authors of the *Roman de la Rose* (1280-1364); Grasseus, nicknamed Hortulanus, commentator of the of *Emerald Table* (1358); finally, the most famous and popular of the French philosophers, the alchemist Nicholas Flamel (1330-1417).

The fifteenth century marks the glorious period of science and surpasses previous ones, both in value and in the number of masters who have illustrated it. Among these, it is worth mentioning in the first row Basil Valentin, Benedictine monk of the Abbey of St. Peter, in Erfurth, electorate of Mainz (about 1413), perhaps the most important artist that the hermetic art has ever produced; his compatriot, the Abbe Tritheme; Isaac the Dutchman (1408); the two English Thomas Norton and Georges Ripley; Lambsprinck; Georges Aurach, of Strasbourg (1415); the Calabrian monk Lacini (1459), and the noble Bernard Trevisan (1406-1490), who spent fifty-six years of his life pursuing the Work, and whose name will remain in alchemical history as a symbol of obstinacy, constancy, irreducible perseverance.

From that moment, hermeticism falls into discredit. Even his partisans, embittered by the lack of success, turn against it. Attacked on all sides, his prestige disappears; enthusiasm decreases, opinion is modified. Practical operations, which had been collected, gathered and then revealed and taught, allow dissenters to support the alchemical nothingness thesis, to ruin philosophy by laying the foundations of our chemistry. Sethon, Vinceslas Lavinius of Moravia, Zachaire, Paracelsus are, in the sixteenth century, the only heirs known to Egyptian esotericism, which the Renaissance denied after corrupting it. Let us make, in passing, a supreme tribute to the ardent defender of the ancient truths that was Paracelsus; the great tribune deserves our eternal gratitude for his ultimate and courageous intervention. Although in vain, his work is nonetheless one of its highest titles to glory.

The hermetic art prolongs its agony until the seventeenth century and finally dies, not without having given to the Western world three large-scale offshoots: Lascaris, the President d'Espagnet and the mysterious Eyrenée Philalèthe, a living enigma of which one never could discover the true personality.

---

6   Lenglet-Dufresnoy, *Histoire de la Philosophie hermétique* (History of Hermetic Philosophy). Paris, Coustelier, 1742.

IV
The Legendary Laboratory

With its procession of mystery and the unknown, under its veil of illuminism and marvel, alchemy evokes a past of distant stories, extraordinary narratives and surprising testimonies. Its singular theories, its strange recipes, the centuries-old renown of her great masters, the passionate controversies it aroused, the favor it enjoyed in the Middle Ages, its obscure, enigmatic, paradoxical literature, seem to us to give off the scent of mold, of rarefied air acquired by the long contact of years, empty sepulchres, dead flowers, abandoned dwellings, yellowed parchments.

The alchemist? – A meditative old man, with a grave forehead and crowned with white hair, a pale and ravaged figure, an original figure of a vanished humanity and a forgotten world; an obstinate recluse, bowed by study, vigils, persevering search, obstinate deciphering of the enigmas of high science. Such is the philosopher whom the imagination of the poet and the brush of the artist were pleased to represent to us.

His laboratory –cellar, cell or old crypt–, is illuminated only by the bleak daylight diffused by many dusty cobwebs. It is there, however, that in the midst of silence, the prodigy, little by little, is accomplished. The tireless nature works –better than in its rocky abysses– under the careful protection of man, with the help of the stars and by the grace of God. Hidden labor, ungrateful and cyclopean task, of a nightmare magnitude! At the centre of this space, *in pace*, a being, a scientist for whom nothing else exists, watches, attentive and patient, over the successive phases of the Great Work...

As our eyes become accustomed, a thousand things come out of the shadows, are born and become more precise. Where are we, Lord? Would it be in the lair of Polyphemus or in the cavern of Vulcan?

Near us, an extinct forge, covered with dust and scales; the anvil, hammer, tongs, shears, clam irons; rusty molds; the rough and powerful tools of the metallurgist came to a standstill. In one corner, large books heavily shod –such as antiphonaries–, with sealed signs of obsolete seals; ashen manuscripts, grimoires piled up, yellowed volumes, riddled with notes and formulas, stained with the incipit to the explicit. Vials, belly full like good monks, filled

19

with opalescent emulsions, gloomy, blue-green or flesh-colored liquids, exhale these acidic odors whose harshness squeezes the throat and bites the nostril.

On the hood of the furnace strange oblong vessels, with short pipes, are aligned, stuffed and encased in wax; matresses, with iridescent spheres of metallic deposits, stretch their necks, sometimes slender and cylindrical, sometimes widened or swollen; the greenish vessels, retorts and pottery spoons rub shoulders with crucibles of red and flamed-like earth. In the background, placed on their straws all along a stone cornice, hyaline and elegant philosophical eggs contrast with the massive and plump squash –*praegnans cucurbita* (big pumpkin).

Damn it! Damn it! Here are now some anatomical pieces, skeletal fragments: blackened skulls, toothless, repulsive in their post-grave smirks; human fetuses suspended, dried up, curled up, miserable waste offering to the eye their tiny bodies, their parchmented, giggling and pathetic heads. These round, glassy, golden eyes are those of a wilted-feathered owl, which stands next the alligator, a giant salamander, another important symbol of the practice. The dreadful reptile emerges from an obscure retreat, stretches the chain of its vertebrae on its stocky legs and directs the bone abyss of fearsome jaws towards the arcatures.

Placed without order, at random, on the hearth of the oven, see these vitrified, aludel or sublimatory pots; thick-walled pelicans; these egg-like burials of which one of the chalazas could be seen; these olive groves buried in the middle of the arena, against the athanor with light smoke climbing the ogival vault. Here the copper still –*homo galeatus*–[1] stained with green smudges; there, the descenders, the curlers and their antenos, the two-brothers or twins of cohobation; serpentine containers; heavy cast iron mortars and marble; a large bellows with wrinkled leather flanks, near a pile of mittens, tiles, cups, evaporators ...

Chaotic mass of archaic instruments, odd materials, old utensils; a confusion of all sciences, clutter of impressive fauna! And, hovering over this disorder, fixed on the keystone, a pendant with outspread wings, is the great raven, a hieroglyph of material death and its decompositions, a mysterious emblem of mysterious operations.

The wall, or at least what is left of it, is strange. Mystical inscriptions fill its voids: *Hic lapis is subtus te, supra te, erga te and circa te*;[2] mnemonic verses are entangled in it, engraved at the whim of the stylus on the soft stone; one of them predominates, carved in Gothic cursive: *Azoth and tibi ignis suffice*;[3] Hebrew characters; triangles cut into circles, interspersed with quadrilaterals in the manner of Gnostic signatures. Here, a thought, based on the dogma of unity, summarizes the whole philosophy: *Omnia ab uno et in unum omnia*.[4] Elsewhere, the image of the scythe, emblem of the thirteenth arcane and the saturnal house; the star of Solomon; the symbol of the crayfish, obsession with the evil spirit; some passages from Zoroaster, testimonies of the high antiquity of the cursed sciences. Finally, located in the luminous field of the basement window, and more readable in this maze of imprecisions, the hermetic ternary: Sal, Sulphur, Mercurius....

This is the legendary picture of the alchemist and his laboratory. Fantastic vision, devoid of truth, out of the popular imagination and reproduced on old almanacs, treasures of peddling.

Puffers, magicians, wizards, astrologers, necromancers?

– Anathema and curse!

---

1   Man wearing a helmet.
2   This stone is directly underneath you, above you, in you, around you.
3   Nitrogen and fire will be enough.
4   All from one and in one all.

V

Chemistry and Philosophy

Chemistry is incontestably the science of facts, as alchemy is that of causes. The first, limited to the material domain, is based on experience; the second preferably takes its directives from philosophy. If one has for object the study of the natural bodies, the other tries to penetrate the mysterious dynamism which presides over their transformations. This is what makes their essential difference and allows us to say that alchemy, compared to our positive science, only admitted and taught today, is a spiritualistic chemistry, because it allows us to glimpse God through the darkness of the substance.

Moreover, it does not seem sufficient to know exactly how to recognize and classify facts; Nature must be questioned in order to learn from her under what conditions, and under the influence of which will, her multiple productions take place. The philosophical mind cannot, in fact, be content with a mere possibility of identifying elements; it demands the knowledge of the secret of their elaboration. To open the door of the laboratory where nature mixes the elements is good; to discover the occult force under the influence of which his labors are accomplished is better. We are, of course, far from knowing all the natural elements and their combinations, since we discover new ones every day.

To say, for example, that two volumes of hydrogen combined with a volume of oxygen give water, is to state a chemical banality. And yet, who will teach us why the result of this combination presents, with a special state, characters which are not possessed by the gases which produced it? What is the agent that imposes on the compound its new specificity and forces the water, solidified by the cold, to always crystallize in the same system? On the other hand, if the fact is undeniable and rigorously controlled, where does it come to be impossible for us to reproduce it simply by reading the formula responsible for explaining its mechanism? Because the H^2O notation lacks the essential agent capable of provoking the intimate union of the gaseous elements, that is, fire. We challenge the most skilful chemist to make synthetic water by mixing oxygen with hydrogen under the indicated volumes: the two gases will always refuse to combine. To succeed the experiment, it is essential to involve the fire, either in the form of a spark, or under that of a body in ignition or likely to be brought to incandescence (*platinum foam*). Thus we recognize, without our least serious argument, that the chemical formula of water is, if not false, at least incomplete and truncated. And the elemental fire agent, without which no combination can be made, being excluded from the chemical notation, the whole science proves lacunous and incapable of providing, by its formulas, a logical and true explanation of the phenomena studied. "Physical chemistry", writes A. Étard, "leads the majority of researching spirits; it is the one who touches closer to the deep truths; it is the one which will slowly deliver the laws capable of changing all our systems and our formulas. But, by its very importance, this kind of chemistry is the most abstract and the most mysterious; the best intelligences cannot, during the instants of creative thought, reach the contention and comparison of all the great known facts. Faced with this impossibility, we resort to mathematical representations. These representations are most often perfect in their methods and results; but in the application to what is profoundly unknown, mathematics can not be made to discover truths whose elements have not been entrusted to them. The best gifted man does not pose the problem he does not understand. If these problems could be correctly equated, we would hope to solve them. But in the state of ignorance where we are, we are inevitably reduced to introducing many constants, to neglect terms, to apply hypotheses ... The setting in equation is perhaps no longer correct in every aspect; we console ourselves, however, because it leads to a solution; but it is a temporary stopping of the progress of science when such solutions are imposed for years upon good minds as a scientific demonstration. Many works are done in this direction, which take time and lead to contradictory theories, destined for oblivion."[1]

These famous theories, which were so long invoked and opposed to hermetic conceptions, nowadays see their solidity greatly compromised. Sincere scientists, belonging to the creative school of these same hypotheses, considered as certainties, give them only a very relative value; their field of action is tightening in parallel with the diminution of their power of investigation. This is what is expressed, with this revealing frankness of the true scientific spirit, Mr. Émile Picard in the *Revue des Deux Mondes*. "As for theories," he writes, "they no longer propose to give a causal explanation of reality itself, but only to translate it into images or mathematical symbols. These working instruments, which are the theories, are asked to coordinate, at least for a time, known phenomena and to predict new ones. When their fertility is exhausted, efforts are made to subject them to the transformations made necessary by the discovery of new facts." Thus, contrary to philosophy, which advances the facts, ensures the orientation of ideas and their practical connection, the theory, conceived after the fact, modified according to the results of the experiment, as acquisitions progress, reflects always the uncertainty of provisional things, and gives to modern science the character of a perpetual empiricism. Numerous chemical facts, seriously observed, resist the logic and defy all reasoning. "Cupric iodide, for example," says Duclaux, "decomposes spontaneously into iodine and cuprous iodide. Since iodine is an oxidant and cuprous salts are reducing agents, this decomposition is inexplicable. The formation of extremely unstable compounds, such as nitrogen chloride, is also inexplicable. Nor is it clear why gold, which is resistant to acids and alkalis, even concentrated and hot, dissolves in a cold, extended solution of potassium cyanide; why hydrogen sulphide is more volatile than water; why sulfur chloride,

---

1   A. Étard, *Revue annuelle de Chimie pure* (Annual review of pure chemistry), in *Revue des Sciences*, 30 sept. 1896, p. 775.

composed of two elements, each of which combines with potassium with incandescence, is without action on this metal."[2]

We have just spoken of fire; still, let us consider it only in its vulgar form, and not in its spiritual essence, which is introduced into bodies at the very moment of their appearance on the physical plane. What we wish to demonstrate, without departing from the alchemical domain, is the grave error which dominates all present science and prevents it from recognizing this universal principle which animates substance, to whatever kingdom it belongs. Yet it manifests itself around us, under our eyes, either by the new properties that matter inherits from it, or by the phenomena that accompany its release. Light, fire rarefied and spiritualized, has the same virtues and the same chemical power as the elemental fire. An experiment, directed towards the synthetic realization of the hydrochloric acid (Cl H) starting from its components, demonstrates it sufficiently. If equal volumes of chlorine gas and hydrogen are enclosed in a glass bottle, the two gases will retain their individuality as long as the vial containing them is kept in the dark. Already, in diffuse light, their combination takes place little by little; but if the ship is exposed to direct sunlight, it shatters under the pressure of a violent explosion.

It will be objected that fire, considered as a simple catalyst, is not an integral part of the substance and consequently cannot be indicated in the expression of chemical formulas. The argument is more specious than real, since experience itself invalidates it. Here is a piece of sugar, the equation of which bears no equivalent of fire; if we break it in the darkness, we will see a blue spark burst forth. Where does it come from? Where was it enclosed, if not in the crystalline texture of sucrose? We talked about water; let's throw a fragment of potassium on its surface: it ignites spontaneously and burns with energy. Where was this visible flame hiding? Whether in water, air or metal, it does not matter; the essential fact is that it potentially exists within one or the other of these bodies, or even all of them. What is phosphorus, light carrier and fire generator? How do noctilucts, glowworms and fireflies transform some of their vital energy into light? Which forces the salts of uranium, cerium, zirconium, to become fluorescent when they have been subjected to the action of sunlight? By what mysterious synchronism does the platinum-cyanide of barium shine in contact with the Rœntgen rays?

And let no one talk to us about oxidation in the normal order of igneous phenomena: it would be to retreat the question instead of solving it. Oxidation is a resultant, not a cause; it is a combination, subject to an active principle, to an agent. If certain energetic oxidations give off heat or fire, it is, most certainly, for the reason that this fire was first engaged in it. The electric fluid, silent, dark and cold, runs through its metallic conductor without influencing it otherwise or showing its passage. But, come to meet a resistance, the energy is revealed immediately with the qualities and under the aspect of the fire. A lamp filament becomes incandescent, the retort coals flare up, the most refractory wire melts on the spot. Now, is not electricity a real fire, a fire in power? Whence does it originate, if not from the decomposition (piles) or the disintegration of metals (dynamos), bodies eminently charged with the igneous principle? Let's detach a piece of steel or iron by grinding it, the shock against a flint, and we will see the spark shine and set free. The pneumatic lighter is well known, based on the property of the atmospheric air to ignite by simple compression. The liquids themselves are often real reservoirs of fire. Just pour a few drops of concentrated nitric

2 J. Duclaux, *La Chimie de la Matière vivante* (The Chemistry of Living Matter). Paris, Alcan, 1910, p. 14.

acid on the essence of turpentine to cause its inflammation. In the category of salts, remember fulminates, nitrocellulose, potash picrate, etc.

Without further multiplication of examples, we see that it would be puerile to maintain that fire, because we cannot perceive it directly in matter, is not really there in the latent state. The old alchemists, who possessed, from a traditional source, more knowledge than we are disposed to grant them, assured that the sun is a cold star and that its rays are dark.[3] Nothing seems more paradoxical or more contrary to appearance, and yet nothing is more true. A few moments of reflection make it possible to be convinced of it. If the sun were a globe of fire, as we are taught, it would be enough to approach it, however little, to experience the effect of increasing heat. It is precisely the opposite that takes place. The high mountains remain crowned with snow despite the heat of summer. In the higher regions of the atmosphere, when the star goes to the zenith, the dome of the aerostats is covered with frost and their passengers suffer from a very cold. Thus, experience shows that the temperature drops as the altitude increases. The light itself is only sensible to us as far as we are placed in the field of its radiance. Are we located outside the radiant beam, its action stops for our eyes. It is a well-known fact that an observer, looking at the sky from the bottom of a well and at the hour of noon, sees the night and starry firmament.

Where do heat and light come from? The simple shock of cold and dark vibrations against the gaseous molecules of our atmosphere. And as resistance increases in direct proportion to the density of the environment, heat and light are stronger at the earth's surface than at higher altitudes, because the layers of air are also denser. That is, at least, the physical explanation of the phenomenon. In reality, and according to the hermetic theory, the opposition to the vibratory movement, the reaction are only the first causes of an effect which results in the liberation of the luminous and igneous atoms of the atmospheric air. Under the action of vibratory bombardment, the spirit, freed from the body, takes on, for our senses, physical qualities characteristic of its active phase: luminosity, brightness and warmth.

Thus, the only reproach that can be addressed to chemical science is to ignore the igneous agent, the spiritual principle and basis of energetics, under the influence of which all transformations take place. It is the systematic exclusion of this spirit, superior will and hidden dynamism of things, which deprives modern chemistry of the philosophical character possessed by ancient alchemy. "You believe," writes M. Henri Helier to ML Olivier, "the indefinite fecundity of experience. Without a doubt; but experimentation has always been guided by a preconceived idea, by a philosophy. Idea often almost absurd in appearance, sometimes bizarre and disconcerting philosophy in his signs. 'If I told you how I made my discoveries,' said Faraday, 'you would take me for a fool'. All the great chemists have thus had ideas in their heads that they have been careful not to make known. It is from their works that we have drawn our methods and our current theories; they are the most valuable result, they were not the origin."[4]

"The alembic, with its grave and posed tones," says an anonymous philosopher, "has gained a vast clientele in chemistry. Just try to trust it; it is an unfaithful depository, and a usurer. You entrust to him a perfectly healthy object, endowed with incontestable natural properties, having a form which constitutes its existence; it returns to you shapeless, as dust or gas, and it pretends to give you everything when it has kept everything, less the weight

---

3   Conf. *Cosmopolite ou Nouvelle Lumière chymique* (Cosmopolitan or New Chemical Light), Paris, 1669, p. 50.

4   Letter on Chemical Philosophy , in the Revue des Sciences, Dec. 30 1896, p. 1227.

which is nothing since it comes from a cause independent of the body itself. And the union of scientists sanctions this horrible usury! You give him wine, he gives you tannin, alcohol and water at equal weight. What is missing? Taste, that is, the only thing that makes it wine, and so on. Since you have obtained three things from wine, chemical gentlemen, you say that wine is composed of those three things. Put it back, then, or I will tell you that three things are obtained from wine. You can undo what you have done, but you will never remake what you have undone in Nature. Bodies resist you only in the proportion in which they are combined with more force, and you call simple bodies all those who resist you: vanity!

"I like the microscope; he is content to show us things as they are, simply by extending our perception; it is therefore the scientists who give him advice. But when, immersed in the last details, these gentlemen come to bring to the microscope the smallest grain or the least droplet, the mocking instrument seems, by showing them living animals, to say to them: Analyze those for me. So, what is the analysis? Vanity, vanity!

"Finally, when a learned doctor slices the scalpel in a corpse to find the causes of the disease that has killed the victim, with his help he finds only results. For the cause of death is in that of life, and true medicine, that which Christ naturally practiced, and which is scientifically reborn with homeopathy, the medicine of similars, is studied on the spot. Now, when it comes to life, as there is nothing that is less like living than death, anatomy is the saddest of vanities.

"Are all the instruments a cause of error? Far from there; but they indicate the truth in so limited a limit that their truth is only vanity. So, it is impossible to attach an absolute truth to it. This is what I call the impossible of the real, and which I take note of to affirm the possible of the marvelous".[5]

Positive in his facts, chemistry remains negative in his spirit. And that is precisely what makes it different from hermetic science, whose own field includes above all the study of efficient causes, their influences, and the modalities they affect according to the environments and conditions. It is this study, exclusively philosophical, that allows the man to penetrate the mystery of the facts, to understand the extent, to identify it finally to the supreme Intelligence, soul of the Universe, Light, God. Thus alchemy, going back from the concrete to the abstract, from material positivism to pure spiritualism, broadens the field of human knowledge, the possibilities of action and realizes the union of God and Nature, of Creation and of the Creator, Science and Religion.

In this discussion, let us not see any unjust or tendentious criticism directed against the chemists. We respect all the industrious, on whatever condition they belong, and personally profess the deepest admiration for the great scientists whose discoveries have so magnificently enriched the science of today. But what men in good faith will regret with us is less the differences of opinion freely expressed than the unfortunate intentions of a narrow sectarianism, throwing discord between the partisans of the one and the other doctrine. Life is too short, time too precious to waste it in vain polemics, and it is scarcely to honor oneself to despise the knowledge of others. It does not matter, moreover, that so many researchers go astray, *errare humanum is*, says the old adage, and illusion often adorns itself with the diadem of truth. Those who persevere despite the lack of success are therefore entitled to all our sympathy.

---

5   *Comment l'Esprit vient aux tables, par un homme qui n'a pas perdu l'esprit* (How the Spirit Comes to Tables). Paris, Librairie Nouvelle, 1854, p. 150.

Unfortunately, the scientific spirit is a rare quality in the man of science, and we find this deficiency at the origin of the struggles we report. From the fact that a truth is neither demonstrated nor demonstrable by the means available to science, it can not be inferred that it will never be. "The impossible word is not French," said Arago; we add that it is contrary to the true scientific spirit. To qualify a thing as impossible because its present possibility remains doubtful is to lack confidence in the future and to deny progress. Does not Lemery commit a grave imprudence, when he dares to write, concerning the alkaest, or universal dissolvent: "To me, I believe him imaginary, for I do not know it."[6] Our chemist, we will admit, overestimated the value and extent of his knowledge. Harrys, brain refractory to hermetic thought, thus defined alchemy, without ever having wanted to study it: *Ars sine arte, cujus principium is mentiri, medium laborare and finis mendicare.*[7]

By the side of these learned men shut up in their ivory towers, beside these men of undoubted merit, certainly, but slaves of tenacious prejudices, others did not hesitate to grant civil rights to the old science. Spinoza and Leibniz believed in the philosopher's stone, the *chrysopoeia.* Pascal is certain of it.[8] Closer to home, some spirits of high order, among others Sir Humphry Davy, thought that hermetic research could lead to unsuspected results. Jean-Baptiste Dumas, in his Lessons on Chemical Philosophy, expresses himself in these terms: "Is it permissible to admit simple isomeric bodies? This question touches closely on the transmutation of metals. Resolved affirmatively, it would give chances of success in the search for the philosopher's stone ... We must therefore consult the experience, and experience, it must be said, is not in opposition until now with the possibility of transmutation simple bodies ... It is even opposed to the fact that we reject this idea as an absurdity that would be demonstrated by the current state of our knowledge". Francois-Vincent Raspail was a convinced alchemist, and the works of classical philosophers occupied a preponderant place among his other books. Ernest Bosc tells that Auguste Cahours, member of the Academy of Sciences, has told him that his revered master Chevreul professed the greatest esteem for our old alchemists; so its rich library contained almost all the important works of hermetic

---

6   Lemery, *Cours de Chymie* (Chemistry Course), Paris, d'Houry, 1757.

7   "An art without art, whose beginning is to lie, the middle is to work, and the end is to beg".

8   Pascal was an alchemist? Nothing authorizes us to claim it. What is most certain is that he himself had to carry out the transmutation, unless he had seen it done before his eyes, in the laboratory of an Adept. The operation lasted two hours. This is what emerges from a curious autograph document on paper, written in mystical style, and found sewn in his coat, during his burial. Here is the beginning, which is also the essential part:

+

The year of grace 1654,

Monday, November 23, St. Clement's Day, Pope and Martyr, and others to the martyrologist,

Eve of St. Chrysogonus, martyr, and others,

From about half past ten in the evening until about half past midnight,

FIRE.

God of Abraham, God of Isaac, God of Jacob,

Not Philosophers and Savans.

Certitude, Certitude, Feeling. Joy. Peace.

We have intentionally pointed out, although it is not in the original piece, the word *Chrysogone*, which the author uses to describe transmutation; it is formed, in fact, of two Greek words, Χρυσός, or, and γονή, generation. Death, which usually carries the secret of men, was to deliver that of Pascal, *philosophus per ignem.*

philosophers.[9] It would even appear that the Dean of the students of France, as Chevreul called himself, had learned a lot in these old books, and that he owed them some of his beautiful discoveries. The illustrious Chevreul, in fact, knew how to read between the lines much information which had passed unnoticed before him.[10] One of the most celebrated masters of chemical science, Marcellin Berthelot, was not satisfied with adopting the opinion of the School. Unlike many of his colleagues, who boldly speak of alchemy without knowing it, he devoted more than twenty years to the patient study of original Greek and Arabic texts. And from this long trade with the old masters, was born in him this conviction that "hermetic principles, as a whole, are as sustainable as the best modern theories". If we were not bound by the promise we made to them, we could add to these scholars the names of certain scientific luminaries, entirely conquered by the art of Hermes, but that their very situation obliges them to practice it only in secret.

In our days, and although the unity of substance –the basis of the doctrine taught since antiquity by all alchemists– is received and officially consecrated, it does not seem, however, that the idea of transmutation has followed the same progression. The fact is all the more surprising because one can not be admitted without considering the possibility of the other. On the other hand, considering the high antiquity of the hermetic thesis, one would have some reason to think that over the centuries it could be confirmed by experience. It is true that scholars generally disregard arguments of this kind; the most credible and well-supported testimonies seem suspicious to them, whether they ignore them or prefer to lose interest in them. In order that we may not be accused of lending them some malicious intention by distorting their thought, and to enable the reader to exercise his judgment freely, we shall submit to his judgment the opinions of modern scientists and philosophers on the subject which we occupy. Jean Finot having appealed to the competent men, asked them the following question: In the present state of science, is metallic transmutation possible or practicable; can it be considered even as realized because of our knowledge? Here are the answers he received:[11]

– Dr. Max Nordeau. - "Let me abstain from any discussion of the transmutation of matter. I adopt the dogma (it is one) of the unity of this one, the hypothesis of the evolution of the chemical elements of the lightest atomic weight, to that of more and more heavy, and even the theory –imprudently termed law– the periodicity of Mendeleeff. I do not deny the theoretical possibility of artificially remaking, by laboratory means, a part of this evolution, naturally produced in billions or trillions of years by cosmic forces and transforming lighter metals into gold. But I do not believe that our century will witness the realization of the dream of the alchemists".

– Henri Poincaré. - "Science cannot and must never say! It may be that one day we will discover the principle of making gold, but for the moment the problem does not seem solved".

– Mrs M. Curie.- "If it is true that spontaneous atomic transformations have been observed with the radioactive bodies (production of helium by these bodies, which you report and which is perfectly exact), one can, on the other hand, ensure that no simple body trans-

9 Chevreul bequeathed his hermetic library to the Museum of Natural History.
10 Ernest Bosc, *Dictionnaire d'Orientalisme, d'Occultisme et de Psychologie* (Dictionary of Orientalism, Occultism and Psychology). Volume I: art. Alchemy
11 Cf. *La Revue* (The Review), No. 18, September 15, 1912, p. 162 et seq.

formation has yet been obtained by the effort of men and thanks to the devices imagined by them. It is therefore quite useless to consider the possible consequences of gold making. "

– Gustave Le Bon.- "It is possible to transform steel into gold, as uranium is said to be transformed into radium and helium, but these transformations are likely to affect only billionths of a milligram, and it would then be much more economical to remove the gold from the sea which contains tons".

Ten years later, a science popularization magazine[12], engaging in the same inquiry, published the following opinions:

– Charles Richet, professor at the Faculty of Medicine, member of the Institute, Nobel Laureate.- "I confess I have no opinion on the question".

– MM. Urbain and Jules Perrin. - "... unless there is a revolution in the art of exploiting natural forces, synthetic gold –if it is not a chimera– will not be worth exploiting industrially."

– Mr. Charles Moureu. - "... The making of gold is not an absurd hypothesis! It is almost the only affirmation that a true scientist can emit ... A scientist affirms nothing a priori ... Transmutation is a fact that we see every day".

To this thought so courageously expressed, thought of brave brain, endowed with the most noble scientific spirit and a deep sense of the truth, we will oppose another, of very different quality. This is the appreciation of Mr. Henry Le Châtelier, member of the Institute, professor of chemistry at the Faculty of Sciences. "I absolutely refuse," writes the illustrious master, "any interview about synthetic gold. I think this has to come from some scam attempt, like the famous Lemoine diamonds".

In truth, one can not with less words and amenity testify so much contempt for the old Adepts, venerated masters of the current alchemists. For our author, who has probably never opened a hermetic book, transmutation is synonymous with quackery. Disciple of these great disappeared, it seems quite natural that we should inherit their unfortunate reputation. What does it matter; that is our glory, the only one we deign to grant to us, when it finds the opportunity, the graduated ignorance, proud of its trinkets: crosses, seals, palms and parchments. But let the donkey carry his relics seriously, and come back to our subject.

The answers just read, except that of M. Charles Moureu, are similar in substance. They flow from the same source. The academic spirit dictated them. Our scholars accept the theoretical possibility of transmutation; they refuse to believe in its material reality. They deny after asserting. It is a convenient means of staying in expectation, of not compromising oneself, or of leaving the domain of relativities.

Can we report atomic transformations on a few molecules of substance? How to recognize them an absolute value, if one can control them only indirectly, by indirect ways? Is this a simple concession that moderns make to the ancients? But we have never heard that hermetic science would have asked alms. We know it rich enough of observations, sufficiently provided with positive facts not to be reduced to begging. Moreover, the theoretical idea that our chemists argue today undoubtedly belongs to the alchemists. It is their own property, and no one can deny them the benefit of a recognized antiquity of fifteen centuries. It is these men

---

12 *Je sais tout* (I know everything) *Is the synthetic manufacture of gold possible?* No. 194, February 15, 1922.

who have, first, demonstrated the actual realization, resulting from the unity of substance, invulnerable base of their philosophy. Moreover, we ask why modern science, endowed with multiple and powerful means, rigorous methods served by precise and perfected tools, has taken so long to recognize the veracity of the hermetic principle? Therefore, we are entitled to conclude that the old alchemists, using very simple processes, had nevertheless discovered, experimentally, the formal proof capable of imposing the concept of metallic transmutation as an absolute truth. Our predecessors were neither foolish nor deceitful, and the mother idea that guided their work, the very one that permeates the scientific spheres of our time, is foreign to the hypothetical principles whose fluctuations and vicissitudes it ignores.

We assure, then, without partiality, that the great scholars whose opinions we have reproduced are mistaken when they deny the lucrative result of transmutation. They misunderstand the constitution and the profound qualities of matter, though they think they have probed all the mysteries. Alas! The complexity of their theories, the mass of words created to explain the inexplicable, and above all the pernicious influence of a materialistic education, push them to look far beyond what is within their reach. Mathematicians for the most part, they lose in simplicity, in a good sense, what they gain in human logic, in numerical rigor. They dream of imprisoning nature into a formula, to put life into a equation. Thus, by successive deviations, do they unconsciously get so far away from the simple truth that they justify the harsh word of the Gospel: "They have eyes so as not to see, and sense not to understand!".

Would it be possible to bring these men back to a less complicated conception of things, to guide those lost to the light of spiritualism which they lack? We are going to try it, and first of all, for the benefit of those who wish to follow us, that we should not study living nature outside of its activity. The analysis of the molecule and the atom learns nothing; it is incapable of solving the highest problem a scientist can offer himself: what is the essence of this invisible and mysterious dynamism which animates the substance? Of life, in fact, what do we know, except that we find its physical consequence in the phenomenon of movement? But everything is life and movement here below. The vital activity, very apparent in animals and vegetables, is hardly less so in the mineral kingdom, although it requires the observer to pay more attention. Metals, in fact, are living and sensible bodies. Proofs are: the mercury thermometer, silver salts, fluorides, etc. What is dilatation and contraction, if not two effects of metallic dynamism, two manifestations of mineral life? However, it is not enough for the philosopher to note only the lengthening of a bar of iron subjected to the heat, it is necessary for him still to seek which occult will forces the metal to dilate. It is known that this, under the impression of caloric radiations, spreads its pores, distends its molecules, increases in surface and volume; it flourishes in a way, as we do ourselves, under the action of the beneficent solar aroma. It can not be denied that such a reaction has a profound cause, immaterial, for we cannot explain, without this impulse, what other force would force the crystalline particles to leave their apparent inertia. This metallic will, the very soul of the metal, is clearly highlighted in one of the beautiful experiments made by Mr. Ch.-Ed. Guillaume. A calibrated steel bar is subjected to a continuous and progressive traction whose power is recorded using the dynamograph. When the bar is going to give way, it manifests a strangulation of which one finds the exact place. We stop the extension and restore the bar in its original dimensions, then the test is resumed. This time, the strangulation occurs at a different point than the first one. By following the same technique, we notice that all the points were successively tested by yielding, one after the other, at the same traction. Now, if we calibrate the steel bar one last time, resuming the experiment at the beginning, we see that we must use a force much greater than the first to cause the return of the symptoms of rupture. Mr. Ch.-Ed. William concludes from these essays, with much reason, that the metal behaved as an organic body would have done; he successively strengthened all his weak parts and intentionally increased his coherence to better defend his threatened integrity. A similar lesson emerges from the study of crystalline salt compounds. If one breaks the ridge of any crystal and plunges it, thus mutilated, into the mother water which produced it, not only is it incontinently seen to repair its wound, but also to increase with a speed greater than that of intact crystals, remained in the same solution. We are still discovering a clear proof of metallic vitality in the fact that in America railroad tracks show, for no apparent reason, the effects of a singular evolution. Nowhere are the derailments more frequent nor the catastrophes more inexplicable. Engineers studying the cause of these multiple failures attribute it to the "premature aging" of steel. Under the probable influence of special climatic conditions, the metal ages quickly, early; he loses his elasticity, his malleability, his resistance; tenacity and cohesion seem diminished to the point of rendering it dry and brittle. This metallic degeneration, moreover, is not only limited to the rails; it also extends its ravages on armor plates armored ships, which are generally put out of service after a few months of use. On trial, we are surprised to see them break into several pieces under the shock of a simple ball-cast iron. The weakening of the vital energy, the normal phase and characteristic of decrepitude, of senility of the metal, is the precursory sign of his impending death. Since death, the corollary of life, is the direct consequence of birth, it follows that metals and minerals manifest their submission to the law of predestination which governs all created beings. To be born, to live, to die or to be transformed are the three stages of a unique period embracing all physical activity. And since this activity has the essential function of renewing itself,

Such is the analogical truth which alchemy has endeavored to practice, and such is also the hermetic idea which it seemed to us necessary to emphasize first of all. Thus, philosophy teaches and experience shows that metals, thanks to their own seed, can be reproduced and developed in quantity. This is what the word of God reveals to us in Genesis, when the Creator transmits a portion of his activity to creatures from his very substance. For the divine word: grow and multiply , does not apply only to man, it refers to all living beings spread in the whole of nature.

VI
Hermetic Cabala

Alchemy is obscure only because it is hidden. The philosophers who wished to transmit to posterity the exposition of their doctrine and the fruit of their labors did not divulge art by presenting it in a common form, so that the profane could not misuse it. Also, it is by its difficulty of comprehension, by the mystery of its enigmas, the opacity of its parables that this science has been relegated among reveries, illusions and chimeras.

Admittedly, these old sepia-toned books are not easily understood. To pretend to read them in the same way as normal books would be to mislead ourselves. However, the first impression one receives, however strange and confusing it may seem, is nonetheless vibrant and persuasive. One can guess, through the allegorical language and the abundance of an ambiguous nomenclature, this ray of truth, this deep conviction born of certain facts, duly observed and which owe nothing to the whimsical speculations of pure imagination.

It will doubtless be objected that the best hermetic works contain strong gaps, accumulate contradictions, and mingle with false recipes; we will be told that the modus operandi varies according to the authors and that, although the theoretical development is the same in all, the descriptions of the elements employed rarely offer a rigorous similarity between them. We will answer that the philosophers did not have other resources, to hide to ones what they wanted to show others, that this jumble of metaphors, of various symbols, this prolixity of terms, capricious formulas traced to the pen, expressed in plain language for the use of greedy or foolish people. As for the argument relating to practice, it falls of itself for the simple reason that the initial subject can be considered in any of the many aspects that it takes in the course of work, and the artists never describe that part of the technique,

For the rest, we must not forget that the treaties which have reached us were composed during the most beautiful alchemical period, that which embraces the last three centuries of the Middle Ages. Now, at that time, the popular spirit, impregnated with oriental mysticism, delighted in the riddle, the symbolic veil, the allegorical expression. This disguise flattered the rebellious instinct of the people, and provided the satirical spirit of the great with a new food. Thus it had won the general favor and was found everywhere, firmly established at different stages of the social ladder. It shone in ingenious words in the conversation of

31

the cultivated people, noble or bourgeois, and was vulgarized in naive puns in the rascals. It adorned the shopkeepers' exhibition with picturesque hieroglyphics and took possession of the blazons, whose esoteric rules and protocol it established. It imposed on art, literature and, above all, esotericism his motley clothing of images, enigmas and emblems.

To alchemy we owe the variety of curious signs, the number and singularity of which add to the strikingly original character of medieval French productions. Nothing shocks our modernism more than these signs of taverns oscillating on an axis of ironwork; we recognize only the letter O followed by a K cut off with a line; but the drunkard of the 14th century was not mistaken and entered, without hesitation, the great cabaret. The "hostelries" often wore a golden lion frozen in a heraldic pose, which, for the wanderer in search of a place to live, meant that one "could sleep there", thanks to the double meaning of the image: in bed one sleeps. Édouard Fournier tells us that in Paris the rue du Bout-du-Monde still existed in the 17th century. "This name," adds the author, "came from the fact that it had long been very close to the city walls, and had been depicted as a hieroglyphic on a cabaret sign. A bone, a goat, a duke (bird), a world had been represented.[1]

Next to the coat of arms of the hereditary nobility, we discover another whose weapons are only speaking and tributary of the hieroglyphic. This last one points out the commoners, arrived by fortune at the rank of personages of condition. François Myron, Parisian builder of 1604, thus wore "gules in the round mirror". A parvenu of the same order, superior of the monastery of St. Bartholomew, in London, Prior Bolton, who held office from 1532 to 1539, had his arms carved on the bow window of the triforium, from which he was watching the pious exercises of his monks. We can see an arrow (bolt) crossing a small barrel (tun), resulting in Bolton (Plate III).

In his *Enigmes des rues de Paris* (Enigmas of the Streets of Paris), Edouard Fournier, to whom we have just quoted, after initiating us in the disputes of Louis XIV and Louvois following the construction of the Invalides, instigated because he wished to place his "weapons" next to those of the king, and thus stumbled upon the opposite orders of the monarch, tells us that Louvois "took his measures in another way to fix, in the Invalides, his memory in an immutable and speaking manner.

"Enter the courtyard of the Hotel, look at the attic which crowns the facades of the monumental quadrilateral; when you look at the fifth of those who line up at the top of the eastern span near the church, look at it well. The ornamentation is very particular. A wolf is carved there, half-body; the paws fall on the opening of the bull's-eye, which they surround; the head is half hidden under a tuft of palms, and the eyes are ardently fixed on the floor of the court. There is, without you doubting it, a monumental pun —as it was so often done for imagery of heraldry–, and in this stone hieroglyphic is the revenge, the satisfaction of the vain minister. This wolf is watching, this wolf is seeing; it's his emblem! So that we cannot doubt, he has carved on the garret which is near, on the right, a barrel of exploding powder, symbol of the war of which he was the impetuous minister; on the garret of the left, a plume of ostrich feathers, attribute of a high and mighty lord, as he claimed to be; and again on two other garrets of the same bay, an owl and a bat, birds of vigilance, his great virtue. Colbert, whose fortune had the same origin as that of Louvois, and who had no less vain pretensions of nobility, had taken for his emblem the snake (coluber), as Louvois had chosen the wolf.

---

1   Edouard Fournier, *Énigmes des rues de Paris* (Enigmas of the streets of Paris). Paris, E. Dentu, 1860.

LONDON - CHURCH OF SAINT BARTHELEMY TRIFORIUM
The Great Window of Prior Bolton - Plate III

The taste of the rebus, the last echo of the sacred language, has considerably weakened these days. It is no longer cultivated, and it is scarcely still of interest to the schoolchildren of the present generation. By ceasing to provide the science of the coat of arms with the means of deciphering the enigmas, the rebus has lost the esoteric value it once possessed. We find him now a refugee on the last pages of magazines, where –recreational hobby– his role is limited to the expression of a few proverbs. One hardly notices, from time to time, a regular application, but frequently directed towards a goal of advertising, of this fallen art. Thus a great modern firm, specialized in the construction of sewing machines, adopted for its publicity a poster well known. She represents a sitting woman, working at the machine, in the center of a majestic S. Above all, we can see the initial of the manufacturer, although the rebus is clear and transparent: this woman sews in her pregnancy, which is an allusion to the gentleness of the mechanism.

Time, which ruins and devours human works, has not spared the old hermetic language. Indifference, ignorance, and forgetfulness have completed the disintegrating action of ages. It cannot be maintained, however, that it is utterly lost; some insiders keep the rules, know how to take advantage of the resources it offers in the transformation of secret truths or use it as a mnemonic key to teaching.

In the year 1843, the conscripts assigned to the 46th Infantry Regiment, garrisoned in Paris, could meet each week, crossing the yard of the barracks Louis-Philippe, an unusual teacher. According to an eyewitness –one of our parents, a non-commissioned officer at the time and who was diligently following his lessons–, he was a man still young, but neglected, with long hair falling in loops on his shoulders, and whose physiognomy, very expressive, bore the mark of remarkable intelligence. In the evening he taught the military, who desired it, the history of France, for a fee, and employed a method he claimed to be known from the highest antiquity. In reality, this course, so attractive to its listeners, was based on the traditional phonetic cabal.

Some examples, chosen from among those whose memory we have preserved, will give an idea of the process.

After a short preamble about a dozen conventional signs destined, by their form and common patterns, to find all the historical dates, the professor drew a very simplified graphic on the blackboard. This image, which was easily engraved in memory, was, in a way, the complete symbol of the reign being studied.

The first of those drawings showed a character standing at the top of a tower and holding a torch with the hand. On a horizontal line, figurative of the ground, three accessories were lined up: a chair, a staff and a footstool. The explanation of the scheme was simple. What the man lifts in his hand serves as a beacon: a beacon of the hand, Pharamond. The tower that holds it indicates the number 1: Pharamond was, it is said, the first king of France. Finally, the chair is the hieroglyphic of the figure 4, the staff is it of the 2 and the footstool is the sign of zero, which gives the number 420, alleged date of the advent of the legendary sovereign.[2]

Clovis, as we didn't know, was one of those rascals with whom there is nothing to do if force is not used. Turbulent, aggressive, battling and ready to break everything, only dreamed of calamities and sprees. His good parents, both to tame him and out of prudence, had tied him to the chair. The whole Court knew that he was locked up and "screwed" (*clos à vis*, Clovis). The chair and two hunting horns placed on the ground gave the date 466.

Clotaire, of indolent nature, walked his melancholy in a field surrounded by walls. The unfortunate man was thus shut up in his land: Clotaire.

Chilperic, –we no longer know for what reason–, was fidgeting in a frying pan, like a simple catfish, screaming in a breathless breath: "I perish," whence Chilperic.

Dagobert adopted the bellicose appearance of a warrior brandishing a dagger and wearing a hauberk, hence Dagobert.

Saint Louis –who would have thought?–, appreciated the polish and brilliancy of the newly struck gold coins; so he used his leisure to melt his old *louis* to have new ones: Louis IX.

As for the little corporal, greatness and decadence, his coat of arms did not require the use of any character. A table covered with its tablecloth and supporting a vulgar pan was enough to identify it. Tablecloth and skillet, Napoleon ...

It is these puns, these games of words associated or not with the rebus, which served to the initiates through their verbal interviews. In acroamatic works, anagrams were reserved, sometimes to hide the personality of the author, sometimes to disguise the title and to subtract from the layman the guiding thought. This is the case in particular, of a small book very curious and so cleverly closed that it is impossible to know what is the subject. It is attributed to Tiphaigne de la Roche, and it bears this singular title *Amilec ou la graine d'hommes* (Amilec or the seed of men).[3] It is an assembly of anagram and pun. You should read instead

---

2 There is here an absolute identity of figuration and meaning with the cabal expressed in the engravings of certain old works, the *Songe de Polyphile* (Dream of Polyphile) in particular. King Solomon is always represented by a hand holding a willow branch: *Saule a main* (willow by hand), Solomon. A daisy means regret me, etc. It is thus necessary to analyze the dictates and ways of speaking of Pantagruel and Gargantua, if one wants to know all that is "mussed" in the work of the powerful initiate that was Rabelais.

3 This little work in-16, very well written, but which carries neither place of edition, nor name of publisher, was published about 1753.

Alcmie ou la crème d'Aum (Alchemy or the Cream of Aum). Neophytes will learn that this is a true treatise on alchemy, because, in the thirteenth century alchemy was written as *alkimie*, *alkemie* or *alkmie*; that the point of science revealed by the author refers to the extraction of the spirit enclosed in the raw material, or philosophical virgin, which bears the same sign as the celestial Virgin, the monogram AUM; that finally this extraction must be done by a process similar to that which makes it possible to separate the cream from the milk, which is also taught by Basil Valentin, Tollius, Philaletes and the characters of *Liber Mutus*. By removing the veil from the title it covers, we can see how suggestive it is, since it announces the disclosure of the secret means of obtaining this cream of virgin milk, which few researchers have had the good fortune to possess. Tiphaigne de la Roche, almost unknown, was however one of the most learned Adepts of the 18th century. In another treatise, entitled *Giphantie* (Tiphaigne's anagram), he describes the photographic process perfectly and shows that he was aware of chemical manipulations concerning the development and fixation of the image, a century before the discovery of Daguerre and Niepce de Saint-Victor.

Among the anagrams intended to cover the name of their authors, we will mention that of Limojon de Saint-Didier: *Dives sicut ardens*, that is to say *Sanctus Didiereus*, and the motto of the President of Espagnet: *Spes mea est in agno*. Other philosophers preferred to wear cabalistic pseudonyms more directly related to the science they professed. Basil Valentin assembles the Greek Βασιλεύς, king, with the Latin *Valens*, powerful, to indicate the surprising power of the philosopher's stone. Eirenea Philaletes appears composed of three Greek words: Εἰρηναῖος, pacific, Φίλος, friend, and ἀλήθεια, truth; Philaletes presents himself as the peaceful friend of the truth. Grassæus signs his works by the name of *Hortulain*, meaning the gardener (*Hortulanus*) –of maritime gardens, he takes care to underline. Ferrari is a blacksmith monk (*ferrarius*) working metals. Musa, disciple of Calid, is Μύστης, the Initiate, while his master, –our master for all–, is the heat released by the athanor (Latin *calidus*, burning). Haly indicates salt, in Greek ἅλς, and the Ovid's Metamorphoses are those of the egg of the philosophers (*ovum, ovi*). Archelaus is rather a book title than an author's name; it is the principle of stone, of the Greek Ἀρχή, principle, and λᾶος, stone. Marcel Palingene combines Mars, iron, ἥλιος, the sun and *Palingenesia*, regeneration, to designate that he realized the regeneration of the sun, or gold, by iron. Jean Austri, Gratian, Étienne share the winds (*austri*), the grace (*gratia*) and the crown (Στέφανος, Stephanus). Famanus takes as its emblem the famous chestnut, so famous among the wise (*Fama-nux*), and John of Sacrobosco has especially in view the mysterious consecrated wood. Cyliani is the equivalent of *Cyllenius*, of Cyllene, a mountain of Mercury, which gave its name to the Cyllenian god. As for the modest Gallinario, it is content with the henhouse and the corral, where the yellow chick, hatched from a black hen's egg will soon become our miraculous golden egg hen...

Without abandoning completely these artifices of linguistics, the old masters, in the drafting of their treatises, used above all the hermetic cabal, which they still called the *language of the birds, of the gods, the gay science* or *gay knowledge*. In this way they could hide from the vulgar the principles of their science, by wrapping them with a cabalistic cover. This is an indisputable and well known fact. But what is generally ignored is that the idiom from which the authors borrowed their terms is the archaic Greek, mother tongue from the plurality of the followers of Hermes. The reason why cabalistic intervention is not noticed is precisely due to the modern French language comes directly from the Greek. As a result, all the words chosen in French to define certain secrets, have their Greek orthographic or phonetic equivalents, it is enough to know these well in order to discover at once the exact, restored meaning of the former. For the substance of the French language, it is indeed Hellenic, its significance has been modified in the course of the centuries, as far it was distancing itself from its source. It is the case of the French, before the radical transformation that made him suffer the Renaissance, hidden decadence under the guise of reform.

The imposition of Greek words hidden under corresponding French terms, of similar texture, but with a more or less corrupted meaning, allows the investigator to easily penetrate the intimate thoughts of the masters and give him the key to the hermetic sanctuary. This is the means we have used, following the example of the elders, and which we will frequently use in the analysis of the symbolic works bequeathed by our ancestors.

Many philologists, no doubt, will not share our opinion and will remain convinced, with the popular mass, that our language is of Latin origin, only because they received the first notion of it on the school bench. We ourselves believed, and for a long time accepted as the expression of the truth, what our teachers taught. Only later, in seeking proof of this very conventional filiation, did we have to recognize the vanity of our efforts and repel the error born of classical prejudice. Today, nothing can undermine our conviction, which has been confirmed many times by the success achieved in the order of material phenomena and scientific results. That is why we affirm highly, without denying the introduction of Latin elements in our idiom since the Roman conquest, that our language is Greek, that we are Greeks or, more precisely, Pelagians.

Defenders of French neolatinism such as Gaston Paris, Littré and Ménage are now opposed by more clairvoyant, open-minded and free masters, such as Hins, J. Lefebvre, Louis de Fourcaud, Granier de Cassagnac, the abbot Espagnolle (J. - L. Dartois), etc. And we are glad to be with them because, despite appearances, we know that they have seen clearly, and that they have judged with a sound spirit and that they follow the simple and upright way of truth, the only one capable of leading to great discoveries.

"In 1872," writes J.-L. Dartois, "Granier de Cassagnac, in a work of marvelous erudition and pleasant style, entitled *History of the Origins of the French Language* , pointed out the inanity of the thesis of neo-Latinism, which claims to prove that French is evolved Latin. He showed that it was not sustainable, that it shocked history, logic, common sense and, finally, that our idiom repulsed it.[4]

A few years later, Mr. Hins in turn proved, in a very documented study published in the *Revue de Linguistique*, that from all the works of neo-Latinism it was only possible to conclude that there was kinship and not the filiation of the so-called neo-Latin languages... Finally, Mr. J. Lefebvre, in two remarkable and widely read articles published in June 1892 in *The New Revue* (The New Review), completely demolished the thesis of neo-Latinism, establishing that the Spanish abbot, in his book *The Origin of French*, was in truth; that our language, as the greatest scholars of the 16th century had foreseen, was Greek; that Roman domination in Gaul had only covered it with a light layer of Latin without altering its genius. "Further on", the author adds: "If we ask neo-Latinism to explain to us how the Gallic people, who included at least seven million people, were able to forget their national language and learn another, or rather change the Latin language into the Gallic language, which is more difficult; how legionaries, most of whom themselves ignored Latin and stationed in entrenched camps separated from

---

4 "Latin, a shameless synthesis of rudimentary Asian languages, but a simple intermediary in linguistics, a kind of curtain drawn on the world scene, was a vast trick favoured by a phonetics different from ours, which concealed its looting and had to be done after Allia, during the Senegalese occupation (390-345 B.C.)." – A. Champrosay, *Les Illuminé de Cabarose* (The Illuminated of Cabarose). Paris, 1920, p. 54.

each other by vast spaces, were nevertheless able to become the teachers of the Gallic tribes and teach them the language of Rome, that is, to work in the Gauls alone a miracle that the other Roman legions could not perform anywhere else, neither in Asia, nor in Greece, nor in the British Isles; how, finally, did the Basques and Bretons manage to keep their idioms, while their neighbors, the inhabitants of Béarn, Maine and Anjou, lost theirs and were forced to speak Latin, what does he tell us?" This objection is so serious that it is Gaston Paris, the head of the School, who is responsible for answering it. "We neo-Latin people," he says, "are not obliged to solve the difficulties that logic and history may raise; we only deal with the philological fact, and this fact dominates the question, since it proves, alone, the Latin origin of French, Italian and Spanish. "... Certainly," replied Mr. J. Lefebvre, "the philological fact would be decisive if it were well and properly established; but it is not at all so. With all the subtleties of the world, neo-Latinism can only actually see this banal truth, namely that there are a fairly large number of Latin words in our language. However, no one has ever contested it."

As for the philological fact invoked, but in no way demonstrated, by Mr. Gaston Paris to try to justify his thesis, J.-L. Dartois shows its non-existence by relying on the work of Petit-Radel. "To the so-called Latin philological fact", he writes, "we can contrast the obvious Greek philological fact. This new philological fact, the only true, the only demonstrable one, is of paramount importance, because it proves, without a doubt, that the tribes that came to populate the West of Europe were Pelagian colonies, and confirms the beautiful discovery of Petit-Radel. We know that this modest scientist read, in 1802, in front of the Institute, a remarkable work to prove that the monuments of polyhedral blocks that we find in Greece, Italy, France, and all the way to the bottom of Spain, and that we attributed to the Cyclops, are the work of the Pelagians. This demonstration convinced the Institute, and no doubt has since been raised about the origin of these monuments... The language of the Pelagians was archaic Greek, composed mainly of Aeolian and Dorian dialects; and it is precisely this Greek that is found everywhere, in France, even in the Argot de Paris."[5]

The language of the birds is a phonetic idiom based solely on assonance. No account is therefore taken of spelling, whose very rigor acts as a brake on curious minds and makes unacceptable any speculation carried out outside the rules of grammar. "I only care about useful things," says St Gregory in the sixth century, in a letter that serves as a preface to his Morals, "without dealing with style, the regime of prepositions or disinences, because it is not worthy of a Christian to subject the words of Scripture to the rules of grammar". This means that the meaning of sacred books is not literal, and that it is essential to know how to recover their spirit through cabalistic interpretation, as is customary to understand alchemical works. The few authors who have spoken about the language of birds give it the first place at the origin of languages. Its antiquity would go back to Adam, who used it to impose, according to God's order, suitable names, suitable to define the characteristics of the created beings and things. De Cyrano Bergerac reports this tradition when, as a new inhabitant of a world close to the sun, he is explained what the hermetic cabal is by "a naked little man sitting on a stone", an expressive figure of simple truth without clothing, sitting on the natural stone of philosophers.

"I don't remember if I spoke to him first," said the great initiate, "or if it was him who questioned me; but I have a fresh memory, as if I was still listening to him, that he spoke to me for three long hours, in a language that I know I never heard, and that has no connection with any of this world, which I understood faster and more intelligibly than that of my

---

5   J.-L. Dartois, *Neo-Latinism*. Paris, Société des Auteurs-Éditeurs, 1909, p. 6.

nurse. He explained to me, when I had inquired about something so wonderful, that in science there was a Truth, outside of which one is always far from simplicity; that the further away an idiom strayed from that Truth, the more it went below our conception, and become less understandable. "Likewise," he continued, "in music, this Truth is never found without our soul, immediately elevated, blindly carries itself there. We do not see it, but we feel that Nature sees it; and, without being able to understand in what way we are absorbed by it, it cannot but delight us, although we do not know where it is. The same applies to languages. Whoever encounters this truth of letters, words and succession can never, when expressing himself, fall below his conception: he always speaks equal to his thought; and it is in order not to have the knowledge of this perfect idiom, that you remain impeded to say anything, not knowing the order or the words that can express what you imagine". I told him that the first man in our world had undoubtedly used this language, because every name he had imposed on everything declared its essence. He interrupted me and continued: "It is not simply necessary to express everything that the mind conceives, but without it one cannot be heard by all. As this idiom is the instinct or voice of nature, it must be intelligible to everything that lives within the jurisdiction of nature. That is why, if you had the intelligence, you could communicate and speak with all your thoughts to the beasts, and the beasts, to you, all theirs, because it is the very language of Nature, by which it is heard by all animals.[6] May the ease with which you hear the meaning of a language that never rang to our ears no longer surprise you. When I speak, your soul encounters, in each of my words, that Truth which it seeks to grope; and even though its reason does not hear it, it has Nature in itself, which cannot fail to hear it."[7]

But this secret, universal, undefined language, despite the importance and truth of its expression, is in reality of Greek origin and genius, as our author teaches us in his History of Birds. He's talking about centuries-old oaks –allusion to the language used by the Druids (Δρυΐδης, de Δρῦς, oak)–, in this way: "Behold the oak trees where we are standing and which you have before your eyes: we are the ones who speak to you; and, if you wonder why we speak a language used in the world from which you come, know that our first fathers came from it; they lived in Epirus, in the forest of Dodona, where their natural kindness invited them to give oracles to the afflicted who consult them. For this purpose, they had learned the Greek language, the most universal language that was then, in order to be heard". The hermetic cabal was known in Egypt, at least in the priestly caste, as evidenced by the invocation of Leiden's Papyrus: "... I invoke you, the most powerful of the gods, who created everything; you, born of yourself, who sees everything, without being able to be seen... I invoke you under the name you possess in the *language of birds*, in the *language of hieroglyphs*, in the *language of Jews*, in the *language of Egyptians*, in the *language of Monkeys*, in the *language of hawks*, in the *language of hieratics*". We still find this idiom among the Incas, sovereigns of Peru until the time of the Spanish conquest; the ancient writers call it *lengua general* (universal language) and *lengua cortesana* (court language), i. e. diplomatic language, because it contains a double meaning corresponding to a double science, one apparent, the other profound (διπλῆ, double, and μάθη, science). "The cabal," said Father Parrot, "was an introduction to the study of all sciences".[8]

---

6 The famous founder of the Franciscan Order, to whom the illustrious Adept Roger Bacon belonged, knew the hermetic cabal perfectly well; Saint Francis of Assisi knew how to speak to birds.

7 From Cyrano Bergerac, *L'Autre Monde. Histoire comique des États et Empires du Soleil* (The Other World. Comic history of the States and Empires of the Sun). Paris, Bauche, 1910.

8 Parrot, priest, *La Vie et le Martyre du Docteur Illuminé, le bienheureux Raymond Lulle* (The Life and Martyrdom of the Illuminated Doctor, Blessed Raymond Lulle). Vendôme, 1667.

In presenting us the powerful figure of Roger Bacon, whose genius shone brightly in the intellectual firmament of the 13th century as a star of first greatness, Armand Parrot described to us how he could acquire the synthesis of ancient languages and possess such extensive practice of the mother tongue that he could, through him, teach in a short time the idioms considered the most ungrateful.[9] This, we will agree, is a truly wonderful particularity of this universal language, which appears to us both as the best key to science and the most perfect method of humanism. "Bacon," wrote the author, "knew Latin, Greek, Hebrew, Arabic; and, having thus put himself in a position to draw a rich education from ancient literature, he had acquired a reasoned knowledge of the two common languages he needed to know, that of his native country and that of France. From these particular grammars, a spirit such as his could not fail to rise to the general theory of language; the two sources from which they derive had been opened up, which are, on the one hand, the positive composition of several idioms, and on the other, the philosophical analysis of human understanding, the natural history of its faculties and concepts. Thus, he is applied almost alone throughout his century to comparing vocabularies, bringing syntaxes closer together, seeking the relationship of language with thought, and measuring the influence that character, movements and so varied forms of discourse have on the habits and opinions of peoples. It thus went back to the origins of all the simple or complex, fixed or variable, true or false notions that speech expressed. This universal grammar seemed to him to be the true logic, the best philosophy; he attributed so much power to it, that with the help of such a science he believed himself capable of teaching Greek or Hebrew in three days, just as his young disciple, John of Paris, had been taught in one year what it had cost him forty to learn.[10] "The speed of common sense education is staggering! Strange power, said Mr. Michelet, to pull, with the electric spark, the pre-existing science to man's brain!".

---

9   Armand Parrot. *Roger Bacon, sa personne, son génie, ses œuvres et ses contemporains* (Roger Bacon, his person, his genius, his works and his contemporaries). Paris, A. Picard, 1894, pp. 48 and 49.

10   See Epist. *De Laude sacrae Scripturae*, ad Clement IV. – De Gérando, *Histoire comparée des systèmes de Philosophie*, t. IV, ch. XXVII, p. 541. – *Histoire littéraire de la France*, t. XX, p. 233-234

Alchemy and Spagyria

It is to be assumed that many learned chemists, and some alchemists as well, will not share our way of seeing things. That will not stop us. Should we regarded as a resolute partisan of the most subversive theories, but we will not be afraid to develop our thinking here, considering that the truth has many other attractions than a vulgar prejudice, and that it remains preferable, in its very nakedness, to the most blatant and sumptuously dressed error.

Since Lavoisier, all the authors who have written on the history of chemistry, agree in professing that our chemistry comes, by direct filiation, from the old alchemy. Consequently, the origin of one is confused with that of the other. Alchemy, it is said, is owed by today's science the positive facts on which it has been built, thanks to the patient work of ancient alchemists.

This hypothesis, to which we could only have given a relative and conventional value, being admitted today as a proven truth, the alchemical science, stripped of its own funds, loses all that was likely to motivate its existence, of justify its reason for being. Seen thus, at a distance, under the legendary mists and the veil of ages, it offers nothing but a vague, nebulous, inconsistent form. An imprecise phantom, a lying specter, the marvelous and disappointing chimera deserves to be relegated to the ranks of the illusions of yesteryear, the false sciences, as a very eminent professor wants.[1]

But where evidence is necessary, where facts are essential, we are content to oppose to hermetic "pretensions" a petition of principle. The School, impatient, does not argue, it slices. Well, we in turn certify, by proposing to demonstrate it, that the learned men who, in good faith, espoused and propagated this hypothesis, have deceived themselves by ignorance or by lack of penetration. Only partially understanding the books they were studying, they took on the appearance of reality. Let us say clearly, since so many learned and sincere people seem to ignore it, that the real grandmother of our chemistry is the old spagyry, and not the hermetic science itself. There is, in fact, a deep chasm between spagyry and alchemy. This is

---

1 Cf. *l'Illusion et les Fausses Sciences* (Illusion and the False Sciences), by Professor Edmond-Marie-Léopold Bouty, in the journal Science et Vie , December 1913.

precisely what we will strive to achieve –at least as far as it will be expedient to do so without exceeding the permitted limits. We hope, however, to go far enough in the analysis and provide sufficient detail to nourish our thesis, and, moreover, happy to give the chemists who are enemies of bias a testimony of our good will and our concern.

There were in the Middle Ages –probably even in Greek antiquity, if we refer to the works of Zozime and Ostanès–, two degrees, two orders of research in chemical science: spagyry and archemy. These two branches of the same exoteric art were diffused in the working class through the practice of the laboratory. Metallurgists, goldsmiths, painters, ceramists, glassmakers, dyers, distillers, enamellers, potters, etc., had to be provided with sufficient spagyric knowledge, as did apothecaries. They then completed them themselves in the exercise of their profession. As for the archemists, they formed a special category, more restricted, also more obscure, among the ancient chemists. The goal they were pursuing was somewhat analogous to that of the alchemists, but the materials and means at their disposal to achieve it were only chemical materials and means. Transmuting metals into each other; producing gold and silver from vulgar ores or saline metal compounds; forcing the gold potentially contained in silver and the silver in tin to become current and extractable, that was what the archemist had in mind. He was, in the end, a spagyrist confined to the mineral kingdom, who voluntarily abandoned animal quintessences and vegetable alkaloids. However, medieval regulations forbidding the possession of chemical stoves and utensils in the home without prior authorization, many craftsmen, their work finished; studied, manipulated, experimented in secret in their cellars or attics. They cultivated the science of the little individuals, according to the somewhat disdainful expression of the alchemists for those unworthy sides of the philosopher. Let us acknowledge, without disregarding these useful researchers, that the happiest often obtained only a mediocre benefit, and that the same process, followed at first by success, afterward only gave null or uncertain results.

Nevertheless, in spite of their mistakes –or rather because of them– it was they, the archemists, who first provided the spagyrists, and later modern chemistry, with the facts, the methods, the operations that they needed. These men, tormented by the desire to search and learn everything, the true founders of a splendid and perfect science, which they endowed with right observations, exact reactions, skillful manipulations, tricks of the hand painfully acquired. Let us humbly greet these pioneers, these precursors, these great laborers and never forget what they did for us.

But alchemy, we repeat, is not part of these successive contributions. Only the hermetic writings, misunderstood by lay investigators, were the indirect cause of discoveries that their authors had never foreseen. Thus Blaise de Vigenère obtained benzoic acid by sublimation of benzoin; Brandt was able to extract phosphorus by looking for alkaest in the urine; that Basile Valentin –a prestigious Adept who did not disregard the spagyric tests–, established the whole series of antimonial salts and created the colloid of ruby gold.[2] Raymond Lulle prepared the acetone and Cassius the golden purple; Glauber obtained sodium sulfate and Van Helmont recognized the existence of gases. But, with the exception of Lulle and Basile Valentin, all these researchers, wrongly classified as alchemists, were mere archemists or

---

2   Starting from pure gold trichloride, separated from chlorauric acid and slowly precipitated by a zinc salt united with potassium carbonate, in a "certain rainwater". Rainwater alone, collected at one time in zinc containers, is enough to form the ruby colloid, which is separated from crystalloids by dialysis, which we have repeatedly experienced and always with equal success.

spagyrist scholars. That is why a famous Adept, author of a classic work,[3] can he say with a lot of reason: "If Hermes, the Father of philosophers, resurfaces today with the subtle Geber, the profound Raymond Lulle, they would not be regarded as Philosophers by our vulgar chemists[4] who would almost deign not to put them among their disciples, because they would not know how to proceed with all these distillations, these circulations, these calcinations, and all these countless operations that our vulgar chemists have invented, for having misheard the allegorical writings of these Philosophers".

With their confusing texts, interspersed with cabalistic expressions, the books remain the efficient and genuine cause of the gross misunderstanding that we are reporting. Because, despite the warnings and abjurations of their authors, students persist in reading them according to the meaning that they have in everyday language. They do not know that these texts are reserved for insiders and that it is essential, in order to understand them properly, to hold the secret key. It is to discover this key that we must first work on. Certainly, these old treaties contain, if not the integral science, then at least its philosophy, its principles, the art of applying them in accordance with natural laws. But if we ignore the occult meaning of the terms –what Ares is, for example, what distinguishes it from Aries and brings it closer to Arles, Arnet and Albait–, strange qualifiers used deliberately in the writing of such works, we must fear that we will not hear a drop or be infallibly deceived. We must not forget that this is an esoteric science. Therefore, strong intelligence, excellent memory, work and attention with strong will are not sufficient qualities to hope to become docile in this area. "These are very mistaken," writes Nicolas Grosparmy, "who claim that we have only made our books for them; but we have made them to throw them out of all those that are not our sect."[5] Batsdorff, at the beginning of his treatise, warns the reader in these charitable terms: "Every prudent man, he says, must first learn Science, if he can, that is, the principles and means of operating, if not remaining there, without foolishly using his time and good... Now, I ask those who will read this little book, to believe my words. I therefore tell them once again that they will never learn this sublime science by means of books, and that it can only be learned by divine revelation, that is why it is called Divine Art, or by means of a good and faithful master; and since there are very few to whom God has given this grace, there are also few who teach it."[6] Finally, an anonymous 18th century author[7] gives other reasons for the difficulty in deciphering the enigma: "But this, he writes, is the first and true cause for which nature has hidden this open and royal palace from so many philosophers, even those with a very subtle mind; is that, departing, from their youth, from the simple path of nature by conclusions of logic and metaphysics and, deceived by the illusions of the best books themselves, they imagine and swear that this art is deeper, more difficult to know than any metaphysics, although the ingenuous nature, in this path as in all the others, walks with a straight and very simple step".

---

3 *Cosmopolite ou Nouvelle Lumière chymique* (Cosmopolitan or New Chemical Light). Paris, Jean d'Houry, 1669.

4 It is the archemists and spagyrists whom the author refers to here as the general epithets of vulgar chemists, to distinguish them from true alchemists, also called Adepts (*Adeptus*, who has acquired) or Chemical Philosophers.

5 Nicolas Grosparmy. *L'Abrégé de Théoricque et le Secret des Secretz* (The Theoretical Abstract and the Secret of Secretz). Ms. de la National Library, nos. 12246, 12298, 12299, 14789, 19072. Arsenal's Library. no. 2516 (166 S. A. A. F.). Rennes, 160, 161.

6 Batsdorff. *Le Filet d'Ariadne* (The net of Ariadne). Paris, Laurent d'Houry, 1695, p. 2.

7 *Clavicula Hermeticae Scientiae, ad hyperbores quodam horis subsecivis consignata.* Anno 1732. Amstelodami, Petrus Mortieri, 1751, p. 51. and note page 343

Such are the opinions of philosophers on their own works. How wonder, then, that so many excellent chemists have gone astray, that they have deceived themselves by discussing a science of which they were incapable of assimilating the most elementary notions? And would it not be a service to others, to neophytes, to engage them to meditate on this great truth proclaimed by *l'Imitation* (Liv. 3, chapter II, v. 2) when speaks about the sealed books):

"They can make the sound of their words heard, but they do not give intelligence. They give the letter, but it is the Lord who discovers its meaning; they propose mysteries, but it is He who explains them. They show the way to go, but He gives strength to walk".

This is the stumbling block against which our chemists have stumbled. And we can affirm that if our scientists had understood the language of the old alchemists, the laws of the practice of Hermes would be known to them and the philosopher's stone would have ceased, for a long time, to be considered as chimerical.

We have stated above that the archemists regulated their work on the hermetic theory –as they understood it– and that this was the point of departure for fruitful experiments in purely chemical results. They thus prepared the acidic solvents which we use, and, by the action of these on the metallic bases, obtained the saline series which we know. By then reducing these salts, either by other metals, by the alkalis or the charcoal, or by the sugar or the fatty substances, they found, without transformation, the basic elements which they had previously combined. But these attempts, as well as the methods they claim, did not differ from those commonly practiced in our laboratories. Some researchers, however, pushed their investigations much further; they extended the field of chemical possibilities singularly, so much so that their results seem to us doubtful if not imaginary. It is true that these processes are often incomplete and enveloped in a mystery almost as dense as that of the Great Work. Our intention being –as we have announced– to be useful to the students, we will enter into this subject in some details and show that these recipes of puffers offer more experimental certainty than one would be inclined to attribute to them. Let the philosophers, our brothers, whose indulgence we ask for, deign to forgive us for these disclosures. But, besides the fact that we only offer our oath to alchemy and that we strictly intend to remain on the spagyric soil, we also wish to keep the promise we made to demonstrate, by real and controllable facts, that our chemistry owes everything to the spagyrists and archemists, and absolutely nothing to the Hermetic Philosophy.

The simplest method consists in using the effect of violent reactions, those of acids on the bases, in order to provoke, in the effervescence, the union of the pure parts, their irreducible assembly in the form of new bodies. It is thus possible, starting from a metal close to gold –preferably silver– to produce a small quantity of precious metal. Here, in this order of research, is an elementary operation which we certify to be successful, if our indications are closely followed.

Pour into a tall tubular glass retort, filling one third of its capacity, pure nitric acid. Fit a container with a release tube and arrange the unit on a sand bath. Operate under a fume hood. Heat the appliance gently and without reaching the boiling point of the acid. Then stop the fire, open the tubing and introduce a small fraction of virgin silver, or a cup, which contains no traces of gold. When the emission of nitrogen peroxide ceases and the effervescence has subsided, let a second portion of pure silver fall into the liquor. Repeat the introduction of the metal, without haste, until the boiling and the evolution of red vapors show little energy, indications of a near saturation. Do not add anything, leave for half an hour, then decant with care, in a beaker, your solution clear and still hot. You will find at the bottom of the retort a thin deposit in the form of black sand. Wash it with lukewarm distilled water and drop it into a small porcelain dish. You will recognize from the tests that this precipitate is insoluble in hydrochloric acid, as it is in nitric acid. Aqua regia dissolves it and gives a magnificent yellow solution, absolutely similar to that of gold trichloride. Dilute this liquor with distilled water; precipitate it with a plate of zinc, it will deposit an amorphous powder, very fine, matte, of reddish-brown color, identical to that which gives the natural gold reduced in the same way. Wash and dry thoroughly this powdery precipitate. By compressing it on a glass sheet or marble, it will give you a brilliant, coherent lamina, with a beautiful yellow sheen by reflection, of green color in transparency, having the appearance and surface characteristics of the purest gold.

In order to increase your tiny deposit by a new amount, you will be able to repeat the process as many times as you like. In this case, resume the clear silver nitrate solution extended from the first wash water; reduce the metal with zinc or copper. Decant and wash thoroughly when the reduction is complete. Dry this powdery silver and use it for your second dissolution. By repeating these steps, you will amass enough metal to make the analysis more convenient. Moreover, you will be assured of its true production, even if the silver first used contains some trace of gold.

But is this simple body, so easily obtained in a small proportion, really gold? Our sincerity commits us to say no, or at least not yet. For if it presents the most perfect external analogy with gold, and even most of its chemical properties and reactions, it nevertheless lacks an essential physical character, density. This gold is lighter than natural gold, although its density is already greater than that of silver. We can therefore consider it not as the representative of an allotropic state, more or less unstable, silver, but as young gold, nascent gold, which further reveals its recent formation. Moreover, the newly produced metal is likely to take and maintain, by contraction, the high density of the adult metal. The archemists used a process which ensured to the nascent gold all the specific qualities of adult gold; they called this technique maturation or firming, and we know that mercury was the main agent. It is still quoted in some ancient Latin manuscripts as *Confirmatio.*

It would be easy for us to make several useful and consequent remarks on the subject of the operation just mentioned, and to show on what philosophical principles the direct production of the metal rests in it. We could also give some alternatives that could increase the yield, but we would go beyond the limits we voluntarily imposed. We will leave it to the researchers to discover them for themselves and to submit the deductions to the control of the experiment. Our role is limited to presenting facts; modern archemists, spagyrists and chemists to conclude.[8]

But archemy has other methods whose results bring the proof of the philosophical affirmations. They allow the decomposition of metal bodies, long considered as simple elements. These processes, which the alchemists know, although they do not have to use them

---

8   In this order of tests, we can note a curious fact and that makes any attempt at industrialization impossible. The result, in fact, varies inversely with the quantity of metal employed. The more we act on large masses, the less produce we harvest. The same phenomenon is observed with the metal and salt mixtures from which small amounts of gold are generally removed. If the experiment usually succeeds in operating on a few grams of initial material, by working a tenfold mass, it is frequent to arrive at a total failure. We have long sought, before discovering it, the reason for this singularity, which lies in the way in which the solvents behave as their saturation progresses. The precipitate appears shortly after the beginning, and until about the middle of the attack; it is redissolved partly or wholly subsequently, according to the very importance of the volume of the acid.

in the elaboration of the Great Work, have for their object the extraction of one of the two metallic radicals, sulfur and mercury.

The hermetic philosophy teaches us that bodies have no action on bodies, and that only spirits are active and penetrating.[9] It is they, the spirits, these natural agents, who cause, within matter, the transformations that we observe there. However, wisdom shows from experience that bodies are only likely to form temporary combinations between themselves that can easily be reduced. This is the case for alloys, some of which are liquefied by simple fusion, and for all saline compounds. Similarly, alloy metals retain their specific qualities despite the various properties they affect in the state of association. We can therefore understand the usefulness of spirits in the release of metallic sulphur or mercury, when we know that only they are capable of overcoming the strong cohesion that closely links these two principles.

First, it is essential to know what the ancients designated by the generic and vague term of spirits.

For alchemists, spirits are real influences, though physically almost immaterial or imponderable. They act in a mysterious, inexplicable, unknowable but effective way, on the substances subjected to their action and prepared to receive them. Moonlight is one of those hermetic spirits.

As for the archemists, their conception turns out to be more concrete and more substantial. Our old chemists include under the same heading all the bodies, simple or complex, solid or liquid, provided with a volatile quality able to make them entirely sublimable. Metals, metalloids, salts, carbides of hydrogen, etc., bring to archemists their contingent of spirits: mercury, arsenic, antimony, and some of their compounds, sulfur, salt, ammonia, alcohol, ether, vegetable essences, etc.

To extract the metallic sulfur, the preferred technique is one that uses sublimation. Here are some indication about the procedure.

Dissolve pure silver in hot nitric acid, as described above, and then dilute this solution with hot distilled water. Decant the clear liquor to separate, if necessary, the slight black deposit we talked about. Let it cool in the dark laboratory and gradually pour into the liqueur either a filtered solution of sodium chloride or pure hydrochloric acid. The silver chloride will fall to the bottom of the vase as a white curdled mass. After letting it rest for twenty-four hours, decant the acidic water that floats, wash quickly with cold water and dry spontaneously in a room where no light enters. Then weigh your silver salt and mix three times as much pure ammonium chloride. Introduce the whole into a glass retort, high, and of such capacity that the bottom alone is occupied by the saline mixture. Give the sand bath a low heat and increase it by degrees. When the temperature is high enough, the ammonia salt will rise and fill the vault and neck of the unit with a firm layer. This sublimated, snow-white, rarely yellowish, would suggest that it contains nothing particular. So cut the retort skillfully, carefully detach this white sublimate, dissolve it in distilled, cold or hot water. Once the dissolution is complete, you will find at the bottom a very fine powder, of a bright red color; it is a part of

---

9   Geber, in his *Summa Perfectionis Magisterii*, thus speaks of the power that spirits have over bodies. "O son of doctrine," he exclaimed, "if you want to make the bodies experience various changes, it is only through the help of spirits that you will succeed (*per spiritus ipsos fieri necesse est*). When these spirits focus on the bodies, they lose their form and nature; they are no longer what they used to be. When it is separated, this is what happens: either the spirits escape alone, and the bodies where they were fixed remain, or the spirits and bodies escape together at the same time".

the silver sulfur, or lunar sulfur, detached from the metal and volatilized by the ammonia salt during its sublimation.

Despite its simplicity, this operation has some major drawbacks. Under its easy appearance, it requires great skill, great caution in the application of the fire. First of all, if we do not want to lose half or more of the metal used, we must avoid melting the salts. However, if the temperature remains below the degree required to determine and maintain the fluidity of the mixture, sublimation will not occur. On the other hand, as soon as it is established, silver chloride, already very penetrating by itself, acquires, in contact with ammonia salt, such a bite that it passes through the walls of the glass.[10] Very often, the retort cracks when the spraying phase begins, and the ammonia salt sublimates outside. The artist does not even have the resource of stoneware, earthenware or porcelain horns, which are even more porous than those of glass, especially because he must be able to constantly observe the progress of the reactions if he wishes to be able to intervene at the appropriate time. There are therefore, in this method as in many others of the same order, some secrets of practice that the archemists have cautiously reserved for themselves. One of the best is to divide the chloride mixture by interposing an inert body, which can impregnate the salts and prevent their liquefaction. This material must have neither reductive nor catalytic properties; it is also essential that it can easily be isolated from the *caput mortuum*. In the past, crushed brick and various absorbents such as tin pot, pumice stone, pulverized flint, etc., were used. These substances unfortunately provide a very impure sublimate. We give preference to certain products, which do not have any affinity for silver and ammonium chlorides, which we extract from Judean bitumen. In addition to the purity of the sulphur obtained, the technique becomes very easy. It is convenient to reduce the residue to metallic silver and repeat the sublimations until the sulphur is completely removed. The residual mass is then no longer reducible and is presented under the appearance of a grey ash, soft, very smooth, greasy to the touch, which retains the fingerprint and which yields, in a short time, half of its weight of specific mercury.

This technique also applies to lead. At a lower price, it offers the advantage of providing salts insensitive to light, which exempts the artist from operating in darkness; it is also not necessary to use impastation; finally, since lead is less fixed than silver, the yield in red sublimated is better and time is shorter. The only unfortunate fact of the operation is that the ammonia salt forms, with the sulphur of lead, a compact and so tenacious saline layer that it looks as if it has melted with the glass. It is therefore difficult to detach it from it without breaking the glass. As for the extract itself, it is a beautiful red, coated in a strongly colored yellow sublimate, but very impure compared to that of silver. It is therefore important to purify it before using it. Its maturity is also less perfect, an important consideration if research is directed towards obtaining particular tinctures.

Not all metals obey the same chemical agents. The process suitable for silver and lead cannot be applied to tin, copper, iron or gold. Moreover, the spirit capable of detaching and isolating sulphur from a given metal will exert its action with another metal, on the mercurial principle of the latter. In the first case, mercury will be strongly retained, while sulphur will sublimate; in the second, the opposite phenomenon will occur. Hence, the diversity of methods and the variety of metal decomposition techniques. It is, moreover, and above all, the affinity that bodies show for each other, and these for spirits, that regulates their application. We know that silver and lead together have a very strong sympathy; silver lead ores prove this quite well. However, since affinity establishes the deep chemical identity of these

---

10 It colours them in the mass with a red tint by transparency, green by reflection.

bodies, it is logical to think that the same mind, when used under the same conditions, will determine the same effects. This is what happens with iron and gold, which are closely related. When Mexican prospectors discover a very red sandy soil, composed mostly of oxidized iron, they conclude that gold is not far away. Therefore, they consider this red earth as the mining and mother of gold, and the best indication of a nearby vein. However, this fact seems quite singular, given the physical differences of these metals. In the category of common metallic bodies, gold is the rarest of them; iron, on the other hand, is certainly the most common, the one found everywhere, not only in mines, where it occupies considerable and numerous deposits, but also scattered on the very surface of the ground. Clay owes its special color to it, sometimes yellow when the iron is divided in the hydrate state, sometimes red if it is in the form of sesquioxide, a color that is still enhanced by firing (bricks, tiles, pottery). Of all the classified ores, iron pyrite is the most vulgar and best known. Black ferruginous masses, in balls of various sizes, in shell-like agglomerates, in nodules, are frequently found in fields, along roads, on chalky soils. Rural children are used to playing with these marcasites, which show a fibrous, crystalline and radiant texture when they are broken. They sometimes contain small amounts of gold. Meteorites, composed mainly of molten magnetic iron, prove that the interplanetary masses from which they originate owe most of their structure to iron. Some plants contain assimilable iron (wheat, watercress, lentils, beans, potatoes). Humans and vertebrate animals owe the red color of their blood to iron and gold. Iron salts are the active ingredient of hemoglobin. They are even so necessary to organic vitality that medicine and pharmacopoeia have always sought to provide depleted blood with the metal compounds suitable for its reconstitution (peptonate and iron carbonate). Among the people, the use of water made ferruginous by dipping oxidized nails has been preserved. Finally, iron salts have such a variety in their coloring that it can be assured that they would be sufficient to reproduce all the tones of the spectrum, from purple, which is the color of pure metal, to the intense red it gives to silica in the various kinds of rubies and garnets.

This was enough to persuade archemists to work on iron, in order to discover the components of their tinctures. Moreover, this metal easily allows its sulphurous and mercurial constituents to be extracted in a single operation, which is already very advantageous. The great, enormous difficulty lies in the combination of these elements, which, despite their purification, energetically refuse to combine to form a new body. But we will not analyze or solve this problem, since our subject is limited to establishing the proof that archemists have always used chemical materials implemented using chemical means and operations.

In the spagyric treatment of iron, it is the energetic reaction of acids, having a similar affinity for the metal, that is used to overcome cohesion. We usually start with iron pyrite or metal reduced to filings. In the latter case, we recommend to exercise prudence and caution. If pyrite is used, it is sufficient to grind it as finely as possible and make it red hot in the fire, only once, by stirring it strongly. When cooled, it is introduced into a large flask with four times its weight of aqua regia, and brought it to a boil. After an hour or two, the liquor is left to rest, decanted, then a similar quantity of new aqua regia is poured over the magma and boiled as before. Boiling and decantation must continue until the pyrite appears white at the bottom of the vessel. All the extracts are then taken up again, filtered on fiberglass and concentrate them by slow distillation in a tubular retort. When only about a third of the original volume remains, open the retort and pour a certain quantity of pure sulphuric acid into it, in successive fractions, at 66° (660 g for a total volume of extract from 500 g of pyrite). Then it is distilled until dry and, after changing the container, the temperature is gradually increased. We will see oily drops, red as blood, which represent the sulphurous tincture, distilled, then a beautiful sublimated white, which attaches to the vault and neck under the appearance of crystalline down. This sublimated is a real salt of mercury –called by some archemists vitriol mercury–, which is easily reduced to fluid mercury by iron filings, quicklime or anhydrous potassium carbonate. We can immediately ensure that this sublimated contains the specific mercury of iron by rubbing the crystals on a copper blade: the amalgam occurs immediately and the metal appears silvery.

As for the filings of iron, they yield a sulfur of a golden color, instead of being red, and a little, very little, of sublimated mercury. The process is the same, but with this slight difference, it is necessary to throw in the aqua regia, previously heated, pinches of filings and wait, at each of them, for the effervescence to subside. It is good to stir the bottom with an agitator to prevent the filings from becoming one single mass. After filtration and reduction by half, we add, very little at a time, because the reaction is violent and the jolts furious, sulfuric acid up to half that weighs the concentrated liquor. This is the dangerous side of handling, because it happens quite often that the retort explodes or cracks at the level of the acids.

We will stop there the description of the processes on the iron, estimating that they amply suffice to support our thesis, and we will finish the exposition of the spagyric processes by that of the gold, which is, according to the opinion of all the philosophers, the body most refractory to dissociation. It is a common axiom in spagyry that it is easier to make gold than to destroy it. But here a brief observation is needed.

Born only our desire to prove the chemical reality of archemical research, we will be careful not to teach, in plain language, how we can make gold. The goal we are pursuing is of a higher order. And we prefer to stay in the pure alchemical field, rather than engage the researcher to follow these paths covered with brambles and bordered by potholes. For the application of these methods, by strengthening the chemical principle of direct transmutations, can not bring the slightest testimony in favor of the Great Work, the elaboration of which remains completely alien to the same principle. That said, let's resume our subject.

An old spagyric proverb claims that the seed of gold is in gold itself; we will not contradict it, provided that we know what gold is in question, or how it is advisable to seize this seed liberated from vulgar gold. If we ignore the last of these secrets, we must necessarily be content to witness the production of the phenomenon, without making any profit other than objective certainty. Observe carefully what happens in the next operation, the execution of which presents no difficulty.

Dissolve pure gold in the aqua regia; pour in sulfuric acid in weight equal to half the weight of gold employed. It will only be a slight contraction. Shake the solution and introduce it into a non-tubulated glass retort, arranged on a sand bath. At first apply a moderate heat, so that the distillation of the acids takes place slowly and without boiling. When nothing will distill more and the gold will appear at the bottom in the aspect of a yellow mass, matte, dry and cavernous, change container and gradually increase the heat of the flame. You will see rising white vapors, opaque, light at first, then more and more heavy. The first will condense into a beautiful yellow oil that will flow to the container; the seconds will sublimate and garnish the vault and the birth of the neck of fine crystals imitating the down of the birds. Their color, a beautiful red blood, takes on the brilliance of the rubies when a ray of sunlight or some bright light comes to strike them. These crystals, very deliquescent, as well as the other salts of gold, disintegrate in yellow liquor as soon as the temperature goes down ...

We will not pursue further the study of sublimations. As for the archemic processes known as Little Particulars, they are, in most cases, random techniques. The best of these processes start from the metal products extracted according to the means we have indicated.

They will be found in abundance in many second-rate books and puffers manuscripts. We will limit ourselves, for documentary purposes, to reproduce the individual mentioned by Basile Valentine, because, unlike the others, he is supported by solid and relevant philosophical reasons. The great Adept states in this passage that a particular tincture can be obtained by combining mercury from silver with sulphur from copper through iron salt. "The Moon, he said, has a fixed mercury by which it underlies the violence of fire longer than other imperfect metals; and the victory it achieves shows how fixed it is, so that the ravenous Saturn cannot take or diminish anything. The lascivious Venus is well colored, and her whole body is almost nothing more than a tincture and color similar to that of the Sun, which, because of its abundance, draws heavily on the red. But all the more so as his body is leprous and sick, the fixed tincture cannot make his home there, and the body flying away, necessarily the tincture must follow, because here the soul cannot remain, his home being consumed by fire, not appearing and fleeing is leaving him no seat and refuge, which on the contrary accompanied remains everything with a fixed body. The fixed salt provides the Mars warrior with a hard, strong, solid and robust body, from which comes his magnanimity and great courage. That's why it's so difficult to overcome this brave captain, because his body is so hard that he can be hurt with great pain. But if someone measures his strength and hardness with the constancy of the Moon and the beauty of Venus, and grants them by a spiritual means, he will be able to do not so much harm to a sweet harmony, by means of which the poor man, having used it, has the effect of a few keys of our Art, after having ascended to the top of this ladder and reached the end of the Work, can particularly gain his life. For the phlegmatic and humid nature of the Moon can be warmed and dried by the hot and angry blood of Venus, and its great darkness corrected by the salt of Mars."[11]

Among the archemists who used gold to increase it, using formulas that led them to success, we quote the Venetian priest Pantheus;[12] Naxagoras, author of Alchymia denudata (1715); de Locques; Duclos; Bernard de Labadye; Joseph du Chesne, Baron de Morance, ordinary physician to King Henry IV; Blaise of Vigenère; Bardin, from Le Havre (1638); Miss de Martinville (1610); Yardley, English inventor of a process transmitted to Mr. Garden, glovemaker in London, in 1716, then communicated by M. Ferdinand Hockley to Dr. Sigismond Bacstrom, and which was the subject of a letter from him to ML Sand in 1804;[13] finally, the pious philanthropist Saint Vincent de Paul, founder of the Fathers of the Mission (1625), the congregation of the Sisters of Charity (1634), etc.

May we allow ourselves to pause for a moment on this great and noble figure, as well as on his occult work, which is generally ignored.

We know that during a trip he made from Marseille to Narbonne, Saint Vincent de Paul was captured by Barbary pirates and taken captive to Tunis. He was then twenty-four years old.[14]

---

11 *Les Douze Clefs de Philosophie* (The Twelve Keys to Philosophy). Paris, Pierre Moët, 1659, Liv. I, p. 34.

12 JA Pantheus, *Ars and Theoria Transmutationis metallicae cum Voarchadumia Veneunt.* Gautherorium Vivantium, 1550.

13 Dr. S. Bacstrom was affiliated with the Hermetic Society founded by the Adept of Chazel, who lived in Mauritius, in the Indian Ocean, at the time of the Revolution.

14 Born in Poux, near Dax, in 1581, biographers say he was born in 1576, although he himself gives his exact age, on various occasions, in his correspondence. This error is explained by the fact that with the complicity of prelates acting against the decisions of the Council of Trent, he was fraudulently passed off as twenty-four years old, whereas he was only nineteen when he was ordained a priest in 1600.

We are also assured that he managed to bring back his last master, a renegade, to the fold of the Church, that he returned to France and stayed in Rome, where Pope Paul V received him with great respect. It was from this moment that he began his pious foundations and his charitable institutions. But what no one told us is that the father of the foundlings, as he was known in his lifetime, had learned archemy during his captivity. Thus it is explained, without the need for miraculous intervention, that the great apostle of Christian charity has had the means to realize his many philanthropic works.[15] He was, besides, a practical man, positive, resolute, not neglecting his affairs, not dreaming or inclined to mysticism. For the rest, a deeply human soul under a rough exterior of an active, tenacious, ambitious man.

We possess two very suggestive letters from him, in regard to his chemical work. The first, written to M. de Comet, a lawyer at the presidential court of Dax, was published several times and analyzed by Georges Bois, in the *Occult Menace* (Occult Peril) (Paris, Victor Retaux, n.d.). It is written from Avignon and dated June 24, 1607. We will take this document, which is quite long, at the moment when Vincent de Paul, having completed the mission for which he was in Marseilles, prepares to return to Toulouse.

"... Being about to leave by land, he said, I was persuaded by a gentleman with whom I was housed, to embark with him until Narbonne, in view of the favorable weather conditions; and I embarked to take advantage of the occasion and to save money, or rather to say, for my misfortune, and to lose everything.. The wind was as favorable as it must be to us to go to Narbonne that day, which is fifty leagues away, if God had only not allowed three Turkish brigantines that were cruising the Gulf of Leon (to catch the boats that come from Beaucaire, where there is a fair that is considered to be one of the most beautiful in Christendom), which hunted and attacked us so fiercely that two or three of our people were killed and all the rest wounded, including myself, that was hit by an arrow, that would serve as a clock for the rest of my life, so we were forced to surrender to those pirates, worse than tigers. Their first outbursts of rage led them to hack our pilot in a thousand pieces, with axes, for having killed one of the principal ones among them, besides four or five criminals that our men had killed. Having done this, they chained us after having treated us rudely and continued their course committing a thousand larcenies, but giving freedom to those who surrendered without fighting, after having stripped them. And finally, loaded with merchandise, after seven or eight days, they took the route of Barbary, lair of the faithless thieves of the worst species of the great Turk, and so we arrived and they put us on sale with the summary of our capture, that they said to have carried out in a Spanish ship, because without that lie we would have been liberated by the consul that the king maintains there to guarantee the free trade of the French. The procedure of our sale consisted in that, after they had left us in live skins, they gave each of us a pair of panties, a linen overvest and a cap, and so they walked us through the city of Tunis, where they had gone to sell us. Having made us go around the city five or six times, with the chain around our necks, they led us to the ship so that the merchants would come to see who could eat and who could not, in order to show that our ailments were not mortal at all. Having done this, they led us to the square, where the merchants went to

---

15 He founded, says the Abbé Pétin (*Dictionary hagiographique*, in the *Encyclopédie de Migne*. Paris, 1850), a hospital for galley slaves in Marseilles, established in Paris the houses of Orphans, Daughters of Providence, and Daughters of the Cross; the Jesus Hospital, Children Found, the General Hospital of Salpêtrière. "Not to mention the general hospital of Sainte-Renne, which he founded in Burgundy, he rescued several provinces, ravaged by famine and plague; and the alms he sent to Lorraine and Champagne amounted to nearly two millions".

examine us just as they is done when purchasing a horse or an ox, making us open our mouth to inspect our teeth, palpating our sides, probing our wounds and making us walk, jog or run, then holding bundles and then struggle to see the strength of each, and a thousand other kinds of brutalities.

"I was sold to a fisherman, who was soon forced to get rid of me, because no one agrees less with the sea than I do. Then, from the fisherman, I became the property of an old man, a spagyric doctor, despotic sovereign of quintessence, a very human and treatable man who, from what he told me, had worked fifty years in search of the philosopher's stone, and although his effort was futile as for the stone itself, it certainly achieved other forms of metal transmutation. And to attest to that, I declare that I often saw him melt as much gold as silver together, place them in little flakes, and then put a layer of some powder, then another layer of powder in a crucible or in a goldsmith's melting pot, keep it on the fire for twenty-four hours and, finally, open it and find the silver turned into gold. And, more often still, I saw him congeal or fix the quicksilver in fine silver that he was selling to give alms to the poor. My occupation was to keep the fire in ten or twelve ovens, which, thank God, did not cause me more pain than pleasure. My owner loved me very much, and he was very pleased to talk to me about alchemy and, moreover, about his law, which he tried to attract me by promising me a lot of wealth and all his your knowledge. God always maintained in me the belief in my liberation, by the assiduous prayers that addressed to him and to the Virgin Mary, through whose sole intercession I firmly believe that I have been saved. The hope and firm belief that I had to see you again, then, sir, moved me to beg my master assiduously to teach me the means of curing lithiasis, in which I saw him operate miracles every day. What he did was to order me to prepare and administer the ingredients ...

"I stayed with this old man since the month of September 1605 until the next month of August, that he was taken and led to the Grand Sultan, to work for him; but in vain, for he died of sorrow on the way. He left me to his nephew, a true anthropomorphist, who sold me after the death of his uncle, because he heard it said that Monsieur de Breve, ambassador of the king of Turkey, came with good and express patents of the great Turk to redeem the Christian slaves. A renegade of Nice in Savoye, enemy of nature, bought me and took me to his *temat* (This is the name of the parcel of land which share croppers held from the great lord, as the village has nothing, as everything belongs to the Sultan). The *temat* of this one was in the mountain, where the country is extremely hot and desert-like".

After converting this man, Vincent left with him, ten months later, "at the end of which", continues the writer, "we ran away with a small skiff and we arrived the twenty-eighth day of June 28 in Aigues-Mortes, and soon after in Avignon, where monseigneur the vice-legat publicly received the renegade, the tear in the eye and the sob in the throat, in the church of St. Peter, to the honor of God and edification of the spectators. This Monsignor honored me with great love and fondness, because some secrets of alchemy that I taught him, which he made more of than *si io gli avessi dato un monte di oro*.[16] Because he has worked all the time of his life, for no other contentment ... - Vincent Depaul.[17]

---

16 If I had given him a mountain of gold.

17 We do not know why historians and biographers persist in maintaining Vincent de Paul's whimsical spelling. This one does not need any particle to be noble among the nobles. All his epistles are signed Depaul. We find this name written in this way on a Masonic convocation reproduced on pages 130-131 of the *Dictionnaire d'Occultisme* (Dictionary of Occultism) of E. Desormes and Adrien Basile (Angers, Lachèse, 1897). It should not be surprising, moreover, that a lodge, obedient to the code of

In January 1608, a second epistle, addressed from Rome to the same addressee, shows Vincent de Paul initiating the vice-legate of Avignon, of which he has just been mentioned, and very well in court, thanks to his spagyric secrets. "My state is thus such, in a word, that I am in that city of Rome, where I continue my studies, maintained by my lord the Vice-Legate, who was of Avignon, who honors my with love and desires my advancement, for having shown him the beautiful and curious things which I learned during my slavery of this old Turkish man, to whom, as I have written to you, I was sold, of the number of which curiosities is the beginning, not the total perfection, the mirror of Archimedes, an artificial resource to make a skull speak, which this wretch used to seduce the people, telling them that his god Muhammad would tell him his will by this skull, and a thousand other beautiful geometrical things, which I have learned from him, of which Monsignor is so jealous that he does not even want me to talk to anyone, for fear that I will teach them, because he wants to be the only one with the reputation of knowing these things, which he sometimes likes to show to His Holiness[18] and to the Cardinals".

Despite the little credit he gives to alchemists and their science, Georges Bois nevertheless acknowledges that one cannot suspect the sincerity of the narrator, nor the reality of the experiences he has seen practiced. "It is a witness, he writes, who brings together all the guarantees that can be expected from an eyewitness, frequent, and particularly unselfish, a condition that does not occur to the same degree among researchers who tell their own experiences and who are always concerned about a particular point of view. He's a good witness, but he's a man: he's not infallible. He could have been mistaken and mistaken for gold what was only an alloy of gold and silver. This is what we are inclined to believe, based on our current ideas, and the habit we owe to our education of classifying transmutation among fables. But if we simply weigh the testimony we are examining, error is not possible. It is clearly stated that the alchemist melted together as much gold as silver: this is the well-defined alloy.[19] This alloy is laminated. Then the laminates are arranged in layers, separated by layers of a certain powder that is not otherwise described. This powder is not the philosopher's stone, but it has one of its properties: it transmutes. It is heated for twenty-four hours, and the silver that entered the alloy is transformed into gold. This gold is sold and so on and so forth. There is no misunderstanding in the distinction of metals. Moreover, it is unlikely, given that the transaction is frequent and the gold traded to merchants, that such a huge error occurred so easily. Because at that time everyone believed in alchemy; and goldsmiths, bankers, merchants, knew very well how to distinguish pure gold from gold alloyed with other metals. Since Archimedes, everyone has known gold by the ratio between its volume and its weight. The princes who forge coins deceive their subjects, but they do not deceive the bankers' scales or the art of the testers. We didn't trade in gold by selling for gold, which was not gold. It was, at the time when we were placing ourselves, in 1605, in Tunis, which was then one of the most famous markets in international trade, a fraud as difficult and dangerous as it would be today, for example, in London, Amsterdam, New York or Paris, where large gold payments are made

charity and high brotherhood which governed masonry of the eighteenth century, was put under the nominal protection of the powerful philanthropist. The document in question, dated February 14, 1835, comes from the lodge *Salut, Force, Union, du Chapitre des Disciples de saint Vincent Depaul* (Salut, Force, Union, of the Disciples' Chapter of St. Vincent Depaul), attached to the East of Paris and founded in 1777.

18 The Pope.

19 It is all the less possible to misunderstand the nature of this alloy since silver causes such discoloration in gold that it cannot go unnoticed. However, it is almost total here, the metals being alloyed with equal weight, and the alloy appears white.

in bullion. This is the most demonstrative, in our opinion, of the facts we have been able to find in support of the alchemists' opinion on the reality of transmutation".

As for the operation itself, it depends exclusively on archemy and is very similar to the one that Pantheus teaches in his *Voarchadumia*, whose result he calls gold of the two cementations. For if Vincent de Paul has given the outline of the process, he has avoided, on the other hand, to describe the order and the way of operating. He who nowadays tries to realize it, even if he had a perfect knowledge of the special cement, should fail. It is because gold, in order to acquire the faculty of transmuting the silver alloyed to it, needs first of all to be prepared, the cement only acting on silver alone. Without this prior arrangement, the gold would remain inert within the electrum and could not transmit to the silver what in the natural state it does not have.[20] Spagyrists call this preliminary work exaltation or transfusion, and it is also by means of a cement applied by stratification that it is executed. So that the composition of this first cement being different from that of the second, the name assigned by Pantheus to the metal obtained is thus fully justified.

The secret of exaltation, without whose knowledge success cannot be obtained, consists in increasing –by a single burst or gradually– the normal color of pure gold by the sulfur of an imperfect metal, usually copper. It gives the precious metal its own blood by a kind of chemical transfusion. The gold, overloaded with tincture, then takes the red aspect of the coral and can give to the specific mercury of silver the sulfur which it lacks, thanks to the mediation of the mineral spirits released from the cement during the work. This transmission of excess sulfur retained by exalted gold is gradually effected by the action of heat; it takes from twenty-four to forty hours, according to the skill of the craftsman and the volume of the treated matter. It is necessary to be extremely careful with the regulation of the fire, which must be continuous and strong enough, without ever reaching the point of fusion of the alloy. By heating too much, one would risk volatilizing the silver and dissipating the sulphur introduced into the gold without this sulphur having acquired a perfect fixity.

Finally, a third manipulation, deliberately omitted because an archemist does not need so much advice, includes the brushing of the extracted laminae, their fusion and cupellation. The pellet of pure gold manifests a more or less noticeable diminution of weight, which generally varies between the fifth and the quarter of the alloyed silver. Whatever the case may be, and despite this loss, the process still leaves a good profit.

We will remark, with regard to exaltation process, that the coralline gold, obtained by any of the various methods advocated, remains capable of transmuting directly, that is to say, without the aid of a subsequent cementation, a certain amount of silver: about a quarter of his weight. However, since it is impossible to determine the exact value of the aurific power coefficient, we circumvent this problem by melting the red gold with a triple proportion of silver (inquartation) and subjecting the laminated alloy to the beginning operation.

After having said that the exaltation, based on the absorption of a certain portion of metallic sulfur by the mercury of gold, has the effect of reinforcing considerably the proper coloration of the metal, we shall give some indications about the methods employed to achieve this purpose. These use the ability of solar mercury to strongly retain a fraction of pure sulfur, when acting on the metal mass, to dissociate the alloy originally formed. Thus, gold melted with copper, if it is separated from it, never entirely abandons a portion of tincture taken from

---

20 Basil Valentine insists on the need to give gold an overabundance of sulfur. "Gold does not dye," he says, "if it has not been dyed before".

it. So that by repeating the same action several times, the gold is enriched more and more and can then yield this excess tincture to the metal that is close to it, that is to say to silver.

An experienced chemist, points out Naxagoras, knows well enough that if gold is purified by antimony sulphide up to twenty-four times or more, it acquires remarkable color, brilliancy, and finesse. But also there is a loss of metal, contrary to what happens with copper, because, in purification, the mercury of gold gives up part of its substance to antimony, and the sulfur is then superabundant, by imbalance of natural proportions. This makes the process unusable and can only be expected to offer a mere satisfaction of curiosity.

It is also possible to exalt the gold by first melting it with three times its weight in copper, and then by decomposing the alloy, converted into filings, by the boiling nitric acid. Although this technique is laborious and costs a lot, given the volume of acid required, it is however one of the best and safest that we know.

However, if one possesses an energetic reducer and knows how to use it in the course of the fusion of gold and the copper, the operation will be greatly simplified and there will be no need to fear loss of material or excessive work, despite the indispensable repetitions that this method still requires. Finally, the artist, by studying these various methods, will be able to discover better, and more effective ones. It will be enough, for example, to use sulphur, directly extracted from the lead, to incinerate it back to a raw state and to project it little by little in the molten gold, which will retain the pure part, unless you prefer to resort to iron, whose specific sulfur is, of all metals, the one for which gold manifests the greatest affinity.

But it's enough. Let whoever wants to work now; let everyone keep their opinion, follow or despise our advice, it doesn't matter to us. We will repeat one last time that, of all the operations voluntarily described in these pages, none of them relate, directly or indirectly, to traditional alchemy; none can be compared to its own operations. A thick wall separates the two sciences, an impassable barrier to those familiar with chemical methods and formulas. We do not want to despair anyone, but the truth forces us to say that those who are engaged in spagyric research will never leave the paths of official chemistry. Many modern people believe, in good faith, that they are resolutely departing from chemical science because they explain its phenomena in a special way, without, however, using any other technique than that of the learned men whom they criticize. There were always, by misfortune, wanderers and deceived of that kind, and for them, no doubt, Jacques Tesson wrote these words full of truth: "Those who want to do our Work by digestion, by vulgar distillation and similar sublimation, and others by trituration; all these are off the right path, in great error and pain, and never will succeed, because all these names, and words, and ways of operating, are names, words and ways of doing things metaphorical".[21]

We believe, that we have fulfilled our intentions and demonstrated, as far as we have been able to do, that the grandmother of present chemistry is not the old and simple alchemy, but ancient spagyria, enriched by the successive contributions of Greek, Arabic and medieval archemy.

And if you wish to have some idea of the secret science, turn your thoughts to the work of the farmer or the microbiologist, because ours is placed under the dependence of analogous conditions. For like Nature gives to the cultivator the soil and the grain, and to the

---

21 Jacques Tesson or Le Tesson. *Le Grand et excellent Œuvre des Sages, contenant trois traités ou dialogues : Dialogues du Lyon verd, du grand Thériaque et du Régime* (The Great and Excellent Work of the Wise, containing three treatises or dialogues: Dialogues of the Green Lyon, the Great Theriac and the Diet. Ms. from the 17th century. Lyon Library, No. 971 (900).

microbiologist the agar and the spore, in the same way it gives the alchemist the appropriate metallic soil and suitable seeds. If all circumstances favorable to the regular march of this special crop are rigorously observed, the harvest cannot but be abundant...

In short, alchemical science, of an extreme simplicity in its materials and its formula, remains however the most thankless, the most obscure of all, considering the exact knowledge of the required conditions, of the required influences. This is his mysterious side, and it is to the solution of this difficult problem that the efforts of all the sons of Hermes converge.

Book II

The Salamander of Lisieux

I

Lisieux is a small Norman town, which owes its picturesque medieval aspect to its many wooden houses and its canopy gables. It is respectful of the past times, and offers us, among so many other curiosities, a pretty and very interesting Alchemist's residence.

A modest house, in truth, but which proves its builder's concern for humility, that the lucky beneficiaries of the hermetic treasure vowed to respect during their whole life. It is generally referred to as "Manor of the Salamander" and occupies the number 19 of rue aux Fèves (see Plate IV, in the next page).

Despite our research, we were unable to get any information about its original owners. We do not know them. No one knows, in Lisieux or elsewhere, by whom it was built, in the sixteenth century, nor who were the artists who decorated it. In order not to fall short of tradition, no doubt, the Salamander jealously keeps its secret and that of the alchemist. It was, however, in 1834, the subject of an article, but it was limited to the description pure and simple carved subjects that the tourist can admire on its facade.[1] This article and some lines inserted in the *Statistique monumentale du Calvados* (Monumental statistics of Calvados), of M. de Caumont (Lisieux, volume V), represent all the published material about the Manor of the Salamander. It is not much, and we regret it. For the tiny, but delightful hotel, built by the will of a true Adept, decorated with motifs borrowed from hermetic symbolism, from traditional allegory, deserves better. Well known to the inhabitants of Lisieux, it is ignored by the general public, perhaps even by many art lovers, although its decoration, both in its abundance and variety, as well as its good conservation, allows it to be ranked first among best buildings of its kind. This is an unfortunate gap, and we will try to fill it by highlighting both the artistic value of this elegant home and the initiatory teaching that emerges from his sculptures.

---

1 Cf. De Formeville, *Notice sur une maison du XVIe siècle, à Lisieux, dessinée et lithographiée par Challamel* (Record on a 16th century house, in Lisieux, drawn and lithographed by Challamel). Paris, Janet and Koepplin; Lisieux, Pigeon, 1834.

A study of the facade's motifs allows us to affirm, with a conviction born of a patient analysis, that the builder of the Manor was an educated alchemist, who gave the measure of his talent; in other words, an adept possessor of the philosopher's stone. We also certify that his affiliation to some esoteric center, having many points of contact with the scattered order of the Knights Templar, proves to be indisputable. But what could be this secret fraternity which was honored to count among its members the learned philosopher of Lisieux? We must confess our ignorance and leave the question unanswered. However, although we have an invincible repugnance for the hypothesis, the likelihood, the relationship of dates, and the proximity of the places suggest certain conjectures.

A century or so before the construction of the Manor de Lisieux, three alchemist companions worked in Flers (Orne) and there accomplished the Great Work in the year 1420. It was Nicolas de Grosparmy, gentleman, Nicolas or Noël Valois, named still Le Vallois, and a priest named Pierre Vicot or Vitecoq. The latter called himself "chaplain and domestic servant

LISIEUX - MANOIR OF THE SALAMANDRE
The Man with the Tree Trunk on the Corner Post - Plate IV

of the Sieur de Grosparmy".[2] Only de Grosparmy possessed some fortune, with the title of Lord and that of Count de Flers. It was, however, Valois who first discovered the practice of the Work and taught it to his companions, as he says in his *Cinq Livres* (Five Books). He was then forty-five, which places the date of his birth to the year 1375. The three Adepts wrote various books between the years 1440 and 1450.[3] None of these books have ever been printed. According to a note appended to manuscript No. 158 (125) of the Rennes Library, it would be a Norman gentleman, M. Bois Jeuffroy, who would have inherited all the original treatises of Nicolas de Grosparmy, Valois and Vicot. He sold the complete copy to the late Count de Flers, for 1500 livres and a prize horse. This Count de Flers and Baron de Tracy is Louis de Pelleve, who died in 1660, who was great-grandson, on the side of women, of the author Grosparmy. [4]

But these three adepts, who lived and worked in Flers in the first half of the fifteenth century, are cited without any reason, as belonging to the sixteenth century. In the copy held by the Rennes library, however, it is clearly stated that they lived in the castle of Flers, of which Grosparmy was the owner, "at which place they did the Philosophical Work and composed their books." The initial error, conscious or not, comes from an anonymous author of notes titled *Remarks*, written in the margin of some handwritten copies of the works of Grosparmy, having belonged to the chemist Chevreul. The latter, without further controlling the whimsical chronology of these notes, gave the dates, systematically set back a century by the anonymous writer, and all the authors, following him, peddled this unforgivable mistake. We will, briefly, restore the truth. Alfred de Caix, after having said that Louis de Pellevé died in distress in 1660, adds:[5] "According to the preceding document, the land of Flers would have been acquired from Nicolas de Grosparmy; but the author of the Notesis here in contradiction with M. de la Ferriere, who quotes at the date of 1404 a Raoul de Grosparmy as lord of the place.[6] Nothing is more true, though, on the other hand, Alfred de Caix seems to accept the falsified chronology of the unknown annotator. In 1404, Raoul de Grosparmy was indeed lord of Beuville and Flers,[7] and although it is not known to what extent he became the owner of it, the fact can not be called into question. "Raoul de Grosparmy," writes Count Hector de la Ferriere, "must be the father of Nicolas de Grosparmy, who, from Marie de Reaux, left three sons, Jehan de Grosparmy, Guillaume and Mathurin de Grosparmy, and a daughter, Guillemette de Grosparmy , married on January 8, 1496 to Germain de Grimouville. On that date, Nicholas Grosparmy was dead, and Jehan de Grosparmy, Baron de Flers, his eldest son, and Guillaume de Grosparmy, his second son, granted to their sister, in consideration of her mar-

2 Cf. National Library, ms. 14789 (3032): *La Clef des Secrets de Philosophie* (The Key of the Secrets of Philosophy), of Pierre Vicot, priest; Eighteenth century.

3 Nicolas de Grosparmy finishes the *l'Abrégé de Théorique* (Abstract of Theoretical), supplying the exact date of completion of this work: "which," he says, "compiled and had it written, and was perfect on the 29th day of December in the year one thousand four hundred and forty-nine." See Rennes Library, ms. 158 (125), p. 111.

4 Cf. Charles Verel. *Les Alchimistes de Flers* (The Alchemists of Flers). Alençon, 1889, in-8 ° of 34 p., in the *Bulletin de la Société historique et archéologique de l'Orne* (Bulletin of the Historical and Archaeological Society of the Orne).

5 Alfred de Caix, *Notice sur quelques alchimistes normands* (Notice on some Norman alchemists). Caen, F. Le Blanc-Hardel, 1868.

6 Count Hector de la Ferriere, *Histoire de Flers, ses seigneurs, son industrie* (History of Flers, his lords, his industry). Paris, Dumoulin, 1855.

7 Laroque, *Histoire de la maison d'Harcourt* (History of the house of Harcourt), t. II, p. 1148.

riage, three hundred livres tournoys, cash , and a pension of twenty pounds a year, redeemable for the price of four hundred livres tournoys.[8]

So that is perfectly well established: the dates on the copies of the various Grosparmy and Valois manuscripts are rigorously exact and absolutely authentic. Therefore, we could dispense with the search for the biographical and chronological concordance of Nicolas Valois, since it is shown that this one was the companion and the commensal of the lord-count of Flers. But it is still necessary to discover the origin of the error attributable to the commentator, so ill-informed, of Chevreul's manuscripts. Let us say immediately that it could come from an unfortunate homonymy, unless our anonymous, faking all the dates, did not want to do honor to Nicolas Valois of the sumptuous hotel of Caen, built by one of his successors.

Nicolas Valois is said to have acquired, towards the end of his life, the four lands of Escoville, Fontaines, Mesnil-Guillaume and Manneville. The fact, however, is by no means proved; no document confirms it, except the free and questionable statement of the author of the aforesaid *remarks*. The old alchemist, craftsman of the fortune of Le Vallois and lords of Escoville, lived as a sage, according to the precepts of philosophical discipline and morality. He who wrote in 1445 for his son that "patience is the ladder of the philosophers, and humility the door of their garden," could hardly follow the example or lead the train of the powerful without failing his convictions. It is therefore probable that at seventy, devoid of any other material preoccupation than that of his works, he finished at Flers Castle an existence of toil, calm, and simplicity, in the company of the two friends with whom he had realized the Great Work. His last years were, in fact, devoted to the writing of works intended to complete the scientific education of his son, known only under the epithet of the "pious and noble knight", to whom Pierre Vicot gave oral initiatory instruction.[9]

It is the priest Vicot who is indeed implied in this passage of the manuscript of Valois: "In the name of Almighty God, know, my son well loved, the intention of nature by the teachings declared hereafter. When, in the last days of my life, my body, giving up my soul, was only waiting for the hour of the Lord and the last breath, desire to leave you as a Testament and last will, these words by which You will be taught many beautiful things touching the very worthy metallic transmutation ... That's why I made you teach the principles of Natural Philosophy, to make you more capable of this holy Science."[10]

The *Cinq Livres* (Five Books) of Nicolas Valois, at the beginning of which figures this passage, bear the date of 1445 –without doubt that of their completion–, which would lead us to believe that the alchemist, contrary to the version of the author of the *Remarks*, died in old age. It may be supposed that his son, brought up and educated according to the rules of hermetic wisdom, had to content himself with acquiring the lands of the domain of Esco-

---

8 *Chartrier du château de Flers* (Chartrier of Flers Castle).

9 *Œuvres manuscrites de Grosparmy, Valois et Vicot* (Handwritten works of Grosparmy, Valois and Vicot). Rennes Library, ms. 160 (124); fol. 90, Second Book of Me Pierre de Vitecoq, Preposter: "To you, noble and valiant horseman, I address and entrust into your hands the greatest secret that has ever been discovered by any living creature ..." Fol. 139, Recapitulation of Me Pierre Vicot, with preface addressed to the "Noble and pious chevallier", son of Nicolas Valois.

10 *Œuvres de Grosparmy, Valois et Vicot* (Works by Grosparmy, Valois and Vicot). National Library, Mss. 12246 (2526), 12298 and 12299 (435), seventeenth century. - Arsenal's Library, ms. 2516 (166, SAF), 17th century. - See Rennes Library; ms. 160 (124), fol. 139: "Follows the recapitulation of Mr. Pierre Vicot, presbyter... on the previous writting that he made to instruct the son of the lord Le Vallois in this Science, after the death of said Le Vallois, his father".

ville, or of receiving the revenues if he had inherited them from Nicholas Valois. Anyway, and although no written testimony comes to help us fill this gap, one thing remains certain is that the son of the alchemist, Adept himself, has never built all or part of this domain; he made no further step for the endorsement of the title which was attached to it; no one, at least, knows whether he lived in Flers, like his father, or whether he fixed his residence at Caen. It is probably the first known owner of the titles of squire and lord of Escoville, of Mesnil-Guillaume and other places that is due the project of construction of the hotel of the Grand-Horse, realized by Nicolas Le Valois, his eldest son, in the city of Caen. In any case, we know from a certain source that Jean Le Valois, first of the name, grandson of Nicolas, "appeared March 24, 1511, in clothing of brigandine and a sallet, at the watch of the nobles of the bailiwick of Caen, following a certificate of Lieutenant General said bailiwick, dated the same day". He left Nicolas Le Valois, lord of Escoville and Mesnil-Guillaume, born the year 1494, and married April 7, 1534 to Marie du Val, who gave him for son Louis de Valois, squire, lord of Escoville, born in Caen on September 18, 1536, which later became secretary-general of the king.

So it was Nicolas Le Valois, great-grandson of the alchemist of Flers, who commissioned the work of the hotel d'Escoville, which required a decade, from 1530 to 1540.[11] It is to the same Nicolas Le Valois that our anonymous, deceived perhaps by the similarity of the names, attributes the works of Nicolas Valois, his ancestor, by carrying to Caen what had Flers for theater. According to the report of de Bras,[12] Nicolas Le Valois would have died young, the year 1541. "Friday day of the Epiphany, 1541", writes the old historian, "Nicolas Le Valois, sir of Escoville, Fontaines, Mesnil-Guillaume and Manneville, and the most opulent of the city at that time, when he had to sit at the table, in the hall of the pavilion of that beautiful and superb dwelling, near the Saint-Pierre crossroads, which he had built the year before, eating an oyster, at the age, more or less, of forty-seven years, fell suddenly dead of a stroke which suffocated him".

In the neighborhood, the hotel d'Escoville was called *Hotel du Grand-Cheval* (Masion of the Great Hourse).[13] According to the testimony of Vauquelin Yveteaux, Nicolas Le Valois, its owner, would have completed the Great Work, "in the city where the hieroglyphs of the house which is there to be built and which one still sees there, in the place Saint-Pierre, facing the large church of this name, beat witness of its science". "There would be hieroglyphs", adds Robillard de Beaurepaire, "in the sculptures of the Hotel du Grand-Cheval; it would then be possible for all these details, which seem incoherent, to have a very precise meaning for the author of the construction and for all the followers of the hermetic science, versed in the mysterious formulas of ancient philosophers, mages, brahmins, and cabalists. Unfortunately, of all the statues which decorated this elegant dwelling, the main room, from the alchemical point of view, "that which, placed above the door, first struck the gaze of the passer-by and gave his name to the habitation, the *Grand-Cheval* (the Great Horse), described and celebrated by all contemporary authors, no longer exists today. " It was ruthlessly broken in 1793. In his book titled *Les Origines de Caen* (The Origins of Caen), Daniel Huet argues that the equestrian statue belonged to a scene of the Apocalypse (chapter XIX, v. 11), against the opinion of Bardou, parish priest of Cormelles, who saw Pegasus there, and of the Roque, who recog-

---

11 Eugene de Robillard de Beaurepaire. *Caen illustré, son histoire, ses monuments* (Caen illustrated, its history, its monuments). Caen, F. Leblanc-Hardel, 1896, p. 436.

12 *Les Recherches et antiquitez de la ville de Caen* (The Research and antique of the city of Caen), p. 132.

13 An inscription, engraved on the beautiful southern facade which forms the bottom of the court, bears the date of 1535.

nized in her the effigy of Hercules. In a letter addressed to Daniel Huet by the father of the Ducquerie, he says that "the figure of the great horse that is at the frontispiece of the house of Mr. Le Valois d'Ecoville is not, as believed M. de la Roque, and after him several others, a Hercules; it is a vision of the *Apocalypse*. This is noted by the inscription which is below. On the thigh of this horseman are written these words of the Apocalypse: *Rex Regum and Dominus Dominantium*, the King of kings and the Lord of lords". Another correspondent of the learned prelate of Avranches, the physician Dubourg, has entered in this respect in more detailed details. "To reply to your letter," he wrote, "I begin to tell you that there are two representations in bas-relief, the one above, where this great horse is represented in the air, with clouds under his front feet. The man who rides it had a sword in front of him, but it is no longer there; in his right hand he holds a long iron rod; above and behind him, there are, in the air, cavaliers who follow him, and before and above him, an angel in the sun. Below the door, there is still a representation of the man on horseback, small, on a pile of dead bodies and horses that the birds eat. He is facing the Orient, in opposition to the other, and in front of him the false prophet is represented, and the dragon with several heads, and cavaliers against whom the cavalier seems to go. His head is turned backwards, as if to see the representation of the false prophet and the dragon, entering an old castle, from where flames come out and by which this false prophet is already half engulfed. There are writings on the thigh of the great Cavalier, and in many places, such as King of Kings, Lord of Lords, and others drawn from Chapter XIX of the *Apocalypse* (Book of Revelation). As these letters are not engraved, I believe they were written not long ago, but there is a marble up and above where it is written: *And it was his name, the Word of God*".[14]

Our intention is not to undertake here the study of the symbolic statuary charged with expressing or exposing the principal mysteries of science. This philosopher's home, well known, often described, may be the subject of personal interpretations of lovers of sacred art. We will confine ourselves to pointing out some particularly instructive and interesting figures. It is first of all the dragon of the mutilated tympanum of the entrance door, on the left, under the peristyle which precedes the turret staircase. On the lateral facade, two beautiful statues, representing David and Judith, must hold our attention; the latter is accompanied by a six verses of that time:

> *Here is the portrait*
> *of Judith the virtuous;*
> *how by a great deed*
> *cut off the inebriated head*
> *of Holofernes, who to the blissful*
> *Jerusalem had defeated.*

Above these great figures, there are two scenes, one depicting the kidnapping of Europe, the other the deliverance of Andromeda by Perseus, which offer a meaning analogous to that of the fabulous Rapture of Dejanira, followed by the death of Nessos, which we will

---

14 This Word of God, which is the *Verbum demissum* of the *Trevisan* and the *Parole perdue* (Lost Word) of the medieval Freemasons, designates the material secret of the Work, whose revelation constitutes the Gift of God, and on the nature, the vulgar name or the use of which all the philosophers preserve a impenetrable silence. It is evident, therefore, that the bas-relief accompanying the inscription must relate to the subject of the wise, and probably also to the manner of working it. Thus one entered the Work, as well as in the hotel of Escoville, by the symbolic door of the Grand-Cheval.

discuss later, speaking of the myth of Adam and Eve. In another pavilion, one reads on the interior frieze of a window: *Marsyas victus obmutescit*.[15] "It is," says Robillard de Beaurepaire, "an allusion to the musical tournament between Apollo and Marsyas, in which, as companions, we find the carriers of instruments that we distinguish above".[16] Finally, to top it all, above the lantern, a small figure, that today looks very worn, in which M. Sauvageon, several years ago, thought he could recognize Apollo, the god of day and light; and, beneath the cupola of the great lantern, in a kind of small wingless temple, the very recognizable statue of Priapus. We would be, for example, adds the author, much embarrassed to explain what precise meaning must be attributed to the character with a grave physiognomy, who wears a Hebrew turban; and to the one who emerges so vigorously from a painted oculus, while his arm crosses the thickness of the entablature; to a very beautiful representation of St. Cecilia playing the theorem; blacksmiths whose hammers, at the bottom of the pilasters, strike on an absent anvil; the exterior decorations, so original, of the service staircase, with the motto: *Labor improbus omnia vincit...*[17] It would perhaps not have been useless, moreover, to penetrate the meaning of all these sculptures, to inquire into the habitual tendencies and habits of the man who had thus lavished them upon his abode. We know that the lord of Escoville was one of the richest men in Normandy; what is less well known is that at all times he had devoted himself passionately to the mysterious quest for alchemy".

From this brief account, we must above all remember that in Flers, in the fifteenth century, existed a nucleus of hermetic philosophers; that these were able to form disciples, –which is confirmed by the science passed on to the successors of Nicolas Valois, the lords of Escoville–, and to create an initiatory center; and the city of Caen being at about equal distance from Flers and Lisieux, it is possible that the unknown Adept, retired from the Manor de la Salamander, might have received his first instruction from some master belonging to the occult group of Flers or Caen.

There is, in this hypothesis, neither material impossibility nor improbability; but we can not, however, attribute to it more value than we might expect from this kind of supposition. So, let us ask the reader to receive it as we offer it to him, that is to say, with all the desirable circumspection, and as mere probability.

II

Here we are at the entrance, closed for a long time, of the pretty manor.

The beauty of the style, the happy choice of motifs, the delicacy of the execution make this little door one of the most agreeable specimens of wood carving in the sixteenth century. It is a joy for the artist, as much as a treasure for the alchemist, as this hermetic paradigm exclusively devoted to the symbolism of the dry way, the only one that the authors have reserved without providing any explanation (see Plate V, in the next page).

---

15 Marsyas, a satyr who was a famous flute player, vanquished remains silent.

16 It is common to meet, on the dwellings of alchemists, among other hermetic emblems, musicians or musical instruments. Between the followers of Hermes, the alchemical science, we will say why in the course of the work, was called the Art of Music.

17 Despised, the work triumphs over everything.

LISIEUX - MANOR OF THE SALAMANDER
Entrance door - Plate V

But, in order to make the particular value of the emblems analyzed more under-standable to students, we will respect the order of work without being guided by consider-ations of architectural logic or aesthetic order.

On the tympanum of the door with carved panels, there is an interesting allegorical group composed of a lion and a lioness facing each other. They both hold, by their forelegs, a human mask personifying the sun, surrounded by a liana curved into a mirror sleeve. Lion and lioness, male principle and female virtue, reflect the physical expression of the two natures, of similar form, but of opposite properties, which art must elect at the beginning of the practice. From their union, accomplished according to certain secret rules, comes this double nature, mixed matter that the sages have named androgynous, their hermaphrodite or Mirror of Art. It is this substance, both positive and negative, patient containing its own agent, which is the basis, the foundation of the Great Work. Of these two natures, considered separately, that which plays the part of feminine matter is alone signed and alchemically named on the raven bearing the projection of a beam of the upper stage. We can see the figure of a winged dragon with a curved tail in a loop. This dragon is the image and symbol of the primitive and volatile body, the true and unique subject on which one must first work. Philosophers have given him a multitude of different names, apart from that under which he is vulgarly known. This is what has caused and still causes so much embarrassment, so much confusion for beginners, especially for those who care little about principles and do not know how far the possibility of nature can extend. In spite of the general opinion that our subject has never been designated, we affirm, on the contrary, that many works name it and that all describe it. But, if it is quoted among good authors, it can not be maintained that it is underlined or shown expressly; it is often even classified among the bodies that have been rejected as unfit or foreign to the Work. A classic procedure that the Adepts have used to divert the profane and hide the secret entrance to their garden.

Its traditional name of stone of the philosophers, portrays with enough fidelity this body to serve as an useful base for its identification. It is, indeed, truly a stone, because it presents, out of the mine, the external characters common to all minerals. It is the chaos of the sages, in which the four elements are contained, but in a confused and disordered manner. He is our old man and the father of metals, and they owe him their origin because it represents the first terrestrial metallic manifestation. It is our arsenic, cadmium, antimony, blende, galena, cinnabar, colcothar, aurichalcum, realgar, orpiment, calamine, tuthie, tartar, etc. All the ores, by the hermetic voice, render homage to it with their names. It is still called black dragon covered with scales, venomous snake, daughter of Saturn and "the most beloved of her children". This primary substance has seen its evolution interrupted by the interposition and penetration of an infectious combustible sulphur that impregnates, retains and coagulates pure mercury. And, although it is entirely volatile, this primitive mercury, materialized by the drying action of arsenical sulfur, takes on the appearance of a solid, black, dense, fibrous, brittle, friable mass, which is of little use and makes it vile, abject, despicable in the eyes of men. In this subject, the poor parent of the family of metals, the enlightened artist nevertheless finds all he needs to begin and perfect his great work, because he enters it, say the authors, at the beginning, in the middle and at the end of the Work. Also, the ancients compared it to the Chaos of Creation, where the elements and the principles, the darkness and the light were confounded, intermingled, and unable to react on each other. This is the reason why they symbolically depicted their matter in its first state, under the figure of the world, which contained in itself the materials of our hermetic globe, or microcosm, assembled without order, without form, without rhythm or measure.[18]

Our globe, reflection and mirror of the macrocosm, is therefore only a parcel of the primordial Chaos, destined, by the divine will, for elementary renewal in the three kingdoms, but which a series of mysterious circumstances has directed and directed towards the mineral kingdom. Thus informed and specified, subject to the laws governing the evolution and the mineral progression, this chaos has become body, and in a confusingly manner, contains the purest seed and the nearest substance there is to minerals and metals. The philosopher's material is therefore of mineral and metallic origin. Therefore, it is necessary to look for it only in the mineral and metallic roots, which, says Basil Valentine in the book of the *Twelve Keys of Philosophy*, was reserved by the Creator and promised only to the generation of metals. Consequently, whoever seeks the sacred stone of the philosophers with the hope of meeting this little world in substances foreign to the mineral and metallic kingdom, this one will never reach the end of his designs. And it is to divert the apprentice from the path of error that ancient writers teach him to always follow nature. Because nature acts only in its own species, it

---

18 Cf. Basil Valentine. *Les douze Clefs de la Philosophie* (The Twelve Keys of Philosophy), Editions de Minuit, 1956, ninth figure, p. 185.

develops and improves only in itself and by itself, without any heterogeneous thing hindering or opposing the effects of its generating power.

On the left door post of the door that we are studying, a subject in high relief attracts and holds our attention. It shows a richly dressed man, wearing a doublet with sleeves, and a mortarboard hat, his breast emblazoned with a shield showing a six-pointed star. This high-class man, placed on the lid of an urn with embossed walls, serves to indicate, according to the custom of the Middle Ages, the contents of the vessel. It is the substance which, during sublimations, rises above the water, floating like an oil on its surface; it is the Hyperion and vitriol of Basil Valentine, the green lion of Ripley and Jacques Tesson, in a word the true unknown of the great problem. This knight, of fine appearance and celestial lineage, is not a stranger to us: several hermetic engravings have made him familiar. Salomon Trismosin, in the *Toyson d'Or* (The Golden Fleece) shows him standing upright, feet resting on the edges of two basins filled with water, which reflect the origin and source of this mysterious fountain; water of nature and double property, issued from the milk of the Virgin and the blood of Christ; igneous water and watery fire, virtue of the two baptisms spoken about in the Gospels: "For me, I baptize you in water; but there will come another more powerful than me, and I am not worthy to untie the cord of his sandals. He will baptize you in the Holy Spirit and in the fire. Whose fan is in his hand, and he will thoroughly purge his floor, and will gather the wheat into his garner; but the chaff he will burn with fire unquenchable.[19] The manuscript of the Philosopher Solidonius reproduces the same subject under the image of a calyx full of water, from which two characters emerge, in the center of a rather dense composition summarizing the whole work. As for the treatise of Azoth, it is an immense angel –that of the parable of St. John, in the *Book of Revelation*–, which treads the earth with one foot and the sea with the other, while raises an inflamed torch with the right hand and compress an air-inflated goatskin with his left one, clear figures of the quaternary of the first elements: earth, water, air, fire. The body of this angel, whose two wings replace the head, is covered by the seal of the open book, adorned with a cabalistic star and the seven-word motto of Vitriol: *Visita Interiora Terrae Rectificandoque, Invenies Occultum Lapidem*.[20] "Then I saw," wrote St. John, "another strong and powerful angel, coming down from heaven, clothed with a cloud, and having a rainbow on his head. His face was like the sun, and his feet like columns of fire. He had a little open book in his hand, and put his right foot on the sea, and his left foot on the ground. And he cried with a loud voice, like a roaring lion; and after he had cried, seven thunders burst forth. And the seven thunders having made their voices ring, I was about to write; but I heard a voice from heaven saying to me: Hold under the seal the words of the seven thunders, and write them not. And that voice that I heard in heaven spoke to me again, and said to me: Go take the little open book that is in the hand of the angel standing on the sea and on the earth. I was going to find the angel and I said: Give me the little book. And he said to me: Take it and devour it; it will cause you bitterness in your belly, but in your mouth it will be sweet as honey."[21]

---

19 Saint Luke, ch. III, v. 16, 17. - Mark, ch. I, v. 6, 7, 8. - John, ch. I, v. 32 to 34.

20 Visit the interior of the earth, purify it and you'll find the hidden stone.

21 *Book of Revelation*, ch. X, v. 1 to 4, 8 and 9. This parable, very instructive, is reproduced with some variations, which specify the hermetic meaning, in the Vision occurred in thinking of Ben Adam, the time of the reign of the king of Adama, which was highlighted by Floretus to Bethabor. Arsenal's Library, ms. 3022 (168, SAF) p. 14. Here is the part of the text that might interest us:

And I heard a voice from heaven, saying to me, saying,

Go and take this open booklet from the hand of this angel who stands on the sea and on the earth. - And I went to the angel and said to him: Lease my this booklet. And I took this booklet from the

This product, allegorically expressed by the angel or man –attribute of the evangelist Saint Matthew–, is none other than the mercury of the philosophers, of double nature and quality, in fixed and material part, in volatile and spiritual part, which is sufficient to begin, complete and multiply the work. This is the one and only material we need, without worrying about seeking any more; but it is necessary to know, so as not to err, that it is from this mercury and its acquisition that authors generally begin their treatises. Mercury is the mine and the root of gold, not the precious metal, absolutely useless and unemployed in the way we are studying. Eyrenée Philalèthe says, with great truth, that our mercury, barely mineral, is even less metallic, because it only contains the spirit or the metallic seed, while the body tends to deviate from the mineral quality. However, it is the spirit of gold, enclosed in a transparent, easily coagulable oil; the salt of metals, because every stone is salt, and the salt of our stone, because the stone of philosophers, which is the mercury we are talking about, is the subject of the philosopher's stone. From this comes the fact that several Adepts, wishing to create confusion, called it nitre or saltpetre (*sal petri,* stone salt), and copied the sign of one on the image of the other. Moreover, its crystalline structure, its physical similarity to molten salt, its transparency have allowed it to be assimilated to salts and have given it all its names. It thus becomes, in turn, according to the will or imagination of the writers, sea salt and rock salt, Alembroth salt, Saturn salt, salt of salts. It is also the famous green vitriol, *oleum vitri,* which Pantheus describes as chrysocolla, others as borax or *atincar,* the Roman vitriol because Ῥώμη, the Greek name of the Eternal City, means strength, vigour, power, domination; Pierre-Jean Fabre's mineral, because in it, he says, gold lives there (vitryol). It is also known as Protée, because of its metamorphoses during work, and also Chameleon (Χαμαιλέων, crawling lion), because it successively covers all the colors of the spectrum.

Here is the last decorative subject of our door. It is a salamander serving as a capital to the column of the right jamb. In a way, it seems to us to be the protective fairy of this pleasant dwelling, as we find it sculpted on the corbel of the middle pillar, located on the ground floor, and even on the skylight of the attic. It would even seem, given the desired repetition of the symbol, that our alchemist would have had a marked preference for this heraldic reptile. We do not pretend to insinuate, by this, that he could attribute to it the erotic and gross sense that Francis I valued so much; this would be tantamount to insulting the craftsman, dishonoring science and insulting the truth, imitating the corrupt but intellectually mediocre avantgarde, to whom we regret owing the paradoxical name of Renaissance.[22]

---

hand of the angel, and gave it to him to swallow it up. And, as he had eaten it, there were trenches in his belly so strong that he came as black as coal; and as he was in this darkness, the sun shone bright as in the warmest midday, and thence changed its black form like a white marble; until at last the sun was at its highest, it became all red like fire ... And then everything vanishes ...

And from the place where the angel spoke, rose a hand holding a glass in which there seemed to be a red pink powder ... And I heard a great echo saying:

Follow nature, followed by nature!"

22 "Francis I is known as the Father of Letters, and this for some favours he granted to three or four writers; but is it forgotten that in 1535, this Father of Letters gave patent letters by which he prohibited printing under penalty of being banned; that after having banned printing he established a censorship to prevent the publication and sale of books previously printed; that he granted the Sorbonne the right of inquisition on consciences; that, according to the Royal Edict, the possession of an ancient book condemned and proscribed by the Sorbonne exposed the owners to the death penalty, if this book were found in his home, where the henchmen of the Sorbonne had the power to search; that he proved, throughout his reign, to be an implacable enemy of the independence of the mind and the progress of enlightenment, as much as a fanatic protector of the most fiery theologians and the scholastic absurdi-

But a singular trait of the human character leads man to become fond of that for which he has suffered most has suffered and toiled most; this reason would undoubtedly allow us to explain the triple use of the salamander, hieroglyph of the secret fire of the sages. Indeed, among the ancillary products that enter the workplace as carers or servants, none is more ungrateful research or more laborious identification than this one. In the accessory preparations, certain substitutes capable of providing a similar result can still be used instead of the required adjuvants; however, in the elaboration of mercury, nothing can replace the secret fire, this spirit capable of animating it, exalting it and becoming part of it, after having extracted it from the filthy matter. "I pity you very much," writes Limojon de Saint-Didier, "if, as a means, after having known the true matter, you spent fifteen years entirely in work, study and meditation, without being able to extract from the stone the precious juice it contains in its bosom, for want of connotation the secret fire of the wise, which makes this dry and arid plant flow a water that does not wet the hands".[23] Without it, without this fire hidden in a saline form, the prepared matter could not be spiked or perform its functions as a mother, and our labor would forever remain chimerical and vain. Every generation requires the help of its own agent, determined to the kingdom in which nature has placed it. And everything carries seeds. Animals are born from an egg or a fertilized ovum; plants come from a seed made prolific; likewise, minerals and metals have as their seed a metallic liquor fertilized by mineral fire. This is therefore the active agent introduced by art into mineral seed, and it is it, Philaletes tells us, "that makes the axle turn first and moves the wheel". By this way, it is easy to understand what use this metallic, invisible, mysterious light is, and with what care we must seek to know it, to distinguish it by its specific, essential and occult qualities.

Salamander, in Latin *salamandra*, comes from *sal*, salt, and *mandra*, which means barn, and also rock hollow, solitude, hermitage. Salamandra is therefore the name of the salt of the barn, rock salt or solitary salt. This word takes in the Greek language another acceptance, revealing the action it provokes. Σαλαμάνδρα appears to be formed of Σάλα, agitation, perturbation, probably used for σάλος or ζάλη, turbulent water, storm, fluctuation, and μάνδρα, which has the same meaning as in Latin. From these etymologies, we can draw this conclusion that salt, spirit or fire, originates in a barn, a hollow of rock, a cave ... That's enough. Lying on the straw of his manger, in the grotto of Bethlehem, is not Jesus the new sun bringing light to the world? Is he not God himself, under his carnal and perishable envelope? Who then said, I am the Spirit and I am the Life; I came to put fire in things?

This spiritual fire, informed and materialized in salt, is the hidden sulfur, because during its operation it never becomes manifest or sensible to our eyes. And yet this sulfur, however invisible, is not an ingenious abstraction, an artifice of doctrine. We know how to isolate it, to extract it from the body which conceals it, by an occult means and in the aspect of a dry powder, which, in this state, becomes improper and without effect in philosophical art. This pure fire, of the same essence as the specific sulfur of gold, but less digested, is, on the other hand, more abundant than that of the precious metal. This is why it easily combines with the mercury of imperfect minerals and metals. Philaletes assures us that we find him hidden in the belly of Aries, or Aries, constellation that runs through the sun in April. Finally, to desig-

ties most contrary to the true spirit of the Christian religion?... What an encouragement for science and literature! All we can see in Francis I is a brilliant madman who made France miserable and ashamed". Abbot of Montgaillard, *Histoire de France* (History of France). Paris, Moutardier, 1827, t. I, p. 183.

23 Limojon de Saint-Didier. *Lettre aux vrays Disciples d'Hermès* (Letter to the true Disciples of Hermes), in the *Triomphe hermétique* (Hermetic Triumph). Amsterdam. Henry Wetstein, 1699, p. 150.

nate it still better, we will add that this Aries, "who hides the magic steel in himself," ostensibly bears on his shield the image of the hermetic seal, a star with six rays. It is therefore in this very common matter, which seems to us merely useful, that we must seek the mysterious solar fire, subtle salt and spiritual sulfur, diffused celestial light in the darkness of the body, without which nothing can be done and nothing can not replace.

We have mentioned above the important place occupied by the salamander, among the emblematic subjects of the little hotel at Lisieux, a particular sign of its modest and learned proprietor. We find it, we said, even on the skylight of the attic, almost inaccessible, rising into the open sky. Supports the two-sided roof between two dragons carved in parallel on the wood of the plays (Plate VI).

LISIEUX - MANOR OF THE SALAMANDER
The Salamander and the two Dragons of the skylight - Plate VI

These two dragons, one wingless (ἄπτεϱος, without wings), the other chrysoptere (χϱυσόπτεϱος, with golden wings), are those of which Nicolas Flamel speaks in his Hierogliphic Figures , and that Michel Maïer (*Symbola aureae mensae*, Frankfurt, 1617) considers as being, along with the globe surmounted by the cross, particular symbols to the style of the famous Adept. This simple observation demonstrates the extensive knowledge that the Exovian artist had of the philosophical texts and the special symbolism of each of his predecessors. On the other hand, the very choice of the salamander leads us to believe that our alchemist had to search for a long time and use many years to discover the secret fire. The hieroglyph conceals the physico-chemical nature of the fruits of the garden of Hespéra, fruits whose late ripeness rejoices the wise only in his old age, and which he only harvests at the end of his life, at sunset (Εσπερίς) of a laborious and painful career. Each of these fruits is the result of a progressive condensation of the solar fire by the secret fire, an incarnate verb, a celestial spirit embodied in all things of this world. And the assembled and concentrated rays of this double fire color and animate a pure, diaphanous, clarified, regenerated body, of brilliance and admirable virtue.

Having reached this point of exaltation, the igneous principle, material and spiritual, by its universality of action, becomes assimilable to the bodies contained in the three kingdoms of nature; it is effective in animals and plants as well as in mineral and metallic bodies. This is the magical ruby, an agent endowed with energy and igneous subtlety, and clothed in the color and multiple properties of fire. This is also the Oil of Christ or crystal, the heraldic lizard that attracts, devours, vomits and provides the flame, stretched on his patience like the old phoenix on his immortality.

III

On the median pillar of the ground floor, the visitor discovers a curious bas-relief. A monkey is busy eating the fruit of a young apple tree, barely higher than him (Plate VII).

Faced with this theme, which translates the perfect realization for the initiate, we look at the finalization of the Work. The bright flowers, whose bright and shimmering colors signify the joy of our artisan, have withered and extinguished one after the other; the fruits have taken shape then and, as they were at the beginning, they are now offered to him adorned with a brilliant purple wrapper, sure indication of his maturity and excellence.

It is because the alchemist, in his patient work, must be the scrupulous imitator of nature, the monkey of creation, according to the genuine expression of many masters. Guided by analogy, he achieves in small scale, with his feeble means and in a limited domain, what God did in greatness in the cosmic universe. Here is the immense; there, the infinitesimal. At both ends, same thought, same effort, similar will in its relativity. God does everything: He creates. Man takes a piece of that whole and multiplies it; he extends and continues. Thus the microcosm amplifies the macrocosm. Such is his purpose, his reason for being; Such seems to us to be his true earthly mission and the cause of his own salvation. Above, God; below, the man. Between the immortal Creator and his perishable creature, all of created Nature. Seek: you will find nothing more, nor discover nothing less, than the Author of the first effort, connected with the mass of beneficiaries of the divine example, subject to the same overriding will of constant activity, of eternal labor.

All classical authors are unanimous in recognizing that the Great Work is an abridgement, reduced to human proportions and possibilities, of the Divine Book. And, as the Adept must bring the best of his qualities to it if he wants to carry it out, it seems fair and equitable that he should collect the fruits of the Tree of Life and make his profit from the wonderful apples of the Garden of the Hesperides.

LISIEUX - MANOR OF THE SALAMANDER
The Salamander and the Monkey by the Apple Tree - Plate VII

But since, obeying the fantasy or desire of our philosopher, we are forced to start at the very point where art and nature complete their work together, would it be acting blindly to worry about knowing first what we are looking for? And isn't it, despite the paradox, an excellent method to start with the end? Those who know exactly what they want to get will find what they need more easily. There is much talk in the occult circles of our time about the philosopher's stone, without knowing what it really is. Many educated people describe the hermetic gem as a "mysterious body"; they have the opinion of certain 17th and 18th century Spagyrists, who classified it among the abstract entities, qualified as non-beings or rational beings. Let us study at our discretion the rare and too succinct descriptions, that some philosophers have left us, and let us see what they have to say about this unknown body, as well as what learned characters and faithful witnesses have to say about it.

Let us say, first of all, that the term philosopher's stone means, according to the sacred language, a stone that bears the sign of the sun. However, this sun sign is characterized by red coloration, which can vary in intensity, as Basile Valentin says: "Its color derives from incarnate red on crimson, or from ruby color on pomegranate color; in terms of weight, it is much more than what corresponds to its volume".[24] So much for color and density. The

---

24 *Les Douze Clefs de Philosophie de Frère Basile Valentin, religieux de l'Ordre Sainct Benoist, traictant de la vraye Medecine metallique* (The Twelve Keys of Philosophy of Brother Basil Valentine, a religious of the Holy Order of Benedict, betraying the true Metal Medicine). Paris, Pierre Moët, 1659; Xe clef, p. 121.

Cosmopolitan, whom Louis Figuier believes to be the alchemist known as Sethon, and others as Michael Sendivogius, describes to us its translucent appearance, its crystalline form and its fusibility in this passage: "If we find our subject in his last state of perfection, made and composed by nature; if he were fusible like wax or butter, and his redness, diaphanousness and clarity appeared outwardly, this would be our benevolent stone".[25] Its fusibility is such that all the authors have compared it to wax (64°C); "it melts with the flame of a candle," they repeat; some, for this reason, have even given it the name of great red wax.[26] With these physical characteristics, the stone combines powerful chemical properties, the power of penetration or ingress, absolute fixity, its inability to be oxidized, that makes it incalcinable, extreme fire resistance, and finally its irreducibility and perfect indifference towards chemical agents. This is also what Henri Khunrath teaches us in his *Amphitheatrum Sapientiae Æternae*, when he writes: "Finally, when the Work has passed from ashen color to pure white, then yellow, you will see the philosopher's stone, our king raised above the overlords, come out of his glassy tomb, rise from his bed and come to our worldly scene in his glorified body, that is, regenerated and more than perfect; in other words, the brilliant carbuncle, very radiant in splendor, and whose very subtle and purified parts, by the peace and harmony of the mixture, are inseparably linked and assembled in one; equal, diaphanous like crystal, compact and very heavy, easily meltable in the fire like resin, fluent like wax and more than the bright silver, but without emitting any smoke; piercing and penetrating solid and compact bodies, as oil penetrates paper; soluble and expandable in any liquor likely to soften it; friable like glass; the color of saffron when sprayed, but red like ruby when it remains in one unadulterated mass (the redness is the signature of perfect fixation and fixed perfection); coloring and dyeing constantly; fixed in the tribulations of all experiences, even in the trials by devouring sulphur and burning waters, and by the very strong persecution of fire; always durable, incalcinable, and, like the Salamander, permanent and just judging all things (because it is in its own way while in all things), and proclaiming: Behold, I will renew all things".

The English adventurer Edward Kelley, known as Talbot, had acquired, by 1585, from an innkeeper, the philosopher's stone found in the tomb of a bishop, who was said to be very rich; the stone was red and very heavy, but without any odor. Bérigard of Pisa says that a skilful man gave him a big (3.82 grams) of a powder whose color was similar to that of the poppy, and which gave off the smell of calcined sea salt.[27]

Helvetius (John Frederick Schweitzer) saw the stone, which was shown to him by a foreign Adept on December 27, 1666, in the form of a metallic body the color of sulfur. This product, pulverized, thus came, as Khunrath says, from a red mass. In a transmutation made by Sethon in July, 1602, in the presence of Dr. Jacob Zwinger, the powder employed was, in Dienheim's report, "rather heavy, and of a color which seemed yellow-lemon." A year later, during a second projection at the house of a silversmith, Hans de Kempen, Cologne, August 11, 1603, the same artist uses a red stone.

According to many worthy witnesses, the stone, obtained directly in powder, could affect a coloring as vivid as that which would have been formed in a compact state. The fact

25 *Cosmopolite ou Nouvelle Lumiere Chymique* (Cosmopolitan or New Chemical Light). Paris, J. d'Houry, 1669. *Traité* du sel, p. 64.

26 In ms. lat. 5614 of the National Library, which is composed of treatises by former philosophers, the third book is entitled: *Modus faciendi Optimam Ceram rubeam*.

27 By evaporating one liter of seawater, heating the crystals obtained to complete dehydration and subjecting them to calcination in a porcelain dish, the characteristic odor of iodine is clearly perceived.

is quite rare, but it can happen and is worth mentioning. Thus an Italian Adept who, in 1658, carried out the transmutation before the Protestant pastor Gros, at the Silversmith Bureau, Geneva, employed, according to the assistants, a red powder. Schmieder describes the stone that Bötticher held of Lascaris as a substance with the appearance of a red-colored glass of fire. However, Lascaris had given Domenico Manuel (Gaëtano) a vermilion-like powder. That of Gustenhover was also very red. As for the sample given by Lascaris to Dierbach, it was examined under the microscope by the adviser Dippel, and appeared composed of a multitude of small grains or red or orange crystals; this stone had a power equal to nearly six hundred times the unit.

Jean-Baptiste Van Helmont, recounting the experience he had in 1618 in his laboratory in Vilvoorde, near Brussels, writes: "I have seen and touched the philosopher's stone more than once; the color was like saffron powder, but heavy and glistening like powdered glass. This product, of which a quarter grain (13.25 milligrams) provides eight ounces of gold (244.72 grams), showed considerable energy: about 18470 times the unit.

In the category of the tinctures, that is to say, of the liquids obtained by solution of oily metallic extracts, we have the account of Godwin Hermann Braun, of Osnabruck, which performed a transmutation, in 1701, with the help of a tincture having the appearance of a "fairly fluid and brown" oil. The famous chemist Henckel reports, according to Valentini, the following anecdote: "There came one day, at a famous apothecary of Frankfort-on-the-Main, named Salwedel, a stranger who had a brown tincture, which had almost smell of hartshorn oil;[28] With four drops of this tincture, he changed a large lead into 7.5 grains of 23-carat gold. This same man gave a few drops of this tincture to this apothecary, who lodged him, and then made such gold, that he keeps in memory of this man, with the little bottle in which it was, and where we can still see marks of this tincture. I had this bottle in my hands and I can testify about it to everyone.[29]

Without contesting the veracity of these last two statements, however, we refuse to place them among the transmutations carried out by the philosopher's stone in the special state of projection powder. All the tinctures are there. Their subjection to a particular metal, their limited power, the specific characteristics they present lead us to consider them as simple metallic products, extracted from vulgar metals by certain processes, called small individuals, which are part of spagyria and not alchemy. Moreover, these tinctures, being metallic, have no other action than to penetrate the metals alone which served as the basis for their preparation.

Let us leave aside these processes and these tinctures. What matters most is to remember that the philosopher's stone is offered to us in the form of a crystalline body, diaphanous, red mass, yellow after spraying, which is dense and very fusible, although fixed at any temperature and whose own qualities make it incisive, ardent, penetrating, irreducible and incalcinable. Let's add that it is soluble in molten glass, but volatilizes instantly when projected onto a molten metal. Here, united in a single subject, we found physico-chemical properties which singularly distance it from a possible metallic nature and render its origin very nebulous. A little thought will help us out. The masters of art teach us that the purpose of their work is threefold. What they seek to achieve in the first place, it is the universal medicine, or the, properly called, philosopher's stone. Obtained in saline form, multiplied or not, it is only useful for the healing of human diseases, the preservation of health and the growth of vegetables. Soluble in any spirituous liquor, its solution takes the name of drinking gold

---

28 This is the characteristic odor of the carbamate of ammonia.
29 J.-F. Henckel. *Flora Saturnisans.* Paris, JT Hérissant, 1760, chap. VIII, p. 158.

(although it does not contain the least atom of gold), because it displays a beautiful yellow color. Its curative value and the diversity of its therapeutic use make it a valuable adjunct in the treatment of serious and incurable conditions. It has no action on metals, except on gold and silver, with which it attaches itself and endows with its properties, but, consequently, is of no use for transmutation. However, if we exceed the maximum number of its multiplications, it changes its form and, instead of returning to the solid and crystalline state while cooling, it remains fluid like quicksilver and absolutely non coagulable. In the darkness, it shines with a soft glow, red and phosphorescent, whose brightness remains weaker than that of an ordinary night light. Universal Medicine has become the unquenchable Light, the illuminating product of these perpetual lamps, which some authors have reported as having been found in some ancient burials. Thus radiant and liquid, the philosopher's stone is hardly susceptible, in our opinion, to be pushed further; to wish to amplify its igneous virtue would seem dangerous to us; the least that could be feared would be to volatilize it and lose the benefit of such considerable labor. Finally, if we ferment the solid Universal Medicine with very pure gold or silver, by direct fusion, we obtain the projection powder, third form of the stone. It is a translucent mass, red or white depending on the chosen metal, pulverizable, useful only for metal transmutation. Oriented, determined and specified to the mineral kingdom, it is useless and without action within the two other kingdoms.

From previous considerations, it is clear that the philosopher's stone, or universal medicine, despite its undeniable metallic origin, is not made only of metallic material. If it were otherwise, and consisted only of metals, it would remain subject to the conditions governing the mineral nature, and would not need to be fermented to effect transmutation. On the other hand, the fundamental axiom that teaches that bodies have no action on the body would be false and paradoxical. Take the time and trouble to experiment, and you will recognize that metals do not act on other metals. Whether they are brought to the state of salts or ashes, glasses or colloids, they will always preserve their nature during the tests and, in reduction.

Only metal spirits have the privilege of altering, modifying and denaturing metal bodies. They are the true promoters of all the physical metamorphoses that can be observed. But as these spirits, thin, extremely subtle and volatile, need a vehicle, an envelope capable of holding them; because this matter must be very pure –to allow the spirit to remain there–, and very fixed, in order to prevent its volatilization; since it must remain fusible, in order to favor the ingress; it is essential to ensure absolute resistance to reducing agents, it is easy to understand that this material can be sought only in the category of metals. That's why Basil Valentine recommends taking the spirit in the metal root, and Bernard the Trevisan forbids the use of metals, minerals, and their salts in the construction of the body. The reason is simple and self-evident. If the stone were composed of a metallic body and a spirit fixed on this body, the latter acting on it as being of the same species, the whole would take the characteristic shape of the metal. In this case, we could obtain gold or silver, or even an unknown metal, and nothing more. This is what archemists have always done, because they did not know the universality and essence of the agent they were looking for. Now, what we are asking, with all philosophers, is not the union of a metallic body and spirit, but rather the condensation, the agglomeration of this spirit in a coherent, tenacious and refractory envelope, capable of coating it, impregnating all its parts and ensuring its effective protection. It is this soul, spirit or fire gathered, concentrated and coagulated in the purest, most resistant and perfect of earthly materials, that we call our stone. And we can certify that any undertaking that does not have this spirit as a guide and this material as a basis will never achieve the proposed goal.

IV

On the second floor of the Lisieux house, and carved into the left pillar of the façade, a man of primitive appearance raises and seems to want to take a trunk of very considerable dimensions (see plate IV, page 58).

This symbol, which seems very obscure, hides however the most important secondary arcane. We may even say that, out of ignorance of this point of doctrine, and also because of having too literally followed the teaching of the old authors, many good artists have not been able to collect the fruit of their labors. And how many investigators, more enthusiastic than penetrating, clash and still stumble today against the stumbling block of specious reasoning! Let us beware of pushing human logic too far, so often contrary to natural simplicity. If we could observe more naively the effects that nature shows around us; if we were content to control the results obtained using the same means; if we subordinate our research to the mystery of the causes to facts, and its explanation to the probable, the possible or the hypothetical, a many truths –which are still to be found– would be discovered. So do not let what you think you know to distort your observations, because you would have to admit that it would have been better to have learned nothing than to have to unlearn everything.

This is perhaps, superfluous advice, because they demand, in their practice, the application of an obstinate will, of which the mediocre are incapable. We know what it costs to trade diplomas, seals and scrolls against the philosopher's humble cloak. When we were twenty-four years old, we had to drain up this chalice filled with bitter beverage. With a broken heart, ashamed of the mistakes of our young years, we had to burn books and notebooks, confess our ignorance and, like a modest neophyte, decipher another science on the benches of another school. And so, for those who have had the courage to forget everything, we take the trouble to study the symbol and strip it of the esoteric veil.

The tree trunk what this artisan of another age has seized, seems hardly to be useful except for his industrious genius. And yet, it is indeed our dry tree, the same one that had the honor of giving its name to one of the oldest streets of Paris, after having figured for a long time on a famous sign. Édouard Fournier informs us that, according to Sauval (v. I, p. 109), this sign still appeared around 1660.[30] It indicated to passers-by "an inn that Monstrele speaks about" (v. I, chapter CLXXVII), and was well chosen for such a lodging, which, as early as 1300, had been used as a lodging for pilgrims from the Holy Land. The Dry Tree was a souvenir of Palestine; it was the tree planted near Hebron,[31] which, having been since the beginning of the world "leafy green", lost its foliage the day that Our Lord died on the cross, and when it dried up; "But to become green again when a lord, prince of the West, will graze the land of promise, with the aide of the Christians, and will have the Mass of the dry wood sung".[32]

This dried-up tree, that sprouts from the arid rock, is represented on the last plate of the Art of the Potter; but it has been represented covered with leaves and fruits, with a banner bearing the motto: *Sic in sterili*.[33] It is also the one that can be found sculpted on the

---

30 Edouard Fournier, *Énigmes des rues de Paris* (Enigmas of the Streets of Paris). Paris, E. Dentu, 1860.

31 We identify it with Membrane Oak, or, more hermetically, dismembered.

32 [*Le Livre de Messire Guill. de Mandeville* (The Book of Messire Guill. from Mandeville). National Library, ms. 8392, fol. 157.

33 *Les Trois Libvres de l'Art du Potier* (The Three Freedoms of the Art of the Potter), by Knight Cyprian Piccolpassi, translated by Claudius Popelyn, Parisian. Paris, Librairie Internationale, 1861.

beautiful door of Limoges Cathedral, as well as in a quatrefoil of the Amiens basement. They are also two fragments of this mutilated trunk, which a stone cleric raises above the large shell used as a holy water basin, in the Breton church of Guimiliau (Finistère). Finally, we also find the dessicated tree on a number of 15th century secular buildings. In Avignon, it surmounts the basket handle gate of the former college of Roure; in Cahors, it serves as a frame for two windows (Verdier House, on the street of Boulevards), as well as a small door belonging to the college Pellegri, located in the same city (plate VIII).

CAHORS - COLLEGE PELLEGRI - DOOR OF THE XVth CENTURY
The Dry Tree - Plate VIII

Such is the hieroglyph adopted by philosophers to express the metallic inertia, that is to say, the special state which human industry has made to the reduced and melted metals. Hermetic esotericism demonstrates, in fact, that metallic bodies remain alive and endowed with vegetative power, as long as they are mineralized in their deposits. They are associated with the specific agent, or mineral spirit, which ensures the vitality, nutrition and evolution to the term required by nature, where they take the appearance and properties of the native silver and gold. Having reached this goal, the agent separates from the body, which ceases to live, becomes fixed and not susceptible of transformation. Although it remained on earth for many centuries, it could not, by itself, change the state or abandon the characters that distinguish metal from the mineral aggregate.

But it is far from being as simple as that inside the metal deposits. Subjected to the vicissitudes of this transitional world, many minerals have their evolution suspended by the action of root causes –nutrient depletion, lack of crystalline inputs, insufficient pressure, heat, etc.–, or external –cracks, water inflows, mine opening. The metals then solidify and remain mineralized with their acquired qualities, without being able to go beyond the evolutionary stage they have reached. Others, younger, still waiting for the agent that must ensure their strength and consistency, retain the liquid state and are completely non coagulable. This is the case for mercury, which is frequently found in its native state, or mineralized by sulphur (cinnabar), either in the mine itself or outside its place of origin.

In this native form, and although the metallurgical treatment did not have to intervene, the metals are as insensitive as those whose ores have undergone roasting and melting. Neither do they possess their own vital agent. The sages tell us that they are dead, at least in appearance, because it is impossible for us, under their solid and crystallized mass, to exert the latent, potential life hidden in the depths of their being. They are dead trees, although they still contain a remnant of moisture, which will give no more leaves, flowers, fruits, or, especially, seed.

It is therefore with great reason that some authors assert that gold and mercury can not contribute, in whole or in part, to the elaboration of the Work. The first, they say, because his own agent was separated when it was completed, and the second because it was never introduced. Other philosophers maintain, however, that gold, though sterile in its solid form, can recover its lost vitality and resume its evolution, if we known how to "put it back in its first state"; but this is an equivocal teaching and one must be careful not to take in the vulgar sense. Let us stop for a moment on this contentious point and let us not lose sight of the possibility of nature: it is the only way we have to recognize our way in this tortuous labyrinth. Most hermetists think that the term "reincrudation" means the return of metal to its original state; they are based on the meaning of the word itself, which expresses the action of rendering raw, or retrograding. This idea is wrong. It is impossible for nature, and even more so for art, to destroy the effect of a secular work. What is acquired remains acquired. And that's why old masters say it's easier to make gold than to destroy it. Nobody will ever flatter himself with giving roasted meats and cooked vegetables the appearance and qualities they possessed before undergoing the action of fire. Here again, the analogy and the possibility of nature are the best and safest guides. There is no example of regression anywhere in the world.

Other researchers believe that it is enough to bathe the metal in the primitive and mercurial substance which, by slow maturation and progressive coagulation, gave birth to it. This reasoning is more specious than real. Even supposing that they knew this first matter and that they knew where to take it, which the greatest masters do not know, they could only obtain, in the end, an increase of the gold employed, and not a new body, of power superior to that of the precious metal. The operation, thus understood, consists of the mixture of the same body taken in two different states of its evolution, one liquid, the other solid. With a little thought, it is easy to understand that such an enterprise cannot lead to the intended goal. It is, of course, in a formal opposition with the philosophical axiom that we have often stated: bodies have no action on bodies; only spirits are active and acting.

We must therefore understand, that the expression: *to put gold back into its first matter*, means the animation of the metal, achieved by the use of this vital agent of which we have spoken. It is the spirit that fled the body during its physical manifestation; it is the metallic soul, or this raw material that has not been otherwise designated, and which dwells in the womb of the undefiled Virgin. The animation of gold, the symbolic vitality of the dry tree, or the resurrection of the dead, is allegorically taught to us by an Arabic author's text. This author, named Kessæus, who has been very busy –Brunet tells us in his notes on the *Gospel of Child-*

hood–, collecting oriental legends about the events told in the Gospels, narrates in these terms the circumstances of Mary's birth: "When the moment of her deliverance approached, she left the house of Zechariah in the middle of the night, and walked out of Jerusalem. And she saw a dried-up palm tree; and when Mary sat at the foot of that tree, it immediately blossomed again and covered himself with leaves and greenery, and bore a great abundance of fruit by the operation of God's power. And God raised up a spring of living water beside it, and when the pains of childbirth tormented Mary, she tightly held the palm tree with her hands".

We can not speak better or speak with more clarity.

V

On the central pillar of the first floor, there is a group quite interesting for lovers and curious about symbolism. Although it suffered a lot and now shows itself mutilated, cracked, corroded by the bad weather, we can still discern the subject. It is a character holding a griffin between his legs, whose paws, equipped with claws, are very visible, as well as the lion's tail extending from the rump, details that allow, on their own, an exact identification. With his left hand, the man grabs the monster towards his head and makes the gesture of hitting him with his right hand (Plate. IX).

LISIEUX - MANOR OF THE SALAMANDER
Baphomet - Combat of the Man and the Griffon - Plate IX

We recognize on this motif one of the major emblems of the science, one which covers the preparation of the raw materials of the Work. But while the fight of the dragon and the knight indicates the initial encounter, the duel of mineral products seeking to defend their integrity threatened, the griffin marks the result of the operation, veiled elsewhere under myths of varied expressions, but all of them having the character of incompatibility, of natural and profound aversion which the substances in contact have for each other.

The astral stone is born from the combat between the knight, or secret sulfur, with the arsenical sulfur of the old dragon; white, heavy, brilliant as pure silver, and which appears signed, bearing the imprint of its nobility, the claw, esoterically translated by the griffin, a sure sign of union and peace between fire and water, between air and earth. However, we cannot hope to attain this dignity from the prime conjunction. Because our black stone, covered with rags, is soiled with so many impurities that it is very difficult to get rid of it completely. That is why it is important to subject it to several levigations (which are Nicolas Flamel's *laveures*), in order to clean it gradually of its defilements, the heterogeneous and tenacious stains that thwart it, and to see it take, to each of them, more splendor, and become more polished and bright.

The initiates know that our science, though purely natural and simple, is by no means vulgar; the terms we use, following the masters, are no less so. That we therefore want to pay attention to it, because we chose them carefully, with the intention of showing the way, to indicate the potholes that pit it, hoping thus to enlighten the studious, and to push away the blinded, the greedy ones and the outrageous. Learn, you who already know, that all our washings are igneous, that all our purifications are done in fire, by fire and with fire. This is the reason why some authors have described these operations under the chemical title of calcinations, because the material, long subjected to the action of the flame, gives up its impure and scorched parts to it. You should also know that our rock –veiled under the figure of the dragon– first lets a dark, stinking and poisonous liquid flow, whose thick and volatile smoke is extremely toxic. This water, whose symbol is the raven, can only be washed and bleached by means of fire. And this is what philosophers tell us when, in their enigmatic style, they recommend that the artist cut off his head. Through these igneous ablutions, the water leaves its black color and turns white. The crow, beheaded, dies and loses its feathers. Thus fire, by its frequent and repeated action on water, forces it to better defend its specific qualities by abandoning its superfluity. The water contracts, tightens to resist Vulcan's tyrannical influence; it feeds on fire, which aggregates its pure and homogeneous molecules, and finally coagulates into a dense body mass, so fiery that the flame remains powerless to exalt it further.

It is for your benefit, unknown brothers of the mysterious solar city, that we have established our purpose to teach the various and successive modes of our purifications. We are sure you will be grateful to us for pointing out to you these reefs, of the hermetic sea, against which so many inexperienced argonauts have come to shipwreck. If then you wish to possess the griffin –which is our astral stone–, by pulling it out of its arsenic gangue, take two parts of virgin earth, our scaly dragon, and one part of the igneous agent, who is this valiant knight armed with the spear and shield. Ἄρης (Ares), more vigorous than Aries, must be in smaller quantities. Spray and add the fifteenth part of the whole of this pure, white, admirable salt, several times washed and crystallized, which you must necessarily know. Mix intimately; then, following the example of Our Lord's painful Passion, crucify it with three iron points, so that the body can die and then rise again. Once this is done, remove the coarsest sediments from the corpse; crush and triturate the bones; knead everything on a low fire with a rod of steel. Then throw half of the second salt, from the dew that fertilizes the soil in May, into this mixture and you will obtain a clearer body than the previous one. Repeat the same technique three times; you will reach the mining of our mercury, and will have climbed the first step of the Staircase of the Sages. When Jesus rose from the dead on the third day after his death, a bright, white-clad angel occupied the empty tomb alone...

But if it is enough to know the secret substance, figured by the dragon, to discover its antagonist, it is indispensable to know what means the wise employ in order to limit, to temper the excessive ardor of the belligerents. For want of a necessary mediator, of which we have never found a symbolic interpretation, the ignorant experimenter would expose himself to grave dangers. An anxious spectator of the drama which he would have unbridledly unleashed, could not direct the phases or regulate the fury. Igneous projections, sometimes even the brutal explosion of the stove, would be the sad consequences of his temerity. Therefore, conscious of our responsibility, let us urge those who do not have this secret to abstain until then. They will thus avoid the unfortunate fate of an unfortunate priest of the Diocese of Avignon, that the following note briefly relates: "Chapaty abbot thought to have found the philosopher's stone, but unfortunately for him, the crucible was broken, the metal jumped against him, attached to his face, his arms and his coat; he thus ran the Infirmaries Street, throwing himself into the streams like a madman, and perished miserably as a damned. 1706".[34]

When you perceive in the vessel a sound like that of the boiling water –the muffled roar of the earth whose fire tears the entrails–, be ready to fight and keep your cool. You will notice smoke and blue, green and purple flames, accompanying a series of precipitous detonations ...

Once the effervescence stops and calm is restored, you can enjoy a magnificent show. On a sea of fire, solid islets form, float, move slowly, take and leave an infinity of bright colors; their surface swells, dies in the center and makes them look like tiny volcanoes. They then disappear to make way for pretty green beads, transparent, which turn quickly on themselves, roll, collide and seem to chase each other, in the midst of multicolored flames, iridescent reflections from the incandescent bath.

In describing the painful and delicate preparation of our stone, we have omitted to speak of the effective contribution that certain external influences must provide. We could, in this sense, content ourselves with quoting Nicolas Grosparmy, adept of the fifteenth century, of whom we have spoken at the beginning of this study, Cyliani, philosopher of the nineteenth century, without omitting Cyprian Piccolpassi, Italian master potter, who devoted a part of his teaching to the examination of these conditions; but their works are not accessible to all. Be that as it may, and in order to satisfy, as far as possible, the legitimate curiosity of the investigators, we shall say that, without the absolute concordance of the superior elements with the inferiors, our matter, devoid of the astral virtues, can be of no use. The body on which we work is, before its treatment, more terrestrial than celestial; art must render it, by helping nature, more heavenly than earthly. Knowledge of the propitious moment, time, place, season, etc., is therefore indispensable for the success of this secret production. Let us foresee the time when the stars will form, in the sky of the fixed heavenly bodies, the most favorable aspect. For they will be reflected in this divine mirror that is our stone and will fix their footprint. And the earthly star, the occult torch of our Nativity, will be the hallmark of the happy union of heaven and earth, or, as Philaletes writes, of the "union of the higher virtues in the lower things". You will have confirmation by discovering, within the igneous water,

---

34 *Recueil de pièces sur Avignon* (Collection of parts on Avignon). Carpentras Library, ms. No. 917, fol. 168.

or this terrestrial sky, following the typical expression of Vinceslas Lavinius of Moravia, the hermetic, centred and radiant sun, made manifest, visible and patent.

Capture a sunbeam, condense it in a substantial form, feed this corporeal spiritual fire with elemental fire, and you will possess the greatest treasure of this world.

It is useful to know that the fight, short but violent, delivered by the knight –either St. George, St. Michael or St. Marcel in the Christian Tradition; Mars, Theseus, Jason, Hercules in the Fable–, ceases only by the death of the two champions (hermetically, the eagle and the lion), and their assembly in a new body whose alchemical signature is the griffon. Remember that in all ancient legends of Asia and Europe, it is always a dragon who is in charge of the treasure. He watches over the golden apples of the Hesperides and the hanging fleece of Colchis. That is why it is necessary, of necessity, to silence this aggressive monster if one wants then to seize the wealth which it protects. A Chinese legend tells about the wise alchemist Hujumsin –elevated to the category of god after his death–, who after killing a horrible dragon that devastated the country, tied the monster to a column. That's exactly what Jason does in the summer forest, and Cyliani in his allegorical tale of Hermes unveiled . The truth, always similar to itself, is expressed by means of analogous means and fictions.

The combination of the two initial materials, one volatile, the other fixed, gives a third body, mixed, which marks the first state of the stone of the philosophers. Such is, as we have said, the griffin, half eagle and half lion, a symbol corresponding to that of the basket of Bacchus and the fish of Christian iconography. We must notice, indeed, that the griffin carries, instead of a lion's mane or a necklace of feathers, a ridge of fish's fins. This detail is important. For if it is expedient to provoke the encounter and to dominate the combat, we must still discover the means of capturing the pure, essential part of the newly produced body, the only one that is useful to us, that is to say the Mercury of the sages. The poets tell us that Vulcan, surprising in adultery Mars and Venus, hastened to surround them with a net, so that they could not avoid his vengeance. In the same way, the teachers advise us to use also a delicate net or a subtle net, to capture the product as and when it appears. The artist fishes, metaphorically, the mystical fish, and leaves the water empty, inert, without soul: the man, in this operation, is thus supposed to kill the griffin. This is the scene reproduced in our bas-relief.

If we search for what secret meaning is attached to the Greek word γρύψ, griffin, whose root is γρυπός, that is, to have the hooked beak, we will find a neighboring word, γρῖφος, whose assonance is closer to the French word. Thus γρῖφος expresses both an enigma and a net. We then see that the fabulous animal contains, in its image and its name, the most ungrateful hermetic enigma to be deciphered, that of the philosopher's mercury, whose substance, deeply hidden in the body, is taken like a fish in the water, using a suitable net.

Basil Valentine, who is usually clearer, did not use the symbol of the Christian, which he preferred to humanize under the cabalistic and mythological name of Hyperion.[35]

This is how he points out this knight, presenting the three operations of the Great Work under an enigmatic formula comprising three succinct sentences, as follows:

"I was born of Hermogenes. Hyperion chose me. Without Jamsuphle, I am forced to perish".

---

35 The Greek name of the Fish is formed by the assembly of the acronyms of this sentence: Ἰησοῦς Χριστός Θεοῦ Υἱός Σωτήρ, which means Jesus Christ, Son of God, Savior. We often see the word Ἰχθύς engraved in the Roman Catacombs; he also appears on the mosaic of St. Apollinaire, at Ravenna, placed at the top of a cross constellation, raised on the Latin words SALUS MUNDI, and having at the end of his arms the letters A and Ω.

We have seen how, and as a result of what reaction, the griffin is born, that comes from Hermogenes, or from the prime mercurial substance. Hyperion, in Greek Ὑπερίων, is the father of the sun; it is he who emerges, out of the second white chaos, formed by art and figured by the griffin, the soul that he holds imprisoned, the spirit, fire or hidden light, and the door above the mass, in the aspect of a clear and limpid water: *Spiritus Domini ferebatur super aquas*. Because the prepared matter, which contains all the elements necessary for our great work, is only a fertilized earth where there is still some confusion; a substance that holds scattered light in itself, that art must gather and isolate by imitating the Creator. This earth, we must mortify and decompose it, which amounts to killing the griffin and fishing the fish, to separate the fire from the earth, the subtle of the thick, "gently, with great skill and caution," according to the Hermes teachings in his Emerald Table.

Such is the chemical role of Hyperion. Its very name, formed of Ὑπ, contraction of Ὑπέρ, above, and ἠρίον, sepulcher, tomb, whose root is ἔρα, earth, indicates what goes up from the earth, above the sepulcher of matter. One may, if one prefers, choose the etymology by which Ὑπερίων, would derive from Ὑπέρ, above, and from ἴον, violet. The two senses have a perfect hermetic concordance; but we only give this variant to enlighten the trainees of our order, following the words of the Gospel: "Take care therefore how you listen, for unto every one that hath shall be given, and he shall have abundance: but from him that hath not shall be taken away even that which he hath".[36]

VI

Carved above the group of the man with the griffin, you will notice a huge grimacing head, embellished with a pointed beard. The cheeks, the ears, the forehead are stretched to take the appearance of flamed expansions. This flamboyant mask, with its unpleasant grin, appears crowned and provided with horned, wrapped appendages, which rest on the twist of the cornice bottom (see Plate IX on page 78).

With its horns and crown, the solar symbol takes on the meaning of a true Baphomet, that is, the synthetic image in which the Initiates of the Temple had gathered all the elements of high science and tradition. A complex figure, in truth, under an exterior of simplicity, a eloquent figure, full of teaching, despite its harsh and primitive aesthetic. If we first find in it the mystical fusion of the natures of the Work symbolized by the horns of the lunar crescent placed on the solar head, we are no less surprised by the strange expression, a reflection of a devouring ardor, that emerges from this inhuman face, the spectre of the last judgment. It is not even up to the beard, hieroglyphic of the beam of light and igneous projected towards the earth, which does not justify what exact knowledge of our destiny the scientist possessed...

Are we in the presence of the dwelling of some affiliate of the sects of the Illuminated or Rosicrucians who descended from the old Templars? The cyclical theory, in parallel with Hermes' doctrine, is so clearly set exposed here that unless ignorance or bad faith is present, one cannot suspect the knowledge of our Adept. For us, our conviction is made; we are certain that we are not mistaken before so many categorical statements: it is indeed a baphomet, renewed from that of the Templars, that we have before us. This image, on which there are only vague indications or simple hypotheses, was never an idol, as some believed, but

---

36 Matthew, XXV, 29 and 30. Luke, VIII, 18, and XIX, 26. Marc, IV, 25.

only a complete emblem of the Order's secret traditions, used especially outside, as an esoteric paradigm, seal of chivalry and sign of recognition. It was reproduced on the jewellery, as well as on the pediment of the commanders' residences and on the tympanum of the Templar chapels. It consisted of an isosceles triangle with a vertex pointing downwards, hieroglyphic of water, the first element created, according to Thales of Milet, who maintained that "God is this Spirit who formed all things of water".[37] A similar second triangle, inverted from the first, but smaller, was inscribed in the centre and seemed to occupy the space reserved for the nose in the human face. It symbolized fire, and more precisely, the fire enclosed in water, or the divine spark, the incarnate soul, the life infused in matter. On the inverted base of the large water triangle, a graphic sign similar to the letter H of the Latins, or to the ἦτα of the Greeks, was supported, with more width however, and whose central bar was intersected by a median circle. This sign, in hermetic steganography, indicates the universal Spirit, the Creator Spirit, God. Within the large triangle, a little above and on either side of the fire triangle, we could see on the left the inscribed crescent lunar circle, and on the right the solar circle with an apparent centre. These small circles were arranged in the same way as the eyes. Finally, welded at the base of the small inner triangle, the cross placed on the globe thus created the double hieroglyph of sulphur, active principle, associated with mercury, passive principle and solvent of all metals. Often, a more or less long segment, located at the tip of the triangle, was carved out of vertically inclined lines where the layman recognized, not the expression of light radiation, but a kind of goatee.

Thus presented, the baphomet affected a coarse, imprecise animal form of difficult identification. This would undoubtedly explain the diversity of the descriptions that we have made of it, and in which we see the baphomet as a haloed death head, or a skull, sometimes an Egyptian Hapi head, a goat head, and, even better, the horrifying face of Satan himself! Simple impressions, far removed from reality, but images so unorthodox that they unfortunately contributed to spreading the accusation of demonology and witchcraft on the Knights of the Temple, which was one of the bases of their trial and one of the reasons for their conviction.

We have just seen what the baphomet was; we must now seek to discover the meaning hidden behind this denomination.

In the pure hermetic expression, corresponding to the work of the Work, Baphomet comes from the Greek roots Βαφεύς, dyer, and μής, set for μήν, the moon; unless one wants to speak to μήτηρ, genitive μητρός, mother or matrix, which amounts to the same lunar meaning, since the moon is really the mother or the mercurial matrix that receives the dye or seed of sulfur, representing the male, the dyer –Βαφεύς–, in the metal generation. Βαφή has the meaning of immersion and tincture. And it may be said, without much disclosure, that the sulfur, father and dyer of the stone, fertilizes the mercurial moon by immersion, which brings us back to the symbolic baptism of Mété expressed again by the word baphomet.[38] This one thus appears well as the complete hieroglyph of the science, figured elsewhere in the personality of the god Pan, mythical image of nature in full activity.

---

37 Cicero. *De Natura Deorum I*, 10, p. 348.

38 The baphomet sometimes offered, as we have said, the character and external appearance of the bucrânes. Presented in this way, it is identified with the watery nature represented by Neptune, the greatest marine deity of Olympus. Ποσειδῶν is, indeed, veiled under the icon of the ox, the bull or the cow, which are lunar symbols. The Greek name of Neptune derives from Βοῦς, genitive Βοός, ox, bull, and εἶδος, εἴδωλον, image, spectrum or simulacrum.

The Latin word *Bapheus*, dyer, and the verb *meto*, to harvest, to gather, to reap, also indicate this special virtue that possesses the mercury or moon of the sages, of collecting the tincture, gradually as it is emitted during the immersion or the bath of the king, and which mother will conserve in her bosom during the required time. Such is the Grail, which contains the eucharistic wine, liquor of spiritual fire, vegetative liquor, alive and vivifying introduced in material things.

As for the origin of the Order, its affiliation, the knowledge and beliefs of the Knights Templar, we can do no better than quote textually a fragment of the study that Pierre Dujols, the scholar and learned philosopher, dedicated to the brothers Knights in his General Bibliography of Occult Sciences.[39]

"The brothers of the Temple," said the author, "we can no longer support the opposite view, were truly affiliated with Manicheism. Moreover, Baron Hammer's thesis is in line with this opinion. For him, the sectarians of Mardeck, the Ismailis, the Albigensians, the Templars, the Freemasons, the Illuminated, etc., are dependent on the same secret tradition emanating from this House of Wisdom (Dar-el-hickmet), founded in Cairo around the 11th century by Hackem. The German academician Nicolaï concludes in a similar sense and adds that the famous baphomet, which he brings from the Greek βαφομητϱός, was a Pythagorean symbol. We will not dwell on the divergent opinions of Anton, Herder, Munter, etc., but we will focus for a moment on the etymology of the word baphomet. Nicolaï's idea is admissible if we accept, with Hammer, this slight variant: Βαφή Μήτεος, which could be translated as Méte's baptism. We have noticed, precisely, a rite of this name among the Ophites. Indeed, Mete was an androgynous deity representing the natural Nature. Proclus says verbatim that Métis, also known as Ἐπικάϱπιος, or *Natura germinans*, was the hermaphroditic god of the Serpent worshippers. It is also known that the Greeks referred to the Prudence revered as Jupiter's wife as the Métis. In short, this philological discussion proves indisputably that the Baphomet was Pan's pagan expression. Now, like the Templars, the Ophites had two baptisms: one exoteric, the baptism of water; the other, esoteric, that of the spirit or fire. The latter was called the baptism of Mete. Saint Justin and Saint Irenaeus call it enlightenment. It is the baptism of the Light of the Freemasons. This purification –the word here is really topical–, is indicated on one of the Gnostic idols discovered by Mr. de Hammer, and whose drawing he gave. She holds in her lap –notice the gesture, it is very revealing–, a basin full of fire. This fact, which should have struck the Teutonic scholar, and with him all the symbolists, does not seem to have told them anything. However, it is from this allegory that the famous myth of the Grail originates. Precisely, the erudite baron speaks abundantly about this mysterious vessel, whose exact meaning is still being sought. It is well known that, in ancient Germanic legend, Titurel erected a temple at the Holy Grail in Montsalvat and entrusted its guard to twelve Templar Knights. Mr. de Hammer wants to see in it the symbol of Gnostic Wisdom, a very vague conclusion after having burned for so long. May we be forgiven if we dare to suggest another point of view. The Grail –who doubts it today?– is the highest mystery of Mystical Knighthood and Masonry which degenerates from it; it is the veil of the Creative Fire, the *Deus absconditus* in the word INRI, engraved above Jesus' head on the cross. When Titurel built his mystical temple, it was to light the sacred fire of the Vestals, Mazdaeans and even the Hebrews, because the Jews maintained a perpetual fire in the Jerusalem temple. The twelve Custodes recall the twelve signs of the Zodiac that the sun, a type of living fire, travels

---

39 *À propos du Dictionnaire des Controverses historiques* (About the Dictionary of Historical Controversies), by SF Jehan. Paris, 1866.

through each year. The vase of the idol of the Baron of Hammer is identical to the pyrogenic vase of the Parses, which is full of flames. The Egyptians also had this attribute: Serapis is often depicted on the banks of the Nile, with the same object on his head, named Gardal. It was in this Gardal that the priests kept the material fire, just as the priestesses kept the heavenly fire of Phtah. For the Initiates of Isis, the Gardal was the hieroglyph of divine fire. Now, this god of Fire, this god of Love is eternally incarnated in each being, since everything in the universe has its vital spark. It is the Lamb sacrificed since the beginning of the world, which the Catholic Church offers to its faithful under the species of the Eucharist enclosed in the *ciborium*, like the Sacrament of Love. The *ciborium* –honoured is whoever misguidedly thinks about it!– as well as the Grail and the sacred craters of all religions, represents the female organ of the generation, and corresponds to the cosmogonic vessel of Plato, the cup of Hermes and Solomon, the urn of the ancient Mysteries. The Egyptian Gardal is therefore the key to the Grail. It is, in short, the same word. Indeed, from deformation to deformation, Gardal became Gradal, then, with a kind of aspiration, Graal. The blood that bubbles in the holy chalice is the igneous fermentation of life or the generating mixture. We could only deplore the blindness of those who would persist in seeing in this symbol, stripped of its veils to nakedness, only a profanation of the divine. The Bread and Wine of Mystical Sacrifice is the spirit or fire in matter, which, by their union, produce life. That is why Christian initiation manuals, called Gospels, make Christ say allegorically: I am the Life; I am the living Bread; I have come to set things on fire , and they wrap him in the sweet exoteric sign of the food par excellence".

VII

Before leaving the pretty Salamander manor house, we will still mention some motifs placed on its second floor, which, without being as interesting as the previous ones, are not devoid of symbolic value.

To the right of the pillar bearing the image of the lumberjack, we see two windows joined, one blind, the other glazed. In the middle of the four centered arches , one distinguishes, on the first, a *fleur-de-lys*, heraldic, emblem of the sovereignty of the science, which became, later, the attribute of the royalty.[40]

The sign of Adepthood and sublime knowledge, appearing in the royal coat of arms at the time of the institution of the coat of arms, did not lose the high meaning which it contained, and has since always been used to designate the superiority, the preponderance, the value and dignity acquired. It is for this reason that the capital of the kingdom was permitted to add to the silver vessel on the field Gules of his arms, three *fleurs-de-lis* on a field of azure. We find, moreover, the meaning of this symbol clearly explained in the Annals of Nangis: "The kings of France used to carry in their weapons the *fleur-de-lys* represented by three leaves, as if they said to the whole world: Faith, Wisdom and Cavalry are, by the provision and grace of God, more abundant in our kingdom than in the others. The two leaves of the *fleur-de-lis* that are equal mean sense and chivalry that preserve faith."

---

40 We keep in the *Fleur de Lys* its ancient spelling, in order to establish clearly the difference of expression that exists between this heraldic emblem, whose design is an iris flower, and the natural *fleur-de-lis* that we give for attribute to the Virgin Mary.

In the second window, a rubicund, round and lunar head, crowned by a phallus, arouses curiosity. In this we discover the very expressive indication of the two principles whose conjunction engenders the philosophical matter. This hieroglyph of the agent and the patient, of sulphur and mercury, of the Sun and the Moon, philosophical fathers of the stone, is eloquent enough to give us the explanation.

Between these windows, the middle column carries, as a capital, an urn similar to that which we have described by studying the grounds of the front door. We do not have to repeat the interpretation already provided. On the opposite pillar, continuing to the right, a little angel figure, with a wrapped forehead, is fixed, with clasped hands, in the attitude of prayer. Further on, two windows, contiguous like the preceding ones, carry over the lintel the image of two crowns on the field adorned with three flowers, which are the emblem of the three reiterations of each work, on which we have frequently spoken about during this analysis. The figures which take the place of capitals on the three columns of the fenestration offer respectively, and from left to right, 1st a head of man, that we believe to be the alchemist himself, whose gaze is directed towards the group of the character straddling the griffin; 2nd a cherub pressing against his chest a quartered shield, which distance and lack of relief prevent us from detailing; 3rd, a second angel exposes an open book, the hieroglyph of the matter of the Work, prepared and capable of manifesting the spirit that it contains. The sages have called their matter *Liber*, the book, because its crystalline and flaky texture is formed of superimposed leaflets like the pages of a book.

Finally, and carved into the mass of the extreme pillar, a kind of Hercules, completely naked, supports with effort the enormous mass of a burning solar baphomet. Of all the subjects carved on the facade, it is the most gross, the one whose execution is the least fortunate. Although being of the same period, it seems certain that this small stocky man, deformed, with a weathered belly, disproportionate genitals, had to be sided by some incompetent and second-rate artist. With the exception of the face, of neutral physiognomy, everything seems struck with pleasure in this unsightly caryatid. It is trampling a curved mass, with many teeth, like the mouth of a cetacean. Our Hercules could thus wish to represent Jonas, the little prophet miraculously saved after having remained three days in the belly of a whale. For us, Jonah is the sacred image of the Green Lion of the Sages, which remains three philosophical days locked in the mother substance, before rising by sublimation and appearing on the waters.

The Alchemic Myth
of Adam and Eve

The dogma of the fall of the first man, says Dupiney de Vorepierre, does not belong only to Christianity; it also belongs to Mosaism and to the primitive religion, which was that of the Patriarchs. This is the reason why this belief is found, though altered and disfigured, among all the peoples of the earth. The authentic history of this decay of man by his sin is preserved in the first book of Moses (Genesis, chapters II and III). "This fundamental dogma of Christianity," wrote Father Foucher, "was not ignored in ancient times. The peoples nearest to us of the origin of the world knew, by a uniform and constant tradition, that the first man had prevaricated, and that his crime had drawn upon him the curse of God upon all his posterity". "The fall of the degenerate man", says Voltaire himself, "is the foundation of the theology of all the ancient nations".

In the report of Philolaus the Pythagorean (5th century BC), the ancient philosophers said that the soul was buried in the body, as in a tomb, in punishment for some sin. Plato thus testifies that such was the doctrine of the Orphics, and he himself professed it. But as it was also recognized that man had gone out of the hands of God, and had lived in a state of purity and innocence (Dicéarque, Plato), it must be admitted that the crime for which he was suffering happened after his creation. The golden age of Greek and Roman mythology is obviously a memory of the first state of man coming out of the hands of God.

The monuments and traditions of Hindus confirm the story of Adam and his fall. This tradition also exists among Tibetan Buddhists; it was taught by the Druids, as well as by the Chinese and ancient Persians. According to Zoroaster's books, the first man and the first woman were created pure and submissive to Orzmuzd, their author. Ahriman saw them and was jealous of their happiness; he approached them in the form of a snake, presented them with fruits, and persuaded them that he himself was the creator of the whole universe. They believed him, and from then on their nature was corrupted, and this corruption infected their posterity. The mother of our flesh or the woman with the snake is famous in the Mexican traditions, which represent her fallen from her primitive state of happiness and innocence. In Yucatan, in Peru, in the Canary Islands, etc., the tradition of decay also existed among the native nations when the Europeans discovered these countries. The expiations that were celebrated among different cultures, to purify the child as he entered this life constitute an irrefutable testimony of the existence of this general belief. "Ordinarily," says the learned Cardinal Gousset, "this ceremony took place on the day when the child was given a name. That day, among the Romans, was the ninth for boys and the eighth for girls; it was called lustricus because of the lustral water that was used to purify the newborn. The Egyptians, the Persians, and the Greeks had a similar custom. In Yucatan, in America, the child was brought into the temple, where the priest poured water on it for the purpose, and gave it a name. In the Canary Islands, it was the women who fulfilled this function instead of the priests. Same expiations prescribed by law among Mexicans. In some provinces a fire was also lit, and the gesture was made to pass the child through the flame, as if to purify it by water and fire. The Tibetans in Asia also have such customs. In India, when the child is given a name, after writing this name on his forehead and throwing it three times into the water, the Brahmin or priest exclaims aloud: "O God, pure, unique, invisible and perfect, we offer you this child, from a holy tribe, anointed with an incorruptible oil and purified with water".

As Bergier points out, this tradition must necessarily go back to the cradle of the human race; for if it had been born in a particular people after the dispersion, it could not have spread from one end of the world to the other. This universal belief in the fall of the first man was, moreover, accompanied by the expectation of a mediator, of an extraordinary personage who was to bring salvation to men and reconcile them to God. Not only was this liberator expected by the patriarchs and the Jews, who knew that he would appear among them, but also by the Egyptians, the Chinese, the Japanese, the Hindus, the Siamese, the Arabs, the Persians, and by various nations of America. Among the Greeks and Romans, this hope was shared by some men, as Plato and Virgil testify. Moreover, as Voltaire remarks: "It was, from time immemorial, a maxim among the Indians and the Chinese, that the Sage would come from the West. Europe, on the other hand, said that it would come from the East".

Under the biblical tradition of the fall of the first man, philosophers have, with their customary skill, hidden a secret truth of an alchemical order. That, no doubt, is what serves and allows us to explain the representations of Adam and Eve that we discovered in some old Renaissance buildings. One of them, clearly characteristic of this intention, will be used as a type for our study. This philosophical residence, located in *Le Mans*, shows us, on the second floor, a bas-relief depicting Adam, his arm raised to pick the fruit of the tree of knowledge, while Eve draws the branch towards him, using a rope. Both hold phylacteries, attributes which express that these characters have an occult meaning, different from that of Genesis. This motif, mistreated by the elements –only larger masses have been spared–, is circumscribed by a crown of foliage, flowers and fruits, hieroglyphics of fertile nature, abundance and production. To the right and above, the image of the sun can be seen among decayed plant motifs, while to the left the image of the moon appears. The two hermetic stars accentuate and further specify the scientific quality and secular expression of the subject borrowed from the Holy Scriptures (Plate X).

Note, by the way, that the secular scenes of temptation conform to those of religious iconography. Adam and Eve are always separated by the trunk of the paradise tree. In the majority of cases, the serpent, wrapped around the trunk, is figured with a human head; this is how it appears on a Gothic bas-relief of the old Fountain of Saint-Maclou, in the church of that name, in Rouen, and on another large stage decorating a wall of the house called Adam and Eve, at Montferrand (Puy-de-Dôme), which seems to date from the end of the 14th century or the beginning of the 15th century. At the stalls of Saint-Bertrand-de-

LE MANS - HOUSE OF ADAM AND EVE
Bas-relief of the 16th century - Plate X

Comminges (Haute-Garonne), the reptile discovers a breasted bust, provided with arms and a woman's head. The snake of Vitre also shows a woman's head.

On the other hand, the solid silver group of the tabernacle of the cathedral of Valladolid (Spain) remains in the realistic note: the snake is represented in its natural aspect and holds, from its wide open mouth, an apple between its fangs.[1]

Adamus, Latin name of Adam, means made of red earth; it is the first being of nature, the only one of the human creatures who has been endowed with the two natures of the androgyne. We can therefore consider it, from the hermetic point of view, as the basic matter joined to the spirit in the very unity of the created, immortal and enduring substance. But as soon as God, according to the Mosaic tradition, gave birth to the woman by individualizing, in separate and distinct bodies, those natures originally associated in a single body, the first Adam had to fade away, specified itself by losing its original constitution and became the second Adam, imperfect and mortal. The Adam principle, of which we have never discovered any figuration anywhere, is called by the Greeks Ἄδαμος or Ἀδαμάς, a word which designates, on the earthly plane, the hardest steel, used for Ἀδάμαστος, that is to say, indomitable and still virgin (roots ἀ, privative, and δαμάω, taming), which characterizes well the deep nature of the first heavenly man and the first terrestrial body, as being solitary and not subject to the yoke of marriage. What is this steel named Ἀδάμας, whose philosophers speak so much? Plato, in his Timaeus, gives us the following explanation.

"Of all the waters which we have called fusible," he says, "that which has the most tenuous and equal parts; which is the densest; this unique kind whose color is a bright yellow;

1 This magnificent art object is the work of the statuary Juan de Arfé, who executed it in 1590.

VITRE (Ille-et-Vilaine) House Door, rue Notre-Dame - Plate XI

the most precious of goods, gold finally, formed itself by filtering through the stone. The knot of gold, become very hard and black because of its density, is called *adamas*. Another body, close to the gold for the smallness of the parts, but which has several species, whose density is lower than the density of the gold, which encloses a weak alloy of very tenuous ground, which makes it harder that gold, and which is at the same time lighter, thanks to the pores of which its mass is hollowed, is one of those brilliant and condensed waters which are called bronze.

When the portion of earth which it contains is separated by the action of time, it becomes visible by itself and is given the name of rust".

This passage of the great initiate teaches the distinction of the two successive personalities of the symbolic Adam, which are described under their own mineral expression of steel and brass. Now, the next body of substance *adamas* –knot or sulfur of gold–, is the second Adam, considered in the organic kingdom as the true father of all men, and in the mineral kingdom as the agent and procreator of the metallic or geological individuals constituting it.

Thus we learn that sulfur and mercury, the generative principles of metals, were at the origin only one and the same matter; for it is only later that they acquire their specific individuality and preserve it in the compounds resulting from their union. And even though it is maintained by a powerful cohesion, art can nevertheless break it and isolate sulfur and mercury in the form that is peculiar to them. Sulfur, the active ingredient, is symbolically designated by the second Adam, and mercury, a passive element, by his wife Eve. This last element, or mercury, recognized as the most important, is also the most difficult to obtain in the practice of the Work. Its utility is such that science owes its name to it, since the hermetic philosophy is based on the perfect knowledge of Mercury, in Greek Ἑρμῆς (Hermes). This is expressed in the bas-relief that accompanies and limits the panel of Adam and Eve on the house of Le Mans. We note Bacchus as a child, provided with the thyrsus,[2] the left hand hiding the opening of a pot, and standing on the lid of a large vase decorated with garlands. Now, Bacchus, the emblematic deity of the mercury of the sages, embodies a secret meaning similar to that of Eve, mother of the living. In Greece, every bacchante was called Εὔα, Ève, a word whose root was Εὔιος, Evius, nickname of Bacchus. As for the vessels intended to contain the wine of the philosophers, or mercury, they speak enough clearly as to dispense us from emphasizing their esoteric meaning.

But this explanation, though logical and consistent with the doctrine, is, however, insufficient to provide the reason for certain experimental peculiarities and some obscure points of practice. It is indisputable that the artist can not claim the acquisition of the original material, that is to say the first Adam "formed of red earth", and that the subject of the sages himself, qualified first subject of art is far removed from the simplicity inherent in that of the second Adam. This subject is, however, and properly the mother of the Work, as Eve is the mother of men. It is she who gives the bodies she gives birth to, or more exactly that she reincrudates, the vitality, the vegetativeness, and the possibility of mutation. We will go further and say, to those who already have some tincture of science, that the common mother of alchemical metals does not enter in substance into the Great Work, although it is impossible, without her, to produce anything or to undertake anything. It is, in fact, through her, that the vulgar metals, real and sole agents of the stone, are changed into philosophical metals; it is through her that they are dissolved and purified; it is in her that they find and resume their lost activity, and, after having been dead, they become alive again; it is the earth that nourishes them, makes them grow, fructify, and allows them to multiply; it is, finally, by returning to the maternal womb which had formerly formed and brought them to light, that they are reborn and recover the primitive faculties which human industry had deprived them of. Eve and Bacchus are the symbols of this philosopher's and natural substance, not, however, first in the sense of unity or universality, commonly known as Hermes or Mercury. Now, we know that

---

2 In Greek θύρσος, to which the Adepts prefer, as being much closer to scientific truth and experimental reality, his synonym θυρσόλογχος, where we can grasp a very suggestive relationship between the rod of Aaron and the javelin of Ares.

the winged messenger of the gods served as intermediary between the powers of Olympus and played, in mythology, a role analogous to that of mercury in hermetic toil. The special nature of his action is better understood, and why he does not abide with the bodies he has diluted, purged, and animated. And it is also understood in what sense it is convenient to hear Basile Valentine, when he asserts that metals are creatures twice born from mercury, children of a single mother, produced and regenerated by her.[3] And we can understand better, on the other hand, where lies this stumbling block that philosophers have thrown in the way, when they affirm, by mutual agreement, that mercury is the only material of the Work, whereas the necessary reactions are only caused by it, what they have said either by metaphor or by considering it from a particular point of view.

It is not useless either to learn that, if we need the cist of Cybele, Ceres, or Bacchus, it is only because it contains the mysterious body which is the embryo of our stone; if we need a vase, it is only for the purpose of placing the body, and no one is ignorant that, without a suitable earth, every seed would become useless. Thus we cannot do without a vessel, although the contents are infinitely more precious than the container, the latter being bound, sooner or later, to separate from that one. Water has no form in itself, although it is likely to marry them all and take that of the container that contains it. This is the reason for our vessel and its necessity, and why the philosophers have so much recommended it as the indispensable vehicle, the obligatory excipient of our bodies. And this truth is justified by the image of Bacchus as a child standing on the lid of the sealed vessel.

From what precedes, it is important to remember that metals, liquefied and dissociated by mercury, regain the vegetative power they possessed at the moment of their appearance on the physical plane. Solvent is, for them, the part of a real fountain of youth. It separates the heterogeneous impurities imported from the mineral deposits, and removes from them the infirmities contracted over the centuries; he revives them, gives them new vigor, and rejuvenates them. It is thus that the vulgar metals are reincrudated, that is, restored to a state close to their original state, and hence called living or philosophical metals. Now, since they resume, in contact with their mother, their primitive faculties, we can be certain that they have taken a nature analogous to hers, becoming close to what she is. But it is obvious, on the other hand, that they can not, as a result of this conformity of complexion, engender new bodies with their mother, the latter having only a renewing and not generating power. From which it must be concluded that the mercury of which we speak, and whose figure is the Eve of the Mosaic Eden, is not the one that the sages have designated as being the matrix, the receptacle, the proper vessel suitable for the reincrudated metal, qualified sulfur, sun of the philosophers, metallic seed and father of the stone.

Let us not be deceived; this is the Gordian knot of the Work, the one that beginners must strive to untie if they do not want to be stopped short at the beginning of the practice. There is therefore another mother, daughter of the first, to whom the masters, with a purpose easy to guess, also called mercury. And the differentiation of these two mercuries, one for renovation and the other for procreation, is the most ungrateful study that science has reserved for the neophyte. It is with the intention of helping him to cross this barrier that we have extended ourselves to the myth of Adam and Eve, and that we will try to shed light on these obscure points, deliberately left in the shadows by the best authors themselves. Most of them were content to describe allegorically the union of sulphur and mercury, generators

---

3   The Adept hears about the alchemical metals produced by reincrudation, or the return to the simple state of vulgar metal bodies.

of stone, which they call sun and moon, philosophical father and mother, fixed and volatile, agent and patient, male and female, eagle and lion, Apollo and Diana (which some convert into Apollonius of Tyana), Gabritius and Beya, Urim and Thumim, the two columns of the temple: Jakin and Bohas, the old man and the young virgin, finally, and more accurately, the brother and sister. For they are, in reality, brother and sister, for they both have a common mother and are indebted to the contrariness of their temperaments rather unlike age and evolution than apart from their affinities.

The anonymous author of the *Ancient Knights' War*, in a speech told by the metal reduced to sulphur under the action of the first mercury, teaches that this sulphur has need of a second mercury with which it must join in order to multiply its species. "Among the artists who have worked with me", he says, "some have pushed their work so far that they have come to the end of separating my spirit, which contains my tincture, from me; so that, by mixing it with other metals and minerals, they have managed to communicate some of my virtues and strengths to those metals who have some affinity and friendship with me. However, the artists who have received this insight and who have surely found a part of art are truly very few. But since they did not know the origin of the tinctures, it was impossible for them to take their work any further, and they did not ultimately find that there was much use in their process. But if these artists had taken their research beyond that, and if they had examined carefully which woman is mine, if they had sought her and united me to her, then I could have tincted a thousand times more".[4] In the *Entretien d'Eudoxe et de Pyrophile* (The Conversation between Eudoxus and Pyrophile), which serves as a commentary to this treatise, Limojon de Saint-Didier writes about this passage: "The woman who is appropriate for the stone and who must be united to it is this fountain of living water whose source, all celestial, which has its centre in the sun and in the moon, produces this clear and precious stream of the Wise, which flows in the sea of philosophers, which surrounds all people. It is not without foundation that this divine fountain is called by the author the woman of the stone; some have represented it in the form of a celestial nymph; some others give it the name of the chaste Diana, whose purity and virginity is not healed by the spiritual bond that unites it to the stone. In a word, this magnetic conjunction is the magical marriage of heaven and earth, of which some philosophers have spoken; so that the second source of the physical tincture, which works such great wonders, is born from this mysterious conjugal union".

These two mothers, or mercuries, which we have just distinguished, appear under the emblem of the two roosters[5] in the stone panel located on the second floor of the house of Le Mans (see Plate XII, in the next page).

They accompany a vase filled with leaves and fruits, a symbol of their life-giving, generative and vegetative capacity, of the fertility and abundance of the resulting productions.[6] On each side of this motif, seated figures –one blowing into a horn, the other pinching a kind of guitar–, perform a musical duet. It is the translation of this Art of Music, the conventional epithet of alchemy, to which the various subjects carved on the facade relate.

---

4   Treaty reprinted in the *Triomphe Hermétique* (Hermetic Triumph) of Limojon de Saint-Didier. Amsterdam, Henry Wetstein, 1699, and Jacques Desbordes, 1710, p. 18.

5   In ancient times, the rooster was attributed to the god Mercury. The Greeks designated it by the word ἀλέκτωρ, which sometimes means virgin and sometimes wife, characteristic expressions of both mercury; Cabalistically, ἀλέκτωρ plays with ἀλεκτρος, which can not or can not be said, secret, mysterious.

6   In Greek, vase is said to be ἀγγεῖον, the body, a word whose root is ἄγγος, the uterus.

LE MANS - HOUSE OF ADAM AND EVE (16th Century)
The Rapture of Dejanire - Plate XII

But before continuing the study of the motives of the house of Adam and Eve, we believe it is our duty to warn the reader that, under the very little veiled terms, our analysis contains the revelation of what is known as the secret of the two mercuries. Our explanation, however, cannot withstand scrutiny, and anyone who takes the trouble to dissect it will encounter certain contradictions, manifest errors of logic or judgment. However, we faithfully acknowledge that there is only one mercury at the base, and that the second necessarily derives from the first. However, attention should be drawn to the different qualities they affect, and care should be taken to show –even at the cost of a deviation from reason or an implausibility–, how they can be distinguished, identified, and how it is possible to extract, directly, the wife herself from the sulphur, mother of the stone, from the womb of our primitive mother. Between the cabalistic narrative, traditional allegory and silence, we did not have to choose. Since our goal was to help workers unfamiliar with parables and metaphors, the use of allegory and cabal was forbidden. Should it be better to act like many of our predecessors and say nothing? We do not think so. What would be the point of writing, if not for those who already know and do not need our advice? We therefore preferred to provide, in clear language, an *ab absurd* demonstration, thanks to which it became possible to unveil the arcane that had hitherto remained stubbornly hidden. The process, moreover, does not belong to us. Let the authors –and there are many of them–, in whom no such discrepancies are noticed, throw us the first stone!

Above the roosters, guardians of the fruiting vase, a larger-sized panel is seen, unfortunately very mutilated, whose scene depicts the kidnapping of Dejanira by the centaur Nessos.

The fable tells that Hercules, having obtained the hand of Dejanira from the Eneo, for having triumphed of the river god Achelaus,[7] wanted to cross the river Evene[8] with his new wife.

Nessos, who was in the neighborhood, offered to transport Deianira to the other bank. Hercules was wrong to consent to it, and was soon aware that the centaur was trying to take it away from him. An arrow, dipped in the blood of the Hydra and thrown with a sure hand, stopped him on the spot. Nessos, feeling herself dying, then handed Dejanira his blood-stained tunic, assuring him that she would serve him to call back her husband if he went away from her to cling to other women. Later, the credulous wife, having learned that Hercules was looking for Iole, the price of his victory over Euryte, his father, sent him the bloody garment; but as soon as he put it on he began to feel atrocious pains.[9]

Unable to resist so much suffering, he threw himself into the flames of a pyre raised on Mount Ota, which he had lit with his own hands.[10] Dejanira, on hearing the fatal news, killed herself in despair.

---

7 The water, the humid or mercurial phase which the metals offer at the origin, and which they gradually lose by coagulating under the desiccating action of the sulfur charged with assimilating the mercury. The Greek term Ἀχελῷος does not apply only to the Achelous river, but is still used to refer to any course of flowing water or river.

8 Εὐήνιος, sweet, easy. It must be remarked that there is no question here of a solution of the principles of gold. Hercules does not enter the waters of the river, and Dejanira crosses it on the crest of Nessos. It is the solution of the stone which is the subject of the allegorical passage of the Evene, and this solution is obtained easily, in a soft and easy way.

9 The Greek word Ἰόλεία is formed of Ἰός, venom, and, λεία, loot, prey. Iole is the hieroglyph of the raw material, violent poison, say the sages, of which one does however the great medicine. The vulgar metals, dissolved by it, are thus the prey of this venom, which changes their nature and decomposes them; this is why the artist must be careful not to combine the sulfur obtained in this way with metallic gold. Hercules, though searching for Iole, does not contract with her.

10 From the Greek Αἴθω, to burn, to ignite, to be ardent.

This narrative relates to the last operations of the Magisterium; it is an allegory of the fermentation of the stone by gold, in order to orient the Elixir towards the metallic kingdom and to limit its use to the transmutation of metals.

Nessos represents the philosopher's stone, not yet determined nor assigned to any of the great natural genera, whose color varies from carmine to brilliant scarlet. Νῆσος, in Greek, means purple garment, and the bloody tunic of the centaur –"which burns the bodies more than the fire of hell"–, indicates the perfection of the completed product, ripe and dyed.

Hercules represents the sulfur of gold, whose refractory virtue to the most incisive agents can only be conquered by the action of the red garment, or the blood of stone. Gold, burnt under the combined effect of fire and stain, takes on the color of the stone and gives it, in exchange, the metallic quality that work had made it lose. Juno, queen of the Work, thus consecrates the reputation and the glory of Hercules, whose mythical apotheosis finds its material realization in the fermentation. The very name of Hercules, Ἡρακλῆς, indicates that he owes to Juno the imposition of the successive works which were to secure him fame and spread his fame; Ἡρακλῆς is formed, indeed, of the roots Ἥρα, Juno, and κλέος, glory, reputation, fame. Deianira, wife of Hercules, personifies the mercurial principle of gold, who struggles in concert with the sulfur to which he is conjoined, but nevertheless succumbs under the ardor of the igneous tunic. In Greek, Δηιάνειρα derives from Δηιοτής, hostility, struggle, agony.

On the two engaged pillars bordering the mythological scene of which we have just studied esotericism, on one side appears a lion's head with wings, on the other a head of a dog or a bitch. These animals are also represented in their complete form on the arches of the Vitré Gate (see Plate XI on page 90).

The lion, a hieroglyph of the fixed and coagulating principle commonly called sulfur, carries wings to show that the primitive solvent, by decomposing and reincruding the metal, gives the sulfur a volatile quality without which its meeting with mercury would become impossible. Some authors have described the manner of carrying out this important operation under the allegory of the fight of the eagle and the lion, the volatile and the fixed, combat sufficiently explained elsewhere.[11]

As for the symbolic dog, the direct successor of the Egyptian cynocephalus, it is the philosopher Artephius who gave him the civil rights among the figures of alchemical iconography. He speaks, in fact, of the dog of Khorassan and the bitch of Armenia, emblems of sulfur and mercury, parents of the stone.[12]

But while the word Ἁρμενος, meaning what is needed, what is prepared and properly arranged, indicates the passive and feminine principle, the dog of Khorassan, or sulfur, derives its name from the Greek word Κόραξ, equivalent of raven, a word which was still used to designate a certain blackish fish on which, if we were allowed, we could say curious things.[13]

---

11 Cf. Fulcanelli. *Le Mystère des Cathédrales* (The Mystery of the Cathedrals). Paris, J. Schemit, 1926, p. 67, and J.-J. Pauvert, Paris, 1964, p. 115.

12 Among the details of the Creation of the World that adorn the north portal of Chartres Cathedral, there is a group of the thirteenth century, representing Adam and Eve having at their feet the tempter, figured by a monster, with the head and torso of a dog, placed on the forelegs and ending in a snake's tail. It is the symbol of mercury-bonded sulfur in the original chaotic substance (Satan).

13 The Latins called the crow *Phoebeius ales*, the bird of Apollo or the Sun (Φοῖβος). At Notre-Dame de Paris, among the chimeras fixed on the guardrails of the high galleries, one notices a curious raven wearing a long veil that covers him halfway.

The "sons of science" whose perseverance has led to the threshold of the sanctuary know that after the knowledge of the universal solvent, the only mother borrowing the personality of Eve, there is not more important knowledge than that of metallic sulfur. Adam's first son, the actual generator of the stone, which received the name of Cain. Now, Cain means acquisition, and what the artist acquires first of all is the black and rabid dog of which the texts speak, the raven first testimony of the Magisterium. It is also, according to the version of the Cosmopolitan, the boneless fish, echelleis or remora "that swims in our philosophical sea", and about which Jean-Joachim d'Estingrel of Ingrofont ensures that "having once the little fish named Remora, which is very rare, not to say unique in this great sea, you will not need to fish anymore, but only to think about the preparation, the seasoning and the cooking of this little fish".[14] And, although it is better not to extract him from the environment he inhabits –leaving him enough water, if necessary, to maintain his vitality–, those who had the curiosity to isolate him could control the accuracy and veracity of philosophical claims. It is a tiny body, in relation to the volume of the mass from which it comes, having the external appearance of a bi-convex lens, often circular, sometimes elliptical. Of rather earthy rather metallic aspect, this light button, infusible but very soluble, hard, brittle, friable, black on one face, whitish on the other, violet in its breaking point, has received various names, relative to its form, to its coloring or certain chemical peculiarities. He is the secret prototype of the popular bather of the king's cake, the bean (κύαμος, paronym of κύανος, bluish black), the sabot or wooden shoe (βέμβιξ); it is also the cocoon (βομβύκιον) and its worm, whose Greek name, βόμβυξ, which resembles so much that of the sabot, has as its root βόμβος, which expresses, precisely, the sound of a spinning top;[15] it is still the little blackish fish called *chabot*, from which Perrault drew his Booted Cat, the famous Marquis of Carabas (from Κάρα, head, and βασιλεύς, king) from the hermetic legends dear to our youth and gathered under the title of *Tales of our mother the Goose;* it is, finally, the basilisk of the fable –βασιλικόν–, our regulator (*regulus*, little king) or king (βασιλίσκος), the fur slipper (because it is white and grey) of the humble Cinderella, the sole, flat fish whose each face is differently colored and whose name refers to the sun (lat. *sol, solis*), etc. In the oral language of the Adepts, however, this body is hardly referred to other than by the term violet, the first flower that the wise man sees born and flourish in the spring of the Work, transforming the greenery of its flower bed into a new color...

We believe that we must suspend this teaching here and keep the prudent silence of Nicolas de Valois and Quercetano, the only ones, as far as we know, who revealed the verbal epithet for sulphur, gold or hermetic sun.

---

14 Jean-Joachim d'Estingrel of Ingrofont. *Traitez du Cosmopolite nouvellement découverts* (Newly Discovered Treatises of the Cosmopolitan). Paris, Laurent d'Houry, 1691. Letter II, p. 46.

15 Conf. Fulcanelli, *Mystery of the Cathedrals*, Jean-Jacques Pauvert, p. 51, what is said about this child's toy, about this main object of the *ludus puerorum*.

Louis D'Estissac

GOVERNOR OF POITOU AND SAINTONGE
GRAND OFFICER OF THE CROWN
AND HERMETIC PHILOSOPHER

I

This is the mysterious side of a historical character who reveals himself to us through one of his works. Louis d'Estissac, a man of high status, turns out to be a practicing alchemist and one of the best-educated Adepts of hermetic arcana.

Where did he get his science? Who gave it to him –by word of mouth, no doubt– the first elements? We do not know it in a relevant way, but we like to believe that the learned doctor and philosopher François Rabelais could well be no stranger to his initiation.[1]

Louis d'Estissac, born in 1507, was Geoffroy d'Estissac's own nephew, and lived in the house of his uncle, superior of the Benedictine abbey of Maillezais, who had established his priory not far from there, in Ligugé (Vienna). Now, it is well known that Geoffroy d'Estissac had for a long time been maintaining relations with Rabelais, marked by the most lively and cordial friendship. In 1525, according to H. Clouzot, our philosopher was in Ligugé, as an attaché "in the service" of Geoffroy d'Estissac. "Jean Bouchet," adds Clouzot, "the procurator-poet, who informs us so well about the life one leads at Ligugé, in the priory of the reverend bishop, does not, unfortunately, specify the functions of Rabelais. Secretary of the prelate? It's possible. But why not tutor his nephew, Louis d'Estissac, who is only eighteen and will not get married until 1527? The author of Gargantua and Pantagruel gives such developments to the education of his heroes, that one must suppose that his erudition is not purely theoretical,

---

1 Gilbert Ducher, in an epigram to philosophy (1538), quotes him among the faithful of divine science:

"In primis sane Rabelæsum, principem eundem
Supremum in studiis diva tuis sophia".

99

but that it is also the fruit of an earlier practice.[2] Moreover, Rabelais does not seem to have ever abandoned his new friend –perhaps his disciple–, because being in Rome in 1536, he sent, says Clouzot, to Mme d'Estissac, the young niece of the bishop, "medicinal plants and a thousand small mireliﬁccs (objects of curiosity) at a cheap price" brought from Cyprus, Candia, Constantinople. It is still in the castle of Coulonges-sur-l'Autize –alled Coulonges-les-Royaux in the Quart Book of Pantagruel –, that our philosopher, pursued by the hatred of his enemies, will come, towards 1550, to seek a refuge near Louis d'Estissac, heir to the protector of Rabelais, the Bishop of Maillezais.

Be that as it may, it leads us to think that the search for the philosopher's stone, in the sixteenth and seventeenth centuries, was more active than one would believe, and that its happy possessors did not represent, in the spagyric world, the tiny minority that we tend to grant them. If they remain unknown to us, it is much less by the absence of documents relating to their science than by our ignorance of traditional symbolism, which does not allow us to recognize them well. It is probable that by prohibiting, by his letters patent of 1537, the use of the printing press, Francis I was the determining cause of this deficiency of works which one notices in the 16th century, and the unconscious promoter of a new symbolic strength worthy of the most beautiful medieval period. Stone replaces parchment, and carved ornamentation comes to the aid of the prohibited impression. This temporary return of thought to the monument, from the written allegory to the stone parable, brought us some brilliant works of real interest for the study of the artistic versions of old alchemy.

Already in the Middle Ages, the masters whose treaties we possess loved to provide their homes with hermetic signs and images. At the time of Jean Astruc, doctor of Louis XV, that is to say about 1720, there was a house in Montpellier, in the street of the Cannau, facing the convent of the Capuchins, which, according to the tradition, would have belonged to master Arnauld de Villeneuve, in 1280, or would have been inhabited by him. On its door two bas-reliefs were carved, one representing a roaring lion, the other a dragon biting its tail, recognized emblems of the Great Work. This house was destroyed in 1755.[3] His disciple, Raymond Lulle, coming from Rome, stops at Milan, in 1296, to pursue his philosophical research there. In this city, in the eighteenth century, people still showed the house where Lulle had worked; the entrance was decorated with hieroglyphic figures referring to science, as it results from a passage of the treatise of Borrichius on the *Origin and Progress of Chemistry.* [4] It is known that the houses, churches and hospitals built by Nicolas Flamel served as facilitators for the diffusion of sacred art images; his own home, "the Flamel hostel", built in 1376, on rue Marivaulx near the church of Saint-Jacques, was, says the chronicle, "all embellished with stories and currencies painted and gilded".

Louis d'Estissac, a contemporary of Rabelais, Denys Zachaire and Jean Lallemant, also wanted to devote to science, which he particularly loved, a residence worthy of it. At the age of thirty-five, he designed a symbolic interior where the secret signs that had guided his work would be cleverly distributed and carefully hidden. The well-established subjects,

    2   H. Clouzot. *Vie de Rabelais, notice biographique écrite pour l'édition des Œuvres de Rabelais* (Life of Rabelais, biographical note written for the edition of the Works of Rabelais). Paris, Garnier Frères, 1926.
    3   Jean Astruc. *Mémoires pour servir à l'Histoire de la Faculté de Médecine de Montpellier* (Memoirs to serve in the History of the Faculty of Medicine of Montpellier). Paris, 1767, p. 153.
    4   "Quod autem Lullius Mediolani et fuerit et chimica ibi tractaverit notissimum est, ostendi-turque adhuc domus illic nobili isto habitatore quondam superbiens; in cujus vestibulo conspicuæ ﬁg-uræ, naturæque ingenium artemque chimici satis demonstrant". (Olaüs Borrichius, *De Orut and Progressu Chemiae*, 133).

suitably veiled –so that the layman could not discern their mysterious meaning–, the main
lines of the architecture decided, he entrusted the execution to an architect who might has
been –at least that is the opinion of M. de Rochebrune–, Philibert de l'Orme. Thus was born
the superb castle of Coulonges-sur-l'Autize (Deux-Sèvres), which took twenty-six years to
build, from 1542 to 1568, but which today offers only an empty interior with bare walls.
The furniture, porches, carved stones, ceilings and even the corner towers, everything was
scattered. Some of these pieces of art were acquired by a famous etcher, Étienne-Octave de
Guillaume de Rochebrune, and were used to repair and beautify his property in Fontenay-le-
Comte (Vendée). It is in the castle of Terre-Neuve, where they are currently preserved, we
can admire and study them at leisure. Moreover, by the abundance, variety and origin of the
artistic pieces that it contains, it is more like a museum than a bourgeois residence from the
time of Henry IV.

The most beautiful ceiling of the castle of Coulonges, the one that once adorned
the vestibule and the treasure room, now covers the grand salon of Terre-Neuve, called the
Atelier. It is composed of nearly a hundred panels, all varied; one of them bears the date of
1550 and the monogram of Diane de Poitiers, like the one in the Castle of Anet. This detail
suggested that the plans for the Château de Coulonges could belong to the architect-canon
Philibert de l'Orme.[5] We will return later to it, when studying a similar residence.

At first a simple farm, the castle of Terre-Neuve was, in its current plan, built in
1595 by Jean Morison, on behalf of Nicolas Rapin, vice-seneschal of Fontenay-le-Comte and
"distinguished poet", as we learn from a manuscript monograph of the Chateau de Terre-
Neuve, probably written by M. De Rochebrune. The inscription, in verse, which is under the
porch, was composed by Nicolas Rapin himself. We quote it here, retaining its layout and
spelling:

WIND. SOVFLEZ. IN . TOVTE. SEASON.
VN. GOOD. AYR. IN . THIS . MAYSON.
QVE. NEVER . NI. FEVER. NI. PESTE.
NI. THE . MAVLX. QVI. ARE COMING . DEXCEZ.
DESIRE . QVERELLE. OV. PROCEED.
CEVLZ. QVI. SY. TIENDRONT. BORN . MOLESTE.[6]

The castle of Terre-Neuve is indebted for its rich collections and its works of art
to the aesthetic sense of the successors of the poet vice-seneschal, and especially to the very
sure taste of M. de Rochebrun.[7] Our intention is not to draw up the catalog of curiosities that
it shelters; Let us announce randomly, for the approval of the amateurs and the dilettantes,
tapestries of high lists, of Louis XIII period, coming from Chaligny, near Sainte-Hermine
(Vendée); a door of the grand salon, from Poitiers; the carrying chair of Bishop de Mercy,
bishop of Luçon in 1773; golden woodwork of Louis XIV and Louis XV styles; some wooden
consoles of Chambord Castle; an armorial panel in Gobelins tapestry (1670), donated by Louis

---

5   On September 5, 1550, Philibert de l'Orme received a cannonicate at Notre-Dame de Paris,
about the same time as Rabelais. Our architect resigned it in 1559, but his name is frequently mentioned
on the capitularies of the cathedral.

6   The winds blow in all seasons / Good air in this house / May fever, plague or evils / Coming
from envy, fights / Or suits never bother / Those who live here.

7   Mr. de Rochebrune, was born in Fontenay-le-Comte in 1824 and died in the castle of Terre-
Neuve in 1900, he was the grandfather of the current owner, M. du Fontenioux.

XIV; very beautiful wood carvings (fifteenth century) from the library of the Hermenault castle (Vendée); Henry II curtains, three of the eight panels of the series entitled "Triumph of the gods", representing the Triumphs of Venus, Bellone and Minerva, woven in silk in Flanders and attributed to Mantegna; very well preserved Louis XIV furniture and Louis XIII sacristy furniture; engravings of the best masters of the sixteenth and seventeenth centuries; a series almost complete of all the offensive weapons in use from the 9th to the 18th century; enameled glazes from Avisseau, Florentine bronzes, Chinese dishes of the green family; library containing the works of the most famous architects of the sixteenth and seventeenth centuries: Ducerceau, Dietterlin, Bullant, Lepautre, Philibert of the Elm, etc.[8]

Of all these wonders, the one that interests us most is, without a doubt, the monumental fireplace in the grand salon, purchased in Coulonges and rebuilt in March 1884 at the Château de Terre-Neuve. Even more remarkable for the accuracy of the hieroglyphs that decorate it, the finishing touch, the "straightness of the carving, sometimes pushed to the limit" and its surprising conservation than for its artistic merit, it constitutes a precious and very useful document to consult for the disciples of Hermes (Plate XIII).

FONTENAY-LE-COMTE - CHATEAU OF NEWFOUNDLAND
Chimney of the Grand Salon - Plate XIII

---

8   René Valette in the *"Revue du Bas-Poitou"* (Review of Bas-Poitou), volume XV, special issue devoted to Octave de Rochebrune, 1901, p. 205.

Certainly, the art critic would have some reason to reproach this lapidary work, common to decorative Renaissance productions, for being heavy, cold and lacking harmony, despite its sumptuous appearance and the display of flashy luxury. He could notice the excessive weight of the coat bearing on thin jambs, the surfaces badly balanced between them, its poverty of form, of invention, painfully masked under the brilliance of ornaments, mouldings, arabesques lavished with a vain ostentation. As for us, we will deliberately leave aside the aesthetic feeling of a brilliant, but superficial era, when affectation and mannerism replaced absent thought and failing originality, to focus only on the initiatory value of symbolism, for which this fireplace serves both as pretext and support.

The mantle, designed like an entablature with interlacing and symbolic figures, is carried by two stone pillars, cylindrical and polished. On their abacuses there is a fluted lintel, under a quarter round ovum and flanked by three acanthus leaves. Above, four caryatids on pedestals –two men and two women– support the cornice; the women's girdles are adorned with fruit, while those of men presents a lion mask, biting, as a ring, the crescent moon. Between the caryatids, three panels of frieze panels develop various hieroglyphs in a decorative form intended to better veil them. The cornice is divided, horizontally, in two stages, by a projecting ridge covering four motives: two vases full of fire and two shields bearing, engraved, the date of execution, March 1563.[9] They serve as a frame for three boxes receiving the three members of a Latin sentence: *Nascendo quotidie morimur.*[10] Finally, the upper part shows six small panels, opposed two-by-two from the ends towards the center; there are kidney-shaped panels, bucranes and, near the middle axis, hermetic shields.

These are, briefly described, the most interesting emblematic pieces for the alchemist; these are the ones we will now analyze in detail.

II

The first of the three panels that separate the caryatids, the one on the left, offers a central flower, our hermetic rose, two shells of the comb type, know as Compostela's meadows, and two human heads, one of the old man at the bottom, the other of the cherub at the top. Here we discover the formal indication of the materials needed for the work and the result that the artist must expect. The old man's mask is the emblem of the primary mercurial substance to which, philosophers say, all metals owe their origin. "You must not be ignorant," writes Limojon de Saint-Didier, "that our old man is our mercury; that this name suits him because he is the raw material of all metals; the Cosmopolite says that he is their water, to which he gives the name of steel and magnet, and he adds, for a greater confirmation of what I have just discovered to you: *Si undecies coit aurum cum eo, emittit suum semen, and debilitatur fere ad mortem usque; concipit chalybs, and generat filium patre clariorem.*[11]

One can see, at the western gate of the cathedral of Chartres, a very beautiful statue of the twelfth century, where the same esotericism is found luminously expressed. It is a tall old man of stone, crowned and haloed, which already signifies his hermetic personality,

9 Louis d'Estissac was then fifty-six years old.
10 Having been born to die daily.
11 "If the gold joins with it eleven times (the water), it emits its seed and is debilitated to death; then steel conceives and begets a son brighter than his father". *Lettre aux Vrays disciples d'Hermes* (Letter to the True Disciples of Hermes), in the *Triomphe hermetique* (Hermetic Triumph), p. 143.

draped in the ample cloak of the philosopher. With his right hand he holds a zither and raises from the left a bulging flask like the calabash of pilgrims.[12]

Standing between the uprights of a throne, he tramples on two human-headed, entwined monsters, one of which has wings and bird's feet (Plate XIV).

CATHEDRAL OF CHARTRES - WESTERN PORTAL
Symbolic Old Man (XIIth century) - Plate XIV

---

12 It is not uncommon to find, in the medieval texts, alchemy qualified as Art of Music. This name motivates the effigy of the two musicians that can be seen among the balusters finishing the upper floor of the manor of the Salamander at Lisieux. We also saw them reproduced on the house of Adam and Eve, in Mans, and we can meet them again so much at the cathedral of Amiens (royal musicians of the high gallery), as with the lodging of the counts of Champagne, called commonly house musicians, in Reims. In the beautiful planks illustrating the *Amphitheatrum Sapientiae Æternae*, from Henri Kunrath (1610), there is one that represents the interior of a sumptuous laboratory; in the middle of it, a table is covered with musical instruments and scores. The Greek μουσικός is rooted μοῦσα, muse, word derived from μῦθος, fable, apologue, allegory, which also means the spirit, the hidden meaning of a story.

These monsters represent the raw bodies whose decomposition and assemblage in another form, of volatile quality, furnish that secret substance which we call mercury, and which alone is sufficient to accomplish the whole work. The calabash, which contains the beverage of the peregrine, is the image of the solvent virtues of this mercury, cabalistically called pilgrim or traveler. It is in the patterns of our fireplace, which also include the scallops of St. Jacques, also called holy water basins, because there is kept holy or blessed water, qualifications that the ancients applied to mercurial water. But here, apart from the pure chemical sense, these two shells still teach the investigator that the regular and natural proportion requires two parts of the solvent against one of the fixed body. From this operation, made according to art, comes a new, regenerated body of volatile essence, represented by the cherub or angel that dominates the composition.[13] Thus, the death of the old man gives birth to the child and ensures its vitality. Philaletes warns us that it is necessary, in order to reach the goal, to kill the living to resurrect the dead. "Taking," he says, "gold that is dead and water that is alive, a compound is formed in which, by a brief decoction, the seed of gold becomes alive, while the living mercury is killed. The spirit coagulates with the body, and both putrefy in the form of silt, until the members of this compound are reduced to atoms. This is the nature of our Magistery".[14] This double substance, this perfectly matured compound, increased and multiplied, becomes the agent of marvelous transformations which characterize the philosopher's stone, *rosa hermetica.* According to the ferment, silver or gold, which serves to orient our first stone, the rose is sometimes white and sometimes red. These two philosophical flowers, blooming on the same rose, are described by Flamel in his *Book of Hieroglyphic Figures.* They embellish the frontispiece of the *Mutus Liber* and we see them bloom in a crucible on Gobille's engraving illustrating the twelfth key of Basil Valentine. We know that the celestial Virgin wears a crown of white roses, and we also know that the red rose is the signature reserved for initiates of the higher order, or Rose-Cross. And this term Rose-Cross will allow us, by explaining it, to complete the description of this first panel.

Apart from alchemical symbolism, the meaning of which is already very transparent, we discover another hidden element, that indicates the elevated rank of the man to whom we owe the motifs of this hieroglyphic architecture in the initiatory hierarchy. It is beyond doubt that Louis d'Estissac had conquered the title par excellence of the hermetic nobility. The central rose, in fact, appears in the middle of a Saint Andrew's cross formed by the elevation of the stone fillets that –we can suppose–, at the beginning covered and enclosed it. This is the great symbol of the manifested light, which is indicated by the Greek letter X (*chi*), initial of words, Χώνη, Χρυσός and Χρόνος, the crucible, the gold and the time, triple unknown of the Great -Artwork.[15] The cross of Saint-André (Χίασμα), which in the form of our French X, is the hieroglyph, reduced to its simplest expression, luminous and divergent radiations emanating from a single focus. It therefore appears as the graph of the spark. We can multiply its radiation, but it is impossible to simplify it further. These intersecting lines give the schema of the glittering stars, the radiant dispersion of all that shines, illuminates, radiates. So we made

---

13 In Greek, ἄγγελος, angel, also means messenger, a function that the deities of Olympus had reserved for the god Hermes.

14 *Introïtus apertus ad occlusum Regis palatium,* in Lenglet-Dufresnoy, *Histoire de la Philosophie Hermétique* (History of Hermetic Philosophy). Paris, Coustelier, 1742, t. II, cap. XIII, 20.

15 The symbol of light is found in the visual organ of man, window of the soul open on nature. It is the X-crossing of strips and optic nerves that anatomists call chiasma (from Greek Χίασμα, cross arrangement, root Χιάζω cross in X). The intercrossing offered by straw chairs gave them, in the Picard dialect, the name of Cayelles (X (α) -εἴλη, ray of light).

the seal, the mark of enlightenment and, by extension, of spiritual revelation. The Holy Spirit is always represented by a dove in full flight, the wings extended along an axis perpendicular to that of the body, that is to say on the cross. For the Greek cross and that of St. Andrew have, in hermetic, a meaning exactly similar. We often find the image of the dove completed by a halo that comes to clarify the hidden meaning, as can be seen on the religious scenes of our Primitives and in many purely alchemical sculptures.[16] The Greek and the French X represent the writing of light by the light itself, the trace of its passage, the manifestation of its movement , the affirmation of its reality. This is his real signature. Until the twelfth century, no other mark was used to authenticate old charters; from the 15th century, the cross became the signature of the illiterate. In Rome, auspicious days were signed with a white cross, and the bad ones of a black cross. This is the complete number of the Work, for unity, the two natures, the three principles and the four elements give the double quintessence, the two Vs, joined in the Roman number X, for the number ten. This number is the foundation of the Kabbalah of Pythagoras, or the universal language, of which a curious paradigm can be seen on the last page of a small alchemy book.[17] Bohemians use the cross or the X as a sign of recognition. Guided by this graphic drawn on a tree or a wall, they always camp exactly where their predecessors stood, next to the sacred symbol they call Patria. This word is believed to be of Latin origin, and apply to nomads this maxim that cats –living art objects– strive to practice: *Patria est ubicumque est bene* –wherever one is well, there is the homeland–; but it is from a Greek word, Πατριά, that their emblem is claimed, with the meaning of family, race, tribe. Therefore, the cross of the Gypsies or Romanies clearly indicates the place of refuge assigned to the tribe. It is peculiar, that almost all the meanings revealed by the sign of the X have a transcendent or mysterious value. X is in algebra the unknown quantity or quantities; it is also the problem to be solved, the solution to be discovered; it is the Pythagorean sign of multiplication and the element to cast out the nines in arithmetic; it is the popular symbol of the mathematical sciences in what they have of superior or abstract. It characterizes what is, in general, excellent, useful and remarkable (Χρήσιμος). In this sense, and in the slang of the students, it serves to distinguish the *École Polytechnique* (French Polytechnic School), by assuring it a superiority that "taupings and dear comrades" would not permit to be discussed. The best pupils (students preparing to enter the School), are united, in each promotion or *taupe*, by a cabalistic formula composed of an X in opposite angles in which the chemical symbols of sulphur and potassium hydrate appear:

$$S X KOH$$

This is stated, in slang of course, "Sulfur and potash for the X". The X is the emblem of the measure (μέτρον), taken in all its acceptances: dimension, extent, space, duration, rule, law, bound or limit. This is the occult reason why the international prototype of the meter, built in platinum iridium and preserved at the pavilion of Breteuil, Sèvres, affects the profile of the X in its cross section.[18] All the bodies of nature, all beings, either in their structure, or in their appearance, obey this fundamental law of radiation, all are subject to this

---

16 The ceiling of the Hotel Lallemant, in Bourges, offers a remarkable example.

17 *La Clavicule de la Science Hermétique* (The Clavicle of Hermetic Science), written by a northerner in his spare time, 1732. Amsterdam, Pierre Mortier, 1751.

18 We are not talking here about copy No. 8, deposited at the *Conservatoire des Arts et Métiers* in Paris, which serves as a legal standard, but of the international prototype.

measure. The canon of the Gnostics is the application to the human body;[19] and Jesus Christ, the incarnated spirit, St. Andrew and St. Peter personify the glorious and painful image. Have we not noticed that the aerial organs of plants, whether they are tall trees or tiny grasses, present with their roots the characteristic divergence of the branches of the X? How do flowers bloom? Cut the plant stems, petioles, veins, etc., examine these sections under the microscope, and you will have, visually, the most brilliant, the most marvelous confirmation of this divine will. Diatoms, sea urchins, starfish will provide you with other examples; but, without seeking further, open an edible shell –either cockle, conch, scallop–, and the two valves, placed on a single plane, will show you two convex surfaces furnished with double-furrowed furrows of the mysterious X. Its whiskers gave the cat its name. There is almost no doubt anymore that they conceal a high point of science, and that this secret reason earned the graceful feline the honor of being elevated to the rank of the Egyptian divinities.[20] About the cat, many of us remember the famous Black Cat, who had so much vogue under the tutelage of Rodolphe Salis; but how many know what esoteric and political center was hidden there, What international masonry was hiding behind the sign of the artistic cabaret? On one hand, the talent of a fervent, idealistic youth, made up of aesthetes in search of glory, carefree, blind, incapable of suspicion; on the other hand, the confidences of a mysterious science mixed with obscure diplomacy, a double-sided painting exposed on purpose in a medieval setting. The enigmatic tour of the Grand Dukes, signed by the cat with its scrutinizing eyes under its night-time livery, with its rigid and excessive X-shaped moustaches, and whose heraldic pose gave the wings of the Montmartre mill a symbolic value equal to its own, was not a pleasure outing for princes![21]

Zeus' lightning, which makes Olympus tremble and sows terror in mythological humanity, either because the god holds them in his hand or crowds them at his feet, or because they spring from the eagle's claws, follows the graphic form of the radiation. It is the translation of the celestial fire or the terrestrial fire, the potential or virtual fire that composes or disintegrates, generates or kills, invigorates or disorganizes. Son of the sun who generates it, servant of man who liberates and maintains it, the divine fire, fallen, decadent, imprisoned in dense matter to determine its evolution and direct its redemption, it is Jesus on his cross, image of the igneous, luminous and spiritual irradiation incarnated in all things. It is the Agnus sacrificed since the beginning of the world, and it is also the Agni, the Vedic god of fire;[22] but if the Lamb of God carries the cross on his banner as Jesus carries it on his shoulder, if he supports it with his foot, it is because he has the sign embedded in the very foot: image outside, reality inside.[23]

---

19 Leonardo da Vinci has taken it up and taught by transporting it from the mystical domain into that of aesthetic morphology.

20 X (ẋ), the sign of light. The Picard dialect, guardian, like the Provençal, of the traditions of the sacred language, has kept the hard primitive sound k for the cat.

21 Rodolphe Salis imposed on Steinlein, the author of the vignette, the image of the Galette mill, that of the cat, as well as the color of the dress, the eyes, and the geometric straightness of the whiskers. The *Chat-Noir* cabaret, founded in 1881, disappeared on the death of its creator –Colette's husband, Mr. Willy–, in 1897.

22 The Hindu svatiska, or swastika, is the sign of the divine, immortal and pure spirit, the symbol of life and fire, and not, as it is wrongly believed, a utensil intended to produce the flame.

23 Let us not be accused of dragging our reader into useless and vain dreams. We say we speak positively, and the initiates will not be mistaken. Let's say this for the others. Boil a sheep's foot in water until the bones can easily separate; you will find one of them, among them, with a medial furrow on one

Those who thus receive the heavenly spirit of the sacred fire, who carry it in them and are marked with its sign, have nothing to fear from the elemental fire. These elect, disciples of Elijah and children of Helios, modern crusaders having for guide the star of their elders, leave for the same conquest with the same cry of God wants it![24]

It is this superior and spiritual force, acting mysteriously within the concrete substance, which compels the crystal to take on its aspect, its immutable characteristics; it this force which is its pivot, its axis, the generating energy, the geometric will. And this configuration, variable to infinity, though always based on the cross, is the first manifestation of the organized form, by condensation and embodiment of light, soul, spirit, or fire. Owing to the same arrangement the spider webs retain midges, the nets grab fish, birds and butterflies without injuring them, the fabrics become translucent, and metal webs cut the flames and prevent the ignition of gases..

Finally, in space and time, the immense ideal cross that shares the twenty-four centuries of the cyclical year (Χιλιασμός), and separates in four age groups the twenty-four elders of the Revelation, twelve of whom sing the praises of God, while the other twelve groan over the decay of man.

What unsuspected truths remain enclosed in this simple sign that Christians renew each day on their own, without always understanding its meaning or hidden virtue! "For the word of the cross is foolishness to those who are lost; but for those who are saved, that is, for us, it is the instrument of the power of God. This is why it is written: I will destroy the wisdom of the wise, and I will reject the science of scholars. What have become of the wise? What have become of the doctors of the law? What has become of those curious minds of the sciences of this century? Has not God convinced the wisdom of this world madly?".[25] How many know more than the wild ass who saw the humble Child God born in Bethlehem, carried him triumphantly to Jerusalem and received, in memory of the King of Kings, the magnificent black cross on his back?[26]

In the alchemical field, the Greek cross and the cross of St. Andrew have some meanings that the artist must know. These graphic symbols, reproduced on a great number of manuscripts, and which, in some printed works, are the object of a special nomenclature, represent, among the Greeks and their successors of the Middle Ages, the melting crucible,

---

side and a Maltese cross on the opposite one. This signed bone is the real knucklebone of the ancients; it is with it that the Greek youth played their favorite game. It was called ἀστράγαλος, a word made up of ἀστήρ, starfish, because of the radiant seal we are talking about, and γάλος, used for γάλα, milk, which corresponds to the milk of the Virgin *(maris stella)* or Mercury of philosophers. We move on to another etymology that is even more revealing, because we must obey the philosophical discipline that forbids us to reveal the entire mystery. Our intention is therefore limited to awakening the investigator's sagacity, enabling them to acquire, through personal effort, this secret teaching whose most sincere authors have never wanted to discover the elements. All their treatises being acroamatic, it is useless to hope to obtain the slightest indication of them, as to the basis and foundation of art. That is why we strive, as far as possible, to make these sealed works useful, by providing the material for what was once the first initiation, that is, the verbal revelation necessary to understand them.

24 Cabalistic expression containing the key to the hermetic mystery. God willing is taken for God the Fire, which explains and justifies the badge adopted by the Crusader knights and its color: a red cross on the right shoulder.

25 St. Paul. First Epistle to the Corinthians, Chap. I, v. 18-20.

26 This signature caused the donkey to be called Saint Christopher of Palm Sunday, because Jesus entered Jerusalem on the day of Palm Sunday, or Easter, the very day when alchemists usually undertake their great work.

which the potters marked always a small cross (*crucibulum*), index of good manufacturing and proven solidity. But the Greeks also used a similar sign to designate a earthenware matrass. We know that this vessel was use for coction, and we think that, given its substance itself, its use must have differed little from the crucible. Moreover, the word matrass, used in the same sense in the 13th century, comes from the Greek μήτρα, matrix, term also used by the blowers and applied to the secret vessel for the maturation of the compound. Nicolas Grosparmy, Norman Adept of the fifteenth century, gives a figure of this spherical utensil, laterally tubulated, and it calls the same matrix. The X also translates the salt ammonia of the sages, or salt of Ammon (ἀμμωνιακός), that is to say of Aries, that one wrote formerly with more harmonic truth, because it realizes the harmony (ἁρμονία, assemblage), the agreement of water and fire, that he is the mediator par excellence between heaven and earth, the spirit and the body, the volatile and the fixed.[27] It is also the Sign, without any other qualification, the seal that reveals to man, through certain superficial lineaments, the intrinsic virtues of the prime philosophical substance. Finally, X is the Greek hieroglyph of glass, a pure material among all, assures us the masters of art, and the one who comes closest to perfection.

We believe that we have sufficiently demonstrated the importance of the cross, the depth of its esotericism and its preponderance in symbolism in general.[28] It does not offer less value or teaching in terms of the practical realization of the Work. It is the first, most important and secret key of all those who can open the sanctuary of nature to man. However, this key always appears in visible characters, drawn by nature itself obeying the divine will, on the cornerstone of the Work, which is also the fundamental stone of the Christian Church and Truth. Therefore, in religious iconography, a key is given to Saint Peter as a particular attribute that distinguishes, among the apostles of Christ, the one who was the humble fisherman Simon (cabalistically, X-μόνος, the only ray) and was to become, after the death of the Savior, his spiritual representative on earth. This is how we find him depicted on a beautiful 16th century statue, carved on oak wood and preserved in the Church of St. Theldreda in London (see Plate XV in the next page).

Saint Pierre, standing up, holds a key and shows the Veronica, singularity that makes this remarkable image a unique work of exceptional interest. It is certain that from the hermetic point of view the symbolism is doubly expressed, since the meaning of the key is repeated in the Holy Face, the miraculous seal of our stone. Moreover, the Veronica is offered here as a veiled replica of the cross, major emblem of Christianity and signature of the sacred art. Indeed, the word veronica does not come, as some authors have claimed, from Latin *vera iconica* (true and natural image) –which teaches us nothing–, but from the Greek φερένικος,

---

27 Ammon-Ra, the great solar divinity of the Egyptians, was usually represented with a ram's head, or, when he kept the human head, with spiraling horns rising above the ears. This god, to whom we dedicated the ram, had a colossal temple at Thebes (Karnak); it was accessed by following an avenue lined with squatting rams. Recall that the ram is the image of the water of the wise, just as the solar disk, with or without the uræus, another attribute of Ammon, is that of the secret fire. Ammon, the saline mediator, completes the trinity of the principles of the Work, of which he realizes concord, unity, perfection in the philosopher's stone.

28 Thus the Gothic cathedrals have their facades built according to the essential lines of the alchemical symbol of the *spirit* and their plan modelled on the imprint of the redemptive cross. All of them feature, inside, these cross-headed warheads, whose invention belongs to the Freemasons, enlightened builders of the Middle Ages. In such a way that the faithful are placed in medieval temples between two crosses, one lower and earthly, on which they walk –an image of their daily calvary–, the other higher and heavenly, towards which they aspire, but which their gaze alone allows them to reach.

LONDON - CHURCH OF SAINT-ETHELDREDA
Saint Peter and the Veronique - Plate XV

which procures the victory (of φέϱω, to wear, to produce, and νίϰη, victory). This is the meaning of the Latin inscription *In hoc signo vinces.* "You will overcome by this sign" placed under the chrism of the *labarum* of Constantine, which corresponds to the Greek formula Ἐν τουτῷ νίϰη. The sign of the cross, the monogram of Christ, of which the X of St. Andrew and the key of St. Peter are two replicas of equal esoteric value, is thus that mark capable of securing victory by the definite identification of the unique substance exclusively devoted to philosopher's labors.

Saint Peter holds the keys of Paradise, although only one is enough to ensure access to the heavenly dwelling. But the first key is duplicated, and these two crossed symbols, one of silver, the other of gold, constitute, with the trireme, the weapons of the sovereign pontiff, heir to the throne of Peter. The cross of the Son of Man, reflected in the keys of the Apostle, reveals the mysteries of universal science and the treasures of hermetic art to the men of good will. It alone allows the one who has the sense to open the door of the closed garden of Hesperides and pick, without fear for his salvation, the Rose of Adepthood.

From what we have said about the cross and the rose which is its center, or, more exactly, the heart –the bloody, radiant and glorious heart of Christ-matter– it is easy to infer that Louis d'Estissac bore the high title of Rose-Cross, a mark of superior initiation, a brilliant testimony of a positive science, concretized in the substantial reality of the absolute.

However, if no one can deny our Adept the grade of Rose-Cross, it cannot be inferred from this fact that he belonged to the hypothetical brotherhood of the same name. To conclude in this way would be to make a mistake. It is important to be able to discern the two Rose Crosses so as not to confuse the true with the false.

We will probably never know what obscure reason guided Valentin Andreae, or rather the German author that used this pseudonym, when he published the booklet entitled *Fama Fraternitatis Rosæ-Crucis* printed in Frankfurt Oder around 1614. Perhaps he was pursuing a political goal, either because he sought to counterbalance, by a fictitious occult power, the authority of the Masonic lodges of the time, or because he wanted to bring about the grouping into a single fraternity, depositary of their secrets, of the Rose Crosses that were scattered everywhere. In any case, if the Manifesto of the Brotherhood could not achieve any of these aims, it nevertheless contributed to spreading the news of an unknown cult, endowed with the most extravagant attributions, among the public. To the testimony of Valentin Andreae, its members, bound by an inviolable oath, subjected to severe discipline, possessed all the wealth and could perform all the wonders. They called themselves invisible, said they could make gold, silver, precious stones; they could heal the paralytics, the blind, the deaf, all the contagious and all the incurable. They claimed to have the means to extend human life beyond its natural limits; to converse with higher and elementary spirits; to discover even the most hidden things, etc. Such a display of prodigies must have struck the imagination of the masses and justified the assimilation of the Rosicrucians soon made, thus presented to magicians, sorcerers, satanists and necromancers.[29] A rather derogatory reputation that they shared, moreover, in a few provinces, with the Masons themselves. Let us add that they had hastened to adopt and introduce this new title into their hierarchy, of which they made a grade, without seeking to know its symbolic meaning or its true origin.[30]

In short, the mystical brotherhood, despite the voluntary affiliation of some learned personalities whose Manifesto surprised good faith, has never existed elsewhere than in the desire of its author. It's a fable and nothing more. As for the Masonic degree, it also has no philosophical importance. Finally, if we announce, without entering, these little chapels where one lazily takes the strip under the Rosicrucian banner, we will have embraced the various modalities of the apocryphal Rose-Cross.

For the rest, we will not argue that Valentin Andreae greatly extolled the extraordinary virtues that certain philosophers, more enthusiastic than sincere, attribute to universal medicine. If he attributes to the brothers what could only belong to the Magisterium, at least we find proof that his conviction was made about the reality of the stone. On the other hand, his pseudonym clearly shows that he knew very well what the symbol of the cross and the rose, the emblem used by the ancient magi and known from all antiquity, contains in occult truth. To such an extent that, after reading the Manifesto, we are led to see only a simple

---

29 Édouard Fournier, in his *Énigmes des Rues de Paris* (Enigmas of the Paris streets). Paris, E. Dentu, 1860), points out the "Sabbath of the Brothers of the Rosicrucians", which took place in 1623 in the rural solitudes of Ménilmontant. In a note (p. 26), he adds: "In a booklet of time, Horrible pactions, etc., reproduced in Volume IX of our historical and literary Varieties (p. 290), it is said that they gathered "the same in the Montmartre quarries as along the Belleville springs, and there they proposed the lessons they should give particularly before making them public".

30 The grade of Rose Cross is the eighth of the French Masonic ritual, and the eighteenth of the Scottish ritual.

treatise on alchemy and interpretation, neither more difficult nor less expressive than so many other writings of the same order. The tomb of the knight Christian Rosenkreuz (the Christian and Rosicrucian cabalist) presents a singular identity with the allegorical cave, furnished with a lead chest, inhabited by the formidable guardian of the hermetic treasure,[31] this fierce genius that the *Songe Verd* (Green Dream) calls Seganissegede.[32] A light, emanating from a golden sun, illuminates the cave and symbolizes this incarnate spirit, a divine spark trapped in things, of which we have already spoken. Multiple secrets of wisdom are enclosed in this tomb, and we cannot be otherwise surprised, since the principles of the Work being perfectly known, analogy naturally leads us to the discovery of truths and related facts.

A more detailed analysis of this pamphlet would not tell us anything new, except for some indispensable conditions of prudence, discipline and silence for the use of the Adepts; judicious advice, undoubtedly, but superfluous. The true Rose Cross, the only ones who can bear this title and provide material proof of their science, do not care. Living in isolation, in their austere retirement, they do not fear to be known, not even by their confreres. Some, however, occupied brilliant situations: d'Espagnet, Jacques Coeur, Jean Lallemant, Louis d'Estissac, the Count of Saint-Germain are among them; but they knew how to mask the origin of their fortune so skillfully that no one could distinguish the Rose Cross in the guise of the gentleman. What biographer would dare to certify that Philaletes –this friend of truth–, was the pseudonym of the noble Thomas of Vaughan and that under the epithet of Sethon (the wrestler) was hidden an illustrious member of a powerful Scottish family, the sirs of Winton? By granting the brothers this strange and paradoxical privilege of invisibility, Valentin Andreæ acknowledges the impossibility of identifying them, as great lords travelling incognito under the habit and in the bourgeois crew. They are invisible because they are unknown. Nothing characterizes them except modesty, simplicity and tolerance, virtues generally despised in our vain civilization, carried to the ridiculous exaggeration of personality.

Besides these upper class men we have just mentioned, how many other scholars preferred to bear without brilliance their Rosicrucian dignity, living among the working people, in a deliberate mediocrity and in the daily exercise of trades without nobility! Such is the case of a certain Leriche, a humble blacksmith, an ignored Adept and owner of the hermetic gem. This good man, of exceptional modesty, would have remained unknown forever if Cambriel had not bothered to name him, by recounting in detail how he went about reviving a man from Lyon, Candy, an eighteen year old who was about to suffer a lethargic crisis (1774).[33] Leriche shows us what the true sage should be and how he should live. If all the Rosicrucians had stood in this prudent reserve, if they had observed the same discretion, we would not have to mourn the loss of so many quality artists, carried away by clumsy zeal, blind trust, or driven by the irresistible need to attract attention. This vain desire for glory led Jean du Châtelet, Baron de Beausoleil, to the Bastille in 1640 and killed him there five years later; Paykul, a Livonian philosopher, transmuted before the Stockholm Senate and was condemned by Charles XII to be beheaded; Vinache, a man of the lower class, who could neither read nor write, but who knew the Great Work to the smallest detail, also cruelly expiated his insatiable desire for luxury and fame. René Voyer de Paulmy d'Argenson approached him to manufacture the gold

---

31 Cf. *Azoth ou Moyen de faire l'Or caché des Philosophes* (Azoth or Means of making the hidden gold of the Philosophers). Paris, Pierre Moët, 1659.

32 Anagram of the Genius of the Wise.

33 See L.-P.-François Cambriel. *Cours de Philosophie Hermétique ou d'Alchimie, en dix-neuf leçons* (Hermetic Philosophy or Alchemy course, in nineteen lessons). Paris, Lacour and Maistrasse, 1843.

that the financier Samuel Bernard had destined to pay France's debts. When the operation was completed, Paulmy d'Argenson, in recognition of his good services, seized Vinache on 17 February 1704, threw him into the Bastille, ordered that his throat be cut on 19 March the following year, and came in person to ensure that the murder was carried out, then had him buried clandestinely on March 22nd, around six o'clock in the evening, under the name of Étienne Durand, aged sixty –whereas Vinache was only thirty-eight–, and completed the crime by publishing that he had died of apoplexy![34] Who, after that, would dare to find it strange that alchemists refuse to reveal their secrets, and prefer to surround themselves with mystery and silence?

The so-called Brotherhood of the Rose-Cross never had a social existence. Adepts with the title are only brothers by the knowledge and success of their work. No oath commits them, no status binds them to each other, no rule other than the hermetic discipline freely accepted, voluntarily observed, influences their free will. All that may have been written or narrated, according to the legend attributed to the theologian of Cawle, is apocryphal and worthy, at most, to feed the imagination, the romantic fantasy of a Bulwer Lytton. The Rose Cross did not know each other; they had no meeting place, no headquarters, no temple, no ritual, no external mark of recognition. They did not pay contributions and would never have accepted the title, given to some other brothers, of *Knights of the Stomach*. The banquets were unknown to them. They were and are still isolated, scattered workers in the world, "cosmopolitan" researchers according to the narrowest acceptation of the term. As the Adepts do not recognize any hierarchical degree, it follows that the Rose-Cross is not a rank, but the only consecration of their secret work, that of experience, a positive light whose existence had been revealed to them by living faith. Certainly, some masters were able to gather around them young aspirants, accept the mission of advising them, directing their efforts and forming small initiation centres of which they were the soul, sometimes recognized, often mysterious. But we certify, and for very relevant reasons we can speak in this way, that there was never, between the owners of the title, any link other than that of scientific truth confirmed by the acquisition of the stone. If the Rose-Cross are brothers through discovery, work and science, brothers through deeds and works, it is in the manner of the philosophical concept, which considers all individuals as members of the same human family.

In short, the great classical authors who have taught, in their literary or artistic works, the precepts of our philosophy and the mysteries of art; those also who left irrefutable proof of their mastery, all are brothers of the true Rose-Cross. And it is to these scholars, famous or unknown, that the anonymous translator of a reputed book is addressed, when he says in his Preface: "As it is only by the cross that the true faithful must be tried, it is to you, Brothers of the True Rose-Cross, who possess all the treasures of the world, it is to you to whom I have recourse. I am completely consumed with your pious and wise counsels; I knew that they would only be good, because I know how much you have virtues over the rest of men. As you are the providers of Science, and therefore I owe you what I know, if I can say I know something, I want (according to the institution that God has established in Nature) things to return to where they came from. *Ad locum*, says the Ecclesiastes, *unde exeunt flumina*

34 *Un mystère à la Bastille. Étienne Vinache, médecin empirique et alchimiste (XVIIe siècle)* (A mystery at the Bastille. Étienne Vinache, empirical doctor and alchemist (17th century)), by Dr Roger Goulard, of Brie-Comte-Robert. In the *Bulletin de la Société française d'Histoire de la Médecine* (Bulletin of the French Society for the History of Medicine), t. XIV, nos. 11 and 12.

revertuntur, ut iterum fluant' . Everything is yours, everything comes from you, so everything will go back to you".[35]

May the reader excuse this digression which has led us further than we desired. But it seemed to us necessary to establish clearly what is the true and traditional hermetic Rose-Cross, to isolate it from other vulgar groups under the same banner, and to make it possible to distinguish the few initiates from impostors who vainly of a title of which they can not justify the acquisition.[36]

III

Let us now return to the study of the curious motifs imagined by Louis d'Estissac for the hermetic decoration of his chimney.

In the right panel, opposite to the one we have just analyzed, we see the mask of old man, previously identified, holding in its jaw two vegetable stems provided with leaves and each one carrying a floral button about to open. These stalks crimp a kind of open almond, inside which we see a vase decorated with scales and containing flower buds, fruits and ears of corn. Here we find the hieroglyphic expression of the vegetation, nutrition, and growth of the infant body of which we have spoken. Corn alone, deliberately placed next to flowers and fruits, is a very telling symbol. Its Greek name, ζέα, derives from ζάω, to live, to subsist, to exist. The scaly vase represents this primitive substance that nature offers to the artist, on leaving the mine, and with which he begins his work. It is from this that he extracts the various elements he needs; it is with it and through it that the whole labor is accomplished. The philosophers have portrayed it under the image of the black dragon covered with scales, which the Chinese call *Long*, and whose analogy is perfect with the hermetic monster. Like him, it is a sort of winged snake, with a horned head, throwing fire and flame through its nostrils, with black and scaly body carried on four stocky legs armed with five claws each. The gigantic dragon of the Scythian banners was called Apophis. Now, the Greek ἀπόφυσις, which means outgrowth, offspring, has for root ἀποφύω, with the sense to push, to grow, to produce, to be born of. The vegetative power **indicated** by the fructifications of the symbolic vase is thus expressly confirmed in the mythical dragon, which doubles as common mercury or first solvent. Subsequently, this primitive mercury, joined to some fixed body, makes it volatile, alive, vegetative and fructifying. It then changes its name by changing its quality and becomes the mercury of the wise, the metallic radical wet, celestial salt or salt flower. *"In Mercurio is quicquid quaerunt Sapientes"* –all that the wise seek is in the mercury, repeat our old writers at will. The nature and function of this vase that so many artists know, without knowing what it is capable of producing, could not be better expressed on stone. Without him, without this mercury from our Magnesia, assures us Philaletes, it is useless to light the lamp or the stove of the Philosophers. We will not say more in this place, because we will have the opportunity to return to this subject and to further develop the major mystery of great art.

---

35 *Le Texte d'Alchymie et le Songe Verd* (The Alchymic Text and the Green Dream). Paris, Laurent d'Houry, 1695. Preface, pp. 25 et seq.

36 In the nineteenth century, two Rosicrucian orders were created and quickly fell into oblivion: 1° Kabbalistic Order of the Rose-Croix, founded by Stanislas de Guaita; 2° Order of the Rose-Cross of the Temple and the Grail, founded in Toulouse, about 1850, by the Viscount de Lapasse, Spagyric doctor, pupil of Prince Balbiani of Palermo, pretended disciple of Cagliostro. Joséphin Péladan, who attributed himself the title of Sar, was one of the aesthetic animators. This idealistic movement, devoid of enlightened initiatic direction and solid philosophical base, could only have a limited duration. The Rosicrucian Salon opened from 1892 to 1897 and ceased to exist.

IV

In front of the central panel, the observer can not defend himself from an instinctive movement of surprise, as his decoration seems singular (Plate XVI).

FONTENAY-LE-COMTE - CHATEAU OF TERRE-NEUVE
Chimney of the Grand Salon - Central motif - Plate XVI

Two human monsters support a crown of leaves and fruit, which circumscribes a simple French shield. One of them presents the horrible feature of a harelip on a hairless, breasted torso. The other has the waking face of a mischievous and mutinous kid, but with the hairy chest of the anthropoids. If the arms and hands offer no other particularity than their excessive thinness, against the lower limbs, covered with long and bushy hairs, end in one in feline claws, in the other in birds of prey claws. These nightmarish creatures, with their long curved tails, are wearing incredible helmets, one scaly, the other striated, the summit of which rolls up in the form of an ammonite shell. Between these "stéphanophores" of repulsive aspect, and placed above them in the axis of the composition, a grinning man's mask, with round eyes and frizzy hair weighing down his low forehead, holds in his open and bestial jaw the central shield by a slight cord. Finally, a bucranium, occupying the lower part of the panel, finishes on a macabre note this apocalyptic quaternary.

As for the shield, the bizarre figures it bears seem to be drawn from some old grimoire. At first glance, they are thought to be borrowed from Solomon's dark clavicle, images drawn with fresh blood on the blank parchment, and which indicate, in their disturbing zigzags, the ritual movements that the forked wand must execute under the fingers of the wizard.

These are the symbolic elements offered to the sagacity of the student and cleverly concealed under the decorative harmony of this strange subject. We will try to explain them as clearly as possible, even if we ask for the help of the philosophical verb, or to resort to the language of the gods when we judge that we cannot overstep this limit and go further.

The two gnomes that face each other translate, as the reader will have guessed, our two metallic principles, bodies or primary natures, with which the Work is begun, perfected and completed.[37] They are the sulphurous and mercurial geniuses who guard the underground treasures, night craftsmen of the hermetic structure, familiar to the wise man they serve, honour and enrich with their unceasing work. They are the owners of earthly secrets, the revealers of the mineral mysteries. The gnome, a fictional creature, deformed but active, is the esoteric expression of metallic life, of the occult dynamism of the raw bodies that art can condense into a pure substance. Rabbinic tradition reports in the Talmud that a gnome cooperated in the building of Solomon's temple, which means that the philosopher's stone had to enter it to some extent. But, closer to home, aren't our Gothic cathedrals, as reported by Georges Stahl, indebted to him for the inimitable color of their stained glass windows? "Our stone," wrote an anonymous man, "still has two very surprising virtues; the first one with regard to glass, to which it gives all kinds of colors inside, such as the windows of the Sainte-Chapelle in Paris, and those of the churches of Saint-Gatien and Saint-Martin in the city of Tours".[38]

Thus, the dark, latent and potential life of the two primitive mineral substances, develops through contact, struggle, the union of their opposite natures, one igneous, the other aqueous. These are our elements, and there are no others. When philosophers speak of three principles, by describing them and distinguishing them by design, they use a subtle device designed to throw the neophyte into the most cruel embarrassment. We therefore certify, with the best authors, that two bodies are enough to fulfill the Magisterium from beginning to end. "It is not possible to acquire possession of our mercury," says the *Old Knights' War*, than by means of two bodies, one of which cannot receive without the other the perfection which is required of it. If we must admit a third, we will find it in the one which results from their assembly and is born of their mutual destruction. For you may seek, multiply the tests, you will never find other relatives of the stone than the two aforementioned bodies, qualified principles, from which comes the third, heir to the qualities and mixed qualities of his parents. This important point deserved to be clarified. Now, these two principles, hostile because contrary, are so expressive on the chimney of Louis d'Estissac, that the beginner will recognize them without difficulty. Here we find, humanized, the hermetic dragons described by Nicolas Flamel, one winged –the hare-lipped monster–, the other wingless –the hairy torso gnome. "Contemplate these two dragons well," says the Adept, "for they are the true principles of philosophy, which the Sages have not dared to show to their own children. The one below, wingless, is the fixed or the male, and the one which is above it is the volatile or the black and dark female, who will take the dominion by several months.[39] The first is called sulphur or heat and dryness, and the last is called quicksilver or coldness and humidity. They are the sun and the moon, of mercurial source and sulphurous origin, which, by continuous fire, are

---

37 The Greek γνῶμα, phonetic equivalent of the French *Gnome*, means the *clue*, which is used to make something known, to classify, to identify something; it is its distinctive sign. Γνώμων is also the indicator sign for the *movement of the sun*, the sundial hand and our *gnomon*. Meditate upon this. An important secret is hidden underneath this cabal.

38 *Clef du Grand-Œuvre, ou Lettres du Sancelrien tourangeau* (Key to the Great Work, or Letters from the Sancelrien Tourangeau). Paris, Cailleau, 1777, p. 65.

39 It is this woman who says of herself, in the *Song of Songs* (chapter I, v. 4): *Nigra sum sed formosa*, I am black, but I am beautiful.

adorned with royal ornaments to conquer, are united, and then change into quintessence, any solid metallic thing, hard and strong. It is these snakes and dragons that the ancient Egyptians painted in a circle, head biting its tail, to say that they came out of the same thing and that it alone is enough, and that in its contour and circulation it is perfect. It is these dragons that the ancient poets have put to keep without sleeping the golden apples of the gardens of the Hesperides virgins. These are the ones on whom Jason, in the adventure of the Golden Fleece, poured the juice prepared by the beautiful Medea, from whose speeches filled the books of the philosophers, that no philosopher has existed that has not written on the subject, from the veridical Trismegist Hermes, Orpheus, Pythagoras, Artephius, Morienus and the others following him up to myself. It is these two serpents sent and given by Juno, which is the metallic nature, that the strong Hercules, that is to say the Wise One, must strangle in his cradle, that is to say defeat and kill, to make them rot, corrupt and engender, at the beginning of his Work. These are the two snakes attached to the Caduceus and Mercury Rod, with whom he exercises his great power and transfigures himself as he wishes. The one, says Haly, who will kill one of them, will also kill the other, because one can only die with his brother; these two (whom Avicenna calls Corascene Dog and Armenian Dog), these two are united together in the vessel of the sepulchre, they both bite each other cruelly, and by their great poison and furious rage, they never let each other go since the moment they entered... It is these two sperm, male and female, described at the beginning of my Philosophical Rosary, that are generated (said Rasis, Avicenna and Abraham the Jew) in the kidneys, bowels, and operations of the four elements. These are the wet metals, Soulphre and Silver, not the vulgar ones, which are sold by merchants and apothecaries, but those given to us by these two beautiful and dear bodies that we love so much. These two sperms, says Democritus, cannot be found in the land of the living".[40]

Serpents or dragons, the hieroglyphic forms indicated by the old masters as figurative materials ready to be worked present, on the work of art of Fontenay-le-Comte, some very remarkable particularities, due to the cabalistic genius, the extended science of their author. What esoterically specifies these anthropomorphic beings is not only their griffin feet and their hairy limbs, but even more importantly their helmet. This hairstyle, finished in the horn of Ammon, and which is called in Greek κράνος, because it covers the head and protects the skull (κρανίον), will allow us to identify them. Already, the Greek word used to designate the head, Κρανίον, brings us a useful indication, because it also marks the place of Calvary, Golgotha where Jesus, Redeemer of men, had to suffer the Passion in his flesh before transfiguring himself in spirit. Now, our two principles, one of which bears the cross and the other the lance that pierces its flank, are an image, a reflection of the Passion of Christ.[41] Just as He, if they are to be resurrected in a new, clear, glorious, spiritualized body, they must together ascend their calvary, endure the torments of fire and die of slow agony, at the end of a bitter fight (ἀγωνία).

We know, on the other hand, that the puffers called their still *homo galeatus* –the man wearing a helmet–, because it was composed of a cucurbite covered with its lid. Our two

---

40 *Le Livre des Figures Hieroglyphiques* (The Book of Hierogliphic Figures) of Nicolas Flamel; In *Trois Traitez de la Philosophie Naturelle* (Three Treatise on Natural Philosophy). Paris, G. Marette, 1612.

41 Longin, in the Passion of N.-S. Jesus Christ plays the same role as St. Michael and St. George; Cadmos, Perseus and Jason make a similar gesture among the pagans. Longin pierces the side of Christ with a spear, as the celestial knights and the Greek heroes pierce the dragon. This is a symbolic act whose positive application to hermetic work is fraught with happy consequences.

helmeted genies can not be anything else than the alembic of the sages, or the two assembled bodies, the container and the contents, the proper matter and his own vessel. Because if the reactions are necessarily caused by the one (agent), they are exerted only by breaking the balance of the other (patient), which serves as receptacle and vase with the contrary energy of the nature opposing.

In the present motif, the agent is distinguished by his striated helmet. In fact, the Greek word ῥαβδοειδής, striated, striped, listed, is rooted ῥάβδος, rod, stick, wand, scepter, caduceus, javelin, dart. These different senses characterize most of the attributes of the active, masculine and fixed material. It is first of all the wand that Mercury throws between the snake and the snake (Rhea and Jupiter), on which they wrap themselves while realizing the Caduceus, emblem of peace and reconciliation. All hermetic writers speak of a terrible struggle between two dragoons, and Mythology tells us that such was the origin of the attribute of Hermes, which provoked their agreement by interposing his staff. It is the sign of union and harmony that must be realized between fire and water. Now, since fire is represented by the hieroglyph Δ, and water by the same inverted graph ∇, the two superimposed form the image of the star, a sure sign of union, pacification and procreation, because star (*stella*) means fixing the sun.[42]

And, in fact, the sign only shows itself after the fight, when everything has become calm and the first effervescence has stopped. The seal of Solomon, geometrical figure resulting from the assembly of triangles of fire and water, confirms the union of sky and earth. It is the messianic star announcing the birth of the King of kings; moreover, κηρύκειον, caduceus, a Greek word derived from κηρυκεύω, to publish, to announce, reveals that the distinctive emblem of Mercury is the sign of the good news. Among the Indians of North America, the pipe they use in their civil and religious ceremonies is a symbol analogous to the caduceus, both in form and in meaning. "It is," says Noel, "a great smoking pipe, of red, black, or white marble. It looks pretty much like a hammer; its head is well polished, and the stem, two and a half feet long, is a strong cane, ornamented with feathers of all kinds of colors, with several braids of women's hair intertwined in many ways. Two wings are attached to it, which makes it rather like the caduceus of Mercury, or the wand that the ambassadors of peace once wore. This cane is implanted in the necks of loons, birds spotted with white and black, and as big as our geese ... This pipe is in greatly venerated among the savages, who respect it as a precious gift that the Sun has made to men; it is also the symbol of peace, the seal of all important business enterprises and public ceremonies".[43] The rod of Hermes is truly the scepter of the sovereign of our art, the hermetic, vile, abject and despised gold, more sought after by the philosopher than pure natural gold; the rod that the high priest Aaron turned into a serpent, and the rod used by Moses (Exodus, XVII, 5, 6) –imitated in this by Jesus–, to strike the rock, that is to say the passive matter, and pure water hidden in his womb, flows;[44] it is Basil

---

42 This esoteric truth is masterfully expressed in the Hymn of the Christian Church:

Latet floor in sidere,	The sun is hidden under the star,
Oriens in vespere,	The Orient in the sunset;
Artifex in opere;	The craftsman is hidden in the work;
Per gratiam	By the help of grace,
Redditur and traditur	He is returned and brought back
Ad patriam	To his homeland.

43 Fr. Noel, *Dictionnaire de la Fable ou Mythologie Grecque, Latine, Égyptienne, Celtique, Persanne, etc.* (Dictionary of Fable or Greek, Latin, Egyptian, Celtic, Persian Mythology, etc.). Paris, Le Normant, 1801.

44 According to the Armenian version of the *Gospel of the Childhood*, translated by Paul Peeters, Jesus, during his stay in Egypt, renews, in the presence of children of his age, the miracle of Moses. "And

Valentine's ancient dragon, whose tongue and tail end in sting, which brings us back to the symbolic snake, the snake *aut draco qui caudam devoravit*.

As for the second body –patient and feminine–, Louis d'Estissac had it represented as the harelip gnome, equipped with breasts and wearing a scaly helmet. We already knew, from the descriptions left by the classical authors, that this mineral substance, as extracted from its mine, is scaly, black, hard and dry. Some have called it leprous. However, the Greek λεπίς, λεπίδος, scale, has among its derivatives the word λέπρα, leprosy, because this dreaded infection covers the epidermis with pustules and scales. It is therefore essential to remove the coarse and superficial impurity from the body by stripping it of its flaky shell (λεπίζω), an operation that can easily be carried out using the active ingredient, the agent with the striated helmet. Following the example of Moses' gesture, it will be enough to hit this rock (λέπας), which looks arid and dry, roughly and three times to see the flow of the mysterious water that it contains. This is the first solvent, the common mercury of the wise, the loyal servant of the artist, the only one he needs and that nothing can replace, according to the testimony of Geber and the oldest Adepts. Its volatile quality, which allowed philosophers to assimilate this mercury to the vulgar hydrargyrus, is underlined, in our bas-relief, by the tiny wings of the lepidoptera (gr. λεπίδος-πτερόν) fixed to the shoulders of the symbolic monster. However, the best name that the authors have given to their mercury seems to us to be that of the Spirit of Magnesia. For they call Magnesia (from the Greek μάγνης, magnet) the raw female matter, which attracts, by an occult virtue, the spirit enclosed under the hard bark of the steel of the wise. It penetrates the body of passive nature like a burning flame, burns, consumes its heterogeneous parts, searching for arsenic sulphur (or leper) and animates the pure mercury it contains, which appears in the conventional form of a liquor that is both wet and igneous –the firewater of the ancients–, that we call the Spirit of Magnesia and universal dissolver. "As steel pulls the magnet to itself", writes Philaletes,[45] "so the magnet turns to steel. This is what the magnet of the wise does to their steel. That is why, having already said that our steel is the mining of gold, it should also be noted that our magnet is the true mining of the steel of the wise".

Lastly –useless detail at work, but which we point out because it comes to support our examination–, a term close to λεπίς, the word λέπορις, used to designate, in the Aeolian dialect, the hare (Latin: *lepus, leporis*), hence this oral deformity, inexplicable a priori, but necessary for the cabalistic expression, which imprints on the face of our gnome with its characteristic physiognomy.

At this point, we have to pause. We wonder. The road, embroiled, covered with brambles and thorns, becomes impracticable. A few steps away, instinctively, we guess the gaping gulf. Cruel uncertainty. To continue going forward, holding the disciple's hand, would it be an act of wisdom? In truth, Pandora accompanies us, but, alas! What can we expect? The fatal box, recklessly open, is now empty. Nothing remains to us but only hope!

It is here, indeed, that the authors, already enigmatic in the preparation of the solvent, keep silent. Covering the process of the second operation with a profound silence, they go directly to the descriptions concerning the third, that is, the phases and regimes of the coction; then, using the terminology used for the first, they make the novice believe that the

---

Jesus rose up and stood among them, and with his rod struck the rock, and at the same time a spring of abundant and delicious water sprang up from it, from which he watered them all. This source still exists today".

45 *Introïtus apertus ad occlusum Regis palatium.* Op. cit., chap. IV, I.

common mercury is equivalent to Rebis or compost and, as such, must be cook, quite simply, in a closed vessel. Philalethes, although writing under the same discipline, claims to fill the void left by his predecessors. Reading his *Introïtus*, one cannot distinguish any cuts; only false manipulations compensate for the defect of the real ones. They fill in the gaps in such a way that they are linked and welded together without leaving any trace of artifice. Such flexibility makes it impossible for the layman to separate the weeds from the wheat, the bad from the good, the error from the truth. We hardly need to say how much we condemn such abuses, which, despite the rule, are nothing more than disguised deceptions. Cabal and symbolism offer enough resources to express what should only be understood by the few; on the other hand, we believe that silence is preferable to the most skillfully presented lie.

You might be surprised that we would make such a harsh judgment on part of the work of the famous Adept, but others, before us, were not afraid to make the same accusations against him. Tollius, Naxagoras, Limojon de Saint-Didier especially, unmasked the insidious and treacherous formula, and we are in perfect agreement with them. It is because the mystery behind our second operation is the greatest of all; it concerns the development of philosophical mercury, which has never been taught openly. Some resorted to allegory, enigmas, parables; but most masters refrained from dealing with this delicate issue. "It is true," writes Limojon de Saint-Didier, "that there are Philosophers who, parodying very sincere, nevertheless throw the artists into this error, underscoring very seriously that those who do not know the gold of the Philosophers can still find it in the common gold, cooked with the Mercury of the Philosophers. Philaletes is of this feeling. He asserts that Le Trevisan, Zachaire and Flamel followed this vision; he adds, however, that it is not the true vision of the Wise, that it leads to the same end. But these assurances, all sincerely expressed, do not let the artists be deceived, who, wanting to follow the same Philaletes in the purification and animation that he teaches of common mercury to make it the Mercury of Philosophers (which is a very gross error under which he hid the secret of the Mercury of the Sages), undertaking on his word a very arduous and absolutely impossible work. Also, after a long work full of troubles and dangers, they have only a slightly more impure mercury than it was before, instead of a mercury animated by the quintessence of heaven. A deplorable mistake, which has lost, ruined, and will ruin many more artists".[46] And yet, the researchers who successfully overcame the first obstacles and drew the living water from the ancient Fountain, possess a key capable of opening the doors of the hermetic laboratory.[47]

If they wander and languish, if they multiply their attempts without discovering a happy outcome, it is probably because they have not acquired sufficient knowledge of the doctrine. Let them not despair, however; meditation, study, and, above all, a living faith, unshakable, will finally draw on their labors the blessing of heaven. "Truly, I say to you," says Jesus (Matt. XVII, 19), "if you have faith the size of a mustard grain, you will say to this mountain, 'Move from here to there,' and it will move, and nothing will be impossible for you". For faith, the spiritual certainty of untested truth, the prescience of the realizable, is the torch that God has placed in the human soul to enlighten, guide, instruct and elevate it. Our senses often mislead us; faith, it never deceives us. "Faith alone", writes an anonymous philosopher, "formulates a positive will; doubt makes it neutral and skepticism negative. To believe before knowing is cruel to scholars; but what do you want? Nature can't change her

---

46 *Le Triomphe Hermétique* (The Hermetic Triumph). Op. cit., p. 71.

47 This key was given to neophytes by the Crater ceremony (Κρατηρίζω, rac. κρατήρ, basin, large bowl or fountain basin), which dedicated the first initiation into the mysteries of the Dionysian cult.

ways, even for them; and she has the pretension to impose on us faith, that is to say, confidence in her, in order to grant us her graces. I confess, as for me, that I have always found her generous enough to forgive this whim of hers".[48]

Let the investigators learn, before incurring new expenses, what differentiates the first mercury from philosophical mercury; when you know what you are looking for, it becomes easier to guide your progress. Let them know that their solvent, or common mercury, is the result of nature's work, while the mercury of the sages remains a production of art. In making it, the artist, applying natural laws, knows what he wants to achieve. The same is not true for common mercury, because God forbids man to penetrate its mystery. All philosophers are unaware, and many admit it, of how the initial materials, brought into contact, react, interpenetrate, finally unite under the veil of darkness that envelops, from beginning to end, the intimate exchanges of this singular procreation. This explains why writers have been so reserved about philosophical mercury, whose successive phases the operator can follow, understand and direct at will. If the technique requires a certain amount of time and effort, it is, on the other hand, extremely simple. Any layman, knowing how to maintain fire, will execute it as well as an expert alchemist. It requires neither special skill nor professional skill, but only the knowledge of a curious device, which constitutes this *secretum secretorum*, which has not been and probably never will be revealed. It is about this operation, whose success ensures the possession of the philosophal Rebis, that Jacques Le Tesson, quoting Damascene, writes that this Adept, at the time of undertaking the work, "looks through the whole room to see if there were no flies in it, meaning that it cannot be kept too secret, for the danger that may arise".[49]

Before going any further, let us say of this unknown artifice –which from a chemical point of view should be described as absurd, bizarre or paradoxical, because its inexplicable action defies any scientific rule–, that it marks the crossroads where alchemical science deviates from chemical science. Applied to other bodies, it provides, under the same conditions, as many unexpected results, substances endowed with surprising qualities. This unique and powerful means thus allows a development of an unsuspected scope, by the multiple new single elements and compounds derived from these same elements, but whose genesis remains an enigma for the chemical reason. This, of course, should not be taught. If we have penetrated into this reserved domain of hermetics; if, more bold than our predecessors, we have pointed it out, it is because we wanted to show: 1° that alchemy is a true science, capable, like chemistry, of extension and progress, and not the empirical acquisition of a trade secret for precious metals; 2° that alchemy and chemistry are two positive, exact and real sciences, although different from each other, both in practice and in theory; 3° that chemistry cannot, for these reasons, claim an alchemical origin; 4° finally, that the innumerable properties, more or less wonderful, attributed en block by the philosophers to the philosopher's stone alone, each belong to unknown substances obtained from materials and chemical bodies, but treated according to the secret technique of our Magisterium.

It is not for us to explain what the artifice used in the production of philosophical mercury consists of. To our great regret, and despite all the concern we have for the "sons of science", we must imitate the example of the wise men, who considered it prudent to reserve

_____

48 *Comment l'Esprit vient aux tables, par un homme qui n'a pas perdu l'esprit* (How the Spirit comes to the tables, by a man who has not lost his spirit). Paris, New Bookstore, 1854.

49 *Le Grand et Excellent Œuvre des Sages* (The Great and Excellent Work of the Sages), by Jacques Le Tesson. Second Lyon Verd dialogue, chap. VI, ms. 17th century, Lyon Library, n° 971.

this badge for themselves. We will limit ourselves to saying that this second mercury, or the next material of the Work, is the result of the reactions of two bodies, one fixed, the other volatile; the first, veiled under the epithet of philosophical gold, is by no means vulgar gold; the second is our living water previously described under the name of common mercury. It is by dissolving the metallic body with the help of living water that the artist comes into possession of the humid radical of metals, its seed, permanent water or salt of wisdom, essential principle, quintessence of the dissolved metal. This solution, executed according to the rules of the art, with all the necessary provisions and conditions, is far from similar chemical operations. It is nothing like them. In addition to the length of time and knowledge of the appropriate means, it requires many painful repetitions. It's a tedious job. Philaletes himself proclaims it when he says: "We who have worked and know the operation, certainly know that there is no more boring work than that of our first preparation.[50] That is why Morien warns King Calid that many Wise Men always complained about the boredom caused to them by this Work. That is why the famous author of the Hermetic Secret told him that the work required for the first operation was a work of Hercules".[51] It is necessary here to follow the excellent advice of the *Hermetic Triumph*, and "not to be afraid to water the earth often with its water, and to dry it many more times". Through these successive lixiviations, or Flamel washings, through these frequent and renewed immersions, the viscous, oleaginous and pure moisture is gradually extracted from the metal "in which", according to Limojon de Saint-Didier, "lies the energy and great effectiveness of philosophical mercury". The living water, "more celestial than terrestrial", acting on the grave matter, breaks its cohesion, softens it, makes it soluble little by little, attaches itself only to the pure parts of the disintegrated mass, abandons the others and rises to the surface, bringing with it what it could grasp in conformity with its ardent and spiritual nature. This important characteristic of the ascent of the subtle by the separation of the coarse, led to the operation of the mercury of the sages to be called sublimation.[52] Our solvent, all spirit, plays the symbolic role of the eagle taking its prey, and this is the reason why Philaletes, the Cosmopolitan, Cyliani, d'Espagnet and several others recommend that we allow it to expand, insisting on the need to make it fly, because the spirit rises and matter precipitates. What is cream, if not the best part of milk? However, Basile Valentine teaches that the "philosopher's stone is made in the same way as the villagers make butter", by beating or shaking the cream, which represents, in this similarity, our philosophical mercury. Therefore, the artist's full attention must be focused on extracting mercury, which is collected on the surface of the dissolved compound by skimming the viscous and metallic unctuousness as it is produced. This is also the case with the two characters in *Mutus Liber*, where a woman is seen skimming off the liquor contained in a bowl that her husband holds within her reach with a spoon.[53] "This", writes Philaletes, "is the order of our operation, and this is our entire philosophy". Hermes, designating the basic and fixed matter by the solar hieroglyph, and its dissolving agent by the lunar symbol, explains it in a few words: "The sun,

---

50 We see that the Adept speaks of the preparation of the philosophical Mercury as the first of all. He deliberately omits the one that provides the universal solvent, which he assumes is known and completed. In reality, this is the first operation of the second work. This is a common philosophical device, of which we would like to warn the disciples of Hermes.

51 *Introïtus apertus ad occlusum Regis palatium.* Op. cit., chap. VIII, 3, 4.

52 "You will separate the earth from the fire, the subtle from the coarse, gently, with great industry". Hermes Trismegistus in the *Emerald Table.*

53 *Mutus Liber, in quo tamen Philosophia Hermetica figuris hieroglyphicis depingitur, ter optimo maximo Deo misericordi consecratus solisque filiis artis dedicatus authore cujus nomen est Altus.*

he says, is his father, and the moon his mother". We will also understand the secret meaning of these words by the same author: "The wind carried him in his belly". Wind or air are epithets applied to living water, which its volatility makes disappear with fire without leaving any residual trace. And like this water –our hermetic moon–, penetrates the fixed nature of the philosophical sun, that it retains and assembles its noblest particles, the philosopher is right to ensure that the wind is the matrix of our mercury, quintessence of the gold of the wise and pure mineral seed. "He who softened the dry Sun", said Henckel,[54] "by means of the wet Moon, to the point that one has become similar to the other and they remain united, found the holy water flowing in the Garden of the Hesperides".

Thus the first term of the axiom *Solve and Coagula* is fulfilled by the regular volatilization of the fixed and by its combination with the volatile; the body is spiritualized, and the metallic soul, abandoning its soiled garment, puts on another of greater value, to which the old masters gave the name of philosophical mercury. It is the water of the two champions of Basil Valentine, whose manufacture is taught by the engraving of his second key. One of them carries an eagle on his sword (the fixed body), the other hides behind his back a caduceus (solvent). The whole bottom of the drawing is occupied by two large wings spread out, while in the center, standing between the combatants, appears the god Mercury in the appearance of a crowned teenager, completely naked and holding between each hand a caduceus. The symbolism of this figure is easily penetrated. The broad wings, which serve as the floor for the fencers, mark the purpose of the operation, that is to say the volatilization of the pure portions of the fixed; the eagle indicates how to proceed, and the caduceus designates the one who must attack the adversary, our dissolving mercury. As for the mythological youth, its nakedness is the translation of the total stripping of impure parts, the crown, the sign of its nobility. It finally symbolizes, by its two caduceus, the *double mercury*, epithet that some Adepts have substituted for that of philosophical mercury, to better differentiate it from simple or common mercury, our living and dissolving water.[55] It is this *double mercury* which we find represented on the mantelpiece of Terre-Neuve by the symbolic human head, which holds between its teeth the small cord of the shield laden with emblems. The animal expression of the mask with the ardent eyes, its energetic face, devoured by appetites, render us sensible the vital power, the generating activity, all those faculties of production which our mercury has received from the reciprocal concurrence of nature and art. We have seen that it is harvested over water, of which it occupies the surface and the highest place; this is what led Louis d'Estissac to place his image at the top of the decorative panel. As for the bucrane, carved on the same axis, but in the bottom of the composition, it indicates this *caput mortuum,* the foul, damned earth of the body, impure, inert and sterile, which the action of the solvent separates, rejects, precipitates as a useless and worthless residue.

The philosophers have translated the union of the fixed and the volatile, of the body and the spirit, by the figure of the serpent devouring its tail. The Ouroboros of the Greek alchemists (οὐρά, tail, βορός, devouring), reduced to its simplest expression, thus takes the circular form, a symbolic trace of infinity and eternity, as well as perfection. It is the central circle of mercury in graphic notation, and the same as we notice, adorned with leaves and fruits to indicate its vegetative faculty and fructifying power, on the bas-relief we are studying. Moreover, the sign is complete, in spite of the care which our Adept made to disguise it. If we examine it well, we will indeed see that the crown carries at its upper curve the two spiral

54 J.-F. Henckel, *Flora Saturnisans.* Paris, J.-T. Herissant, 1760, chap. IV, p. 78.
55 *Les Douze Clefs de la Philosophie* (The Twelve Keys of Philosophy), op. cit. supra.

expansions and, at the lower end, the cross, represented by the horns and the frontal axis of the skull, complements the circle in the astronomical sign of the planet Mercury.

We still have to dissect the central shield, which we have seen carried by the human head (and consequently placed under its dependence), an image of philosophical mercury, dominating the various motifs on the panel. This relationship between the mask and the shield shows the essential role of hermetic matter in the cabalistic exposition of these singular coats of arms. These mysterious characters express, in short, all philosophical labour, no longer using forms borrowed from flora or fauna, but by graphic notation figures. This paradigm thus constitutes a true alchemical formula. First of all, let us note three stars, characteristic of the three degrees of the Work or, if we prefer, of the three successive states of the same substance. The first of these asterisks, isolated towards the lower third of the shield, refers to our first mercury, or this living water whose composition was taught by the two stephanophore gnomes. By the solution of philosophical gold, which nothing indicates here or elsewhere, we obtain philosophical mercury, composed of fixed and volatile, not yet radically united, but capable of coagulation.[56] This second mercury is expressed by the two intertwined V's of the tip, a known alchemical sign of the alembic. Our mercury is, as we know, the alembic of the sage, whose cucurbite and lid represent the two spiritualized and assembled elements. It is with philosophical mercury alone that the wise men undertake this long work made of numerous operations, which they have called coction or maturation.[57]

Our compound, subjected to the slow and continuous action of fire, distils, condenses, rises, lowers, bloats, becomes pasty, contracts, decreases in volume and, agent of its own cohobations, acquires little to little solid consistency. Thus raised a degree, this mercury, which has become fixed by habituation to fire, again needs to be dissolved by the first water, hidden here under the sign I, followed by the letter M, that is Spirit of Magnesia, another name for the solvent. In alchemical notation, any bar or stroke, whatever its direction, is the conventional graphic signature of the mind, which is worth retaining if one wants to discover which body is hidden under the epithet of gold philosophical, father of mercury and sun of the Work.[58] The capital letter M serves to identify our Magnesia of which it is, moreover, the initial letter. This second liquefaction of the coagulated body is intended to increase and fortify it, by feeding it mercurial milk to which it must be, life, vegetative power. It becomes a second time volatile, but to resume, in contact with the fire, the dry and hard consistency that he had previously acquired. And so we come to the top of the shaft of the bizarre character whose appearance recalls the number 4, but which is, in fact, the way, the path we must follow. Having reached this point, a third solution, similar to the first two, brings us, always by the straight path of the regime, and the linear path of fire, to the second star,

---

56 "You must know that this solution and separation has never been described by any of the ancient Philosopher Wise Men who lived before me and who received this Magisterium. And if they talked about it, it was only by enigmas and figures, and not to discover it". Basil Valentine, *Testamentum*.

57 The artists who believed that the third work was completed by a continuous coction, requiring no help other than that of a given fire, of equal and constant temperature, were greatly mistaken. The real coction is not made in such a way, and it is the ultimate stumbling block against which those who, after long and painful efforts, have finally arrived at the possession of the philosophical mercury, stumble. A useful indication may correct them: colors are not the work of fire; they appear only by the will of the artist; they can only be observed through the glass, that is to say in each coagulation phase. But will we understand each other well?

58 The father of the Greek Hermes was Zeus, the master of the gods. Gold, Ζεύς is neighbor of Ζεῦξις, which marks the action of joining, uniting, assembling, marrying.

seal of the perfect and coagulated matter, which will be enough to cook while continuing the required degrees without ever deviating from this linear path that is completed by the bar of the spirit, fire or incombustible sulfur. Such is the ardently desired sign of stone or medicine of the first order. As for the flowering branch of a star, located separately, it shows that, by reiteration of the same technique, the stone can be multiplied in quantity and quality, thanks to the exceptional fertility it has received from the nature and art. Now, as its exuberant fertility comes from the primitive and celestial water, which gives the metallic sulfur the activity and the movement, in exchange for its coagulating virtue, it is understood that the stone differs from the philosophical mercury only in perfection and not essentially. The sages are therefore right to teach that "the stone of the philosophers, or our mercury, and the philosopher's stone are one and the same thing, of one and the same kind", though one is more mature and more excellent than the other. Touching this mercury, which is also the salt of the sages and the cornerstone of the Work, we will quote a passage of Khunrath, very transparent despite his emphatic style and the abuse of incidental sentences. "The Stone of the Philosophers", says our author, "is Ruach Elohim (who rested –*incubebat*–, on the waters [Genesis, I]), conceived by the mediation of heaven (God alone, by his pure goodness, so wishing it) and made true body and falling under the senses, in the virginal womb of the world or of the created chaos, i.e. the earth, empty and inane, and the water. It is the son born in the light of Macrocosmos, vile in appearance (in the eyes of fools), deformed and almost minute; consubstantial, however, and similar to its author (*parens*), little World (do not imagine here that it is about the man or something else, of or by him), catholic, three in one, hermaphrodite, visible, sensitive to touch, hearing, smell and taste, local and finished, manifested regeneratively by itself, and, by means of the obstetrical hand of the art of physico-chemistry, glorified in his body from his assumption; which can be used for almost infinite commodities or uses, and miraculously beneficial to microcosm and macrocosm in the Catholic trinity. Oh you, son of perdition, surely leave the quicksilver (ὑδράργυρος) and leaves with him all things, whatever they may be, which have been prepared by you as elixirs. You are the type of the sinner, not the Savior. You can and should be liberated, but not by yourself. You are the figure of the mediator who leads to error, ruin and death, not the one who is good and leads to truth, growth and life. He has ruled, reigns and will naturally and universally over natural things; he is the Catholic son of nature, the salt (know it) of Saturn, fusible according to his particular constitution, permanent everywhere and always in nature by himself; and, by his origin and virtue, universal. Listen and be careful: this salt is the very ancient stone. It is a mystery! whose kernel (*nucleus*) is in the denarius. Shut up harpocratically! Who can understand, understands. I said. The Salt of Sapience, not without serious cause, was adorned by the sages with many nicknames; they said that there was nothing more useful in the world than it and the sun. Study this".[59]

But before going further, we will allow ourselves to make a remark of some importance to our brothers and men of good will. For our intention is to give here the complement of what we have taught in a previous work.[60]

The most educated of ours in the traditional cabal have undoubtedly been struck by the relationship existing between the way, the path drawn by the hieroglyph which borrows the form of the number 4, and the antimony mineral or *stibium*, clearly indicated under this term topographic . Indeed, the natural antimony oxysulphide was called, in the Greeks, Στίμμι or

59 Henri Khunrath. *Amphitéâtre de l'Éternelle Sapience* (Amphitheatre of the Eternal Sapience. Paris), Chacornac, 1900, p. 156.
60 Cf. Fulcanelli, *Le Mystère des Cathédrales* (The Mystery of the Cathedrals). Paris, J. Schemit, 1926.

Στίβι; Now, Στίβία is the path, the path, the path that the investigator (Στιβεύς) or pilgrim travels on his journey; it is she who tramples underfoot (Στείβω). These considerations, based on an exact correspondence of words, have not escaped the old masters or the modern philosophers, who, by supporting them with their authority, have contributed to spreading this harmful error that the vulgar antimony was the mysterious subject of art. Unfortunate confusion, invincible obstacle against which hundreds of researchers have come up against. Since Artephius, who begins his treatise with these words: "Antimony is made up of parts of Saturn",[61] to Philaletes, who entitled one of his works: *Experiments on the preparation of the Philosophical Mercury by the Regulation of Starry Martial Antimony and Silver*, passing by *The triumphal chariot of the Antimony* of Basil Valentine, and the dangerous affirmation, in his hypocritical positivism, of Batsdorff, the number of those who have allowed themselves to be caught in this rude trap is simply prodigious. The Middle Ages saw puffers and archimists volatilize, without any result, tons of mercury amalgamated with stibiated gold. In the eighteenth century, the scientist chemist Jean-Frédéric Henckel admits, in his *Treaty of Appropriation*, that he has long given himself up to these costly and vain experiments. "The regulator of antimony," he says, "is regarded as a means of union between mercury and metals; and here is the reason: it is no longer mercury and it is not yet perfect metal; he ceased to be one and began to become the other. However, I must not overlook the fact that I have undertaken in vain great works to unite gold and mercury more closely by means of the antimony regulator".[62] And who knows if good artists do not yet follow the deplorable example of medieval spagirists? Alas! Each one has his tricks, each one attaches himself to his idea, and what we can say will not prevail against a prejudice so tenacious. It doesn't matter; our duty being above all to help those who do not feed on chimeras, we will write for those alone, without caring more about others.

Recall that another similarity of words would also infer that the philosopher's stone could come from antimony. We know that the alchemists of the fourteenth century called *Kohl* or *Kohol* –from the Arabic words *al cohol*– their universal medicine, which means subtle powder, a term that later took, in our language, the meaning of spiritus (of alcohol). In Arabic, *Kohl* is said to be pulverized antimony oxysulfide, which is used by Muslim women to dye their eyebrows black. Greek women used the same product, which was called Πλατυόφθαλμον, that is to say, big eye, because the use of this article made their eyes appear larger (from πλατύς, large, and ὀφθαλμός, eye). This, it will be thought, is suggestive of relations. We would certainly be of the same opinion, if we did not know that there was not a single molecule of stibnite in the platyophthalmon of the Greeks (sublimated mercury sulphide), the *Kohl* of the Arabs and the *Cohol* or *Cohel* of the Turks. The last two, in fact, were obtained by calcination of a mixture of peened granulated and gall-nuts. Such is the chemical composition of the *Kohl* of Eastern women, whose ancient alchemists have used as a term of comparison to teach the secret preparation of their antimony. This is the solar eye that the Egyptians called oudja; it still appears, among the masonic emblems, surrounded by a halo in the center of a triangle. This symbol has the same meaning as the letter G, seventh of the alphabet, initial of the vulgar name of the Subject of the sages, figured in the middle of a radiant star. It is this matter which is Artephius' Saturnine antimony. Tollius' antimony regulate, the true and only stibium of Michel Maier and all the Adepts. As for the mineral stibnite, it possesses none of

---

61 *Le Secret Livre du Tres-ancien philosophe Artephius* (The Secret Book of the Very Old Philosopher Artephius), in *Trois Traitez de la Philosophie naturelle*. Paris, Guillaume Marette 1612.

62 J.-F. Henckel, *Opuscules Minéralogiques* (Mineralogical Opuscules), chap. III, 404. Paris, Herissant, 1760.

the required qualities, and, however it may be treated, it will never obtain either the secret solvent or the philosophical mercury. And if Basil Valentine gives him the name of pilgrim or traveler (στιβεύς), because he must, he tells us, cross six cities of heaven before setting his residence in the seventh;[63] if Philaletes assures us that he alone is our path (στίβία), these are not sufficient reasons to invoke that these masters have claimed to designate common antimony as generator of philosophical mercury. This substance is too far removed from the perfection, the purity, and the spirituality possessed by the moist radical or metallic seed, which cannot be found on earth, to be really useful to us. The antimony of the sages, a raw material extracted directly from the mine, "is not properly mineral and less metallic, as Philaletes teaches us; but, without participating in these two substances, he holds the middle between the two. It is not nevertheless corporeal, since it is entirely volatile; he is not a spirit, since he liquefies himself in the fire like a metal. It is therefore a chaos that takes the place of mother to all metals.[64] It is the metallic and mineral flower (ἄνθεμον), the first rose, black in truth, which has remained here below as a parcel of elementary chaos. It is from her, this flower of flowers (*flos florum*), that we first draw our white frost (στίβη), which is the spirit that moves on the water, and the white face of the angels; reduced to this sparkling whiteness, it is the mirror of art, the torch (στίλβη), the lamp or the lantern, the brightness of the stars and the splendor of the sun (*splendor solis*);[65] it is she who, united with the philosophical gold, will become the metallic planet Mercury (Στίλβων ἀστήρ), the nest of the bird (στιβάς), our Phoenix and its small stone (στία); it is, finally, the root, subject or pivot (Latin: *stipes, stirps*) of the Great Work, and not common antimony. Know then, brethren, that we may no longer err, that our term antimony, derived from the Greek ἄνθεμον, designates, by a play of words familiar to philosophers, the ane-Timon, the guide who leads, in the Bible, the Jews at the fountain. It is the mythical Aliboron, Ἀέλι-φορόν, the sun's horse. One more word. You must not be ignorant that in the primitive language the Greek Cabalists used to substitute figures for certain consonants for the words whose ordinary meaning they wanted to hide in an hermetic sense. They thus used the episemon (σταγιον), the Koppa, the sampi, the digamma, to which they adapted a conventional value. The names, modified by this process, constituted true cryptograms, although their form and pronunciation did not appear to have undergone any alteration. Now, the term antimony, στίμμι, was always written with the episemon (ς), equivalent to the two assembled consonants sigma and tau (στ), when it was used to characterize the hermetic subject. Written in this way, ςίμμι is no longer the stibine of mineralogists, but a matter signed by nature, or better a movement, dynamism or vibration, sealed life (ς-ίμμεναι), in order to allow man the identification, signature very particular and subject to the rules of the number six. Ἐπίσεμον, word formed of Ἐπί, on and σῆμα, sign, signifies *marked with a distinctive sign*, and this sign must correspond to the number six. Moreover, a related term,

---

63 Old prints bearing the legend *Icon peregrini* represent the hermetic Mercury under the image of a pilgrim climbing a steep and rocky path, in a site of rocks and chasms. Wearing a broad flat hat, he leans one hand on his staff and holds on the other a shield with the sun and three stars. Sometimes young, alert and dressed with research, sometimes old, weary and miserable, he is always followed by a faithful dog who seems to share his good or his bad fortune.

64 *Introïtus apertus ad occlusum Regis palatium*. Op. Cit., Chap. II, 2.

65 A drawing in the goose quill, executed by the Adept Lintaut, in his manuscript entitled *L'Aurore* (Arsenal's Library, 17th century, n ° 3020), shows the soul of a crowned king, extinct, inert, on a large slab, rising, in the aspect of a winged child, towards a lantern suspended in the midst of thick clouds. We also note, for hermetists, what Rabelais said about the trip to the land of *Lanternois*, which he had the heroes of his Pantagruel accomplish.

frequently used for assonance in phonetic cabal, the word Ἐπιστήμων, indicates the one who knows, who is instructed in, skilled at. One of the important characters of *Pantagruel*, the man of science, is called Epistemon. And he is the secret craftsman, the spirit enclosed in the raw substance, named epistemon by the Greeks,, because only the spirit is capable of executing and perfecting the entire work, with no other help than that of the elementary fire.

It would be easy for us to complete what we have said about philosophical mercury and its preparation; but it is not up to us to fully disclose this important secret. The written teachings cannot go beyond what the proselytes once received at the Little Mysteries of Agra. And if we willingly give in to the ungrateful task of the ancient Hydranos, on the other hand the esoteric domain of the Great Eleusinies is strictly forbidden to us. It is because before receiving the supreme initiation, the Greek mystes swore on their life and in the presence of the Hierophant, never to reveal anything of the truths that would be entrusted to them. Now, we do not speak to a few reliable and tested disciples, in the shadow of an enclosed sanctuary, before the divine image of a venerable Ceres –black stone imported from Pessinonte–, or of the sacred Isis, sitting on the cubic block; we speak at the threshold of the temple, under the peristyle and in front of the crowd, without requiring our listeners to take any prior oath. In the presence of such conflicting conditions, why should we be surprised to see ourselves using caution and circumspection? Certainly, we deplore the fact that the initiatory institutions of antiquity have forever disappeared and that a narrow exotericism has replaced the broad spirit of the Mysteries of yesteryear; for we believe, with the philosopher, "that it is more worthy of human nature, and more instructive, to admit the wonderful by seeking to extract the true from it, than to first treat it as a lie, or to canonize it as a miracle, to escape its explanation".[66] But these are superfluous regrets. Time, which destroys everything, has wiped out ancient civilizations. What remains of it today, if not the historical testimony of their greatness and power, a memory buried at the bottom of the papyrus or piously exhumed from arid soils, populated by moving ruins? Alas! The last Mystagogues took away their secret; it is only from God, father of light and dispenser of all truth, that we can ask for the grace of the high revelations.

This is the advice we allow ourselves to give to the sincere investigators, to the sons of science for whom we write. Only, the divine illumination will bring them the solution of the obscure problem: where and how to obtain this mysterious gold, unknown body likely to animate and to fertilize the water, first element of the metallic nature? The ideographic sculptures of Louis d'Estissac remain silent on this essential point, but since our duty is oriented towards respect for the will of the follower, we will limit our request to pointing out the obstacle by putting it in the context of practice.

Before proceeding to the examination of the upper motifs, we must still say a word about the central shield, laden with hieroglyphs, which we have just analyzed. The monograph quoted from the Chateau de Terre-Neuve, which we believe to have been written by the late M. de Rochebrune, contains a rather singular passage concerning the symbols in question. The author, after a short description of the chimney, adds: "This is one of the beautiful stone works executed by the decorators of Louis d'Estissac. The shield placed under that of the lord of this beautiful castle is decorated in its center with the monogram of the master image carver; it is surmounted by a four, a symbolic figure which is almost always attached to all these monograms of artists, engravers, printers or glass painters, etc. We are still looking for the key to this strange sign of companionship. Here, in truth, a thesis for the least surprising.

---

66 *Comment l'Esprit vient aux tables* (How the Spirit comes to the tables). Op. cit., p. 25.

It is possible that its author sometimes encountered a four-sided symbol used to classify or identify certain pieces of art. As for us, who have noticed it on a number of curious objects, of a clearly hermetic character —prints, stained glass, earthenware, goldsmith's work, etc.– we cannot admit that this figure constitutes a figure of companionship. It does not belong to the coat of arms of the guild, because these should present, in this case, the tools and badges related to the given guild. This coat of arms cannot be classified in the category of revealing weapons, nor marks of nobility, since these do not obey the heraldic rules, and that these are deprived of the image meaning, which characterizes the hieroglyphs. On the other hand, we know that the artists to whom Louis d'Estissac entrusted the decoration of his home are quite forgotten, their names have not been preserved. Does this gap allows the hypothesis of a personal mark of an artist, while these same characters, provided with a precise meaning, are commonly found in alchemical formulas? Moreover, how to explain the indifference of the scholarly scientist who was the Adept of Coulonges, in front of his work, while, being contented himself with a modest shield, he abandons to the whim of his artisans a space more spacious than his own? Why would the organizer and creator of such a harmonious hermetic paradigm, so in accordance with pure doctrine even in its smallest details, have tolerated the application of strange hieroglyphics if the latter were to be in flagrant disagreement with the rest? We conclude that the hypothesis of any guild's sign cannot be sustained. There is no example where the thought of a work has been concentrated in the very signature of the craftsman, although this is the mistake made by a faulty interpretation of the analogy.

V

A Latin inscription, which occupies the whole width of the entablature, can be seen above the symbolic panels, which have furnished us so far the subject of our study. It comprises three words, separated from each other by two pyrogenic vases, forming the following epigraph:

NASCENDO QUOTIDIE MORIMUR[67]

Being born, we die every day. Grave thought of Seneca the Philosopher, axiom that one would hardly expect to meet here.

It is obvious that this profound truth, but of a moral nature, seems discordant and has no direct connection with the symbolism that surrounds it. What value can the severe exhortation to meditate on the miserable fate that life holds for us, on the implacable destiny that imposes death as the real goal of existence on humanity, the march to the tomb as the essential condition of the earthly sojourn, the coffin as the cradle's purpose, take amidst hermetic emblems? Could it simply be to remind us –a salutary deviation–, that it is useful to keep in mind the image of anguish, supreme uncertainty, fear of the unsettling Unknown, necessary obstacles to our passions and misguided actions? Or did the scientist who authorized the monument, by incidentally provoking this awakening of conscience, by inviting us to reflect, to look at what we fear most, want to persuade us of the vanity of our desires, of our hopes, of the impotence of our efforts, of the nothingness of our illusions? We do not believe so. For, however expressive and rigorous the literal meaning of the epigraph may be for the common man, it is certain that we must discover another, adequate and in conformity

---

67 *Morimur* is an ancient form of *moriemur.*

with the esotericism of this masterly work. We believe that the Latin axiom borrowed by Louis d'Estissac from Néron's stoic preceptor was not inappropriate. It is the only written word in this *mutus liber*. There is no doubt that it is not substantial, and is deliberately used to teach what the image cannot translate.

A simple examination of the inscription shows that, of the three terms that contribute to its formation, two are preceded by a special sign, the words *quotidie* and *morimur*. This sign, a small diamond, was called by the Greeks ῥόμβος, from ῥέμβω, to make mistakes, get lost, turn around. The indication of a misleading meaning, which may lead to error, is therefore very clear. And two signs were used to indicate that there are two meanings (ἀμφίβολος) in this diplomatic sentence. Therefore, if we determine which of the three members has a double meaning, we will easily discover the secret meaning hidden in the literal sense. However, the same character engraved in front of *quotidie* and *morimur* attests that these words remain invariable and retain their ordinary value. *Nascendo*, on the contrary, being devoid of any evidence, contains another meaning. By using it with gerunds, it invokes, without spelling modification, the idea of production, of generation. We should no longer read it as *being born*, but instead *to produce, to generate*. Thus the mystery, freed from its matrix, reveals the hidden reason for the amphibological axiom. And the superficial formula reminding man of his mortal origin fades away and disappears. It is now symbolism, in its figurative language, that addresses the reader and teaches him: *To produce we die every day*. It is the parents of the hermetic child who speak. And their language is true; they really die together, not only to give it being, but also to ensure its growth and develop its vitality. They die every day, that is, on each of the six days of the Work that govern the increase and multiplication of the stone. The child is born from their death and feeds on their bodies. We see how the alchemical sense is expressive and luminous. Limojon de Saint-Didier therefore states a fundamental truth when he asserts that the "stone of philosophers is born from the destruction of two bodies". We will add that the philosopher's stone –or our mercury, its next material–, is also born from the struggle, mortification and ruin of two opposing natures. Thus, in the essential operations of art, we see that it is always two principles that produce a third, and that this generation depends on a prior decomposition of its agents. Moreover, philosophical mercury itself, the only substance of the Magisterium, can never give anything if it does not die, ferment and putrefy at the end of the first stage of the Work. Finally, whether it is a question of obtaining sulphur, the Elixir or Medicine, we will only succeed in transforming each other, either in power or in quantity, if we have restored them to their mercurial state, close to the original rebis and, as such, directed towards corruption. For it is a fundamental hermetic law that expresses the old adage: *Corruptio unius est generatio alterius*. Huginus a Barma tells us, in the chapter on Hermetic Positions, that "whoever ignores the means of destroying bodies, also ignores the means of producing them"; elsewhere, the same author teaches that "if mercury is not dyed, it will not dye".[68] However, philosophical mercury inaugurates with black, the seal of its mortification, the chromatic series of the philosophical spectrum. This is his first tincture, and it is also the first favorable indication of the technique, the harbinger of success, the one that consecrates the craftsman's mastery. "Certainly", writes Nicolas Flamel in the *Book of Hieroglyphic Figures*, "who does not see this darkness at the beginning of his operations, during the days of the stone, whatever other color he sees, he is completely missing from the

---

68 Huginus à Barma, *Le Règne de Saturne changé en Siècle d'or* (The Kingdom of Saturn changed into the Golden Age). S. M. I. I. S. S. P. or the *Magistère des Sages* (Magisterium of the Wise). Paris, Pierre Derieu, 1780.

Magisterium and can no longer do so with this perfect chaos. For he does not work well, he does not putrefy; especially since if one does not putrefy, one does not corrupt, nor generate, and therefore the stone cannot come to life vegetatively to grow and multiply." Further on, the great Adept affirms that the solution of the compound and its liquefaction under the influence of fire causes the disintegration of the assembled parts, of which the black color is the certain proof. "So, he said, this darkness and color clearly teach that in this beginning the matter and compound begins to rot and dissolve into a smaller powder than the atoms of the Sun, which then change into permanent water. And this dissolution is called by the envious philosophers, death, destruction and perdition, because natures changes form. From there came out so many allegories about the dead, tombs and sepulchres. The others called it Calcination, Denudation, Separation, Crushing, Assation, because the confections are altered and reduced to very small pieces and parts. Others, Reduction in first matter, Mollification, Extraction, Commixtion, Liquefaction, Conversion of Elements, Subtiliation, Division, Humation, Impastation and Distillation, because the confections are liquefied, reduced in seed, softened and circulated in a matrass. Others still, Xir, Putrefaction, Corruption, Cymmerian Shadows, Abbyss, Hell, Dragons, Generation, Ingression, Submersion, Complexion, Conjunction and Impregnation, because matter is dark and aqueous, and natures are perfectly measured and retain each other". A number of authors –Philaletes in particular–, demonstrated the necessity, the utility of mineral death and putrefaction using a similarity drawn from wheat seed. They probably took the idea from the Gospel parable collected by Saint John (chap. XII, v. 24); the apostle transcribed these words of Christ: "Verily I say to you, unless the grain of wheat dies after it has been cast into the ground, it remains alone; but when it is dead, it bears much fruit".

We think we have sufficiently developed the secret meaning of the epigraph: *Nascendo quotidie morimur*, and showed how this classic axiom, skillfully used by Louis d'Estissac, sheds new light on the lapidary work of the hermetic scientist.

VI

We only need to talk about the cornice of the symbolic fireplace. It is divided into six oblong boxes, decorated with symmetrical patterns repeated two by two, and summarizes the main points of the practice.

Two kidney-shaped shields occupy the corners and have their concave edges stretched into the shape of a shell. Their field offers the image of a jellyfish head, with its snake hair, from which spring two lightning bolts. These are the emblems of the initial materials, one ardent, igneous, represented by the Gorgon marks and its lightning bolts; the other aqueous and cold, passive substance represented under the aspect of a marine shell, which the philosophers call Mérelle, Greek words μήτηρ and ἕλη, mother of light. The mutual reaction of these raw elements, water and fire, provides the common mercury of mixed quality, which is the igneous water or aqueous fire that we use as a solvent for the preparation of philosophical mercury.

Following the shields, the bucranes indicate the two mortifications that appear at the beginning of the preliminary work: the first creates common mercury and the second gives birth to the hermetic rebis. These emaciated heads of the solar ox take the place of human skulls, crossed femurs, scattered bones or complete skeletons of alchemical iconography; they are, like them, called raven heads. It is the ordinary epithet applied to materials in the process of decomposition and corruption, which are characterized in philosophical work by their oily and greasy appearance, strong and offensive odor, viscous and adherent quality, mercurial consistency, blue, violet or black coloration. Note the cords that bind the horns of these bucranes; they are crossed in the shape of an X, divine attribute and first manifestation of light, previously diffused in the darkness of the mineral earth.

As for philosophical mercury, the development of which is never revealed, not even under the hieroglyphic veil, we find, however, the effect on one of the decorative shields surrounding the median acanthus. Two stars are engraved above the lunar crescent, images of double mercury or Rebis, which the coction first transforms into white sulphur, half fixed and fusible. Under the action of the elementary fire, the operation resumed and continued leads to the great final achievements, represented, on the opposite shield, by two roses. These, as we know, mark the result of the two small and great magisteries, white Medicine and red Stone, whose *fleur-de-lis*, which we see below them, consecrates absolute truth. It is the sign of perfect knowledge, the emblem of Wisdom, the crown of the philosopher, the seal of Science and Faith united with the double power, spiritual and temporal, of Knighthood.

The Man of the Woods
Mystical Herald of Thiers

Picturesque sub-prefecture of Puy-de-Dôme, Thiers has a remarkable and very elegant specimen of civil architecture in the fifteenth century. It is the so-called house of the Man of the Woods, a vaulted building, reduced today to the first and second floors only, but its surprising conservation makes it precious to art lovers and dilettantes of our middle ages (Plate XVII).

THIERS (Puy-de-Dôme)
House of the Man of the Woods (XVth century) - Plate XVII

Four bays closed with braced arches, with threaded and retooled ribs, open on the facade. They are separated from each other by attached columns with capitals made up of grotesque masks touched with long ear caps, and support as many figurines protected under light and delicate canopies. The upper bays correspond, in the basement, to panels decorated with parchments; but the bevelled columns that border them, overhanging the columns, show devouring dragon mouths as capitals.

The main subject, which serves as a sign for the old house, is a personage analogous to the one we have seen, maneuvering an stump, on the corner post of the manor of Lisieux. Carved in the same place, almost with the same gestures, he seems to claim the same tradition. Nothing is known about him, except that he is finishing his fifth centenary and that generations of Thiers inhabitants have always seen it, since its construction, backed by the sign of its old house. This bas-relief on wood, of large size, but rather rudimentary, with the naive drawing, whose age and weathering accentuate its harsh character, represents a man of tall stature, shaggy, dressed with skins sewn transversely, the hair outside. Head naked, he smiles, enigmatic, somewhat distant, and leans on a long stick finished, at its upper end, by an old, hooded and ugly face. The bare feet bear flat on a mass of rough sinuosities, which their coarseness of execution makes it difficult to identify. Such is this Man of the Woods that a local chronicler calls the *Thiers Sphinx*. "The local people, he writes, are not concerned about his origins, his gesture or his silence. They know only one thing about him, and that is the name he bears in their memory, the wild and graceless name they use to talk about him, and which perpetuates his memory through the ages. Foreigners and tourists are more friendly and curious. They stop in front of him like they are in front of a prized object. They detail at leisure the features of his physiognomy and anatomy. They smell a story full of local interest and perhaps of general interest. They question their guides. But these guides are as ignorant and almost as mute as the local people, who guard this solitary. And he takes revenge for the ignorance of some and the stupidity of others by keeping his secret".

We wondered if this image would not represent Saint Christopher, opposite that of a Child Jesus who would have occupied the opposite and empty panel of the facade. But, apart from the fact that no one remembers the subject who once concealed the right vault –assuming it could have existed–, it would have to be admitted that the base bearing our hermit represented waves. Nothing is less certain than such an assumption. How can we explain, in fact, its miraculous station on the waters –on waters whose surface is convex? Moreover, the very absence of Jesus from the colossus' shoulders justifies the exclusion of a possible resemblance to Saint Christopher. Even assuming that he could embody Offerus –the first personality of the Christian giant before his conversion–, no satisfactory reason can be given for the simian clothing that gives our statue its particular character. And if the legend asserts that took Jesus across had to uproot a tree in order to fight against the violence of the current and the inexplicable weight of his divine burden, it does not indicate that this tree was provided with an effigy, with any distinctive mark. However, we know too much about the high consciousness, the scrupulous fidelity that medieval imagers brought to the translation of their subjects, to accept such an unfounded assumption.

The Man of the Woods, the result of a clear and thoughtful will, necessarily expresses a precise and strong idea. It will be agreed that it cannot have been realized and placed there without purpose, and that, in this spirit, the decorative concern seems to be of secondary importance. In our opinion, what was meant to be stated, what the bas-relief of Thiers clearly indicates, is that it designates the home of an unknown alchemist. It seals the former philosophical residence and reveals its mystery. His undeniable hermetic individuality is completed, accentuated even more by the contact with the other figurines that escort him. And, if they have neither the scale nor the expressive energy of the main subject, these small actors of the Great Work are no less instructive. To such an extent that it would be very difficult to solve the enigma if these symbolic characters were not compared to each other. As for the literal meaning of the Man of the Woods, it is mainly concentrated in the head of the matron who finishes his rustic scepter. The duenna face with the skull tightened with a hood, such appears here, in its plastic form, a version of our crazy Mother. This is how the people referred –at the time of the joyful parodies of the Donkey Festival–, to the high dignitaries and masters of certain secret institutions. The Dijon Infantry, or Brotherhood of the Crazy Mother, a group of insiders masked under Rabelaisian exterior and pantagruelic eccentricities, is the latest example. However, the mother of the madmen, the Crazy Mother, is none other than the hermetic science itself, considered in all the scope of its teaching. And, as this science confers on the one who embraces and cultivates it, the complete wisdom, it follows that the tall madman sculpted on the Thiers facade is in reality a wise man, since he rests on the Sapience, dry trees and scepter of the Crazy Mother. This simple man, with abundant and poorly combed hair, with an uncultivated beard, this man of nature whose traditional knowledge leads him to despise the vain frivolity of the poor fools who think they are wise, dominates from above the other men, as he dominates the heap of stones he treads on his feet.[1]

He is the Illuminate, because he has received light, spiritual illumination. Behind a mask of indifferent serenity, he keeps his muteness and protects his secret from the vain curiosities, the sterile activity of the histrions of the human comedy. It is he, the silent, who represents for us the ancient Myste (Greek Μύστης, leader of the initiates), Greek incarnation of mystical or mysterious science (μυστήριον, secret dogma, esoterism) (see Plate XVIII in the next page).[2]

But, beside its esoteric function, which shows us what the alchemist must be, a simple-minded scientist, an attentive investigator of nature, whom he will always try to imitate, just as the monkey imitates man,[3] the Man of the Woods reveals another. The other function completes the first one. For the madman, the humanized emblem of the children of Hermes, still evokes mercury itself, unique and proper matter of the wise. It's this *artifex in opere* of which the Hymn of the Christian Church speaks, this craftsman hidden in the center of the book, able to do everything with the outside help of the alchemist. He is therefore the absolute master of the Work, the obscure and never idle worker, the secret agent, the faithful and loyal servant of the philosopher. And this incessant collaboration of human foresight and natural activity, this duality of effort combined and directed towards the same goal, expresses the great symbol of Thiers. As to the means by which the philosophical mercury makes itself known and can be identified, we will now discover it.

In an old almanac which, together with Solomon's Clavicles and the Secrets of the Great Albert, once constituted the clearest part of the scientific background of the peddlers,

---

1   Note, by the way, that it is indeed hoarded stones, or some cracked rock, and not waves, which are reproduced here. We find the obvious evidence on a subject of the sixteenth century, located in the same region: the bas-relief of Adam and Eve, in Montferrand (Puy-de-Dome). We notice our first parents, tempted by the snake with human head, wrapped around the tree paradise. The soil of this beautiful composition is treated in the same way, and the tree of life develops its roots around a mound in all respects similar to that on which stands the Man of the Woods.

2   Μύστης has for root μύω, to be silent, to remain silent, to conceal, from where our old word musser, corresponding to the woodpecker mucher, to hide, to dissimulate.

3   This is the reason for its sartorial appearance and local name.

THIERS (Puy-de-Dôme)
The Man Of Wood - Plate XVIII

there is, among the plates illustrating the text, a singular woodcut.[4] It represents a skeleton surrounded by images intended to mark planetary correspondences "with those of the parts of the body that look at and dominate it". Now, while the Sun offers us, in this drawing, its radiant face, and the Moon its profile set with the crescent, Mercury appears under the aspect of a court jester. We see him, wearing the pilgrim's cap from which two long pointy ears –like the capitals we have mentioned at the base of the figurines–, holding a caduceus as a jester's scepter. In order to make no mistake, the artist has taken care to inscribe the name of each planet under his own sign. There is therefore a real symbolic formula here, used in the Middle Ages for the esoteric translation of the celestial Mercury and the quicksilver of the sages. Moreover, it is enough to remember that the French word *sou* (one upon a time *fol*, meaning crazy) comes from the Latin *follies*, bellows used to blow in the fire, to suggest the idea of the

---

4   The Great Calendar or Compost of the Shepherds, composed by the Shepherd of the Great Mountain, very useful and profitable to people of all states, reformed according to the Calendar of His Holiness Pope Gregory XIII. In Lyon, at Louys Odin's house, 1633.

puffer, a contemptuous epithet given to medieval Spagyrists. Even later, in the 17th century, it is not uncommon to find, in the caricatures of Jacques Callot's emulators, some grotesque figures executed with the symbolic spirit whose philosophical manifestations we study. We still remember some drawings of a sitting buffoon with his legs crossed in an X-shape and a large bellow behind his back. It should therefore come as no surprise that court jesters, many of whom have remained famous, have a hermetic origin. Their colorful costumes, their strange costumes –they wore a bladder on their belts which they described as a lantern–, their projections, their mystifications prove it, as well as this rare privilege, which linked them to philosophers, to say bold truths with impunity. Finally, mercury, called the Madman of the Great Work, because of its inconsistency and volatility, has its meaning confirmed in the first card of the Tarot, called the Fool or Alchemist.[5]

In addition, the Jester's scepter, which is positively a rattle (κρόταλον), object of amusement for the little ones and toy of the first age, does not differ from the caduceus.[6] The two attributes offer an obvious analogy between them, although the rattle expresses, moreover, that native simplicity which the children possess, and which science requires of the wise. One and the other are similar images. Momos and Hermes wear the same instrument, a tell-tale sign of mercury. Draw a circle at the top end of a vertical, add two horns to the circle, and you will have the secret graphic used by the medieval alchemists to designate their mercurial material.[7] Now, this schema, that reproduces faithfully enough the jester's scepter, and the caduceus was known from antiquity; it was discovered engraved on a Punic stele of Lilybee.[8] In short, the scepter of the jester seems to us to be a caduceus, of esotericism more transparent than the serpents' rod, surmounted or not by the winged petasos[9]. Her name, diminutive of *merotte*, little mother, according to some, or of Mary, the universal mother, according to others, emphasizes the feminine nature and the generating virtue of the hermetic mercury, mother and nurse of our king.

Less evocative is the word caduceus, which retains, in the Greek language, the meaning of annunciator. The words κηρύκειον and κηρύκιον, caduceus, both mark the herald or public barter; only their common root, κῆρυξ, the cock (because this bird announces the dawn of the day and the light, the dawn), expresses one of the qualities of secret quicksilver. This is the reason why the rooster, herald of the sun, was consecrated to the god Mercury and appears on our church steeples. If nothing in the bas-relief of Thiers recalls this bird, it can not be denied, however, that it is hidden under the name of the caduceus, held by our herald in both hands. Because the staff or scepter worn by the heraldry officers was called caduceus like

---

5 Some occultists place the Fool or Alchemist at the end of the twenty-one cards in the game, i.e. after the one showing the World, to which the highest value is assigned. Such an order would be without consequence –the Fool, without a number, being out of series–, if we did not know that the Tarot, a complete hieroglyph of the Great Work, contains the twenty-one operations or phases through which philosophical mercury passes before reaching the final perfection of the Elixir. However, since the work is carried out precisely by the Fool or mercury prepared, subject to the will of the operator, it seems logical to us to name the craftsmen before the phenomena that must arise from their collaboration.

6 In Greek, κρόταλον, rattle, corresponds to our crotale, or rattlesnake, and we know that in hermetism, all serpents are hieroglyphs of the mercury of the sages.

7 Only in the sixteenth century a crossbar was added to the primitive stem, so as to depict the cross, image of death and resurrection.

8 Philippe Berger, *Revue archéologique* (Archeological Review), April, 1884.

9 A *petasos* or *petasus* (Greek: πέτασος) is a sun hat of Thessalian origin worn by the ancient Greeks.

the rod of Hermes. It is also known that one of the attributions of the heralds was to build, as a sign of victory or a happy event, memorials called *Mont-joie*. They were simple mounds or heaps of stones, mountains of joy. The Man of the Woods appears to us to be at once the representative of mercury, or a madman of nature, and the mystic herald, a marvelous workman whom his masterpiece raises on the mount-joy, a sign revealing his material victory. And if this king at arms, this triumphant one, prefers his faunal tunic to the opulent uniform of the heralds, it is in order to show others the right path he himself has taken, the prudent simplicity he has observed, the indifference he shows towards earthly goods and the glory of the world.

Beside a subject of such noble bearing, the little characters who accompany him have only a very effaced role; it would be wrong, however, to neglect its study. No detail is superfluous in hermetic iconography, and these humble depositories of arcana, modest images of ancestral thought, deserve to be questioned and examined with care. It is less for a decorative purpose, than with the charitable intention of enlightening those who will show their interest for them, that they have been placed there. As far as we are concerned, we have never repented of having spent too much time and attention on the analysis of hieroglyphs of this kind. Often, they brought us the solution of abstruse problems and, in the practice, the success that we vainly sought to obtain without the help of their teaching.

There are five figurines sculpted under the canopy that support the heads of the capitals. Four of them wear the philosopher's mantle, which they discard to show the different emblems of their office. The farthest from the Man of the Woods stands in the corner formed by the return of a small modern niche, in Gothic style, which houses behind its windows a statuette of the Virgin Mary. He is a very hairy man with a long beard, who holds a book in his left hand and holds the shaft of a spike or spear with his right hand. These attributes, highly suggestive, formally designate the two materials, active and passive, whose mutual reaction provides, at the end of the philosophical struggle, the first substance of the Work. Some authors –Nicholas Flamel and Basile Valentine in particular–, have given these elements the conventional epithet of dragons; the celestial dragon, which they represent winged, characterizes the volatile body, the terrestrial wingless dragon, designates the fixed body. "Of these two dragons or metallic principles," wrote Flamel, "I told the aforementioned Summary that the enemy would ignite by its ardor the fire of his enemy, and that then, if one were careful, one would see through the air a poisonous and malodorous smoke, too much worse in flame and poison than the poisonous test of a Babylonian snake and dragon".[10] Generally, and when they only talk about the dragon, it is the volatile that philosophers consider. It is him they recommend to kill, with a blow of a spear; and this operation makes them the subject of many fables, of various allegories. The agent is veiled under various names of similar esoteric value: Mars, Marthe, Marcel, Michel, Georges, etc., and these knights of sacred art, after a fiery struggle from which they always emerge victorious, opening, on the flank of the mythical snake, a large wound from which a thick and viscous black blood flows.[11]

---

10 *Le Livre des Figures Hierogliphiques* (The Book of Hierogliphic Figures). Op. cit.

11 The myth of the dragon and the knight who attacks it plays an important role in the heroic or popular legends, as well as in the mythologies of all peoples. Scandinavian accounts, as well as Asians, describe these exploits. In the Middle Ages, the knight Gozon, the knight of Belzunce, St. Romain, etc., fights and kills the dragon. The Chinese fable takes a closer look at reality. She tells us that the famous alchemist Hujumsin, put in the rank of the gods for having discovered the philosopher's stone, had killed a horrible dragon that ravaged the country and attached the remains of this monster to the shaft of a column "that we still see today",says the legend. After which he had risen in the sky.

Such is the secret truth that proclaims, from the pulpit, the secular herald, inert and mute, pegged to the body of his old home.

The second character is more discreet and more reserved; he barely raises the skirt of his cloak, but this gesture makes it possible to distinguish a closed big book which he keeps pressed against his belt. We will talk about it again soon.

This character is followed by a knight of energetic attitude, who grabs the hilt of his sword. Necessary weapon, which he will use to remove life from the terrestrial lion and flying lion, or griffin, mercurial hieroglyph that we studied on the manor of Lisieux. Here we find the emblematic presentation of an essential operation, that of the fixation of mercury and its partial mutation into fixed sulfur. "The fixed blood of the red Lyon," says Basil Valentine, "is made of the volatile blood of the verdant Lyons, for which they are both of the same nature.[12] Note that there are a few different versions in the parables used by the authors to describe this work; most, in fact, are limited to representing the combat of the knight and the lion, as can be seen in the castle of Coucy (tympanum of the dungeon door), and on one of the bas-reliefs of the *Carrior Doré*,[13] of Romorantin (see plate XIX, on the next page).

From the figurine that follows, we cannot give an exact interpretation. It is unfortunately mutilated, and we do not know what emblems she presented with her hands now broken. Only of the symbolic procession of the Man of the Woods, this young woman with wide open, haloed, meditative, affects a distinctly religious character and could possibly represent a virgin. In this case, we would see the humanized hieroglyph of our first subject. But this is only a hypothesis, and nothing allows us to develop the argumentation. We will thus pass on this graceful motive, regretting that it is incomplete, to study the last of the extras, the Pilgrim.

Our traveler, without a doubt, has walked for a long time; yet his smile shows how happy and satisfied he is to have fulfilled his wish. For his empty satchel, the pilgrim staff without calabash indicate that this worthy son of Auvergne no longer has to worry about drinking or eating. In addition, the shell attached to the hat, the special badge of the pilgrims of Saint-Jacques, proves that it returns to us straight from Compostela. The indefatigable pedestrian carries the open book –this book adorned with beautiful images that Flamel could not explain– that a mysterious revelation now allows him to translate and put into action. This book, although it is very common, and everyone can easily acquire it, cannot be opened, that is to say understood, without prior revelation. God alone, by the intercession of "Monsieur Saint Jacques," only those who are judged to be worthy of it are given the indispensable enlightenment. It is the book of the Revelation, whose pages are closed with seven seals, the initiatory book that presents the characters responsible for exposing the high truths of science. Saint James, a disciple of the Savior, does not leave him; with the calabash, the blessed staff and the shell, he possesses the attributes necessary for the hidden teaching of the pilgrims of

---

12 *Les Douze Clefs de Philosophie* (The Twelve Keys of Philosophy). Op.cit., Liv II, p. 140.

13 The *Carroir Doré* is a 15th century wooden dwelling, includes a ground floor of which only the structure remains and a later added gabled attic. Houses, like books and men, sometimes have a strange destiny. The curse was that this pretty house lost its corner turrets. Built at the intersection of two streets, it forms a cut-off corner, and we know what advantage medieval builders knew to take from such a layout, by beveling edges, by rounding of the lateral projections of the corbels, with the help of turrets, ramps or watchtowers. It is to be assumed that the golden square, if we judge by the flared shape of the cantilevered horn posts, should have had that harmonious and original aspect that medieval aesthetics loved. Unfortunately, today there are only the scruffy, rough, half worm-eaten supports, miserable bony extensions, emaciated patella of a wooden skeleton.

ROMORANTIN
The Carroir Doré - Plate XIX

the Great Work. This is the first secret, that which philosophers do not reveal and which they reserve under the enigmatic expression of the Path of St. James.[14]

All alchemists are obliged to undertake this pilgrimage. At least figuratively, because this is a symbolic journey, and whoever wishes to benefit from it cannot, even for a moment, leave the laboratory. He must watch without pause the vessel, the matter and the fire. He must, day and night, stay at the Work. Compostela, an emblematic city, is not situated in Spanish territory, but in the very land of the philosophical subject. Hard road, painful, full of surprises and danger. Long and tiring road, by which the potential becomes realized and the occult manifested! It is this delicate preparation of the first matter, or common mercury, that the sages have veiled under the allegory of the pilgrimage of Compostela.

---

14 This is what is still called the Milky Way. The Greek mythologists tell us that the gods took this route to go to the palace of Zeus and that the heroes also took it to enter Olympus. The Path of St. James is the starry road, accessible to the elect, valiant mortals, scholars and persevering.

Our mercury, we believe to have said it, is this pilgrim, this traveler to whom Michel Maïer devoted one of his best treaties.[15] Now, by using the dry path, represented by the terrestrial road followed at first by our peregrine, we manage to exalt little by little the diffuse and latent virtue, transforming into activity that which does was only potential. The operation is completed when a shining star appears on the surface, formed of rays emanating from a single center, prototype of the great roses of our Gothic cathedrals. This is the sure sign that the pilgrim arrived happily at the end of his first voyage. He received the mystical blessing of St. James, confirmed by the luminous impress which radiated, it is said, above the tomb of the apostle. The humble and common shell which he wore on his hat turned into a bright star, a halo of light. Pure matter, whose hermetic star consecrates perfection: it is now our compost, the holy water of Compostela (Latin: *compos*, which received, possesses, – *stella*, the star), and the alabaster of the wise (*albastrum*, contraction of *alabastrum*, white star). It is also the vase of perfumes, the alabaster vase (gr. ἀλάβαστρον, lat. *alabastrus*) and the blooming bud born from the flower of wisdom, the hermetic rose.

The return from Compostela can be made either by the same way, following a different route, or by the wet or maritime way, the only one that the authors indicate in their works. In this case, the pilgrim, choosing the sea route, embarks under the guidance of an expert pilot, tried mediator, able to ensure the safeguarding of the ship during the whole crossing. Such is the ungrateful role assumed by the *Pilote de l'Onde vive* (Pilot of the living wave)[16], because the sea is strewn with reefs and storms are frequent there.

These suggestions help to understand the error into which many occultists have fallen, by taking the literal meaning of purely allegorical narratives, written with the intention of teaching some what is hidden from others. Albert Poisson himself got caught up in the scheme. He believed that Nicholas Flamel, leaving Lady Pernelle, his wife, his school and his illuminations, had really accomplished, on foot and by the Iberian road, the vow made before the altar of Saint-Jacques-la-Boucherie, his parish. However, we certify, and we can be confident in our sincerity, that Flamel never left the cellar where his stoves were burning. Whoever knows what the pilgrim staff, the calabash and the shell on the hat of St. James are, also knows that we are telling the truth. By substituting himself for materials and taking inspiration from the internal agent, the great Adept observed the rules of philosophical discipline and followed the example of his predecessors. Raymond Lulle tells us that in 1267, immediately after his conversion and at the age of thirty-two, he made the pilgrimage to Santiago de Compostela. All the masters, therefore, used allegory; and those imaginary relationships, which the laymen would mistake for ridiculous realities or tales, according to the meaning of the versions, are precisely those where truth is most clearly affirmed. Basile Valentine finished his first book, which served as an introduction to the *Douze Clefs* (Twelve Keys), with an escape into Olympus. He makes the gods speak, and each of them, beginning with Saturn, gives his opinion, gives his advice, explains his own influence on the progress of great labor. Bernard Trévisan says very little in forty pages; but the interest of his *Livre de la Philosophie naturelle des métaux* (Book of the Natural Philosophy of Metals) emerges from the few pages that make up his famous Parable. Vinceslas Lavinius of Moravia gives the secret of the Work, in about fifteen lines, in the *Enigme du Mercure Philosophal* (Enigma of the Philosopher Mercury) found in the Treaty of Earthly Heaven. One of the most famous

15 *Viatorium: Hoc is from Montibus Planetarum septem seu metallorum.* Rouen, Jean Berthelin, 1651.
16 This is the title of an alchemical work by Mathurin Eyquem, Sieur de Martineau, published by Jean d'Houry. Paris, 1678.

alchemical manuals of the Middle Ages, the *Code de Verite* (Code of Truth), also known as *Turba Philosophorum*, contains an allegory in which several artists, in a pathetic scene animated by the spirit of Pythagoras, play the chemical drama of the Great Work. A classic anonymous work, generally attributed to the Trevisan, *Le Songe Verd* (The Green Dream), exposes the practice under the traditional formula of the craftsman transported, during his sleep, to a heavenly land, populated by unknown inhabitants living among a wonderful flora. Each author chooses the theme he likes and develops it according to his imagination. The Cosmopolitan takes up the familiar dialogues of the medieval era and is inspired by Jehan de Meung. More modern, Cyliani hides the preparation of mercury under the fiction of a nymph, who guides and directs him in this work. As for Nicholas Flamel, he departs from the beaten track and the consecrated fables; more original if not clearer, he prefers to disguise himself as the subject of the wise and leave to whomever will understand it this autobiography, revealing but supposed.

All the effigies of Flamel represented him as a pilgrim. This is how he appeared on the porch of Saint-Jacques-la-Boucherie and Sainte-Geneviève-des-Ardents churches; it is in the same costume that he had himself painted on the arch of the Innocents cemetery. Louis Moreri's *The Dictionnaire Historique* (The Historical Dictionary) cites a painted portrait of Nicholas Flamel, which was exhibited at the time of Borel, i. e. around 1650, at the home of M. des Ardres, a doctor. Here again, the Adept had put on the costume he particularly liked. A singular detail, "his cap was in three colors, black, white, red and white", the colors of the three main phases of the Work. By imposing this symbolic formula on statues and painters, Flamel alchemist concealed the bourgeois personality of Flamel the writer, under that of Saint James the Major, hieroglyph of the secret mercury. These images no longer exist today, but we can have a fairly accurate idea of them from the statues of the apostle, executed at the same time. A masterly 14th century work, belonging to Westminster Abbey, shows us Saint James dressed in a mantle, a satchel on his side, wearing a large hat decorated with a shell. In his left hand, he holds the closed book, wrapped in a case cover. Only the pilgrim staff, on which he leans with his right hand, disappeared (see the plate XX).

This closed book, clear symbol of the subject used by alchemists, who carried it at the beginning, is the one that the second character of the Man of the Woods holds with such fervor; the book signed with figures allowing him to be recognized, to appreciate his virtue and object. The famous manuscript of Abraham the Jew, of which Flamel takes a copy with him, is a work of the same order and quality. Thus fiction, substituted for reality, takes shape and asserts itself in the hike to Compostela. We know how stingy the Adept is with information about his trip, which he makes in one go. "So in this very way",[17] he just writes, "I set out on my journey and arrived at Montjoye and then at Saint-Jacques, where, with great devotion, I fulfilled my wish". This is, of course, a description reduced to its simplest expression. No itinerary, no incidents, no indication of the duration of the trip. The English occupied the whole territory at that time: Flamel said nothing about it. Only one cabalistic term, that of Montjoye, which the Adept, of course, deliberately uses. This is the sign of the blessed stage, long awaited, long hoped for, where the book is finally opened, the joyful mountain at the top of which shines the hermetic star.[18]

---

17 That is, under the pilgrim's habit with which he was later represented at the mass grave of the Innocents

18 The legend of St. James, reported by Albert Poisson, contains the same symbolic truth. "In 835, Theodomir, bishop of Iria, was informed by a mountaineer that, on a wooded hill, some distance to the west of Mount Pedroso, one perceived at night a soft, slightly bluish light, and when the sky was

LONDON - ABBEY OF WESTMINSTER
Statue of Saint James the Greater - Plate XX

Matter has undergone a first preparation, the vulgar quicksilver has turned into philosophical hydrargyrum, but we learn nothing more. The route followed is knowingly kept secret.

The arrival in Compostela implies the acquisition of the star. But the philosophical subject is too impure to undergo maturation. Our mercury must gradually rise to the supreme degree of purity required by a series of sublimations requiring the help of a special substance, before being partially coagulated into *living sulphur*. To introduce his reader to these operations, Flamel tells us that a merchant from Boulogne –whom we identify with the essential mediator– put him in contact with a Jewish rabbi, Master Canches, "a strong man who knew the sublime sciences".[19] Our three characters have their respective roles perfectly established. Flamel, as we

---

without clouds, there was a star of marvelous splendor above this same place. Theodomir went with all his clergy to the hill; Excavations were made at the place indicated, and a perfectly preserved body was found in a marble coffin, which certain indications revealed to be that of the Apostle St. James". The present cathedral, intended to replace the primitive church, destroyed by the Arabs in 997, was built in 1082.

19 Boulogne presents some analogy with the Greek Βουλαῖος, which presides over the councils. Diane was nicknamed Βουλαία, goddess of good advice.

have said, represents philosophical mercury; its very name speaks as a pseudonym chosen on purpose. Nicholas, in Greek Νικόλαος, means winner of the stone (from Νίκη, victory and λᾶος, stone, rock). Flamel is similar to the Latin *Flamma*, flame or fire, expressing the igneous and coagulating virtue of prepared matter, a virtue that allows it to fight against the heat of fire, to feed itself and to triumph over it. The merchant acts as an intermediary in sublimation, which requires violent fire.[20] In this case, ἔμπορος, merchant, is put for ἔμπυρος, which is worked by means of fire. It is our secret fire, called lunatic Vulcan by the author of the *Ancient War of Knights*. Master Canches, whom Flamel presents to us as his initiator, expresses white sulphur, the principle of coagulation and dryness. This name comes from the Greek Κάγκανος, dry, arid, from καγκαίνω, heating, desiccating, words whose meaning expresses the styptic quality that the ancients attribute to the sulphur of philosophers. Esotericism is completed by the Latin word *Candens*, which indicates what is white, pure, bright white, obtained by fire, what is ardent and burning. One word could not be better characterized as sulphur in the physico-chemical plane, and the Initiate or Cathar in the philosophical plane.

Flamel and Master Canches, allied by an unfailing friendship, will now travel together. Mercury, sublimated, manifests its fixed part, and this sulphurous base marks the first stage of coagulation. The intermediary is abandoned or disappears: it will not be questioned anymore. The three are reduced to two, sulfur and mercury, which produce what is commonly called the philosophical amalgam, a simple chemical combination not yet radical. It is here that the coction intervenes, an operation responsible for ensuring that the newly formed compost has the indissoluble and irreducible union of its elements, and their complete transformation into fixed red sulfur, a first-order medicine according to Geber.

The two friends agreed to return by sea, instead of by land. Flamel does not tell us the causes of this resolution, which he simply submits to the investigators for their consideration. In any case, the second part of the journey is long, dangerous, "uncertain and futile," says an anonymous author, "if there is the slightest mistake". Certainly, in our opinion, the dry method would be preferable, but we have no choice. Cyliani warns his reader that he only describes the wet path, full of difficulties and unexpected events, out of duty. Our Adept judges the same, and we must respect his will. It is well known that a large number of inexperienced sailors were shipwrecked on their first crossing. One must always ensure the orientation of the ship, manoeuvre with caution, fear wind shifts, anticipate storms, be on the alert, avoid the abyss of Charybdus and the reef of Scylla, and fight constantly, night and day, against the violence of the waves. It is no small task to direct the hermetic vessel, and Master Canches, whom we suspect to have served as pilot and conductor for the Argonaut Flamel, must have been very skilled in this matter. Such also is the case of sulphur, which energetically resists attacks, the detersive influence of mercurial humidity, but ends up being defeated and dying under its blows. Thanks to his companion, Flamel was able to land safely in Orléans (or-léans, *l'or est là*, the gold is there), where the sea voyage should, naturally and symbolically, end. Unfortunately, barely on land, Master Canches, the good guide, died, victim of the great vomiting he had suffered on the water. His grieving friend had him buried in the Church of the Holy Cross and returned home alone, but instructed and satisfied that he had achieved the goal of his desires. Similar to that of Christ, the passion for sulphur, which dies in order to redeem its metal brothers, ends with the redemptive cross.

---

20 Intermediate, in Greek, is μεσίτης, from μέσος, which is in the middle, which stands between two extremes. He is our Messiah, who fulfils in the Work the mediating function of Christ between the Creator and his creature, between God and man.

The vomitings of sulphur are the best indicators of its dissolution and mortification. Once this phase is reached, the Work takes on the surface the appearance of a "grassy broth sprinkled with pepper" –*brodium saginatum piperatum*, the texts say. From then on, the mercury gets darker every day and its consistency becomes syrupy and then pasty. When the black reaches its maximum intensity, the putrefaction of the elements is accomplished and their union achieved; everything appears firm in the vase until the solid mass cracks, chips, crumbles and finally falls into an amorphous powder, black as coal. "Then you will see," wrote Philaletes, "a remarkable black color, and the whole earth will be dried up. The death of the compound has arrived. The winds cease and all things enter into rest. It is the great eclipse of the sun and the moon; no luminary shines on the earth anymore, and the sea disappears".[21] We thus understand why Flamel recounts the death of his friend; why the latter, having suffered the dislocation of his parts by a kind of crucifixion, had his grave placed under the invocation and sign of the Holy Cross. What we do not understand as much is the rather paradoxical eulogy pronounced by our Adept in favour of the Rabbi: "May God have his soul," he shouts, "for he died a good Christian". Undoubtedly, he had in mind only the fictional ordeal endured by his philosophical companion.

These are, studied in the very order of the narrative, the reports –too eloquent to be accused of mere coincidences– which have contributed to establishing our conviction. These singular and precise concordances show that Flamel's pilgrimage is a pure allegory, a very clever and ingenious fiction of the alchemic labor of the charitable and learned man. We now have to speak of the mysterious work of this Liber, who was the initial cause of the imaginary journey, and to say what esoteric truths he is responsible for revealing.

In spite of the opinion of certain bibliophiles, we confess that it has always been impossible for us to believe in the reality of the Book of Abraham the Jew, nor in what his happy owner says about it in his *Figures Hieroglyphiques*. In our opinion, this famous manuscript, as unknown as it is undiscoverable, seems to be only another invention of the great Adept, destined, like the preceding one, to instruct the disciples of Hermes. It is a precise character that distinguishes the raw material from the Work, as well as the properties it acquires by its preparation. In this connection, we will enter into some details which will justify our thesis and provide useful indications to the amateurs of sacred art. Faithful to the rule that we have imposed on ourselves, we will limit our explanation to the important points of the practice, carefully avoiding to substitute new figures for those which we will have unveiled. These are certain, positive and real things that we teach, things seen with our eyes, a thousand times touched by our hands, sincerely described.

The legendary work of Abraham is only known to us from the description that Nicholas Flamel left in his famous treatise.[22] It is to this unique relation, which includes an alleged copy of the title, that our bibliographical documentation is limited.

At the testimony of Albert Poisson,[23] Cardinal Richelieu would have had it in his possession; he bases his hypothesis on the seizure of the papers of a certain Dubois,

---

21 *Introïtus apertus ad occlusum Regis palatium*. Op. cit., ch. XX, 6.
22 *Le Livre des Figures Hieroglyphiques de Nicolas Flamel, escrivain…* (The Book of Hieroglyphic Figures by Nicolas Flamel, a writer...), translated from Latin into French by P. Arnauld, in *Trois Traitez de la Philosophie naturelle* (Three Treatises of Natural Philosophy). Paris, Guil. Marette, 1612.
23 Albert Poisson, *L'Alchimie au XIVe siècle. Nicolas Flamel* (Alchemy in the fourteenth century. Nicolas Flamel). Paris, Chacornac, 1893.

hanged after having been tortured, who passed, rightly or wrongly, to be the last descendant of Flamel.[24]

However, there is no evidence that Dubois inherited the singular manuscript, much less that Richelieu took it, since this book has never been reported anywhere since Flamel's death. It is true that sometimes we see, from far and wide, so-called copies of the Book of Abraham being sold; these, in very small numbers, have no connection with each other and are distributed in a few private libraries. The ones we know are only attempts at reconstitution according to Flamel. In all of them, we find the title, in French, very precisely reproduced and in conformity with the translation of the Hieroglyphic Figures, but it serves as a sign for versions so diverse, so far removed especially from the hermetic principles, that they *ipso facto* reveal their sophistic origin. However, Flamel exalts precisely the clarity of the text, "written in beautiful and highly intelligible Latin", to the point that he takes note of it in order to refuse to transmit the slightest extract to posterity. Consequently, there can be no correlation, and for good reason, between the claimed original and the apocryphal copies we report. As for the images that would have illustrated the book in question, they were also made according to Flamel's descriptions. Designed and painted in the 17th century, they are currently part of the French alchemical collection of the Arsenal's Library.[25]

In short, both for the text and for the figures, we have been content to respect, in these attempts at reconstitution, the little that Flamel has left; everything else is pure invention. Finally, as no bibliographer has ever been able to discover the original, and we are in the material impossibility of collating the relation of the Adept, we are compelled to conclude that this is indeed the case, a work that is inexistent and presumed.

The analysis of the text of Nicholas Flamel reserves us, moreover, other surprises. Here is first the passage of the Hieroglyphic Figures which contributed to spread, among the alchemists and bibliophiles, the near-certainty of the reality of the book called of Abraham the Jew. "So, I, Nicholas Flamel, scrivener, when after the death of my parents I made my living with our art of writing, making inventories, keeping accounts and subtracting the expenses of tutors and minors, when, for the sum of two florins, a large and very old gilded book fell into my hands. It was not made of paper or parchment at all, like the others, but it was made, simply of thin bark (it seemed to me) of tender little trees. Their cover was made of very fine copper, all engraved with strange letters or figures. As for me, I think they could very well be Greek characters or characters from another similar ancient language. So much that I do not know how to read them, and that I know well that they were not notes, nor Latin or Gallic letters, because we understand a little of both. As for the interior, the bark is engraved, with a very great workmanship, written with a iron point, in beautiful and very colorful colored Latin letters. It contained three times seven sheets".

Do we need to emphasize already the strangeness of a work made up of such elements? Its originality borders on the bizarre, almost extravagant. The very large volume thus resembles Italian-style albums containing reproductions of landscapes, architectures, etc.,

---

24 Flamel died on March 22, 1418, feast day of the traditional alchemists. It is indeed the spring equinox that opens the era of the Great Work.

25 *Recueil de Sept Figures peintes* (Collection of Seven Painted Figures). Arsenal's Library, No. 3047 (153, S. A. F.), 0m365 × 0m225. On the back of folio A is a note from the secretary of Mr. de Paulmy, to whom this collection belonged, corrected by Paulmy, in which it is stated that: "The seven illuminated figures in this volume are the famous Figures that Nicholas Flamel found in a Book whose author was Abraham the Jew".

prints usually presented in landscape format. It is, we are told, golden, although its cover is copper, which is not clearly explained. Let's move on. The leaves are made of the bark of young trees; Flamel no doubt wants to designate the papyrus, which would give the book a respectable antiquity; but these barks, instead of being written or painted directly, are engraved with a point of iron before they are colored. We do not understand anymore. How does the narrator know that the stylus Abraham would use was iron, rather than wood or ivory? For us, it is an enigma as indecipherable as this other one: the legendary rabbi writing, in Latin, a treatise dedicated to his fellow believers, Jews like him. Why did he use Latin, the common scientific language of the Middle Ages? He could have dispensed, using the less widespread Hebrew language, from throwing the anathema and shouting out Maranatha at those who would try to study it. Finally, and despite Flamel's assurance, this old manuscript –one cannot think of everything–, had just been written when he acquired it. Indeed, Abraham says he only wants to reveal his secret to help the sons of Israel, persecuted at the very time when the future Adept was reading his text: "To the gentleman of the Jews, by the wrath of God scattered among the Gauls, salvation," cried the Levite, Prince, Hebrew priest and astrologer, at the beginning of his *grimoire.*

Thus, the great master Abraham, doctor and light of Israel, reveals himself, if we take it literally, for a mystifier emeritus, and his work, fraudulently archaic, devoid of authenticity, as incapable of supporting criticism. But if we consider that the book and the author have never had any other existence than in Nicholas Flamel's fertile imagination, we must think that all these things, so diverse and so singular, contain a mysterious meaning that it is important to discover.

Let's start the analysis by the alleged perpetrator of the fictional book. What is Abraham? The Patriarch par excellence; in Greek Πατριάρχης is the first author of the family, roots πατήρ, father, and ἀρχή, beginning, principle, origin, source, foundation. The Latin name Abraham, which the Bible gives to the venerable ancestor of the Hebrews, means Father of a multitude. It is therefore the first author of created things, the source of all that lives here below, the only primordial substance whose different specifications populate the three kingdoms of nature. The *Book of Abraham* is, therefore, the *Book of the Principle* and as this book is devoted, according to Flamel, to alchemy, part of the science which studies the evolution of mineral bodies, we learn that it deals with the original metallic matter, the basis and foundation of sacred art.

Flamel buys this book for the sum of two florins, which means that the overall price of materials and fuel needed for the work was estimated at two florins in the fourteenth century. The raw material alone, in sufficient quantity, was then worth ten sols. Philaletes, who wrote his treatise on the Introitus in 1645, brings the total expense to three florins. "Thus," he says, "you will see that the Work, in its essential materials, does not exceed the price of three ducats or three florins of gold. Even more, the cost of making water is just over two crowns per pound.[26]

The volume, gilded, very old, and very large, bears no resemblance to ordinary books; no doubt because it is made and composed of other matter. The gilding that covers it gives it the metallic aspect. And if the Adept assures that he is old, it is only to establish the high antiquity of the hermetic subject. "I will say then," asserts an anonymous author, "that the matter of which the stone of the philosophers is made was made at the same time as man, and that it is called philosopher's earth. But no one knows it, except the true philosophers,

---

26 *Introïtus apertus ad occlusum Regis palatium.* Op. Cit., Chap. XVII, 3.

who are the children of Art".[27] Although this book, unknown, is very common, it contains many things and contains great hidden truths. Flamel is therefore right in saying that he is broad; indeed, the Latin *largus* means abundant, rich, hearty, word derived from the Greek λα, many, and ἔργον, thing. Further, the Greek πλατύς, broad, also has the sense of usability, widespread, exposed to all eyes. The universality of the subject of the wise cannot be better defined.

Continuing his description, our writer thinks that the book of Abraham "was made of thin barks of tender saplings", or so it seemed to him. Flamel is not very assertive, and for good reason: he knows very well that with very few exceptions, the medieval parchment had replaced, for the past three centuries, the Egypian papyrus.[28] And, although we cannot paraphrase this laconic expression, we must recognize that this is where the author speaks the most clearly. A sapling is a small tree, just as a mineral is a young metal. The bark or gangue, which serves as an envelope for this mineral, allows the man to identify it with certainty, thanks to the external characters of which it is coated, which is called *liber*, the book. This mineral has a particular configuration; the crystalline blades which form its texture are, as in mica, superimposed in the manner of the leaflets of a book. Its outward appearance has earned it the epithet of leprous, and that of Dragon covered with scales, because its gangue is flaky, unpleasant and rough to the touch. A simple advice about this: choose preferably the samples with the largest and most pronounced scales.

"... Its cover was made of very fine copper, all engraved with strange letters or figures".

The ore often affects a pale color such as brass, sometimes reddish like copper; in all cases, its scales appear to be covered with entangled lineaments, having the appearance of odd, varied, and ill-defined signs or characters. We have noted above the evident contradiction which exists between the golden book and its copper binding, because it cannot describe here its internal structure. It is probable that the Adept wishes to attract our attention, on the one hand, to the metallic specification of the substance figured in his book, and, on the other hand, on the faculty that this mineral possesses to be partially transmuted into gold. This curious property is indicated by Philaletes in his Commentary on the Epistle of Ripley addressed to King Edward IV. "Without using the transmutatory elixir," says the author, speaking of our subject, "I can easily extract the gold and silver which it contains, which may be certified by those who have seen it, as well as me". This operation is not advisable, because it deprives it of any value for the Work; but we can assure that the philosopher's material truly contains the gold of the sages, gold imperfect, white and raw, vile with regard to the precious metal, much superior to gold even if we only envisage the hermetic work. In spite of its humble copper cover, with engraved scales, it is indeed a golden book, a book of gold, that of Abraham the Jew, and the famous fine gold small book mentioned by Bernard the Trevisan in his Parable. In addition, it seems that Nicholas Flamel had understood what confusion could result, in the mind of the reader, of this duality of meaning, when he writes in the same treatise: "Let no one blame me if he does not understand me, for he will be more blameworthy than I, as he

---

27 *Discours d'Autheur incertain sur la Pierre des Philosophes* (Speeches of anonymous authors on the Philosophers' Stone). Manuscript of National Library, dated 1590, no. 19957 (former French Saint-Germain). A handwritten copy of the same treaty, dated April 1, 1696, belongs to the Library of Arsenal, no. 3031 (180, SAF).

28 The use of papyrus was completely abandoned at the end of the 11th century or the beginning of the 12th century.

has not being initiated into those sacred and secret interpretations of the first agent (which is the key to opening the doors of all sciences), yet he wants to hear the more subtle conceptions of the most envious philosophers, who are only written for those who already know these principles, which are never found in any book".

Finally, the author of the *Figures Hieroglyphiques* completes his description by saying: "As for the interior, the bark pages are engraved, with a very great workmanship, written with a iron point".

Here, it is no longer the physical aspect that is at issue, but rather the very preparation of the subject. To reveal a secret of this order and importance would be to cross the boundaries imposed on us. Therefore, we will not seek, as we have done so far, to comment in clear language on the ambiguous and highly allegorical phrase of Flamel. We will simply draw attention to this iron point, whose secret property changes the intimate nature of our Magnesia, separates, orders, purifies and assembles the elements of mineral chaos. To succeed in this operation, it is necessary to know the sympathies of things well, to have a lot of skill, to be a "great industry", as the Adept tells us. But, in order to provide some help to the artist in resolving this difficulty, we will point out to him that, in the early language, which is archaic Greek, all words containing the diphthong ἤρ must be taken into consideration. 'Ηρ has remained, in the phonetic cabal, the sound expression dedicated to active light, the incarnate spirit, the manifest or hidden bodily fire. 'Ηρ, contraction of ἔαρ, is the birth of light, spring and morning, the beginning, the dawn, the dawn. The air –in Greek ἀήρ–, is the support, the vehicle of light. It is through the vibration of the atmospheric air that the dark waves, emanating from the sun, become luminous. The ether or the sky (αἰθήρ) is the place of election, the domicile of pure clarity. Among metal bodies, the one containing the highest proportion of fire, or latent light, is iron (σίδηρος). We know how easily the internal fire can be released, by shock or friction, in the form of bright sparks. It is this active fire that must be communicated to the passive subject; it alone has the power to modify its cold and sterile complexion, making it ardent and prolific. It is him that the wise call the green lion, a wild and ferocious lion –cabalistically λέων φήρ– which is quite suggestive and dispenses us from insisting.

We have, in a previous work, pointed out the implacable struggle of the bodies in contact with a bas-relief of the basement of Notre-Dame de Paris.[29] Another translation of the hermetic combat exists on the facade of a wooden house, built in the fifteenth century, at Ferté-Bernard (Sarthe). There we find, other time, the jester, the man with a tree trunk, the pilgrim, familiar images and which seem to enter into an applied formula, towards the end of the Middle Ages, the decoration of the modest houses of alchemists without pretension. In addition, there is the Adept in prayer, as well as the siren, emblem of united and pacified natures, the meaning of which is commented on elsewhere. But what interests us above all –because the subject relates directly to our analysis– are two snarling, counterfeit and grimacing marmosets, carved on the extreme abutments of the cornice, on the second floor (see plates XXI and XXII, on the next page).

---

29 Cf. *Le Mystère des Cathédrales* (The Mystery of the Cathedrals), p. 79 (ed., 1926).

LA FERTE-BERNARD (Sarthe) - HOUSE OF THE XVth CENTURY
Marmousets and sculptures of the facade (left side) - Plate XXI

LA FERTE-BERNARD (Sarthe) - HOUSE OF THE XVth CENTURY
Marmousets and sculptures of the facade (right side) - Plate XXII

Too far from each other to come to blows, they try to satisfy their native aversion by throwing stones. These grotesques have the same hermetic meaning as that of the children of the porch of Notre-Dame. They attack with frenzy and seek to stone themselves. But while at the cathedral of Paris the indication of opposite tendencies is furnished to us by the different sex of the young pugilists, it is only the aggressive nature of the characters which appears on the Sarthe residence. Two men, of similar appearance and costume, express, one the mineral body, the other the metallic body. This external similarity brings fiction closer to physical reality, but resolutely departs from operational esotericism.

If the reader has understood what we wish to teach, he will easily find, in these various symbolic expressions of the combat of the two natures, the secret materials whose mutual destruction opens the first door of the Work. These bodies are the two dragons of Nicholas Flamel, the eagle and the lion of Basil Valentine, the magnet and the steel of Philaletes and the Cosmopolite.

As for the operation by which the artist inserts into the philosopher's subject the igneous agent who is its animator, the ancients have described it under the allegory of the fight of the eagle and the lion, or both natures, one volatile, the other fixed. The Church has veiled it in the dogma, all spiritual and rigorously true, of the Visitation. At the end of this artifice, the book, open, shows its engraved leaves of bark. It appears then, for the wonder of the eyes and the joy of the soul, clothed with the admirable signs which manifest its change of constitution.

Prostrate yourself, wise men of the East, and you doctors of the Law; bow down your foreheads, sovereign princes of the Persians, of the Arabs and of India! Look, adore and be silent, for you could never understand. This is the divine, supernatural, ineffable Work, of which no mortal will ever penetrate the mystery. In the nocturnal firmament, silent and deep, shines a single star, an immense star, resplendent, composed of all the celestial stars, your luminous guide and the torch of universal Wisdom. See: the Virgin and Jesus rest, calm and serene, under the palm tree of Egypt. A new sun shines in the centre of the wicker cradle, a mystical basket once worn by the cystophores of Bacchus, the priestesses of Isis, the Ichthus of the Christian Catacombs. The ancient prophecy has finally come true. Oh miracle! God, master of the Universe, incarnates himself for the salvation of the world and is born, on the earth of men, in the frail form of a very small child.

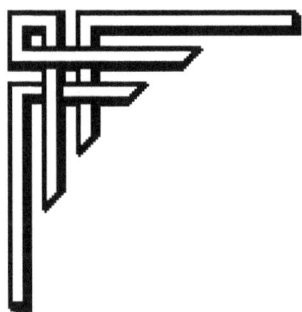

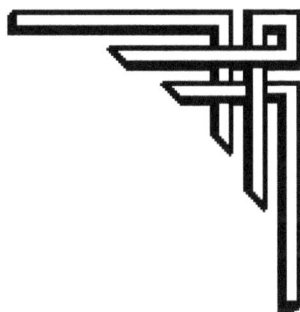

SECOND
VOLUME

The Wonderful Grimoire of the Castle of Dampierre

I

In the Santoine region to which Coulonges-sur-l'Autize belongs –chief town of the canton where formerly rose the beautiful residence of Louis d'Estissac–, the forewarned tourist can discover another castle, whose conservation and the importance of a singular decoration makes it even more interesting, that of Dampierre-sur-Boutonne (Charente-Inferieure). Built at the end of the 15th century, under François de Clermont, the castle of Dampierre is currently the property of Dr. Texier, of Saint-Jean-d'Angély.[1] By the abundance and the variety of the symbols which he proposes, like so many enigmas, to the sagacity of the researcher, he deserves to be better known, and we are happy to point it out particularly to the attention of the disciples of Hermes.

Externally, its architecture, although elegant and of good taste, remains very simple and possesses nothing remarkable; there are some buildings, like certain men: their discreet dress, the modesty of their appearance, only serve to veil in them what they have of superior.

Between round towers topped by conical roofs and provided with barbicans, lies a Renaissance building whose facade opens, outward, by ten lowered arches. Five of them form a colonnade on the ground floor, while the five others, directly superimposed on the previous ones, open the second floor. These openings light up galleries of access to the interior rooms, and all thus offers the appearance of a large loggia crowning the ambulatory of a cloister. Such is the humble cover of the magnificent album, the stone pages of which fill the vaults of the upper gallery (see the plate XXIII on the next page).

But, although we know today who was the builder of the new buildings intended to replace the old feudal burg of Château-Gaillard, we still do not know the mysterious individual to whom the hermetic philosophers are indebted for the symbolic pieces they shelter.[2]

---

1 Compendium of the Commission for Arts and Historic Monuments of Charente-Inferieure, t. XIV. Saintes, 1884.

2 "We used to see, above the front door of the Richard House, rebuilt about fifteen years ago, a stone of a rather respectable dimension on which was read this Greek word, engraved in large characters:

155

DAMPIERRE-SUR-BOUTONNE (Charente-Inférieure)
The 16th Century Castle - Plate XXIII

It is almost certain, and we share on this point the opinion of Leon Palustre, that the paneled ceiling of the upper gallery, where all the interest of Dampierre lies, was executed from 1545 or 1546 to 1550. Less sure, however, is the attribution that has been made of this work to some characters, notorious without a doubt, but who are completely foreign to it. Some authors have, indeed, claimed that the emblematic motifs emanated from Claude de Clermont, Baron Dampierre, governor of Ardres, colonel of Graubünden and gentleman of the room of the king. Now, in his *Vie des Dames Illustrtres* (Life of the Illustrious Ladies), de Brantome tells us that during the war of the King of England and the King of France, Claude de Clermont fell into a "snare" set up by the enemy, and died there in 1545. He could not, therefore, intervene, however little, in the work performed after his death. His wife, Jeanne de Vivonne, daughter of André de Vivonne, lord of Châteigneraye, d'Esnandes, Ardelay, councilor and chamberlain of the king, seneschal of Poitou, etc., and Louise de Daillon du Lude, was born in 1520. She remained a widow at twenty-five. Her spirit, his distinction, her high virtue earned her such a reputation that, like Brantome, praising the extent of his erudition, Leon Palustre does her the honor of being the instigator of the bas-reliefs of

ΑΝΑΛΩΤΟΣ, that is to say, impregnable. It came, it seems, from the old castle. This stone was later used for the construction of a shed pier. "Compendium of the Commission of Arts and Historic Monuments of Charente-Inférieure, note of Mr. Serton father, communicated by Mr. Fragnaud, former mayor of Dampierre.

Dampierre. "It is here," said he, "that Jeanne de Vivonne amused herself by having sculptors of ordinary merit execute a whole series of compositions in the more or less clear sense".[3]

Finally, a third attribution does not even deserve to be considered.[4] Father Noguès, by putting forward the name of Claude-Catherine de Clermont, daughter of Claude and Jeanne de Vivonne, expresses an absolutely unacceptable opinion, as Palustre says: "This future châtelaine of Dampierre, born in 1543, was a child at the time the work was completed".

So, in order not to fall into anachronisms, we are obliged to grant Jeanne de Vivonne alone the authorship of the symbolic decoration of the upper gallery. And yet, however likely this hypothesis may seem, it is impossible for us to subscribe to it. We strongly refuse to recognize a 25-year-old woman as a beneficiary of a science that requires more than twice as much sustained effort and persistent study. Even supposing that in his first youth she had been able, and with contempt for any philosophical rule, to receive the oral initiation of some unknown artist, she would not have been able to do without controlling, by means of tenacious and personal labor, the truth of that teaching. However, nothing is more painful, more discouraging, than to pursue, for many years, a series of experiments, trials, attempts requiring constant attendance, the abandonment of all business, all relationships, all external concerns. Voluntary confinement and renunciation of the world are essential to observe if we want to obtain, with practical knowledge, the notions of this symbolic science, even more secret, which covers them and steals them from the vulgar. Did Jeanne de Vivonne submit to the demands of an admirable mistress, prodigious of infinite treasures, but uncompromising and despotic, wanting to be loved exclusively for herself and imposing blind obedience and fidelity to all tests on her worshippers? We find nothing in her that would justify such a concern. On the contrary, her life is only worldly. Admitted to court, written by Brantôme, "from the age of eight, she had been nurtured by it and had forgotten nothing. And it was pleasant to hear her speak, and I have seen our king and our queens experience a singular pleasure in listening to her, for she knew everything about her time and the past, to the point that she was regarded as an oracle. Also our most recent king, Henry III of France, made her lady-in-waiting to the queen, his wife". Living at the court, she successively saw five monarchs succeed one another on the throne: Francis I, Henry II, Francis II, Charles IX and Henry III. Her virtue is recognized and reputed to be respected by the irreverent Tallemant des Réaux; as for her knowledge, it is exclusively historical. Facts, anecdotes, chronicles, biographies constitute her only baggage. She was, in short, a woman of excellent memory, having listened a lot, retained a lot, to the point that Brantôme, her nephew and historiographer, speaking of Madame de Dampierre, said that she "is a true register of the court". The image speaks for itself; Jeanne de Vivonne was a register, pleasant, informative to consult, we have no doubt about it, but she was no other thing. Having entered so young into the intimacy of the sovereigns of France, had she only more or less resided, later, at the Château de Dampierre? This was the question we were asking ourselves as we leaf through Jules Robuchon's beautiful collection, when a notice from Mr. Georges Musset, a former student of the École des chartes and a member of the Société des Antiquaires de l'Ouest, came along to solve it and support our conviction. "But," writes G. Musset, "unpublished documents complicate the issue and seem to create impossibilities. A declaration from Dampierre is sent to the king, because of his castle of Niort, on August 9, 1547, with the advent of Henry II. The declarants are Jacques de Clermont, usufructuary of

---

3   Léon Palustre, *La Renaissance en France* (The Renaissance in France); Aunis et Saintonge, p. 293.

4   Abbot Noguès, *Dampierre-sur-Boutonne. Monographie historique et archéologique* (Dampierre-sur-Boutonne. Historical and archaeological monograph). Saintes, 1883, p. 53.

the land, and François de Clermont, his emancipated son, for the bare ownership. The debt consists of a yew bow. From this record it appears: 1st, that it is not Jeanne de Vivonne who enjoys Dampierre, nor his daughter Catherine who owns it; 2nd, that Claude de Clermont had a younger brother, François, who was a minor, but emancipated in 1547. Indeed, there are no grounds to suppose that Claude and François were the same person, since Claude died during the Boulogne campaign, which ended, as we know, by the treaty between Francis I and Henry VIII on 7 June 1546. But then, what happened to François, who is not mentioned by Anselme? What happened, with respect to that land, from 1547 to 1558? How could such an association of persons incapacitated for possession, usufructuaries or minors, produce such a luxurious dwelling? These are mysteries that we cannot clarify. It's a great deal already, even to understand the complexity of the situation".[5]

Thus is confirmed the opinion that the philosopher to whom we owe all the embellishments of the castle –paintings and sculptures– is unknown to us and will remain so perhaps forever.

II

In a spacious room on the first floor, a large and very beautiful fireplace, gilded and covered with paintings, is particularly noteworthy. Unfortunately, the main frame of the mantelpiece has lost the subjects that decorated it, under a dreadful reddish brush. Only a few isolated letters remain visible in its lower part. On the other hand, both sides have kept their decoration and make us deeply regret the loss of the main composition. On each of these sides the pattern is similar. At the top, a forearm appears with a raised sword and a pair of scales in its hand. Towards the middle of the sword is the central part of a floating phylactery, covered with the inscription:

DAT JVSTVS FRENA SVPERBIS[6]

Two chains of gold, connected to the top of the scale, are connected below, one to the collar of a mastiff, the other to the shackles of a dragon whose tongue comes out of its open mouth. Both raise their heads and point their eyes towards the hand. The two weighing pans of the scale carry rolls of gold coins. One of these scrolls is marked with the letter L surmounted by a crown; on another, there is a hand holding a small scale with, below it, the image of a dragon of menacing appearance.

Above these large motifs, that is to say, at the upper end of the lateral faces, two medallions are painted. The first shows a Maltese cross flanked at the corners by fleurs-de-lis; the second bears the effigy of a graceful figurine.

As a whole, this composition presents itself as a paradigm of hermetic science. Mastiff and dragon take the place of the two material principles, assembled and retained by the gold of the sages, according to the required proportion and the natural equilibrium, as the image of the scales teaches us. The hand is that of the craftsman; firm to maneuver the sword, hieroglyph of fire which penetrates, mortifies, changes the properties of things, prudent in the distribution of matters according to the rules of weight and philosophical measures. As for

---

5   *Paysages et Monuments du Poitou* (Landscapes and Monuments of Poitou), photographed by Jules Robuchon. T. IX: Dampierre-sur-Boutonne, by Georges Musset. Paris, 1893, p. 9.

6   The just puts a brake on the proud.

the gold coin rolls, they clearly indicate the nature of the final result and one of the objectives of the Work. The mark formed of a crowned L has always been the traditional sign, in graphic notation, to designate projection gold, that is to say, alchemically manufactured gold.

Equally expressive are the small medallions, one of which represents Nature, which must constantly serve as a guide and mentor to the artist, while the other proclaims the Rose-Cross quality that the scientist who created these varied symbols had acquired. The heraldic fleur-de-lis corresponds to the hermetic rose. Joined to the cross, it serves, like the rose, as an ensign and coat of arms for the practising knight who, by divine grace, made the philosopher's stone. But, if this emblem provides us with proof of the knowledge possessed by the unknown Adept of Dampierre, it also serves to convince us of the vanity, of the uselessness of the attempts we could make in the search for his true personality. We know why the Rosicrucians called themselves invisible; it is therefore likely that, during his lifetime, ours had to take the necessary precautions and take all necessary measures to hide his identity. He wanted man to erase himself before science and his lapidary work to contain no other signature than the high, but anonymous, title of Rosicrucian and Adept.

On the ceiling of the same room where the large fireplace that we are signalling stands, there was once a beam decorated with this curious Latin inscription:

Factorum claritas fortis animus secundus famæ sine villa fine cursus modicæ opes bene partæ innocenter amplificatæ semper habita numera Dei sunt extra invidiæ injurias positæ æternum ornamento et exemplo apud suos futura.

"Illustrious deeds, a magnanimous heart, a glorious fame, which does not end in shame; a modest fortune well acquired, honorably increased, and always regarded as a gift from God, that is what injustice and envy can not attain, and which must be eternally, for the family, a glory and an example".

On the subject of this text, which has long since disappeared, Dr. Texier has kindly communicated some details to us: "The inscription about which you speak", he writes, "existed on a beam of a room on the first floor, which, falling from old age, had to be changed sixty or eighty years ago. The inscription was exactly raised, but the fragment of beam, where it was painted in golden letters, was lost. My father-in-law, who owned the castle, remembers seeing it very well".[7]

Paraphrasing Solomon in Ecclesiastes, where it is said (chapter III, v. 13) that "everyone must eat and drink, and enjoy the produce of all his labor, for it is a gift of God," this coin determines in a positive way and suffices to explain what was the mysterious occupation to which the enigmatic lord of Dampierre gave himself up under cover. The inscription reveals, in any case, in its author, an unusual wisdom. No labor, whatever it may be, can procure a better acquired comfort; the worker receives from nature the full wages to which he is entitled, and this is offered to him in proportion to his skill, his efforts, his perseverance. And as practical science has always been recognized as a true gift of God by all the possessors of the Magisterium, the fact that this profession of faith considers fortune acquired as a gift from God is sufficient to detect its alchemical origin. Its steady and honorable growth can not surprise anyone in these circumstances.

Two other inscriptions from the same house are worthy of mention here. The first, painted on the mantel of a fireplace, has a six-line stanza dominated by a subject composed of the letter H, holding two D intertwined and adorned with human figures, seen in profile,

---

7   We later found the plate with the inscription that we reproduce, in the middle of other boards forming, in a sheep pen, used as a partition wall.

one of old man, the other of young man. This small room, briskly written, exalts the happy existence, imbued with calm and serenity, of benevolent hospitality, which led our philosopher in his seductive home:

DOVLCE . EST . LA . VIE . A . LA . BIEN . SVYVRE .	SWEET IS LIFE IF YOU FOLLOW IT WELL
EMMY . SOYET . PRINTANS . SOYET . HYVERS .	WHETHER IN SPRING OR IN WINTER,
SOVBS.BLANCHE.NEIGE.OV.RAMEAVX.VERTS.	UNDER WHITE SNOW OR GREEN BRANCHES
QVAND . VRAYS . AMIS . NOVS . LA . FONT . VIVRE .	WHEN TRUE FRIENDS MAKE US LIVE IT.
AINS . LEVR . PLACE . A . TOVS . EST . ICI .	SO, HERE EVERYONE HAS THEIR PLACE,
COMME . AVX . VIEVLS . AVX . JEVNES . AVSSI .	BOTH OLD AND YOUNG.

The second one, which is furnished with a larger chimney, ornamented with red, gray and gold ornaments, is a simple maxim of a fine moral character, but which the superficial and presumptuous humanity of our epoch is reluctant to practice:

SE.COGNESTRE.ESTRE.AND.NON.PARESTRE.   TO KNOW ONESELF, TO BE AND NOT SHOW OFF.

Our Adept is right; the knowledge of oneself allows one to acquire the science, purpose and reason of life, the basis of all real value; and this power, elevating the laborious man who can acquire it, incites him to abide in a modest and noble simplicity, eminent virtue of the higher minds. It was an axiom that the teachers repeated to their disciples, and by which they indicated to them the only way to reach the supreme knowledge: "If you wish to know wisdom," they said to them, "know yourselves well and you will know it".

III

The high gallery, whose ceiling is so curiously decorated, occupies the entire length of the high building between the towers. As we have said, it opens to the outside through five bay windows separated by stocky columns, equipped inside with engaged supports receiving the fallout of arches. Two straight mullioned windows and straight lintels open at the ends of this gallery. Transverse ribs take the lowered shape of the bay windows and are cut by two parallel longitudinal ribs, thus determining the frame of the panels which are the subject of our study (Plate XXIV).

The panels were described long before us by Louis Audiat.[8] But the author, unaware of the science to which they refer, and the essential reason that links so many strange images together, has endowed his book with the character of incoherence that the figures themselves affect for the profane. From reading the *Epigraphy Santone*, it seems that whim, fantasy and extravagance presided over their execution. Also, the least that can be said of this work is that it doesn't seem to be very serious, is devoid of substance, baroque, with no other interest than an excessive singularity. Some inexplicable errors add to the negative impression we receive. For example, the author takes a cubic stone, cut and placed on the water (series I, box 5), for "a ship shaken on the waves"; elsewhere (series IV, box 7), a stooped woman, planting pits near a tree, becomes "a traveller who travels painfully through a desert". In the first box of the fifth series –may our readers forgive him for this involuntary comparison–, he sees a woman instead of the devil himself, hairy, winged, horned, perfectly clear and visible.

---

8   Louis Audiat, *Epigraphy Santone and Aunisian*. Paris, J.-B. Dumoulin, and Niort, L. Clouzot, 1870.

DAMPIERRE-SUR-BOUTONNE
Upper Gallery - Plate XXIV

Such misunderstandings denote an inexcusable stupidity in an epigraphist conscious of his responsibility and the accuracy that his profession demands.

According to Dr. Texier, to whom we owe this information, the figures of Dampierre never have been published in their entirety. However, there is a reproduction drawn from the original and kept in the museum of Saintes. It is to this drawing that we have resorted, for some patterns that were not clear, in order to render our description as complete as possible.

Almost all the emblematic compositions have, apart from a subject sculpted in bas-relief, an inscription engraved on a phylactery. But while the image refers directly to the practical side of science, the epigraph offers above all a moral or philosophical meaning; it is addressed to the worker rather than to the work, and, sometimes using an apophthegm, sometimes a parable, defines a quality, a virtue that the artist must possess, a point of doctrine that he cannot ignore. However, by the very fact that they are equipped with phylacteries, these figures reveal their secret scope, their assignment to some hidden science. Indeed, the Greek φυλακτήριον, formed by φυλάσσω, keep, preserve, and τηρέω, conserve, indicates the function of this ornament, responsible for keeping and preserving the occult and mysterious meaning hidden behind the natural expression of the compositions it accompanies. It is the sign, the seal of this Wisdom who stands on guard against the wicked, as Plato says: Σοφία η περὶ περὶ τοὺς πονηροὺς φυλακτική. Whether it bears an epigrapher or not, it is enough to find the phylactery on any subject to be assured that the image contains a hidden meaning, a secret meaning proposed to the researcher and marked by its simple presence. And the truth of this meaning, the reality of this meaning is always found in the hermetic science, described by the ancient masters as eternal wisdom. It should therefore come as no surprise to find banners and parchments, abundantly represented among the attributes of religious scenes or secular compositions of our great cathedrals, as well as in the less severe framework of civil architecture.

Arranged in three rows, perpendicular to the axis, the panels of the upper gallery are 93 in number. Of these, 61 relate to science, 24 offer monograms to separate them into series, 4 have only geometric ornaments, of later execution, and the last 4 show their empty and smooth slab. The symbolic panels, on which the interest of the Dampierre ceiling is concentrated, constitute a set of figures divided into seven series. Each series is isolated from the next by three panels, arranged in a transverse line, alternately decorated with the monogram of Henri II and the intertwined croissants of Diane de Poitiers or Catherine de Médicis, figures that can be seen on many buildings of the same period. However, we have made the rather surprising observation that most hotels or castles carrying the double D linked to the letter H and the triple crescent, have an undeniably alchemical decoration. But why are these same dwellings qualified as "castles of Diane de Poitiers" by the authors of the monographs, and on the mere existence of the figure in question?

However, neither the home of Louis d'Estissac, at Coulonges-sur-l'Autize, nor that of the Clermont, both placed under the aegis of the too famous favorite, ever belonged to him. On the other hand, what reason could be given for the monogram and crescents that were likely to justify their presence in the middle of hermetic emblems? To what thought, to what tradition did the initiates of the nobility obey, placing under the fictitious protection of a monarch and his concubine, objects of general reprobation, their hieroglyphic work painted or carved? "Henry II," wrote the Abbé de Montgaillard, "was a stupid prince, brutal and profoundly indifferent to the good of his people; this bad king was constantly dominated by his wife and his old mistress; he abandoned to them the reins of the state, and did not shrink from any of the cruelties exercised against the Protestants. We can say that he continued the reign of Francis I, in fact political despotism and religious intolerance.[9] It is therefore impossible to admit that educated philosophers, people of study and high morality, had the thought of offering the homage of their labors to the royal couple whose debauchery made them shamefully famous.

Different is the truth, for the crescent does not belong to either Diane de Poitiers or Catherine de Medici. It is a symbol of the highest antiquity, known to the Egyptians and Greeks, used by the Arabs and by the Saracens long before its introduction into our Western Middle Ages. It is the attribute of Isis, of Artemis or of Diana, of Selene, Phoebe or the Moon, the spagyric emblem of silver and the seal of the color white. Its meaning is threefold: alchemical, magical, cabalistic, and this triple hierarchy of meaning, synthesized in the image of intertwined crescents, embraces the extent of ancient and traditional knowledge. It will be less surprising, therefore, to see appearing the symbolic triad next to obscure signs, since it serves as a support and allows the investigator to orient the investigator towards the science to which they belong.

As for the monogram, it is easily explicable and shows, once again, how philosophers have used emblems of known significance, endowing them with a special meaning generally ignored. It is the surest way they have had to hide from the layman a science figuratively exposed to all eyes; a renewed process of the Egyptians whose teaching, translated into hieroglyphics outside the temples, remained a dead letter for those who did not have the key. The historical monogram is formed of two D's, interlaced and united by the letter H, initial of Henry II. Such is, at least, the ordinary expression of the figure which, under its image, hides a very different thing.

9   Abbot of Montgaillard. *Histoire de France* (History of France), t. I, p. 186. Paris, Moutardier, 1827.

It is known that Alchemy is based on the physical metamorphoses effected by the spirit, the name accorded to the universal dynamism emanating from the divinity, which maintains life and movement, causes it to stop or die, evolves the substance, and affirms as the only animator of all that is. Now, in the alchemical notation, the sign of the spirit does not differ from the letter H of the Latins and the eta of the Greeks. We will give further, by studying one of the panels where this character is figured crowned (series VII, 2), some of its symbolic applications. For the moment, it is enough to know that the spirit, universal agent, constitutes, in the realization of the Work, the principal unknown whose determination ensures the complete success. But this one, exceeding the limits of the human understanding, can only be acquired by divine revelation. "God", the masters repeat, "gives wisdom to whom he pleases and transmit it by the Holy Spirit, light of the world; this is why science is called a gift of God, formerly reserved for its ministers, hence the name of the sacerdotal art it originally bore". Let us add that in the Middle Ages the gift of God applied to the *secretum secretorum*, which is precisely the secret par excellence, that of the universal spirit.

Thus, the *Donum Dei*, a revealed knowledge of the science of the Great Work, the key to the materializations of the mind and the light (Ἥλιος), undeniably appears under the monogram of the double D (Donum Dei) united to the sign of the spirit (H), Greek initial of the sun, father of light, Ἥλιος. The alchemical character of the figures of Dampierre cannot be better indicated, of which we are now going to undertake the study.

IV

First series (Plate XXV).

DAMPIERRE-SUR-BOUTONNE
Panel of the Upper Gallery – First Series – Plate XXV

Panel 1 – Two trees of the same size and similar size appear side by side on the same site; one is green and vigorous, the other inert and dry.[10] The banner which seems to bring them together bears these words:

. SOR. NO . OMNIBVS. ÆQVE.   FATE IS NOT THE SAME FOR ALL

The fate is not the same for all. This truth, limited to the period of human existence, seems to us all the more relative because destiny, sad or smiling, quiet or upset, leads us all, without distinction or privilege, towards death. But if we transpose it into the hermetic domain, it then takes on a clearly marked positive meaning which must have assured the preference of our Adept.

According to the alchemical doctrine, common metals, torn from their lodgings to meet the needs of industry, forced to comply with the demands of man, thus appear as the victims of a blatant curse. While in the state of ore they lived at the bottom of the rock, evolving slowly towards the perfection of the native gold, they are condemned to die immediately after their extraction and perish under the harmful action of the reducing fire. The melting, by separating them from the nutrients associated with the mineralizing elements responsible for maintaining their activity, kills them by fixing the temporary and transient form they had acquired. This is the meaning of the two symbolic trees, one of which expresses mineral vitality and the other expresses metallic inertia.

From this simple image, the intelligent investigator, sufficiently educated in the principles of art, can draw a useful and profitable consequence. If he remembers that the old masters recommend to begin the work at the very point where nature finishes his; if he knows how to kill the living in order to resuscitate the dead, he will certainly discover what metal he must take and what mineral he must elect in order to begin his first work. Then, reflecting on the operations of nature, he will learn from her how to unite the revived body with another living body –for life desires life–, and, if he understands us, he will see from his eyes and touch with his hands the material testimony of a great truth ...

These are words too succinct, no doubt, and we regret it; but our submission to the rules of traditional discipline does not allow us to specify or develop them further.

Panel 2 (Plate XXV) - A fortress tower, built on a glacis, crowned with battlements and barbican, provided with loopholes and topped by a dome, is pierced by a narrow grilled window and a solidly locked door. This building, with its powerful and boring appearance, receives a shower from the clouds, which the inscription refers to as a golden rain:

. AVRO. CLAVSA. PATENT.   GOLD OPENS CLOSED DOORS

Gold opens closed doors. Everyone knows it. But this proverb, the application of which is found at the basis of privilege, favoritism, and all other rights, cannot, in the mind of the philosopher, have the figurative meaning that we assign to it. It is not corruptive gold that we are talking about here, but rather the mytho-hermetic episode contained in the fable of Jupiter and Danae. The poets recount that this princess, daughter of the king of Argos, Acrisius, was locked in a tower because an oracle had announced to his father that he would be killed by his grandson. Now, the walls of a prison, however thick, cannot constitute a serious

---

10 At the foot of this tree covered with foliage, the earth is dug in the shape of a bowl, so that the water poured for its watering is better retained. In the same way, the metal, dead by the reduction, will recover the existence, in frequent imbibitions.

obstacle to the will of a god. Zeus, a great lover of romantic adventures and metamorphosis, always preoccupied with deceiving Hera's vigilance and extending his offspring, noticed Danae. Little troubled about the choice of means, he introduced himself to her in the form of a shower of gold, and at the expiration of the term required, the prisoner gave birth to a son who received the name of Perseus. Acrisius, very dissatisfied with this news, had the mother and the child shut up in a chest which was thrown into the sea. Carried by the currents to the island of Sériphe, fishermen collected the singular vessel, then opened and presented its contents to the King Polydectus, who received Danae and Perseus with great hospitality.

Beneath this wonderful story hides an important secret, that of the preparation of the hermetic subject, or raw material of the Work, and the obtaining of sulfur, the stone's *primus ens.*

Danae represents our raw mineral, as extracted from the mine. It is the earth of the wise that contains within it the active and hidden spirit, the only one capable, says Hermes, of performing "by these things the miracles of one thing". Indeed, Danae comes from the Dorian Δᾶν, earth, and from ἄη, breath, spirit. Philosophers teach that their raw material is a fragment of the original chaos, and this is what the Greek name Acrisius, king of Argos and father of Danae, says: Ἀκρισία means confusion, disorder; Ἀργός means raw, uncultivated, unfinished. Zeus, for his part, marks the sky, the air and the water; to such an extent that the Greeks, to express the action of raining, said: Ὕει ὁ Ζεύς, Jupiter sends rain, or more simply, it rains. This god therefore appears as the personification of water, of water capable of penetrating the bodies, of metallic water, since it is of gold or at least golden. This is exactly the case with hermetic solvent, which, after fermentation in an oak barrel, takes on the appearance of liquid gold when settling. The anonymous author of an unpublished manuscript from the 18th century writes on this subject: "If you let this water flow, you will see with your own eyes the gold shining in his first being, with all the colors of the rainbow".[11] The very union of Zeus and Danae indicates the way in which the solvent must be applied; the body, reduced to a fine powder, digested with a small quantity of water, is then moistened, watered little by little, as it is absorbed, a technique that the sages have called imbibition. The result is an increasingly soft paste, which becomes syrupy, oily, fluid and clear. Then, under certain conditions, subjected to the action of fire, part of this liquor coagulates into a mass that falls to the bottom and is carefully collected. This is our precious sulphur, the newly born child, the little king and our dolphin, a symbolic fish otherwise known as échénéis, remora or pilot, Perseus or Red Sea fish (in Greek Περσεύς), etc.[12]

Panel 3 (Plate XXV). - Four blooming and erect flowers on their stems are in contact with the edge of a bare sword. This motive has for motto:

. NVTRI. ETIAM. RESPONSA. FERVNTVR.   ALSO DEVELOP THE ANNOUNCED ORACLES

Also develop the announced oracles. It is a piece of advice given to the artist, so that, while practicing it, can be assured to direct suitably the coction, or second operation of the Magisterium. *Nutri etiam responsa feruntur*, entrusts to him the spirit of our philosopher, through the petrified characters of his work.

---

11 *La clef du Cabinet Hermétique* (The key to the Hermetic Cabinet), manuscript copied from the original belonging to Mr. Desaint, doctor, rue Hiacinthe in Paris.

12 The remora is famous for the tales it has been the subject of. Among other ridiculous fables, Pliny certifies that, if this fish is kept in salt, its simple proximity is enough to extract from the deepest well the gold that could have fallen on it.

These oracles, four in number, correspond to the four flowers or colors that appear during the evolution of the Rebis and reveal to the alchemist from the outside the successive phases of the internal work. These phases, variously colored, are called Regimes or Kingdoms. There are usually seven of them. To each regime the philosophers attributed one of the higher deities of Olympus, and also one of the celestial planets whose influence is exerted parallel to their own, in the very time of their domination. According to the generally widespread idea, planets and deities develop their simultaneous power according to an invariable hierarchy. The reign of Mercury (Ἑρμῆς, base, foundation), the first stage of the Work, is followed by that of Saturn (Κρόνος, the old man, the madman); Jupiter then governs (Ζεύς, union, marriage), then Diana, (Ἄρτεμις, whole, complete) or the Moon, whose sparkling dress is sometimes woven of white hair, sometimes made of snow crystals; Venus, destined for the green (Ἀφροδίτη, beauty, grace), then inherited the throne, but Mars soon hunted her down (Ἄρης, adapted, fixed), and this bellicose prince, in clothes dyed with coagulated blood, was himself overthrown by Apollo (Ἀπόλλων, the triumphant), the Sun of the Magisterium, emperor dressed in brilliant scarlet, who definitively established his sovereignty and his power over the ruins of his predecessors.[13]

Some authors, comparing the colorful phases of the coction to the seven days of creation, have designated the whole work by the expression *Hebdomas hebdomadum*, Week of weeks, or simply the Great Week, because the alchemist must follow as closely as possible in its microcosmic realization, all the circumstances that accompanied the Great Work of the Creator.

But these various schemes are more or less clear and vary a great deal, both for duration and intensity. Thus the masters have been content to point out only four colors, essential and preponderant, because they offer more sharpness and permanence than others, namely: black, white, yellow or citrine and red. These four flowers of the hermetic garden must be cut successively, in order and at the end of their flowering, which explains the presence of the weapon on our bas-relief. Therefore, it is necessary to fear too much hastening, with the vain hope of shortening the time, sometimes very long, besides passing the degree of fire required by the regime of the moment. Old writers advise caution and warn apprentices against any prejudicial impatience; *præcipitatio a diabolo* (precipitous action goes to the devil) they say; for, in seeking to reach the goal too soon, they would succeed only in burning the flowers of the compost, and would cause the irremediable loss of the work. It is therefore preferable, as the Adept of Dampierre teaches, to develop the oracles, which are the predictions or the colored presages of the regular operation, with patience and perseverance, as long as nature can demand it.

Panel 4 (Plate XXV) – An old dismantled tower, whose door, torn from its hinges, leaves the entrance free. That's how the artist represented the open prison. Inside, one still can sees a pair of shackles, as well as three stones indicated in the upper part. Another pair of shackles, extracted from the jail, are noticeable alongside the ruin. This composition marks the completion of the three stones or medicines of Géber, successively obtained, which are designated by the philosophers under the names of Sulfur philosophical for the first; Elixir or Gold drinking for the second; Philosopher's Stone, Absolute or Universal Medicine for the

13 We will limit ourselves here to list the successive stages of the second Work without making any special analysis of it. Great Adepts, and especially Philaletes, in his *Introïtus*, have taken the study very far. Their descriptions reflect such a consciousness that it would be impossible for us to say more or say it better.

last. Each of these stones had to undergo the coction in the Athanor, prison of the Great Work, and that is the reason why a last obstacle is still sealed there.

The motto of the little bas-relief is the word of the apostle Peter (Acts xiii, v. 11), which was miraculously delivered from his prison by an angel:

. NV (N) C. SCIO. VERE.   NOW I REALLY KNOW

Now, I really know! Word of lively joy, outburst of intimate satisfaction, cry of joy that the Adept utters before the certainty of the prodigy. Until then, doubt could still assail him; but, in the presence of a perfect and tangible realization, he no longer fears wandering; he discovered the way, recognized the truth, inherited the *Donum Dei* (Gift of God). Nothing of the great secret is now ignored. Alas! How many, among the crowd of researchers, can flatter themselves to reach the goal, to see, with their own eyes, open the prison, forever closed for the greatest number!

The prison also serves as an emblem for the imperfect body, the initial subject of the Work, in which the aqueous and metallic core is strongly attached and retained. "It is this trapped water, says Nicolas Valois, that constantly shouts: Help me and I will help you, that is, free me from my prison, and if you can get me out once, I will make you the owner of the fortress where I am. The water that is in this enclosed body is the same nature of water that we give it to drink, which is called Mercury Trismegistus, of which Parmenides speaks, when he says: Nature has rejoiced in Nature. Nature surmounts Nature and Nature contains Nature. Because this enclosed water rejoices with his companion who comes to deliver it from its irons, struggles with it and finally, converting the said prison into themselves, rejecting what is contrary to them, which is the preparation, are converted into mercurial and permanent water. It is therefore at good right that our divine Water is called the Key, Light, Diana who shines in the thick of night. For it is the entrance of the whole Work and the one that illuminates every man".[14]

Panel 5 (Plate XXV) – To have found it experimentally, the philosophers certify that their stone is nothing else than a complete coagulation of mercurial water. This fact is reflected in our bas-relief, where we see the cubic stone of the old Freemasons floating on the sea waves. Although such an operation seems impossible, it is nevertheless natural, because our mercury carries in itself the sulphurous principle, rendered soluble, to which it is indebted for its subsequent coagulation. It is regrettable, however, that the extremely slow action of this potential agent does not allow the observer to record any sign of any reaction during the early stages of the work. This is the cause of failure of many artists, who, quickly disappointed, give up hard work, that they judge vain, although they have followed the right path and operated on clean, canonically prepared materials. It is to them that the word of Jesus is addressed to Peter walking on the water, and that St. Matthew relates (chapter XIV, 31):

. MODICE. FIDEI. QVARE. DVBITASTI.   WHY DO YOU DOUBT, MAN OF LITTLE FAITH?

Why do you doubt, man of little faith? In truth, we can know nothing without the help of faith, and whoever does not possess it can not do anything. We have never seen that skepticism and doubt would have built anything stable, noble, lasting. It is often necessary to remember the Latin saying: *Mens agitat molem* (mind moves the mass) because it is the profound conviction of this truth that will lead the wise worker to the happy end of his labors. It is from

---

14 Nicolas Valois. *Les Cinq Livres. Livre I : De la Clef du Secret des Secrets* (The Five Books. Book I: On the Key to the Secret of Secrets). Ms. quoted.

it, his robust faith, that he will draw the virtues indispensable to the resolution of this great mystery. The term is not exaggerated: we find ourselves in front of a real mystery, as much by its development contrary to the chemical laws as by its obscure mechanism, a mystery that the best educated scholar and the most expert Adept cannot explain. So true is it that nature, in its simplicity, seems to take pleasure in proposing to us enigmas before which our logic recedes, our reason is disturbed, our judgment is lost.

Now this cubic stone, which the industrious nature engenders water alone –the universal material of the Peripatics– and whose art is to cut the six faces according to the rules of occult geometry, appears in the process of formation in a curious bas-relief of the 17th century decorating the fountain of Vertbois, in Paris (Plate XXVI).

PARIS – MUSEUM AND COLLEGE OF ARTS AND CRAFTS
Original Bas-relief of the Fountain of Vertbois – Plate XXVI

As the two subjects have a close correspondence between them, we will study here the larger Parisian emblem, hoping thus to throw some clarity into the concise symbolic expression of the ornamental image.

Built in 1633 by the Benedictines of Saint-Martin-des-Champs, this fountain was originally built inside the priory and leaned against the wall. In 1712, the religious offered it, for public use, to the city of Paris, with the necessary location for its reconstruction, under this condition "that the site would be established in one of the old towers of their convent", and that "There would be an outer door".[15] The fountain was thus placed against the so-called Vertbois tower, located on rue Saint-Martin, and took the name of Saint-Martin fountain, which it kept for more than a century.

---

15 Fountains of Paris, designed by Moisy. Notices by Amaury Duval . Paris, 1812.

The small building, restored at the expense of the State in 1832, has "a shallow rectangular niche, framed by two Doric pilasters, with vermiculated embossments, which support an architraved cornice. On the cornice rests a kind of small helmet crowned by a cartridge with wings. A marine conch surmounts this cartridge. The upper part of the niche is occupied by a frame in the center of which a vessel is carved".[16] This bas-relief, in stone, measures 80 cm in height by 105 cm in width; its author is unknown.

Thus, all the descriptions of the fountain of Vertbois, plausibly copied one from each other, are limited to indicate, without further specifying, a vessel as the main motif. Moisy's drawing, which is responsible for illustrating Amaury Duval's instructions, does not tell us any more. His fanciful vessel, represented in profile, bears no trace of its singular cargo, and one would search in vain, among the scrolls of the marine volutes, for the beautiful and large dolphin that accompanies it. Moreover, many people, who are not very attentive to detail, see in this subject the heraldic nave of Paris, without suspecting that it offers the curious the enigma of a completely different truth and a less vulgar order.

Admittedly, we could question the accuracy of our observation and, where we recognize a huge stone, attached to the building with which it forms a body, notice only an ordinary bundle of some kind of merchandise. But one would be, in this case, very embarrassed to give the reason of the raised sail, incompletely carved on the yard of the main mast, a feature which sheds light on the unique and voluminous package, thus unveiled on purpose. The intention of the creator of the work is therefore manifest; it is an occult cargo, normally hidden from prying eyes, and not a bundle traveling on deck.

In addition, the vessel, seen from behind, seems to move away from the spectator and shows that its movement is provided by the mizzen sail, to the exclusion of others. Alone, it receives the force of the wind, blowing at the stern; alone, it transmits energy to the ship sliding on the waves. Now cabalists write *artimon* and pronounce *antemon* or *antimony*, a term behind which they hide the name of the subject of the sages. Ἄνθεμον, in Greek, means flower, and we know that the raw material is called the flower of all metals; it is the flower of flowers (*flos florum*); the root of this word, ἄνθος, also expresses the youth, the glory, the beauty, the most noble part of things, everything that has brilliance and shines like fire. It will not be surprising, then, that Basil Valentine, in his *Triumphal Chariot Of Antimony*, has given to the prime substance of the particular work that he describes as fire-stone.

As long as it remains fixed to the hermetic vessel, this stone, as we have said, is to be considered in process of elaboration. It is therefore necessary, with all precision, to help it to continue its crossing so that neither the storms, neither the pitfalls nor the thousand incidents of the route delay its arrival at the blessed inlet towards which, little by little, Nature guides it. Facilitate your trip, foresee and avoid possible causes of shipwreck and maintain the vessel, loaded with precious cargo in its straight line, such is the task of the craftsman.

This gradual and slow formation explains why the stone is here figured under the aspect of a roughhewn block, called to receive the definitive size which will make our cubic stone. The cables which fasten it to the building indicate, by their crossing on its visible faces, the transient state of its evolution. We know that the cross, in the speculative order, is the figurative of the spirit, a dynamic principle, while it serves, in the practical domain, as a graphic sign in the crucible. It is in it, in this vessel, that the concentration of the mercurial water takes place, by the bringing together of its constitutive molecules, under the will of the metallic

---

16 *Inventaire général des Richesses d'Art de la France. Paris. Monuments civils* (General Inventory of the Riches d'Art of France. Paris. Civil monuments), Paris, Plon, 1879, t. I.

spirit and thanks to the permanent help of the fire. For the spirit is the only force capable of moving the dissolved bodies into new compact masses, just as it forces crystals from stock solutions to take the specific, invariable form by which we can identify them. This is why the philosophers have assimilated the molecular aggregation of the mercurial solid, under the secret action of the spirit, to that of a bag, squeezed by interlaced ligatures. The stone seems bound as a *secchina* (from the Greek σηκάζω, to enclose, to close), and this embodiment is made sensitive by the cross, image of the Passion, that is to say during the work in the crucible, whenever the heat is cautiously applied in the degree required and at the proper pace. Thus it is necessary to specify the particular meaning of the cable, which the Greeks called κάλως, the homonym of the adverb καλῶς, which means in a suitable and effective way.

This is the most delicate phase of the work, when the stone's first coagulation, which is unctuous and light, appears on the surface and floats on the water. It is then necessary to be more careful and cautious in the application of fire, if we do not want to redden it before term and precipitate it. At first it appears as a thin film, very quickly broken, whose fragments detached from the edges shrink, then weld, thicken, take the form of a flat islet –the island of the Cosmopolitan and the mythical land of Delos–, animated by gyratory movements and subjected to continuous movements. This island is just another figure of the hermetic fish, born from the Sea of the Wise –our mercury, which Hermes calls *mare patens*–, the pilot of the Work, the first solid state of the embryonic stone. Some have named it *échénéis*, others dolphin, with just as much reason; for if the *échénéis* is used, in legend, to stop and fix the strongest ships, the dolphin, whose head can be seen emerging in our bas-relief, has an equally positive meaning. Its Greek name, δελφίς, refers to the matrix, and it is well known that mercury is called by philosophers the receptacle and matrix of the stone.

But in order that no one may be deceived, let us repeat again that this cannot be about vulgar mercury, although its liquid quality may give the change and allow its assimilation with secret water, the metallic humid radical. The powerful initiate who was Rabelais provides, in a few words, the true characteristics of philosopher's mercury.[17]

In his description of the underground temple of the Holy Bottlee (*Pantagruel*, Liv. V, ch. XLII), he refers to a circular fountain that occupies the centre and the deepest part of it. Around this fountain are seven columns "which are stones, says the author, which the ancient Chaldeans and magi attributed to the seven planets of heaven. For which, to hear more of the rude Minerva, above the first of sapphire is the roof above the capital, with the bright and centred perpendicular line raised, in precious lead, the image of Saturn holding her scythe, having at her feet a golden crane artificially enamelled according to the proper naively attributed to the saturnine bird, in their proper order. Above the second of hyacinth, turning to the left, there is a Jupiter of tin, jovial, above the chest an eagle of gold enamelled according to the natural. On the third, Phoebus in gold, in his right hand a white cock. On the fourth, in Corinthian brass, Mars, and at his feet a lion.[18] On the fifth, Venus in copper,

---

17 His works are signed by the pseudonym Alcofribas Nasier, anagram of François Rabelais, followed by the title of abstraction of quintessence, which served, in the Middle Ages, to designate in popular language the alchemists of time. The famous doctor and philosopher declares himself, without doubt, Adept and Rose-Cross, and places his writings under the aegis of the sacred Art. By the way, in the Prologue of Gargantua, Rabelais shows sufficiently that his work belongs to the category of closed, hermetic and acroamatic books, for the understanding of which strong symbolic knowledge is absolutely indispensable.

18 The attribution of bronze to Mars proves that Rabelais knew perfectly the alchemical correspondence of planets and metals. In Greek, χαλκός, which means copper or bronze, was used by the

of the same material as the one for which Aristonides made the statue of Athamas... A dove at her feet. On the sixth, Mercury in hydrargyre, fixed, firm, maleable and motionless, with a stork at his feet". The text is formal and cannot be confusing. The mercury of the sages, all the authors certify it, is presented as a body of metallic aspect, of solid consistency, consequently immobile compared to the strong silver, of mediocre volatility to the fire, susceptible finally to fix itself by simple coction in a closed cup. As for the stork, which Rabelais attributes to mercury, it takes its meaning from the Greek word πελαργός, stork, formed by πελός, livid brown or black, and ἀργός, white, which are the two colors of the bird and those of philosophical mercury; πελαργός also refers to a pot made of white and black earth, emblem of the hermetic vase, i. e. mercury, whose water, alive and white, loses its light, its brightness, mortifies itself and becomes black, leaving its soul to the embryo of the stone, which is born from its decomposition and feeds on its ashes.

In order to bear witness that the Vertbois fountain was originally dedicated to philosophical water, the mother of all metals and the basis of sacred art, the Benedictines of Saint-Martin-des-Champs had carved on the cornice serving as a support bas-relief, various attributes relating to this fundamental liquor. Two oars and a crossed caduceus carry the petasus of Hermes, figured under the modern aspect of a winged helmet, on which a small dog watches. Some ropes, coming out of the visor, unfurl their spirals on the oars and the winged rod of the god of the Work.

The Greek word πλάτη, by which rowing was designated, simultaneously offers the meaning of vessel and winnowing basket.[19] The latter is a kind of wicker shell attributed to mercury, and that cabalists write *vent* (wind). This is why the Emerald Table says allegorically, speaking of the stone, that "the wind carried it in its belly". This winnowing basket is nothing else than the matrix, the vessel carrying the stone, emblem of mercury and main subject of our bas-relief. As for the caduceus, it is well known that it belongs to the messenger of the gods, with the winged helmet and talaria. We will only say that the Greek word Κηρύκειον, caduceus, recalls by its etymology the cock, Κῆρυξ, consecrated to Mercury as harbinger of light. All these symbols converge, one sees it, towards one and the same object, also indicated by the small dog, placed on the vault of the small helmet, whose special meaning (κράνος, head, vertex) marks the important part, in other words, it is the culmination of art, the key to the Great Work. Noel, in his *Dictionnaire de la Fable* (Dictionary of the Fable), writes that "the dog was consecrated to Mercury as the most vigilant and most cunning of all the gods". According to Pliny, the flesh of young dogs was so pure that it was offered to the gods as a sacrifice, and served in meals prepared for them. The image of the dog placed on the protective helmet of the head is, moreover, a real hieroglyphic still applicable to mercury. It is a figurative translation of the cynocephalus (κυνοκέφαλος, which has a dog's head), a mystical form very venerated by the Egyptians, who gave it to some higher divinities, and especially to the god Thoth, who later became the Hermes of the Greeks, the Trismegistus of the philosophers, the Mercury of the Romans.

---

ancient Hellenic poets to define not copper or one of its compounds, but iron. The author is therefore right to assign it to the planet Mars. As for the brass of Corinth, Pliny assures that it presents itself in three aspects. It had sometimes the brilliancy of silver, sometimes gold, and could be the result of an alloy in roughly equivalent proportions of gold, silver, and copper. It is this last brass that was believed to have been fortuitously produced by the melting of precious metals and copper, during the burning of Corinth by Mummius (146 BC).

19 In phonetic cabal, oar, equivalent of rowing, also means philosopher's water. Ῥάμα, put for ῥάσμα, means sprinkling, watering, rac. ῥέω, to sink.

Panel 6 (Plate XXV) – A dice to play is placed on a small garden table; in the foreground vegetate three herbaceous plants. For any sign, this bas-relief bears the Latin adverb:

.VTCVMQVE.   IN SOME WAY

In some way, that is, in a similar way, which could lead us to believe that the discovery of the stone was due to chance, and that thus the knowledge of the Magisterium would remain dependent on a happy stroke of the dice. But we know full well that science, the true present of God, the spiritual light obtained by revelation, cannot be subject to such hazards. It is not that we cannot accidentally find, here as elsewhere, the trick that the rebel operation requires; however, if alchemy were limited to the acquisition of a special technique, of some laboratory device, it would be reduced to very little and would not exceed the value of a simple formula. However, science goes far beyond the synthetic manufacture of precious metals, and the philosopher's stone itself is only the first positive step allowing the Adept to rise to the most sublime knowledge. By remaining even in the physical realm, which is that of material manifestations and fundamental certainties, we can ensure that the Work is not subject to the unexpected. It has its laws, principles, conditions, secret agents and results from too many combined actions and diverse influences to obey empiricism. It must be discovered, understood the process, well known its causes and accidents before proceeding to its execution. And anyone who cannot see it "in spirit" is wasting his time and oil wanting to find it through practice. "The wise man has his eyes in his head", says the Ecclesiastes (ch. II, 14), "and the fool walks in darkness".

The gambling dice has another esoteric significance. His figure, which is that of the cube (κύβος, gambling dice, cube), refers to the cubic or carved stone, our philosopher's stone and the cornerstone of the Church. But, to be regularly trained, this stone requires three successive repetitions of the same series of seven operations, bringing their total to twenty-one. This number corresponds exactly to the sum of the points scored on the six faces of the dice, since by adding the first six numbers we obtain 21. And the three series of seven will again be found by totaling the same numbers of points to boustrophedon:[20]

1 2 3
6 5 4

Placed at the intersection of the sides of an inscribed hexagon, these figures will translate the circular movement proper to the interpretation of another figure, emblematic of the Great Work, that of the serpent Ouroboros, *aut serpens qui caudam devoravit*[21]. In any case, this arithmetic peculiarity, in perfect harmony with the work, devotes the attribution of the cube or dice to the symbolic expression of our mineral quintessence. This is the Isiac table made by the cubic throne of the great goddess.

It is therefore enough, analogously, to throw the dice three times on the table, which amounts, in practice, to redissolve the stone three times, to obtain it with all its qualities. These are the three vegetative phases that the artist represented here by three plants. Finally, the reiterations indispensable to the perfection of hermetic labor furnish the reason of the

---

20 Boustrophedon is a kind of bi-directional text, mostly seen in ancient manuscripts and other inscriptions. Every other line of writing is flipped or reversed, with reversed letters.

21 The Ouroboros serpent, or "the serpent which devours its tail". The philosophers have trans-lated the union of the fixed and the volatile, of the body and the spirit, by the figure of the serpent devouring its tail.

hieroglyphic book of Abraham the Jew, composed, says Flamel, of three times seven pages. Likewise, a splendid illuminated manuscript, executed in the early eighteenth century, contains twenty-one painted figures each adapted to the twenty-one operations of the Work.[22]

V

Second series (Plate XXVII).

DAMPIERRE-SUR-BOUTONNE
Panel of the Upper Gallery – Second Series – Plate XXVII

Panel 1 – Thick clouds intercept the light of the sun and cover with shade an agrarian flower that accompanies the motto:

. REVERTERE. AND. REVERTAR.   COME BACK AND I WILL RETURN

Come back and I will return. This fabulous herbaceous plant, was called Barras by the elders. It was found, it is said, on the flanks of Mount Lebanon, above the road that leads to Damascus (that is, cabalistically, to the mercurial female principle: Δάμαρ, woman, wife). It was only seen in the month of May, when spring removes from the earth its shroud of snow.

As soon as night comes, Noel tells us, "this plant begins to ignite and to render light like a little torch; but as soon as day comes, this light disappears, and the grass becomes invisible; the leaves that have been wrapped in handkerchiefs are no longer there, which authorizes the opinion of those who say that this plant is obsessed with demons, because it also has, according to them, an occult property to break the charms and the spells. Others

---

22 *La Génération et Opération du Grand-Œuvre* (The Generation and Operation of the Great Work), ms. of the library from the Palais des Arts, in Lyon, n ° 88 (Delandine, 899), in-folio.

assert that it is suitable for transmuting the metals into gold, and it is for this reason that the Arabs call it the grass of gold; but they would not dare to pluck it, or even to approach it, to have, they say, experienced several times that this plant suddenly kills the one who tears it from the ground without taking the necessary precautions, and, as they ignore these precautions, they leave it without touching it".

From this little subject emerges esoterically the artifice of the solution of sulfur by mercury, the plant expressing the vegetative virtue of it, and the sun, the igneous nature of that one. The operation is all the more important because it leads to the acquisition of philosophical mercury, a living substance, animated, issuing from pure sulfur radically united with primitive and heavenly water. We have said previously that the external character, allowing the certain identification of this water, is a starry and radiant figure which the coagulation made appear on its surface. Let us add that the astral signature of mercury, as it is customary to name the imprint in question, asserts itself with all the more clarity and vigor as the animation progresses and is more complete.

However, the two paths of the Work require two different ways to operate the animation of the initial mercury. The first belongs to the short way and involves a single technique by which the fixed is gradually moistened –for all dry matter eagerly drinks its own humidity–, until the repeated affusion of the volatile on the body makes the compound to swell and converts it into a pasty or syrupy mass, as appropriate. The second method is to digest all the sulfur in three or four times its weight in water, then decant the solution, then dry the residue and resume with a proportional amount of new mercury. When the dissolution is complete, the feces, if any, are separated, and the collected liquors are subjected to a slow distillation in the bath. This releases excess moisture, leaving the mercury in the required consistency, without any loss of its qualities and ready to undergo hermetic coction.

It is this second practice that our bas-relief expresses symbolically.

It is easy to understand that the star –the external manifestation of the internal sun– is represented each time a new portion of mercury comes to bathe the undissolved sulphur, which then ceases to be visible and reappears in the decantation, that is, at the starting point of the astral matter. "Return", says the fixed, "and I'll come back". Seven successive times, the clouds conceal the star from view, sometimes the flower, depending on the phases of the operation, so that the artist can never, during the work, simultaneously see the two elements of the compound. And this truth is confirmed until the end of the Work, since the coction of philosophical mercury, otherwise known as the star or star of the wise, transforms it into fixed sulphur, the fruit of our emblematic plant, whose seed is thus multiplied in quality, quantity and virtue.

Panel 2 (plate XXVII) – In the center of this box, a fruit, which one generally takes for a pear, but which can, with so much likelihood, be an apple or a pomegranate, takes its meaning from the legend under which it appears:

. DIGNA. MERCES. LABORE.   WORK HONORABLY REWARDED

This symbolic fruit is none other than the hermetic gemstone, the philosopher's stone of the Great Work or Medicine of the ancient sages, still called Absolute, Little Coal or Precious Carbuncle (*carbunculus*), the brilliant sun of our microcosm and the star of the eternal wisdom.

This fruit is twofold, because it is gathered from the Tree of Life, reserving it especially for therapeutic uses, and from the Tree of Science, if one prefers to use it to for metallic transmutation. These two faculties correspond to two states of the same product, the first of which characterizes the red, translucent and diaphanous stone, intended for medicine in the quality of drinking gold, and the second, the yellow stone, whose metallic orientation and its fermentation by natural gold have made it opaque. For this reason, De Cyrano Bergerac gives two colors to the fruit of the Magisterium in its description of the emblematic tree at the foot of which it rests. "It was," he writes, "an open country, so open that my sight, from its longest reach, couldn't find a single bush; and yet when I woke I found myself under a tree, in comparison of which the tallest cedars would but appear like grass. Its trunk was solid gold, its branches of silver and its leaves emerald, which, above the brilliant verdure of their precious surface, represented as in a mirror the images of the fruit which hung around it. But judge if the fruit has nothing to do with the leaves! The inflamed scarlet of a big carbuncle made up half of each, and the other was suspended if it held its matter of a chrysolite or a piece of golden amber; the blooming flowers were very broad diamond roses, and the buttons were large pear-shaped pearls".[23]

According to the craftsman skill, care and prudence, the philosophical fruit of the *arbor scientiae* (tree of knowledge) testifies to a more or less extensive virtue. For it is indisputable that the philosopher's stone, used to transmute metals, is never endowed with the same power. Historical projections provide us with clear evidence of this. In the operation carried out by J.-B. Van Helmont, in his laboratory in Vilvoorde, near Brussels, in 1618, the stone transformed into gold 18,740 times its weight of flowing mercury. Richtausen, using the product provided by Labujardière, obtained a result equivalent to 22,334 times the unit. Sethon's 1603 projection at the Frankfurt am Main merchant Coch's in 1603 was 1,155 times. At Dippel's report, the powder Lascaris gave to Dierbach transmuted about 600 times its weight in silver. However, another piece, provided by Lascaris, proved more efficient; in the operation carried out in Vienna in 1716, in the presence of Councillor Pantzer of Hesse, Count Charles-Ernest of Rappach, Count Joseph of Würben and Freudentahl, the brothers Count and Baron of Metternich, the coefficient reached a power of about ten thousand. Moreover, it is worth knowing that the maximum production is achieved by using mercury, and that the same quality of stone provides variable results depending on the nature of the metals used as the base for the projection. The author of the Letters of the Cosmopolitan states that if one part of Elixir converts a thousand parts of ordinary mercury into perfect gold, it will transform only twenty parts of lead, thirty parts of tin, fifty parts of copper and one hundred parts of silver. As for the white stone, it can only act on about half of these quantities at the same degree of multiplication.

But, if the philosophers have spoken little about the variable yield of the chrysopoeia, on the other hand they have been very prolix on the medical properties of the Elixir, as well as on the surprising effects that it allows to obtain in the vegetable kingdom.

"The white elixir," says Batsdorff, "is a marvel of the diseases of all animals, and especially of women, for it is the true drinking moon of the ancients.[24] The Anonymous Author of the Key to the Great Work, taking up Batsdorff's text, asserts that "this medicine has other even more incredible virtues. When it is at the white stage of the elixir, it has so much sympathy with the ladies, that it can renew and make their bodies as robust and

---

23 From Cyrano Bergerac, *L'Autre Monde. Histoire comique des États et Empires du Soleil* (The Other World. Comic history of the States and Empires of the Sun). Paris, Bauche, 1910, p. 42.

24 Batsdorff, *Le Filet d'Ariadne, pour entrer avec seureté dans le Labirinthe de la Philosophie Hermetique* (The Net of Ariadne, to enter safely into the Labyrinth of Hermetic Philosophy). Paris, Laurent d'Houry, 1695, p. 136.

vigorous as they were in their youth. For this purpose, first of all a bath is prepared with many odoriferous herbs with which they must be rubbed well in order to degrease themselves; then they enter a second bath without herbs, but in which three grains of the white elixir have been dissolved in a measure of alcohol, which are then poured into the water. They remain a quarter of an hour in this bath; after which, without wiping, a large fire is made to dry this precious liquor. The ladies then feel so strong in themselves, and their bodies are rendered so white that they cannot imagine it without having experienced it. Our good father Hermes remains in agreement with this operation, but he wishes, besides these baths, that at the same time, for the next seven days, the elixir should be taken internally; and he adds: if a lady does the same thing every year, she will live free from all the diseases to which the other ladies are subject, without feeling any discomfort".[25]

Huginus a Barma certifies that "the stone fermented with gold can be used in medicine in this way: one will take a scruple or twenty-four grains, which one will solve according to the art in two ounces of spirit of wine, and from two or three to four drops, according to the exigency of the disease, in a little wine or some other suitable vehicle".[26] According to the ancient authors, all the affections would be radically cured in a day for those which are a month old; in twelve days if they are one year old; in one month if their origin goes back beyond a year.

But in this, as in many other things, it is necessary to know how to guard against the excesses of imagination; too enthusiastic, the author of *The Key of the Great Work* sees wonders even in the spiritual dissolution of the stone: "ardent golden sparks", claims this writer, "must come out of it, and an infinite number of colors must appear in the vessel". It is going a little far in describing phenomena that no philosopher has ever mentioned. Moreover, he does not recognize any limits to the virtues of the Elixir: "leprosy, gout, paralysis, kidney stone, epilepsy, dropsy, could not resist the virtue of this medicine". And since the cure of these illnesses, which are considered incurable, does not seem sufficient to him, he hastened to add even more admirable properties. "This medicine makes the deaf hear, the blind see, the mute speak, the lame walk; it can renew the whole man, making him change his skin, falling old teeth, nails and white hair, in whose place it makes new ones grow, according to the color you desire". In this way, we fall into humour and buffoonery.

According to the majority of wise men, stone can give excellent results in the vegetable kingdom, especially for fruit trees. In the spring, if the soil is watered near their roots with a highly diluted solution of elixir and rainwater, they are made more resistant to all the causes of wasting and sterility. They produce more and carry healthy, tasty fruits. Batsdorff goes so far as to say that it would be possible, using this process, to cultivate exotic plants under our latitude. "The delicate plants," he wrote, "which have difficulty in coming into climates of a temperament contrary to that which is natural to them, being watered, become as vigorous as if they were in their own land and soil as ordered by Nature".

Among the other wonderful properties attributed to the philosopher's stone, very old authors cite many examples of transformation from crystal to ruby and from quartz to diamond, by means of a sort of progressive soaking. They even consider the possibility of making the glass ductile and malleable, which, despite the affirmation of Cyliani, we will

---

25 *La Clef du Grand-Œuvre, ou Lettres du Sancelrien Tourangeau* (The Key to the Great Work, or Letters from Sancelrien Tourangeau). Paris, Cailleau, 1777, p. 54.

26 *Huginus a Barma, Le Règne de Saturne changé en Siècle d'Or* (The Reign of Saturn changed to Golden Age). Paris, Pierre Derieu, 1780, p. 190.

be careful not to certify, because the way of acting specific to the Elixir –contraction and hardening–, seems contrary to obtain a similar effect.[27]

Anyway, Christophe Merret quotes this opinion and speaks of it in the Preface to his treatise: "As for the malleability of glass," he says, "on which the alchemists base the possibility of their Elixir, it appears supported, but not firmly, on the next passage of Pliny, liv. XXXVI, ch. XXVI: 'It is asserted that in the time of Tiberius there was found a mean of rendering the glass flexible, and that the whole workshop of the worker who was the inventor of it was destroyed, for fear that this discovery would not detract from the price of gold, silver and copper. But this rumor, although quite widespread, is no more true because of it'."

Other authors have recounted the same fact after Pliny, but with a few different circumstances. Dion Cassius, liv. LVII, says: "At the time when the great portico tipped, an architect whose name is unknown (because the jealousy of the emperor prevented it being put in the registers), straightened it and strengthened its foundations. Tiberius, after having paid him, banished him from Rome. This workman came back under the pretext of asking the Emperor's favor, and dropped a glass in his presence, which was hobbled, and which he immediately mended with his hands, hoping thus to obtain what he asked, but he was sentenced to death. Isidore confirms the same thing; he adds only that the emperor, indignant, threw the glass on the pavement, but that the workman having drawn a hammer and having recomposed it, Tiberius asked him if there was anybody who knew this secret, and that the workman having sworn that no one but himself possessed him, the Emperor cut off his head lest he divulged, he did not make gold fall into contempt, and remove their value from metals.[28]

In making allowance for exaggeration and legendary contributions, it is none the less true that the hermetic fruit bears in itself the highest reward that God, through nature, can bestow on men of good will.

Panel 3 (plate XXVII) – The effigy of the Ouroboros serpent stands on the capital of an elegant column. This curious bas-relief is distinguished by the axiom:

. NOSCE. TE. IPSVM.   KNOW THYSELF.

Latin translation of the Greek inscription which appeared on the pediment of the famous temple of Delphi:

ΓΝΩΘΙ ΣΕΑΥΤΟΝ

Know thyself. We have already met, on some ancient manuscripts, a paraphrase of this maxim thus conceived: "You who want to know the stone, know thyself well and you shall know it". Such is the affirmation of the law of analogy which gives, in fact, the key to the mystery. Now, what characterizes our figure precisely is that the column responsible for supporting the emblematic serpent is reversed in relation to the meaning of the inscription. A deliberate, thoughtful, premeditated disposition, giving the whole appearance of a key and that of the graphic sign with which the ancients used to note their mercury. The key and column of the Work are, moreover, epithets applied to mercury, for it is in it that the elements assemble

---

27 "I will not describe here very curious operations which I have made, to my astonishment, in the vegetable and animal kingdoms, as well as the means of making malleable glass, pearls and precious stones more beautiful than the those of nature ... not wishing to be perjured and appear here to pass the limits of the human mind". Cyliani, *Hermès dévoilé* (Hermes unveiled).

28 Neri, Merret and Kunckel, *L'Art de la Verrerie* (The Art of Glassware). Paris, Durand and Pissot, 1752.

in their proper proportion and natural quality; it is from him that everything comes, because, alone, he has the power to dissolve, mortify and destroy the bodies, to dissociate them, to separate the pure portions, to join them to the spirits and thus to generate new metallic beings different from their parents. The authors are therefore right in asserting that all that the wise seek is to be found in mercury alone, and this is what must bring the alchemist to direct his efforts towards the acquisition of this indispensable body.

But in order to achieve this, we advise him to act methodically by studying, in a simple and rational way, the way in which nature operates, in living beings, to transform the absorbed food, freed by digestion of useless substances, into black blood, then in red blood, generator of organic tissues and vital energy. *Nosce te ipsum.* He will thus recognize that the mineral producers of mercury, who are also the artisans of his nutrition, his growth and his life, must first be chosen with discernment and worked with care. For although, theoretically, all can be used for this composition, some are nevertheless too far removed from the active metallic nature to be really useful either because of their impurities or because their maturation was stopped or pushed beyond the term required. Rocks, stones, metalloids belong to the first category; gold and silver enter the second. In the metalloids, the agent we need is lacking in vigor, and his weakness could not be of any use to us; in gold and silver, on the contrary, one would look for it in vain: since Nature has separated him from the perfect bodies because of his appearance on the physical plane.

In stating this truth, we do not mean to say that it is absolutely necessary to proscribe gold and silver, nor to pretend that these metals are excluded from the Work by the masters of science. But we fraternally warn the disciple that there is no gold or silver, even modified, in the composition of mercury. And if we find, in classical authors, some assertion to the contrary, we should believe that the adept means, like Philaletes, Basil Valentine, Nicholas Flamel and Trevisan, philosophical gold or silver, and not precious metals with which they have and have nothing in common.

Panel 4 (plate XXVII) – Put on the bottom of an inverted bushel, a candle burns. This rustic motif has for epigraph:

. SIC. LVCEAT. LVX. VESTRA.   LET YOUR LIGHT SHINE LIKE THIS

Let your light shine like this. The flame indicates for us the metallic spirit, which is the purest, the clearest part of the body, its soul and its own light, although this essential part is the least, considering the quantity . We have often said that the quality of the spirit, being aerial and volatile, always obliges it to rise, and that its nature is to shine, as soon as it is separated from the coarse and corporeal opacity which coats it. It is written that one does not light a candle to put it under the bushel, but on a candlestick, so that it can light all that surrounds it.[29]

In the same way, let us see in the Work the necessity of making manifest this internal fire, this light or this soul, invisible under the hard crust of dense matter. The operation which served the old philosophers to realize this design, was named by them sublimation, although it offers only a distant relation with the ordinary sublimation of the Spagyrists. Because the spirit, quick to disengage itself as soon as it is provided with the means, cannot, however, completely abandon the body; but it makes itself a garment closer to his nature, more supple to its will, from the clear and purified particles that he can reap around itself, in order to use it as a new vehicle. It then reaches the outer surface of the agitated substance and continues to move over the waters, as is said in Genesis (chapter I, 2), until the light appears.

---

29 Matthew, ch. V, 15; Marc, ch. IV, 21; Luke, ch. VIII, 16.

Let us learn, so that the student cannot ignore anything of the practice, that this separation, or sublimation of the body and manifestation of the spirit, must be done gradually and that it must be repeated as many times as it will be judged expedient. Each of these reiterations is called an eagle, and Philaletes tells us that the fifth eagle resolves the moon, but that it is necessary to use seven to nine to reach the characteristic splendor of the sun. The Greek word αἴγλη, from which the sages drew the term of eagle, signifies brightness, bright clarity, light, torch. To fly the eagle, according to the hermetic expression, is to shine the light by uncovering it from its dark envelope and bringing it to the surface. But we will add that, unlike chemical sublimation, the mind being small in relation to the body, our operation provides little of the invigorating and organizing principle we need. Thus, according to the advice of the philosopher of Dampierre, the cautious artist should endeavor to make the occult manifest, and to make that "make that which is below to be above", if he wishes to see the internal metallic light radiate to the outside.

Panel 5 (plate XXVII) – A moving banner highlights here the symbolic meaning of a drawing that has now disappeared. If we believe the *Epigraphie Santone*, it was "a hand holding a spade". There is currently nothing left of it but the phylactery and its inscription, amputated by the last two letters:

. NON . SON . TALES . NVS . AMORES(ES) .   THERE ARE NOT OUT LOVES

These are not our loves. But this solitary Spanish phrase, of vague meaning, hardly allows serious comment. Rather than spreading an erroneous version, we prefer to remain silent on this incomplete ground.

Panel 6 (plate XXVII) – The reasons of impossibility invoked for the precedent bas-relief are also valid for this one. A small quadruped, which the leprous condition of the limestone does not allow to identify, appears enclosed in a bird cage. This motive has suffered a lot. From his motto, one hardly reads two words:

LIBERTA . VER

Belonging to this phrase preserved by some authors:

. AMPANSA. LIBERTA. VERA. CAPI. INTVS.   THIS IS WHERE THE ABUSE OF FREEDOM LEADS

It is probably a reference about the spirit, first free, then imprisoned inside the body as if in a very strong cage. But it also seems obvious that the animal, holding the ordinary place of a bird, brought, by its name or by its species, a special meaning, precise, easy to locate in the work. These elements, essential for the exact interpretation, are missing, so we have to move on to the next box.

Panel 7 (plate XXVII) – Lying on the ground, a unhooked lantern half-open door shows its extinguished candle. The phylactery which signs this subject contains a warning for the use of the impatient and versatile artist:

. SIC . PERIT . INC(N)STANS .   THUS PERISHES THE INCONSTANT

Like the lantern without light, his faith ceases to shine; easily vanquished, unable to react, he falls and vainly seeks, in the darkness that surrounds him, that clarity that can only be found in himself.

But if the inscription offers nothing ambiguous, the image, on the other hand, is much less transparent. This stems from the fact that the interpretation can be given in two ways, regarding which method is employed as well as to the path followed. We first discover an allusion to the fire of the wheel, under pain of being stopped resulting in the consequent loss of materials, cannot cease its action for a moment. Already, in the long way, a slowing of its energy, the lowering of the temperature, are accidents prejudicial to the regular march of the operation; for, if nothing is lost, the time, already considerable, is still increased. An excess of fire spoils everything; however, if the philosophical amalgam is simply reddened, and not calcined, it is possible to regenerate it by dissolving it again, according to the advice of the Cosmopolite, and resuming the coction with more caution. But the complete extinction of the hearth irremediably causes the ruin of the contents, although this one, at the analysis, does not appear to have undergone modification. Also, during the whole course of work, should we remember the hermetic axiom reported by Linthaut, which teaches that "gold, once resolved in spirit, if it feels the cold, is lost with all the Work". Do not, therefore, activate too much the flame inside your lantern, and take care not to let it go out: you will fall from Charybdis into Scylla.

Applied to the short way, the lantern symbol gives us another explanation of one of the essential points of the Great Work. It is no longer the elementary fire, but the potential fire –the secret flame of the very matter–, that the authors steal from the profane under this familiar image. What is this mysterious, natural, unknown fire that the artist must know how to introduce into his subject? This is a question that no philosopher has ever wanted to resolve, even by claiming the help of allegory. Artephius and Pontanus talk about it so obscurely that this important thing remains incomprehensible or passes unanswered. Limojon de Saint-Didier assures that this fire is of the nature of lime. Basile Valentine, usually more prolific, simply writes: "Turn on your lamp and look for the lost drachma". Trismosin is hardly any clearer: "Make a fire in your glass, or in the earth that keeps him locked up". Most of the others refer to this inner light, hidden in the darkness of the substance, under the epithet of lamp fire. Batsdorff describes the philosophical lamp as always having to be abundantly supplied with oil, and its flame fed by an asbestos wick. However, the Greek ἄσβεστος means unquenchable, of unlimited duration, indefatigable, inexhaustible, qualities attributed to our secret fire, which, says Basil Valentine, "does not burn and is not burned". As for the lamp, we find it in the Greek word λαμπτήρ, lantern, torch, which designated the fire vase where wood was burned for lighting. Such is our vessel, the dispenser of the fire of the wise, that is, our matter and its spirit, or, to put it bluntly, the hermetic lantern. Finally, a term similar to λαμπάς, lamp, the term λάμπη, expresses everything that comes and goes to the surface, foam, scum, froth, etc.. And this indicates, for those who possess some kind of scientific tincture, the nature of the body, or, if you prefer, of the mineral envelope containing this lamp fire which only needs to be excited by the ordinary fire to carry out the most surprising metamorphoses.

One more word addressed to our brothers. Hermes, in his Table of Emerald, utters these grave, true and consequent words: "You will separate the earth from the fire, the subtle from the thick, gently, with great industry. He ascends from earth to heaven, and descends from heaven to earth, and thus receives the virtue of higher things and those of inferior things". Notice, then, that the philosopher recommends separating, dividing, not destroying, or sacrificing one to preserve the other. For if it were to be so, we ask you, from what body would the spirit rise, and in what earth would the fire descend?

Pontanus affirms that all superfluousness of the stone are converted, under the action of fire, into a single essence, and that consequently, whoever claims to separate a thing from it, understands nothing of our philosophy.

Panel 8 (Plate XXVII) – Two vases, one in the form of a embossed and engraved flagon, the other, a vulgar pot of earth, are figured in the same frame occupied by this word of Saint Paul:

. ALIVD. VAS. IN. HONOREM. ALIVD. IN. CONTVMELIAM.

ONE VESSEL FOR HONORABLE USE AND ANOTHER FOR VILE EMPLOYMENT.

One vessel for honorable use and another for vile employment. "In a big house, says the Apostle, there are not only vessels of gold and silver, there are also wood and earth; some are reserved for honorable uses, and others for vile uses".[30]

Our two vases thus appear clearly defined, clearly distinguished, and in absolute concordance with the precepts of the hermetic theory. One is the vessel of nature made of the same red clay that served God to form the body of Adam; the other is the vase of art, of whose entire matter is composed of pure gold, clear, red, incombustible, fixed, diaphanous and of incomparable brilliance. And these are our two vessels, which really represent only two distinct bodies containing metal spirits, the only agents we need.

If the reader is aware of how to philosophers write –the traditional way that we will try to imitate as best we can, so that the Ancients can be explained through us, and we can be controlled by them– it will be easy for him to understand what Hermetists hear by their vessels. For these are not only two subjects –or rather the same two-state material of its evolution– but they still symbolize our two paths, based on the use of these different bodies.

The first of these ways, which uses the vase of the art, is long, laborious, ungrateful, accessible to wealthy people, but in great honor, despite the expense it requires, because it is it that the authors preferably describe. It serves as a support for their reasoning, as for the theoretical development of the Work, requires an uninterrupted work of twelve to eighteen months, and starts from the prepared natural gold, dissolved in the philosophical mercury, which is then cooked in a glass matrass. This is the honorable vessel reserved for the noble use of these very precious substances, which are the exalted gold and the mercury of the wise.

The second way requires, from beginning to end, only the help of a vile ground, abundantly spread, so cheap that at our time ten francs are enough to acquire a quantity greater than what is needed. It is the land and the way of the poor, the simple and the modest, those whom nature amazes to its humblest manifestations. Extremely easy, she only asks for the presence of the artist, because the mysterious work is perfect on its own and is completed in seven or nine days at most. This path, ignored by the majority of practicing alchemists, is fully developed in a single crucible of refractory earth. It is the way that the great masters called woman's work and child's play; it is to it that they apply the old hermetic axiom: *una re, una via, una dispositione.* One matter, one vessel, one furnace. Such is our earthen vessel, a despised, vulgar vase of common use, "which everyone has before the eyes, which costs nothing and is found among all people, but which no one can know without revelation".

Panel 9 (Plate XXVII) – Cut by the middle, a snake, in spite of the fatal nature of its wound, thinks however to be able to live a long time in this state.

. DVM. SPIRO. SPERABO.   AS LONG AS I BREATHE, I HOPE

He is told to say. As long as I breathe, I hope.

---

30 Second Epistle of St. Paul to Timothy, ch II, 20.

The serpent, an image of mercury, expresses, by its two sections, the two parts of the dissolved metal, which will later be fixed one by the other, and from the assemblage of which it will take its new nature, its physical individuality, its effectiveness.

Because the sulphur and mercury of metals, extracted and isolated under the disintegrating energy of our first agent, or secret solvent, reduce themselves, by simple contact, to a viscous, greasy and coagulable oil, which the ancients called metallic humid radical and mercury of the sages. It follows that this liqueur, despite its apparent homogeneity, is really composed of the two fundamental elements of all metallic bodies, and that it can logically be considered as representing a liquefied and reincrudated metal, i.e. artificially restored to a state close to its original form. But these elements, being simply associated and not radically united, it seems reasonable that our symbolist should have considered representing mercury as a severed reptile, whose two parts each retain their activity, their mutual virtues. And this is what justifies the exclamation of trust fixed on the lapidary emblem: as long as I breathe, I hope. In this state of simple mixing, philosophical mercury preserves the balance, stability and energy of its constituents, although they are nevertheless destined to mortification and decomposition, which prepare and realize their mutual and perfect interpenetration. Therefore, as long as the mercury has not experienced the embrace of the igneous mediator, it can be stored indefinitely, provided that it is carefully removed from the combined action of air and light. This is what some authors suggest, when they claim that "philosophical mercury always retains its excellent qualities if it is kept in a well sealed bottle"; and we know that in alchemical language any container is said to be sealed, covered, sealed or lined, when it is kept in complete darkness.

VI

Third series (plate XXVIII).

DAMPIERRE-SUR-BOUTONNE
Panel of the Upper Gallery – Third Series – Plate XXVIII

Panel 1 – Standing on its frame, and half dipping into the bucket, a sandstone grinding wheel is waiting for the grinder to put it into action. However, the epigraph of this subject, which should underline its meaning, seems, on the contrary, to have no relation with it; and it is with a certain surprise that one reads this singular inscription:

. DISCIPVLVS. POTIOR. MAGISTRO.

IS THE STUDENT SUPERIOR TO THE MASTER?

We will easily agree that there is little need for serious learning to turn a wheel, and we have never heard that the most skillful of the lowest-income earners, on his rudimentary machine, would have acquired celebrity rights. However useful and honourable it may be, the job of the grinder does not require the contribution of innate gifts, special knowledge, rare technique or the slightest master's certificate. It is therefore certain that the inscription and the image have another meaning, clearly esoteric, which we will interpret.[31]

Considered in its various uses, the millstone is one of the philosophical emblems charged with expressing the hermetic solvent, or that first mercury without which it is quite useless to undertake or hope anything profitable. It is our only material capable of exerting, animating and revivifying the common metals, because they are easily solved in it; they can be divided and adapt to it under the effect of a mysterious affinity. And although this primitive subject does not present the qualities or the power of the philosophical mercury, it nevertheless possesses all that is needed to become it, and it becomes so, provided that the metallic seed, which it lacks, is added to it. Art thus comes to help nature, allowing this clever and wonderful worker to perfect what, for lack of means, of material or favorable circumstances, she must have left unfinished. Now, this initial mercury, subject of art and our true solvent, is precisely the substance that philosophers named the unique matrix, the mother of the Work; without it, it would be impossible for us to achieve the preliminary decomposition of metals, nor, consequently, to obtain the humid radical or mercury of the sages, which is really the stone of the philosophers. So those who pretend to make mercury or stone with all metals are right, and so are those who hold the unity of the raw material and mention it as the only thing necessary.

It is not by chance that the hermetists chose the millstone as the hieroglyphic sign of the subject, and our Adept certainly obeyed the same traditions by giving it a place in the Dampierre panels. We know that the wheels have a circular shape, and that the circle is the conventional signature of our solvent, as well as all bodies likely to evolve by igneous rotation. We find mercury, indicated in this way, on three plates of the *Art of the Potter*,[32] that is to say under the aspect of a millstone, sometimes moved by a mule –cabalistic image of the Greek word μύλη, millstone–, sometimes by a slave or a character of condition, dressed like a prince.

---

31 We can never blame enough those who, hidden and almighty, decided, in Paris, the inexplicable destruction of the very old rue des Nonnains-d'Hyères, which in no way opposed health and offered the remarkable harmony of its 18th century facades. This vandalism, perpetrated on a large scale, led to the loss of the curious sign that adorned the building at No. 5 on the first floor, at the corner of the narrow rue de l'Hôtel-de-Ville, formerly a mortar's shop. Freed from the stone, in a round bump, the motif, of large dimensions, which had kept its original colors, showed a grinder, in his period costume: black tricorn, red frock coat, and white stockings. The man was busy sharpening the iron, in front of his sturdy wheelbarrow, activating the two major elements, namely the hidden fire of his wheel and the rare water that a large hoof seemed to deliver in a thin stream.

32 Cyprian Piccolpassi. *Les Trois Libvres de l'Art du Potier* (The Three Libres of the Potter's Art), translated from Italian into French by Maistre Claudius Popelyn, Parisian. Paris, Librairie Internationale, 1861.

These engravings reflect the double power of the natural solvent, which acts on metals such as grinding on grain or sandstone on steel: it divides them, grinds them, sharpens them. So much so that, after dissociating and partially digesting them, it becomes acidified, takes on a caustic virtue and becomes more penetrating than it was before.

The alchemists of the middle ages used the verb *acuer* (to sharpen) to express the operation which gives the solvent its incisive properties. Now, *acuer* comes from the Latin *acuo*, honing, sharpening, becoming sharp and penetrating, which corresponds not only to the new nature of the subject, but also accords with the role of the grinding wheel.

Who is the master of this work? Obviously, the one who sharpens and turns the wheel –this grinder absent from the bas-relief–, i. e. the active sulphur of the dissolved metal. As for the disciple, he represents the first mercury, of cold and passive quality, which some call faithful and loyal servant, and others, in view of its volatility, *servus fugitivus*, the runaway slave. We can therefore answer the philosopher's question that, given the very difference in their conditions, the student will never be able to rise above the master; but we can assure, on the other hand, that with time, the disciple, who has become master in his turn, will become the alter ego of his preceptor. For while the master lowers himself to the level of his inferior in dissolution, he will elevate him with him in coagulation, and the fixation will make them similar to each other, equal in virtue, value and power.

Panel 2 (plate XXVIII) – The head of Medusa, placed on a pedestal, shows her severe grin and her hair interlaced with serpents; it is decorated with the Latin inscription:

. CVSTOS. RERVM. PRVDENTIA.   PRUDENCE IS THE GUARDIAN OF THINGS

Prudence is the guardian of things. But the word prudential has a wider meaning than prudence or foresight; it still denotes science, wisdom, experience, knowledge. Epigram and figure agree to represent, in this bas-relief, the secret science concealed under the multiple and varied hieroglyphs of the panels of Dampierre.

Indeed, the Greek name Μέδοισα, Medusa, has for root μῆδος and expresses the thought of which one deals, the favorite study; μῆδος has formed μηδοσύνη, whose meaning evokes prudence and wisdom. On the other hand, the mythologists teach us that Medusa was known to the Greeks under the name of Γοργώ, that is to say the Gorgon, which also served to qualify Minerva or Pallas, goddess of Wisdom. Perhaps the secret reason of the aegis, shield of Minerva, covered with the skin of Amalthea, nurse's goat of Jupiter, and decorated with the mask of Medusa Ophiotrix, would be discovered in this connection. In addition to bringing together the goat and the ram –the latter wearing the golden fleece, the one provided with the cornucopia– we know that the attribute of Athena had the petrifying power. Jellyfish, it is said, changed into stone those whose eyes met his. Finally, the very names of the sisters of Medusa, Euryale and Stheno, also bring their share of revelation. Euryale, in Greek Εὐρύαλος, means that the area is wide, vast, spacious; Stheno comes from Σθένος, strength, power, energy. This is how the three Gorgons symbolically express the idea of power and scope proper to natural philosophy.

These convergent relations, which we are forbidden to expose more clearly, make it possible to conclude that, apart from the precise esoteric fact but barely scratched, our motive is to indicate wisdom as the source and guardian of all our knowledge, the sure guide of the industrious to whom she discovers the secrets hidden in nature.

Panel 3 (Plate XXVIII) – On the altar of sacrifice, a forearm is consumed by fire. The sign of this igneous emblem is in two words:

. FELIX. INFORTVNIVM.   HAPPY MISFORTUNE

Although the subject seems, a priori, very obscure and unparalleled in hermetic literature and iconography, it nevertheless gives way to analysis and accords perfectly with the technique of the Work.

The human forearm, which the Greeks simply called the arm, βραχίων, serves as a hieroglyph for the short and abbreviated way. In fact, our Adept, playing on words as the learned cabalist he is, conceals under the substantive βραχίων, arms, a comparative of βραχύς, which is written and pronounced in the same way. This one means short, in short, of short duration, and forms several compounds, of which βραχύτης, brevity. Thus the comparative βραχίων, in short, homonymous of βραχίων, arm, takes the particular meaning of brief technique, ars brevis.

But the Greeks still used another expression to describe the arm. When they evoked the hand, χείρ, they applied, by extension, the idea to the whole upper limb, and gave it the figurative value of an artistic production, skilful, of a special process, in a personal way of work, in a nutshell of a hand acquired or revealed. All these acceptations characterize exactly the finesse of the Great Work in its prompt, simple and direct realization, since it only requires the application of a very energetic fire, which is reduced to the whim of the hand in question. Now, this fire is not only figured, on our bas-relief, by the flames, it is still represented by the member itself, which the hand indicates as being the right arm; and it is well known that the proverbial phrase "to be the right arm" always refers to the agent in charge of executing the wishes of a superior –the fire in this case.

Alongside these reasons –necessarily abstract because they are veiled in the lapidary form of a concise image–, there is another, concrete reason which supports and confirms, in the practical field, the esoteric filiation of the former. We will state it by saying that anyone who, ignoring the trick of the operation, risks undertaking it, must fear everything from the fire; it is in real danger and can hardly escape the consequences of an ill-considered and reckless act. Why, then, will we be told not to divulge this method? We will answer that to reveal such a manipulation would be to reveal the secret of the short way, and that we have not received from God or from our brothers the authorization to discover such a mystery. It is already a lot that we push solicitude and charity to the point of alerting the beginner, that his lucky star would lead to the door of the lair, to be on his guard and to redouble his caution. A similar warning is hardly found in the books, which are very succinct on all that concerns the brief Work, but which the Dampierre Adept knew as well as Ripley, Basil Valentine, Philaletes, Albert the Great, Huginus a Barma, Cyliani or Naxagoras.

However, and because we consider it useful to warn the neophyte, it would be wrong to conclude that we were trying to repel him. If he wants to risk the adventure, let it be for him the test of fire, to which the future initiates of Thebes and Hermopolis were to submit, before receiving the sublime teachings. Is not the fiery arm on the altar an expressive symbol of the sacrifice, the renunciation required by science? Everything is paid here below, not with gold, but with pain, with suffering, often leaving a part of oneself; and one cannot pay too dearly for the possession of the least secret, the most minute truth. If, therefore, the aspirant feels endowed with the faith and armed with the necessary courage, we will wish him fraternally to come out safe from this harsh experience, which ends most often by the explosion of the crucible and the projection of the oven. Then will he be able to exclaim, like our philosopher: happy misfortune! For the accident, compelling him to reflect on the fault committed, will undoubtedly reveal to him the means of being able to avoid it, and the trick of the regular operation.

Panel 4 (plate XXVIII) – Fixed on a tree trunk covered with leaves and loaded with fruit, an unrolled banner bears the inscription:

. MELIVS. SPE. LICEBAT.   SOMETHING BETTER COULD BE EXPECTED.

This is an image of the solar tree that the Cosmopolite points out in his allegory of the green forest, which he tells us belongs to the nymph Venus. About this metal tree, the author, recounting how the old Saturn works in the presence of the lost puffer, says that he took fruit from the solar tree, put it in ten parts of a certain water –very rare and difficult to obtain–, and easily dissolved it.

Our Adept thus intends to speak of the first sulfur, which is the gold of the sages, green, unripe fruit of the tree of knowledge. While the Latin phrase betrays some disappointment with a normal result, which many artists would be very happy to obtain, it is because by means that we cannot achieve the transmutation with this sulfur. The philosophical gold, in fact, is not the stone; Philaletes is careful to warn the student that this is only the first matter. And as this sulfur principle, according to the same author, requires an uninterrupted labor of about a hundred and fifty days, it is logical, and especially human, to think that such a mediocre result in appearance cannot satisfy the artist, who expected to reach the elixir in one go, as it happens in the short way.

At this point, the apprentice must recognize the impossibility of continuing the work, by continuing the operation that provided him with the first sulphur. If he wants to go further, he must go back on his steps, undertake a second cycle of new trials, plough a year and sometimes more before reaching the first order stone. But if discouragement does not reach him, let him follow the example of Saturn and dissolve again in mercury, in the proportions indicated, this green fruit that divine goodness has allowed him to pick, and he will then see, with his own eyes, all the appearances of a progressive and perfect maturation. We cannot remind him enough, however, that he is on a long and painful path, strewn with brambles and dug by potholes; that art, having more to do with it than nature, and with opportunities to wander, there are also more schools. He should preferably direct his attention to the mercury which the philosophers have sometimes called double, not without cause, and other times ardent or sharp and actuated with its own salt. You must know, before you make the sulphur solution, that your first water –the one that gave you the philosophical gold– is too simple and weak to serve as food for this solar seed. And in order to overcome the difficulty, let him try to understand the allegory of Nicolas Flamel's *Massacre of the Innocents*, as well as Limojon's explanation, as clearly as an art master can do.[33] As soon as he knows what these spirits of the bodies designated by the blood of the innocent slaughtered are, in metal terms, how the alchemist differentiates between the two mercuries, he will have overcome the last obstacle and nothing, afterwards, except his impatience, will be able to frustrate him with the expected result.

Plate 5 (plate XXVIII) – Two pilgrims, each provided with a rosary, meet near a building –church or chapel–, which can be seen in the background. Of these very old men, bald, with long beards and the same clothes, one supports his march with the help of a stick;

---

33 Limojon de Saint-Didier. *Lettre aux vrays Disciples d'Hermès* (Letter to the true Disciples of Hermes), in the *Triomphe Hermétique* (Hermetic Triumph). Amsterdam, Henry Wetstein, 1699.

the other, whose skull is protected by a thick cap, seems to manifest a lively surprise at the adventure, and exclaims:

.TROPT.TARD.COGNEU. TROPT.TOST . LAISSE.　　*KNOW TOO LATE, ABANDONED TOO EARLY*

Word of a disappointed puffer, happy to finally recognize, at the end of his long journey, this humid radical so ardently desired, but sorry to have lost, in vain work, the physical strength essential to the realization of the Work with this best companion. For it is indeed our faithful servant, mercury, who is shown here as the first old man. A slight detail points it out to the discerning observer: the rosary it holds forms, with the drone, the image of the caduceus, a symbolic attribute of Hermes. On the other hand, we have frequently said that dissolving matter is commonly recognized, among all philosophers, as the old man, the pilgrim and the traveller of the great Art, as Michel Maïer, Stolcius and many other masters teach.

As for the old alchemist, so happy of this meeting, if he has not known so far where to find the mercury, it shows enough how yet matter is familiar to him, because his own rosary, hieroglyph speaking, represents the circle surmounted by the cross, symbol of the globe and signature of our little world. We understand then why the unfortunate artist regrets this too late knowledge, and his ignorance of a common substance, which he had within reach, without ever thinking that it could provide him the mysterious water vainly sought elsewhere ...

Panel 6 (plate XXVIII) – In this bas-relief are three neighboring trees, and of such magnitude; two of these show their trunks and their dried branches, while the last, remaining healthy and vigorous, seems to be both the cause and the result of the death of others. This motive is adorned with the motto:

. SI . IN . VIRIDI . IN . ARIDO . QUID .
IF IT IS SO IN THE GREEN THINGS, WHAT WILL IT BE IN THE DRY?

Our philosopher thus lays down the principle of the analogical method, the only means, the only resource available to the hermetist for the resolution of natural secrets. We can therefore answer, according to this principle, that what happens in the plant kingdom must find its equivalence in the mineral kingdom. Consequently, if the dry and dead trees give up their share of food and vitality to the survivor planted next to them, it is logical to consider the latter as their heir, the one to whom, by dying, they bequeathed the full enjoyment of the means from which they derived their livelihood. From this perspective and from this point of view, he appears to us as their son or descendant. The three trees thus constitute a transparent emblem of the way in which the stone of philosophers is born, the first being or subject of the philosopher's stone.

The author of *Le Triomphe Hermétique* (The Hermetic Triumph), correcting the erroneous assertion of his predecessor, Pierre-Jean Fabre, says clearly that "our stone is born from the destruction of two bodies".[34] We will specify that, of these bodies, one is metallic, the other mineral, and that they both grow in the same soil. The tyrannical opposition of their contrary temperament prevents them from ever agreeing, except when the artist's will obliges them to do so, by subjecting these resolved antagonists to the violent action of fire. After a long and hard struggle, they perished exhausted; from their decomposition a third body was born, heir to the vital energy and mixed qualities of his deceased parents.

---

34 Limojon de Saint Didier, *Le Triomphe Hermétique* (The Hermetic Triumph). Amsterdam, Desbordes, 1710, p. A 4.

Such is the origin of our stone, provided from birth with the double metallic disposition, which is dry and igneous, and the double mineral virtue, whose essence is to be cold and damp. Thus it achieves, in its state of perfect equilibrium, the union of the four natural elements, which are found at the base of all experimental philosophy. The heat of the fire is tempered by the frigidity of the air, and the drought of the earth neutralized by the humidity of the water.

Panel 7 (Plate XXVIII) – The geometrical figure we meet here frequently adorned the frontispieces of the alchemical manuscripts of the Middle Ages. It was commonly called Solomon's Labyrinth , and we have elsewhere reported that it was reproduced on the pavement of our great Gothic cathedrals. This figure carries for motto:

. FATA. VIAM. INVENIENT.   THE FATES WILL FIND THEIR WAY.

Our bas-relief, characterizing only the long path, reveals the formal intention, expressed by the plurality of Dampierre's motifs, to teach above all the Work of the Rich. For this labyrinth offers us only one entrance, while the drawings of the same subject generally show three of them, which correspond, moreover, to the three porches of the Gothic cathedrals placed under the invocation of the Virgin Mother. One, absolutely straight, leads directly to the middle chamber –where Theseus kills the Minotaur–, without encountering the slightest obstacle; it reflects the short, simple, easy path of the Work of the poor. The second, which also leads to the center, only leads to it after a series of detours, returns, convolutions; it is the hieroglyph of the long way, and we have said that it refers to the preferred esotericism of our Adept. Finally, a third gallery, whose opening is parallel to the previous ones, suddenly ends in a dead end, at a short distance from the threshold, and leads to nothing. It causes the despair and ruin of the wandering, the presumptuous, of those who, without serious study, without solid principles, nevertheless set out on their journey and risk adventure.

Whatever their shape, the complication of their layout, the labyrinths are the talking symbols of the Great Work considered in relation to its material realization. We therefore see them as responsible for expressing the two major difficulties involved in the work: 1° access to the inner chamber; 2° the possibility of leaving it. From these two points, the first looks at the knowledge of the material –which ensures the entry–, and that of its preparation –which the artist accomplishes at the centre of the maze. The second concerns the mutation, by the help of fire, of the prepared matter. The alchemist therefore repeats, in the opposite direction, but with caution, slowness, perseverance, the journey quickly made at the beginning of his work. In order not to get lost, philosophers advise him to locate his path at the beginning –for the operations that we could call analytical–, by using this Thread of Ariadne,[35] without which he would most likely not be able to return from it –that is to say to get lost in the work of synthetic unification. It is to this second phase or period of the Work that the Latin sign of the labyrinth applies. Indeed, from the moment when compost, made up of vitalized bodies, begins to evolve, the most impenetrable mystery then covers with its veil the order, measure, rhythm, harmony and progress of this admirable metamorphosis that man does not have the ability to understand or explain. Abandoned to its own fate, subjected to the torments of fire in the darkness of its narrow prison, the regenerated matter follows the secret path traced by destinies.

---

35 Ariadne gave Teseo a ball of red thread, which allowed him to escape from the Labyrinth after he killed the Minotaur, a beast half bull and half man.

Panel 8 (Plate XXVIII) – Drawing erased, sculpture disappeared. Only the inscription remains, and the sharpness of its engraving contrasts with the bare uniformity of the surrounding limestone; it reads:

. MICHI. CELVM.   THE SKY IS MINE

Exclamation of ardent enthusiasm, of exuberant joy, cry of pride, it will be said, of the Adept in possession of the Magisterium. Perhaps. But is this what the author's thought is meant to imply? We allow ourselves to doubt this because, based on so many serious and positive motives, epigraphs in the weighted sense, we prefer to see there the expression of a radiant hope directed towards the knowledge of celestial things, rather than the presumptuous and baroque idea of an illusory conquest of the empyrean.

It is obvious that the philosopher, having achieved the tangible result of hermetic labor, no longer ignores the power, the preponderance of the spirit, nor the truly prodigious action he exerts on the inert substance. Strength, will, science itself belong to the spirit; life is the consequence of its activity; movement, evolution, progress are the results. And since everything comes from it, that everything is generated and discovered by it, it is reasonable to believe that in the end everything must necessarily return to it. It is therefore sufficient to observe its manifestations in the serious matter, to study the laws to which it seems to obey, to know its directives to acquire some notion of the things and the first laws of the universe. Thus, it is possible to maintain the hope of obtaining, by simply examining spiritual labor in the hermetic work, the elements of a less vague conception of the divine Great Work, the Creator and the things created. What is below is similar to what is above, said Hermes; and it is by the persevering study of all that is accessible to us, that we can elevate our intelligence to the understanding of the inaccessible. This is the idea that emerged, in the ideal of the philosopher, of the fusion of the human spirit and the divine spirit, of the return of the creature to the Creator, to the ardent, unique and pure focus from which the martyred, laborious, immortal spark had to escape, on God's command, to associate itself with the vile matter, until the past accomplishment of its earthly journey.

Panel 9 (Plate XXVIII) – Our predecessors have recognized, in this little subject, only the symbol attributed to the King of France Henry II. It consists of a simple lunar crescent, which this motto accompanies:

. DONEC. TOTVM. IMPLEAT. ORBEM.   UNTIL HE FILLS THE WHOLE EARTH

We do not believe that the interpretation of this emblem, to which Diane de Poitiers remains completely foreign, can lend itself to the slightest ambiguity. The youngest of the "sons of science" is well aware that the moon, the spagyric hieroglyphic of silver, marks the final goal of the *Work to White* and the transition period of the *Work to Red*. It is in the reign of the moon that the characteristic colour of silver, i. e. white, appears. Artephius, Nicholas Flamel, Philaletes and many other masters teach that at this phase of coction, the rebis offers the appearance of fine, silky threads, hair stretched to the surface and moving from the periphery to the centre. Hence the name capillary whiteness, which is used to describe this coloring. The moon, the texts say, is then in its first quarter. Under the influence of fire, the whiteness increases in depth, reaches the entire mass and turns, on the surface, to lemon yellow. It is the full moon; the crescent has grown to form the perfect lunar disc: it has completely filled the orb. The material is provided with a certain degree of fixity and dryness, which are sure signs of the completion of the little Magisterium. If the artist does not wish to go any further or cannot lead the Work to the red, all he has to do is multiply this stone, starting again with the same operations, to increase it in power and virtue. And these repetitions can be renewed as many times as the matter allows, that is, as long as it is saturated with its spirit and that it "fills the whole earth with it". Beyond the saturation point, its properties change; too subtle, it can no longer be coagulated; it remains in thick oil, bright in the dark, now without any action on living beings or metal bodies.

What is true for the White Work is also true for the Grand Magisterium. In the latter, it is sufficient only to increase the temperature, as soon as the citrine whiteness has been obtained, without however touching or opening the vessel, and on condition that the red ferment has initially been substituted for white sulphur. This is, at least, what Philaletes recommends and does not do Flamel, although their apparent disagreement is easily explained if the guidelines of the ways and operations are well known. In any case, by continuing the action of the fourth degree of fire, the compost will dissolve itself, new colors will follow one another until a weak red, called peachtree flower, gradually becoming more intense as the dryness spreads, announces the success and perfection of the work. When cooled, the material offers a crystalline texture, made, it seems, of small agglomerated rubies, rarely free, always of high density and brightness, frequently embedded in an amorphous, opaque and red mass, called by the ancients the damned earth of stone. This residue, which is easy to separate, is of no use and must be discarded.

VII

Fourth series (Plate XXIX).

DAMPIERRE-SUR-BOUTONNE
Panel of the Upper Gallery – Fourth Series – Plate XXIX

Panel 1 – This bas-relief presents us with a rock which the furious sea attacks and threatens to engulf; but two cherubim blow on the waves and soothe the storm. The phylactery that accompanies this figure exalts *constancy in the perils*:

. IN. PERICVLIS. CONSTANTIA.   CONSTANCY IN THE PERILS

A philosophical virtue that the artist must know to keep during the course of the coction, and especially at the beginning of it, when the unleashed elements collide and repel each other with violence. Later, despite the length of this ungrateful phase, the yoke is less painful to bear, because the effervescence calms down, and peace is finally born from the triumph of the spiritual elements –air and fire–, symbolized by the angels, agents of our mysterious elementary conversion. But, with regard to this conversion, perhaps it is not superfluous to provide here some details on how the phenomenon is carried out, on which the elders have shown, in our opinion, an excessive reserve.

Every alchemist knows that stone is composed of the four elements united, by a powerful cohesion, in a state of natural and perfect balance. What is less well known is the way in which these four elements are resolved into three physical principles, which the artist prepares and assembles according to the rules of the art, taking into account the required conditions. However, these primary elements, represented in our box by the sea (water), the rock (earth), the sky (air), and the cherubs (light, spirit, fire), are reduced to salt, sulphur and mercury, material and tangible principles of our stone. Of these principles, two are considered simple, sulphur and mercury, because they occur naturally combined in the body of metals; only one, salt, appears to consist partly of a fixed substance, partly of volatile matter. In chemistry, we know that salts, formed by an acid and a base, reveal, by their decomposition, the volatility of one, as well as the fixity of the other. As salt participates in both the mercurial principle through its cold and volatile humidity (air) and the sulphurous principle through its igneous and fixed dryness (fire), it therefore acts as a mediator between the sulphur and mercury components of our embryo. Thanks to its double quality, salt makes it possible to achieve the conjunction, which would be impossible without it, between one and the other of the antagonists, effective parents of the hermetic little king. Thus, the first four elements are assembled in pairs in the stone in formation, because the salt has in it the fire and air necessary for the assembly of sulphur-earth and mercury-water.

However, and although the saline components are close to the sulphurous and mercurial natures (because fire always seeks earthly food and the air willingly mixes with water), they do not have such an affinity for the material and weighting principles of the Work, sulphur and mercury, that their presence alone, their catalysis, is capable of avoiding any disagreement in this philosophical marriage. On the contrary, it is only after long debates and multiple shocks that air and fire, breaking their saline association, act together to restore harmony between enemies separated by a simple difference in evolution.

Hence we must conclude, in the theoretical explanation of the conversion of the elements and their indissoluble union to the state of Elixir, that salt is the only instrument of lasting harmony, the instigator of a stable and fruitful peace into happy results. And this peaceful mediator, not content to intervene constantly during the slow, tumultuous and chaotic elaboration of our mixtion, still contributes, of his own substance, to nourish and strengthen the newly formed body. Image of the Good Shepherd, who gives his life for his sheep, the philosophical salt, his role finished, dies so that our young monarch can live, grow, extend his sovereign will over all metallic nature.

Panel 2 (plate XXIX) – Moisture gnawed the bottom table by depriving it of the relief it once had. The imprecise and frustrated roughness that still exists could belong to some plants. The inscription has suffered a lot; some letters only have been able to resist the insult of time:

. . M. RI. . . V. RV. .

It is impossible, with so few elements, to restore the sentence; however, according to the book entitled *Landscapes and Monuments of Poitou*, which we have already mentioned, the plants are ears of wheat and the inscription should be read

. MIHI. MORI. LVCRVM.   DEATH IS A GAIN FOR ME

It is an allusion to the necessity of the mortification and the decomposition of our mineral seed. For just as a grain of wheat could not germinate, produce, and multiply if it had not previously been liquefied in the earth, so is it essential to cause the disintegration of the philosopher's rebis, where the seed is included, to generate a new being, of a similar nature, but capable of increasing itself, both in weight and volume as in power and virtue. In the center of the compound, the enclosed, living, immortal spirit, always ready to manifest its action, only waits for the decomposition of the body, the dislocation of its parts, to work on the purification and then the repair of the substance and clarified with the help of fire.

It is therefore the matter, still gross, of the philosophical mercury which speaks in the epigraph *Mihi mori lucrum*. Not only does death give him the benefit of a corporal envelope much more noble than the first, but it also gives him a vital energy which she did not possess, and the generative faculty of which a bad constitution had so far then private

This is the reason why our Adept, in order to give a sensible image of the hermetic regeneration by the death of compost, has carved ears under the parabolic motto of this little subject.

Panel 3 (plate XXIX) – Leaving thick clouds, a hand whose forearm is ulcerated, holds an olive branch. This coat of arms, of a morbid character, has for sign:

. PRVDENTI. LINITVR. DOLOR.   THE SAGE KNOWS HOW TO APPEASE THE PAIN

The olive branch, a symbol of peace and concord, marks the perfect union of the generative elements of the philosopher's stone. Now this stone, by the certain knowledge that it brings, by the truths that it reveals to the philosopher, enables him to dominate the moral sufferings which affect other men, and to overcome the physical pains by suppressing the cause and the effects of a large number of diseases.

The very elixir's elaboration shows him that death, a necessary transformation, but not a real annihilation, must not afflict him. On the contrary, the soul, liberated from the bodily burden, enjoys, in full swing, a marvelous independence, bathed in that ineffable light, accessible only to pure spirits. He knows that the phases of material vitality and spiritual existence succeed each other according to the laws which govern its rhythm and periods. The soul leaves its earthly body only to animate a new one. The old man of yesterday is the child of tomorrow. The missing ones are found again, the lost ones get closer, the dead are reborn. And the mysterious attraction which binds together beings and things of similar evolution unites those who are still alive and those who are no longer. There is no true, absolute separation for the initiate, and the absence alone cannot cause him grief. He will easily recognize the objects of his affections, even though they are clothed in a different envelope, because the spirit, of immortal essence and endowed with eternal memory, will know how to make them be discerned...

These certainties, materially controlled throughout the labor of the Work, assure him an undeniable moral serenity, calm amidst human agitations, contempt for worldly joys, resolute stoicism and, above all, the powerful comfort that the secret knowledge of his origins and destiny gives him.

On the physical level, the medicinal properties of the Elixir protect its lucky possessor from defects and physiological misery. Thanks to it, the wise man knows how to ease his pain. Batsdorff certifies that it cures all external diseases of the body, ulcers, scrofula, excrescences, paralysis, wounds and such other conditions, being dissolved in a suitable liquor and applied to the evil, by means of a cloth soaked in the liquor.[36] For his part, the author of an illuminated alchemical manuscript also praises the high virtues of the sages' medicine. "The Elixir," he wrote, "is a divine ash, more miraculous than otherwise, and leaves, as we can see, according to the necessity that arises, and refuses no one, both for the health of the human body and the nourishment of this decaying and transitory life, and for the resurrection of imperfect metallic bodies... In truth, it exceeds all the most excellent theriaca and medicines that men can do, however subtle they may be. It makes the man who possesses it blessed, grave, prosperous, notable, bold, robust, magnanimous".[37] Finally, Jacques Tesson gives the new converts wise advice on the use of the universal balm. "We have spoken" –says the author, addressing the object of art–, "of the fruit of blessing that came from you; now we will say how you should apply; it is to relieve the poor, not the worldly pumps; it is to heal the needy cripples, not the great and powerful of the earth. For we must be careful who we give to, and know who we must relieve, in the infirmities and diseases that afflict the human race. Administer this powerful remedy only through an inspiration from God, who sees everything, knows everything, orders everything".[38]

Panel 4 (plate XXIX) – Here is one of the major symbols of the Great Work: the figure of the Gnostic circle, formed by the body of the serpent that devours its tail, with, for motto, the Latin word

. AMICITIA.   FRIENDSHIP

The circular image is, in fact, the geometric expression of unity, affinity, balance and harmony. All the points of the circumference being equidistant from the center and in close contact with each other, they realize a continuous and closed orb, which has no beginning and can not have an end, just as God in metaphysics, infinity in space and eternity in time.

The Greeks called this snake Ouroboros, the words οὐρά, tail, and βορός, devouring. In the Middle Ages, it was assimilated to the dragon by imposing on it an esoteric attitude and value similar to that of the Hellenic snake. This is the reason for the associations of reptiles, natural or fabulous, that are almost always found among old authors. *Draco aut serpens qui caudam devoravit; serpens aut lacerta viridis quæ propriam caudam devoravit*, etc.,[39] they frequently write. On monuments, on the other hand, the dragon, allowing more movement and picturesque in the decorative composition, seems to appeal more to artists; it is the one they prefer to

---

36 *Le Filet d'Ariadne* (The Thread of Ariadne), Op. cit., p. 140.

37 *La Génération et Opération du Grand-Œuvre* (The Generation and Operation of the Great Work). library of Lyon. Ms. cité.

38 Jacques Tesson. *Le Grand et Excellent Œuvre des Sages, contenant trois traités ou dialogues. Dialogues du Lyon verd, du Grand Thériaque et du Régime* (The Great and Excellent Work of the Wise, containing three treatises or dialogues. Dialogues of the Lyon verd, the Grand Thériaque and the Diet). Ms. from the 17th century. Library de Lyon, n° 971 (900).

39 Dragons or serpents that swallow its own tail; serpents or green lizards swallowing their own tails.

represent. This can be seen at the north portal of Saint-Armel church in Ploermel (Morbihan), where several dragons clinging to the crawling gables make the wheel by biting their tails. The famous Amiens stalls also offer a curious figure of a horse-headed dragon with a winged body, finished by a decorative tail whose end is devoured by the monster.

Given the importance of this emblem –it is, with the seal of Solomon, the distinctive sign of the Great Work–, its meaning remains open to varied interpretations. Hieroglyph of absolute union, of indissolubility of the four elements and of the two principles brought back to unity in the philosopher's stone, this universality allows its use and attribution to the various phases of the Work, since all aim at the same goal and are oriented towards the assembly, the homogeneity of the first natures, the mutation of their native antipathy into solid and stable friendship. Generally, the head of the dragon or the Ouroboros marks the fixed part, and its tail the volatile part of the compound. This is how Marc Fra Antonio's commentator hears it: "This earth, he says of sulphur, by its igneous and innate dryness, draws its own wetness to itself and consumes it; and because of this, it is compared to the dragon that devours its tail. Moreover, it only attracts and assimilates its wetness because it is of the same nature".[40] Other philosophers make a different application, witness Linthaut, who relates it to the colored periods: "There are, he writes, three main colors that must be shown in the Work, black, white, red. The darkness, the first color, is called the Ancient Poisonous Dragon, when they say: the dragon will devour its own tail".[41] Esotericism is equivalent in Georges Aurach's *The Most Precious Gift of God*. David de Planis Campy, further from the doctrine, sees only a version of spagyric cohobations.

As for us, we have always understood the Ouroboros as a complete symbol of the alchemical work and its result. But, whatever may be the opinion of the scientists of our time in this figure, we may at least be certain that all the attributes of Dampierre, placed under the aegis of the snake biting its tail, are exclusively related to the Great Work and present a particular character, conforming to the secret teaching of hermetic science.

Panel 5 (plate XXIX) – Another vanished subject from which we cannot decipher anything. Some incoherent letters appear only on the disintegrating limestone:

... CO. PIA...

Panel 6 (plate XXIX) – A large star with six rays shines on the waves of a moving sea. Above her, the banner bears the Latin motto, the first word of which is written in Spanish:

. LVZ. IN. TENEBRIS. LVCET.   THE LIGHT SHINES IN THE DARKNESS

It will probably come as a surprise that we take for waves what others think are clouds. But by studying the way in which the sculptor represents water and clouds elsewhere, we will quickly be convinced that there is no error, misunderstanding or bad faith on our part. By this sea star, however, the author of the image does not claim to represent the common asteria, commonly known as a starfish. It has only five radiant arms, while ours has six distinct branches. We must therefore see here the indication of starry water, which is none other than

---

40 *La Lumière sortant par soy-mesme des Ténèbres, ou Véritable Théorie de la Pierre des Philosophes, écrite en vers italiens...* (The Light Coming Out by Itself from the Darkness, or True Theory of the Stone of Philosophers, written in Italian verses...). Paris, L. d'Houry, 1687, p. 271.

41 Henri de Lintaut. *Commentaire sur le Trésor des Trésors de Christophe de Gamon* (Commentary on Christophe de Gamon's Treasure of Treasures). Paris, Claude Morillon, 1610, p. 133.

our prepared mercury, our Virgin Mother and her symbol, *Stella Maris*,[42] mercury obtained in the form of white and brilliant metallic water, which philosophers still call the star (from the Greek ἀστήρ, brilliant, radiant). Thus the work of art makes manifest and external what was previously diffused in the dark, coarse and vile mass of the primitive subject. From the dark chaos, he brings forth the light after gathering it, and this light now shines in the darkness, like a star in the night sky. All chemists have known and know this subject, although very few know how to extract the radiant quintessence, so strongly buried in the earth and the opacity of the body. This is why Philaletes recommends that the student not despise the astral signature, which reveals the prepared mercury. "Take care," he said, "to set your course by the North Star, which our magnet will make you appear. Then the wise man will rejoice; the fool, however, will regard this as a small thing. He will not learn wisdom and will even look at, without understanding its value, this central pole made of intersecting lines, a wonderful mark of the Almighty".[43]

Highly intrigued by this star, whose importance and meaning he could not explain to himself, Hoefer addressed the Hebrew Cabala. "Iesod (דסֹי), he writes, means both foundation and mercury, because mercury is the foundation of transmutatory art. The nature of mercury is indicated by the names יח לא (Living God), whose letters produce, by their summation, the number 49, which is also given by the letters בכוב (cocaf), star. But what meaning should be attached to the word בכוב? Let us listen to Kabbalah: "The character of true mercury consists in covering itself, by the action of heat, with a film more or less approaching the color of gold; and this can be done even in the space of a single night. "This is the mystery indicated by the word בכוב, star".[44] This exegesis does not satisfy us. A film, of whatever color it may be, bears no resemblance to starry radiation, and our own work guarantees us an effective signature, which has all the geometric and regular characters of a perfectly drawn star. Therefore, we prefer the language, less chemical but more true, of the ancient masters, to this cabalistic description of the red oxide of hydrargyrum. "It is the nature of light, says the author of a famous book, not to be able to appear in our eyes without being clothed in some body, and this body must also be able to receive light; where light is, therefore, there must also necessarily be the vehicle of this light. This is the easiest way to avoid wandering. Seek therefore with the light of your spirit, the light that is enveloped in darkness, and learn from there that the most vile subject of all according to the ignoramuses, is the most noble according to the sages".[45]

In an allegorical account of the preparation of mercury, Trismosin is even more categorical; he affirms, as we do, the visual reality of the hermetic seal. "On the spot of the day," said our author, "we empty a very shining star over the king's person, and the daylight illuminated the darkness".[46] As for the mercurial nature of the support of the star (which is the sky of philosophers), Nicolas Valois gives us a clear idea of it in the following passage: "The wise men", he said, "call their sea the whole Work, and as soon as the body is reduced to water, of which it was first composed, this is called sea water, because it is truly a sea, in which many wise navigators have been shipwrecked, not having this star as their guide, which will never fail those who once knew it. It is this star that leads the Wise Men to the birth of the

---

42 The Star of the Sea.
43 Philaletes, *Introïtus apertus*. Op. cit., ch. IV, 3.
44 Ferdinand Hoefer, *Histoire de la chimie* (History of Chemistry), Paris, Firmin Didot, 1866, p. 248.
45 *La Lumière sortant par soy-mesme des Ténèbres* (The Light Coming Out by Itself from the Darkness). Op. cit.
46 Salomon Trismosin, *La Toyson d'Or* (The Golden Fleece). Paris, Ch. Sevestre, 1612.

Son of God, and this same soul that makes us see the birth of this young king".[47] Finally, in his Catechism or Instruction for the rank of Adept, annexed to his book entitled *The Flaming Star*, Baron Tschoudy informs us that the star of philosophers was so named among Masons. "Nature", he said, "is not visible, although it acts visibly, for it is only a volatile spirit, which performs its function in the bodies, and which is animated by the universal spirit, which we know, in vulgar Masonry, under the respectable emblem of the flaming Star".

Panel 7 (plate XXIX) – At the foot of a tree laden with fruit, a woman plants in the ground several pits. On the phylactery, one end of which is on the trunk, and the other on the top of the figure, we read this Latin phrase:

. TV. BORN . CEDE. MALIS.   DO NOT GIVE IN TO MISTAKES

It is an encouragement to persevere in the path followed and the method used, which gives our philosopher to the good artist, who likes to naively imitate the simple nature, rather than pursue vain chimeras .

The ancients often called alchemy the celestial agriculture, because it offers, in its laws, circumstances, and conditions, the closest relation to terrestrial agriculture. There is scarcely any classical author who takes his examples and establishes his demonstrations of field work. The hermetic analogy thus appears to be based on the art of the farmer. Just as a seed is needed to obtain an ear or corn –*nisi granum frumenti* (unless a grain of wheat). In the same way, it is essential to first have the metallic seed, in order to multiply the metal. Now, every fruit carries its seed in itself, and every body, whatever it is, has its own. The delicate point, which Philaletes calls the pivot of art, consists in knowing how to extract from metal or mineral this first seed. This is the reason why the artist must, at the beginning of his work, completely decompose what has been assembled by nature, because "whoever ignores the means of destroying the metals, also does not know how to perfect them". Having obtained the ashes of the body, these will be subjected to the calcination, which will burn the heterogeneous, combustible parts, and will leave the central salt, incombustible and pure seed that the flame can not overcome. The sages called it sulphur, first agent or philosophical gold.

But any seed capable of germinating, growing and fructifying requires proper soil.

The alchemist also needs soil appropriate to the species and nature of the seed; here again, he will have to ask only the mineral kingdom. Certainly, this second job will cost him more fatigue and time than the first. And this is also in line with the art of the farmer. Do we not see all the care of the latter directed towards an exact and perfect preparation of the soil? While sowing is quick and effortless, the soil, on the contrary, requires several ploughings, a fair distribution of fertilizers, etc., laborious and time-consuming work whose analogy is found in the Great Philosopher's Work.

May the true disciples of Hermes therefore study the simple and effective ways of isolating metallic mercury, mother and nurse of this seed from which our embryo will be born; may they endeavour to purify this mercury and enhance its faculties, like the peasant who increases the fertility of humus by aerating it frequently, by incorporating the necessary organic products. Above all, they should be wary of sophistic procedures, capricious formulas for the use of the ignorant or greedy. That they question nature, observe how it operates, know how to discern what its means are and strive to imitate it closely. If they do not let themselves be discouraged and do not give in to mistakes, which are widespread in the best

---

47 *Les Cinq Livres de Nicolas Valois* (The Five Books of Nicolas Valois). Ms. cité.

books themselves, they will undoubtedly finally see success crown their efforts. The whole art is to discover the seed, sulphur or metal nucleus, to throw it into a specific earth, or mercury, and then to subject these elements to fire, according to a regime of four increasing temperatures, which constitute the four seasons of the Work. But the great secret is that of mercury, and it is in vain that we will seek its operation in the works of the most famous authors. It is therefore preferable to go from the known to the unknown, by the analogical method, if one wishes to approach the truth about an object that has made despair, and caused the ruin of so many investigators more enthusiastic than deep.

Panel 8 (plate XXIX) – This bas-relief bears only the image of a circular shield, and the historical injunction of the Spartan mother:

. AVT. HVNC. AVT. SVPER. HVNC.   EITHER WITH HIM, OR ON HIM

Nature is here for the son of science preparing to undertake the first operation. We have already said that this manipulation, very delicate, involves a real danger, since the artist must provoke the old dragon, guardian of the Hesperides orchard, force him to fight, then kill him mercilessly if he does not want to be its victim. To conquer or to die is the veiled meaning of the inscription. Our champion, despite his valor, cannot act with too much caution, because the future of the Work and his own destiny depend on this first success.

The figure of the shield –in Greek ἀσπίς, shelter, protection, defence–, indicates to him the need for a defensive weapon. As for the attack weapon, it is the spear –λόγχη, fate, destiny–, or the estoc –διάληψις, separation–, that he must use. Unless he prefers to use the means Bellerophon used, riding Pegasus, to kill the Chimera. The poets pretend that he pushed a wooden spike, hardened by fire and filled with lead, deep into the monster's throat. The Chimera, irritated, vomited flames; the lead melted, sank to the entrails of the beast, and this simple device was quickly proved right.

We call specially the attention of the beginner on the spear and the shield, which are the best weapons that the expert and sure knight can use, and that will appear, if he comes out victorious of the combat, in his symbolic shield, assuring him the possession of our crown.

Thus, from plowman, one becomes herald (Κῆρυξ, Greek root of Κηρυκιοφόρος, which carries the Caduceus). Others, of the same courage and ardent faith, more confident in the divine mercy than assured by their own strength, abandoned the sword, the lance, and the sword for the cross. These were even better, for the dragon, material and demonic, never resisted the Savior's spiritual and omnipotent effigy, the ineffable sign of the incarnated Spirit and Light: *In hoc signo vinces.*[48]

To the wise, it is said, few words suffice, and we think we have spoken enough for those who will take the trouble to understand us.

Panel 9 (plate XXIX) – A country flower, having the aspect of the poppy, receives the light of the sun shining above it. This bas-relief has suffered from adverse weather conditions, or, perhaps, the poor quality of the stone; the inscription which adorned a banner of which we still see the trace is completely erased. Since we have previously analyzed a similar subject (series II, panel I), and this motif is susceptible of several very different interpretations, we will remain silent, for fear of a possible error, given the absence of its particular inscription.

---

48 In this sign you will conquer.

VIII

Fifth series (plate XXX).

DAMPIERRE-SUR-BOUTONNE
Panels of the Upper Gallery - Plate XXX

Panel 1 – A horny and hairy vampire, with membranous, nervated and clawed wings, feet and hands in the form of talons, is shown crouching. The inscription makes this nightmare character speak in Spanish verses:

.MAS . PENADO . MAS . PERDIDO .Y . MENOS . AREPANTIDO .

MORE PUNISHED MORE LOST AND LESS REPENTANT

This devil, an image of material grossness opposed to spirituality, is the hieroglyph of the first mineral substance, such as it is found in ore deposits where the miners will tear it away. It was formerly represented, under the figure of Satan, in Notre-Dame de Paris, and the faithful, in testimony of contempt and aversion, came to extinguish their candles by plunging them into its mouth, which it held open. For the people it was Master Pierre of Coignet, our corner stone, and the original block on which the whole Work is built.

It must be admitted that, to be symbolized in this way under deformed and monstrous exterior –dragon, snake, vampire, devil, *tarasque*,[49] etc.–, this unfortunate subject must be very disgraced by nature. In fact, there is nothing attractive about its appearance. Black, covered with scaly flakes often coated with red dots or with yellow, friable and lacklustre wrappers, with a strong and foul odor, which philosophers define as *toxicum and venenum*, it stains

---

[49] The Tarasque is a fearsome and legendary mythological dragon-like beast of Provence, in the south of France.

fingers when touched and seems to bring together everything that may displease. Yet it is he, this primitive subject of the sages, vile and despised by the ignorant, which is the only one, the only dispenser of celestial water, our first mercury and the great Alkaest.[50] He is the loyal servant and salt of the earth whom Mrs. Hillel-Erlanger calls Gilly, and who makes his master triumph over Vera's hold.[51] So it was called the universal solvent, not because it was capable of solving all the bodies of nature, which many mistakenly believed, but because it could do everything in this small universe that is the Great Work. In the 17th century, a time of heated discussions between chemists and alchemists on the principles of old science, the universal solvent was the subject of fierce controversy. J.-H. Pott, who worked hard to identify the many formulas of menstrual and tried to give a reasoned analysis of them, proves above all that none of their inventors understood what the Adepts mean by their solvent.[52] Although they claim that our mercury is metallic and homogeneous to metals, most researchers have persisted in extracting it from materials more or less distant from the mineral kingdom. Some thought they were preparing it by saturating some acid with volatile urinary spirit (ammonia), and then circulating this mixture; others exposed thickened urine to the air, with the intention of introducing the aerial spirit, etc. Becker (*Physica subterranea, Francofurti*, 1669) and Bohn (*Epistle on the insufficiency of acid and alkali*) believe that "alkaest is the purest mercurial principle that is removed from either mercury or sea salt, by particular processes". Zobel (*Margarita medicinalis*) and the author of *Lullius redivus* prepare their dissolvent by saturating the spirit with ammonia salt (hydrochloric acid) with tartar spirit (potash tartrate) and raw tartar (impure potassium carbonate). Hoffmann and Poterius volatilize the salt of tartar by first dissolving it in water, exposing the liquor to putrefaction in an oak wood vessel, then sublimating the soil that has precipitated from it. "A solvent that leaves all the others far behind," says Pott, "is the precipitate that results from mixing the corrosive sublimate and ammonia salt. Anyone who knows how to use it properly will be able to see it as a real alkaest".[53] Le Fèvre, Agricola, Robert Fludd, de Nuysement, Le Breton, Etmuller and others, prefer the spirit of dew, as well as similar extracts prepared "with storm rain or with the oily film that floats mineral waters". Finally, according to Lenglet-Dufresnoy, Olaüs Borrichius (*De Origine Chemiæ et in conspectu Chemicorum celebriorum*, num. XIV) "notes that Captain Thomas Parry, Anglois, saw this same science (alchemy) practiced in 1662 in Fez in Barbary, and that the great alchemy, the first material of all philosophers, has long been known in Africa by the most skilled Mahoman artists".[54]

In summary, all alkaest recipes proposed by authors, especially those who have in mind the liquid form attributed to the universal solvent, are useless, if not false, and good only for spagyria. Our raw material is solid; the mercury it supplies is always salty and has a hard consistency. And this metallic salt, as Bernard Trévisan rightly says, is extracted from Magnesia "by repeated destruction of the latter, by dissolving and sublimating". At each operation the body gradually splits up, disintegrates, without apparent reaction, abandoning a quantity of

---

50 The term *alkaest*, attributed sometimes to Van Helmont, sometimes to Paracelsus, would be the equivalent of the Latin *alkali est* and would give the reason why many artists have worked to obtain it from alkalis. For us, *alkaest* derives from the Greek words ἀλκά, Dorian word used for ἀλκή, force, vigour, and εἰς, the place or ἑστία, home, place or home of energy.

51 Irene Hillel-Erlanger. *Voyages en kaléidoscope* (Kaleidoscope journeys). Paris, Georges Crès, 1919.

52 J.-H. Pott. *Dissertations chymiques. T. I. Dissertation sur les soufres des Métaux, soutenue à Hall, en 1716* (Chemical essays. T. I. Dissertation on the sulphur of metals, supported at Hall, in 1716). Paris, Th. Hérissant, 1759.

53 Hoffmann. *Notes on Poterius*, in *Opera omnia*, 16 vol. Geneva, 1748 to 1754.

54 *Histoire de la Philosophie Hermétique* (History of Hermetic Philosophy.) Paris, Coustelier, 1742, t. I, p. 442.

impurities; the extract, purified by sublimation, also loses heterogeneous parts, so that its virtue is condensed at the end into a small mass, of volume and weight much lower than that of the primitive mineral subject. This is exactly what justifies the Spanish axiom, because the more numerous the repetitions, the more the broken and dissociated body is harmed, and the less opportunity to repent has the quintessence that comes from it; on the contrary, it increases in strength, purity and activity. Therefore our vampire acquires the power to penetrate metallic bodies, to attract its sulfur or its true sulfur, blood, and allows the philosopher to assimilate it to the nocturnal vampire of Eastern legends.

Panel 2 (plate XXX) – A crown made of leaves and fruits: apples, pears, quince, etc., is bound by ribbons whose knots also clasp four small branches of laurel. The epigraph which frames it tells us that no one will obtain it if he does not fulfill the laws of combat:

. NEMO. ACCIPIT. QVI.

NO . LEGITIMATE. CERTAVERIT.

NO ONE WILL GET IT IF

DOES NOT COMPLY WITH THE LAWS OF COMBAT

Mr. Louis Audiat sees in this subject a laurel wreath; this should not surprise us: his observation is often imperfect and the study of detail does not concern him much. In reality, it is neither the ivy with which the ancient poets were crowned, nor the sweet laurel on the foreheads of the victors, nor the palm tree dear to the Christian martyrs, nor the myrtle, the vine or the olive tree of the gods, which are represented here, but quite simply the fruitful crown of the wise. Its fruits mark the abundance of earthly goods, acquired through the skilful practice of celestial agriculture: this is for profit and utility; a few branches of laurel, of such discreet relief that they can hardly be distinguished: this is for the honour of the laborious. And yet, this rustic garland, which wisdom offers to learned and virtuous investigators, is not easily won. Our philosopher tells us bluntly: the artist must fight the elements if he wants to overcome the great trial. Like the stray knight, he must direct his walk towards the mysterious garden of the Hesperides and provoke the horrible monster that defends its entrance. This is, to remain in tradition, the allegorical language by which the sages intend to reveal the first and most important of the Work's operations. In truth, it is not the alchemist himself who defies and fights the hermetic dragon, but another beast, equally robust, in charge of representing it and that the artist, as a prudent spectator, constantly ready to intervene, must encourage, help and protect. He is the master of arms in this strange and merciless duel.

Few authors have spoken of this first meeting and the danger it entails. To our knowledge, Cyliani is certainly the Adept who pushed the furthest in the metaphorical description he gives of it. However, nowhere have we discovered such a detailed account, so accurate in its images, so close to truth and reality as that of the great hermetic philosopher of modern times: Cyrano Bergerac. We do not know enough about this brilliant man whose work, deliberately mutilated, was probably intended to embrace the entire scope of science. As for us, we hardly need the testimony of Mr. de Sercy, affirming that Cyrano "received from the Author of the Light and from this Master of Science (Apollo), lights that nothing can obscure, knowledge where no one can happen", to recognize in him a true and powerful initiate.[55]

---

55 Dedication of the *Histoire comique des Etats et Empires du Soleil* (Comic History of the States and Empires of the Sun), addressed by M. de Sercy to M. de Cyrano Mauvières, the author's brother. Paris, Bauche, 1910.

De Cyrano Bergerac depicts two fantastic beings, representing the principles of Sulfur and Mercury, from the four primary elements: the sulphurous Salamander, which thrives in the middle of the flames, symbolizes the air and fire whose sulfur has the dryness and igneous ardour, and the Remora, the mercurial champion, heir of the earth and water by its cold and humid qualities. These names are chosen on purpose and do not owe anything to whim or fantasy. Σαλαμάνδρα, in Greek, appears as σαλ, anagram of ἄλς, salt, and μάνδρα, stable; it is the stable salt, the urine salt of artificial saltpeter bed, the saltpeter of old spagyrists –*sal petri*, stone salt–, that they still referred to under the Dragon epithet. The Remora, in Greek Ἐχενηΐς, is the famous fish that used to stop (according to some) or direct (according to others) ships sailing on the northern seas, subject to the influence of the North Star. It is the *échénéis* of which the Cosmopolitan speaks, the royal dolphin that the characters of the *Mutus Liber* strive to capture, the one represented by the alchemical poet of P. F. Pfau, at the Winterthur Museum (canton of Zurich, Switzerland), the same one who accompanies and pilots, on the bas-relief adorning the fountain of the Vertbois, the ship loaded with an enormous cut stone. The *échénéis* is the pilot of the living wave, our mercury, the alchemist's faithful friend, the one who must absorb the secret fire, the igneous energy of the salamander, and, finally, remain stable, permanent, always victorious under the protection and protection of his master. These two principles, of opposite nature and tendencies, of opposite complexity, manifest an irreducible antipathy and aversion towards each other. In the presence of each other, they attack each other furiously, defend themselves ruthlessly, and the combat, without truce or quarter, does not cease except by the death of one of the antagonists. Such is the esoteric duel, terrible but real, that the illustrious De Cyrano narrates to us in these terms:.

"I walked about four hundred stadiums, at the end of which I saw, in the middle of a very large countryside, like two balls which, after having rustled around each other for a long time, approached and then backed away. And I observed that, when the collision occurred, it was then that one heard these great blows; but after walking further, I recognized that what, from afar, had seemed to me two balls, were two animals; one of which, although round from below, forms a triangle in the middle, and its very high head, with its red hair that floats against it, sharpens into a pyramid; its body is perforated like a screen, and, through these loose holes that serve as pores, we see sliding small flames that seem to cover it with a plumage of fire.

"As I walked around there, I met a very venerable Old Man who watched this famous battle with as much curiosity as I did. He waved to me to come closer: I obeyed and we sat down next to each other...

"Here is how he spoke to me: 'In this globe where we are, the forests would be very thin because of the great number of beasts of fire that desolate them, without the ice cube animals, that every day, at the request of their friends the forests, come to heal the sick trees.

"In the world of the Earth from where you are and where I am, the fire beast is called Salamander, and the ice cube animal is known there as Remora. However, you will know that the Remoras live towards the end of the pole, deep in the freezing sea, and it is the evaporated coldness of these fish, through their scales, that makes the sea water, although salty, freeze in these districts...

"This stigiad water, from which the great Alexander was poisoned, and whose coldness petrified his entrails, was the urine of one of these animals... So much for the ice cubes.

"But as for the fire animals, they live in the earth, under mountains of lit asphalt, like Etna, Vesuvius and Cap Rouge. These pimples, which you see at his throat, which are the result of inflammation of his liver, are...'

"After this, we remained speechless to pay attention to that famous duel. The salamander attacked with much ardor, but the remora defended impenetrably. Each attack they made gave rise to a thunder, as happens in the worlds around here, where the encounter of a warm cloud with a cold excites the same noise. From the eyes of the salamander, a red light appeared, an angry look that it directed at its enemy, which seemed to inflame the air. As it flew, he was sweating boiling oil and urinating nitric acid. The Remora, by its part, corpulent, heavy and square, showed a completely scaly body of icicles. Her wide eyes looked like two crystal plates, whose glances carry such a mortifying light, that I feel the shiver of winter on what member of my body where it fixed them. If I thought of putting my hand in front, my fingers were numbed; the very air around it, infected with its rigour, thickens into snow; the earth hardened under its steps, and I can count the tracks of the beast by the number of chilblains that I got when I walked on them.

"At the beginning of the battle, the Salamander, because of the vigorous restraint of its first ardor, had made the Remora sweat; but, in the long run, this sweat having cooled, enamelled the whole plain with such a slippery ice storm, that the Salamander could not get up to the Remora without falling. The Philosopher and I knew well that after falling and getting up so many times, she became tired; because the thunderstorms, once so dreadful, which were caused by the shock with which he charged his enemy, were no more than the dull sound of these taps which mark the end of a storm, and this dull sound, muffled little by little, degenerated into a snorting sound like a red iron immersed in cold water. When the Remora realized that the combat was coming to an end due to the weakening of the shock because of which she felt barely broken, it raised itself upon an angle of its cube and dropped down onto the stomach of the salamander, with such success that the heart of the poor salamander, where it is he had concentrated all the rest of his ardor, broke down and gave such a frightful burst that I know nothing in nature that can be compared to him. Thus died the beast of fire, under the lazy resistance of the ice cube animal.

"Some time after the Remora withdrew, we approached the battlefield, and the Old Man then coated his hands with the earth on which the Remora had walked, like a condom against burning, and he grabbed the corpse of the Salamander. 'With the body of this animal, he told me, I have no use for fire in my kitchen; for, as long as it is hung from my rack, it will boil and roast everything I had put in the fireplace. As for the eyes, I keep them carefully; if they are cleaned of the shadows of death, you would take them for two little suns'. The Ancients of our World know how to implement them well; this is what they call the Burning Lamps,[56] and they were only appended to the pompous graves of famous people. Our modern contemporaries met some of them while searching some of these famous tombs; but their ignorant curiosity pierced them, thinking they would find, behind the ruptured membranes, that fire that they saw shining brightly there".[57]

---

56 From Cyrano Bergerac, *Histoire des Oiseaux, dans l'Autre Monde. Histoire comique des États et Empires du Soleil* (History of Birds, in the Other World. Comic history of the States and Empires of the Sun). Paris, Bauche, 1910, p. 79.

57 Burning lamps, still called perpetual or inextinguishable, are one of the most surprising achievements of hermetic science. They are made of liquid Elixir, brought to the radiant state and maintained in a high vacuum as far as possible. In his *Dictionnaire des Arts et des Sciences* (Dictionary of Arts and Sciences), (Paris, 1731), Thomas de Corneille says that in 1401, "a peasant dug up a Pallas lamp near the Tiber, some distance from Rome, which had burned for more than two thousand years, as seen through the inscription, without anything having been able to extinguish it. The flame went out as soon as a small hole was made in the ground. A perpetual lamp, still burning and giving a bright light, was also discovered in the

Panel 3 (plate XXX) – A 16th century piece of artillery is represented at the moment of firing. It is surrounded by a phylactery bearing this Latin phrase:

. SI . NON . PERCVSSERO . TERREBO .   IF I REACH NO ONE, AT LEAST I WILL TERRIFY

It is quite obvious that the creator of the subject meant to speak figuratively. We understand that it is addressed directly to the laymen, the instigators devoid of science, unable consequently to understand these compositions, but which will nevertheless be astonished of their number as much as of their singularity and their incoherence. The wise moderns will take this old labor for a work of madness. And, just as the ill-tuned cannon surprises only by its noise, our philosopher rightly thinks that if it can not be understood by all, everyone will be astonished by the enigmatic, strange and discordant character that so many symbols and scenes affect.

We also believe that the curious and picturesque aspect of these figures retains above all the attention of the spectator, although without illuminating it. This is what seduced M. Louis Audiat and all the authors who took care of Dampierre. Their descriptions are not, at heart, but a rumor of confused, vain and pointless words. But, though they are no good for the instruction of the inquisitive, they bring us the testimony, however, that no observer, in our opinion, has been able to discover the general idea hidden behind these motives, nor the high significance of the mysterious teaching which in release.

Panel 4 (plate XXX) – Narcissus strives to seize, in the basin where he has been mirrored, his own image, because of his metamorphosis into a flower, so that he can revive thanks to the waters that gave him death:

. VT . PER . QVAS . PERIIT . VIVERE . POSSIT .AQVAS .

TO REVIVE THANKS TO THOSE WATERS THAT HAVE CAUSED HIS DEATH

Narcissus are plants with white or yellow flowers, and it is these flowers which made them distinguished by mythologists and symbolists; they offer, in fact, the respective colors of the two sulphurs charged with orienting the two Magisteries. All the alchemists know that it is necessary to use exclusively the white sulfur for the Work with the silver and the yellow sulfur for the Solar Work, carefully avoiding to mix them, according to the excellent advice of Nicholas Flamel: it would result in a monstrous generation, without a future and without virtue.

Narcissus is here the emblem of dissolved metal. Its Greek name, Νάϱκισσος, comes from the root Νάϱκη or Νάϱκα, numbness, torpor. However, reduced metals, whose lives are latent, concentrated, sleepy, appear to remain in a state of inertia similar to that of hibernating animals or patients under the influence of a narcotic (ναϱκωτικός, from νάϱκη). They are therefore said to be dead, compared to the alchemical metals that art has tested and vitalized. As for the sulphur extracted by the solvent –the mercurial water of the basin–, it remains the only representative of Narcissus, i. e. dissociated and destroyed metal. But just as the image reflected by the water mirror carries all the apparent characteristics of

tomb of Tullia, daughter of Cicero, during the pontificate of Paul III (1534-1549), although this tomb had not been opened for fifteen hundred and fifty years". The Reverend S. Mateer, of the Missions in London, reports a lamp from the Temple of Trevaudrum, Kingdom of Travancore (South India); this gold lamp has been shining "in a hollow covered with a stone" for more than one hundred and twenty years, and is still burning today.

the real object, so too does sulphur retain the specific properties and metallic nature of the decomposed body. So that this sulphur principle, a true seed of the metal, finding in mercury living and invigorating nutrients, can then generate a new being, similar to it, but of a higher essence, and capable of obeying the will of evolutionary dynamism.

It is therefore with reason that Narcissus, metal transformed into flower, or sulfur –for sulfur, say the philosophers, is the flower of all metals–, hopes to find existence, thanks to the particular virtue of the waters which have caused his death. If it cannot extract its image from the wave that imprisons it, at least that wave will allow it to materialize into a "double" in which it will find its essential characteristics preserved.

Thus, what causes the death of one of the principles gives life to the other, since the initial mercury, living metallic water, dies to provide the sulfur of the dissolved metal with the elements of its resurrection. That's why the ancients always said that you had to kill the living in order to resurrect the dead. The practice of this axiom assures the sage of the possession of the live sulfur, the principal agent of the stone and the transformations that can be expected. It still allows him to realize the second axiom of the Work: to join life to life, uniting the firstborn mercury of nature, to this active sulfur to obtain the mercury of the philosophers, pure substance, subtle, sensitive and alive. This is the operation that the sages have reserved under the expression of the chemical marriage, the mystical marriage of brother and sister –because they are both of the same blood and have the same origin– of Gabritius and Beya, of the Sun and the Moon, of Apollo and Diana. This last word furnished the cabalists with the famous Apollonian sign of Tyana, under which they believed to recognize a pretended philosopher, although the miracles of this fictitious personage, of incontestably hermetic character, were, for the initiated, clothed with the symbolic seal and devoted to alchemical esotericism.

Panel 5 (plate XXX) – The ark of Noah floats on the waters of the Flood, while beside it a boat threatens to sink. In the sky of the subject read the words

. VERITAS. VINCIT.   TRUTH PREVAILS

We believe that we have already said that the ark represents all the materials prepared and united under the various names of compound, rebis, amalgam, etc., which properly constitute the *archaea*, igneous matter, base of the philosopher's stone. The Greek ἀρχή means beginning, principle, source, origin. Under the action of external fire, exciting the internal fire of the *archaea*, the whole compost is liquefied, takes on the appearance of water; and this liquid substance, which the fermentation agitates and swollen, assumes, in the authors, the character of the diluvian flood. At first yellowish and muddy, it is given the name of brass or laton, which is none other than that of the mother of Diana and Apollo, Latona. The Greeks called it Λητώ, of λῆτος put for λήϊτος, with the Ionian meaning of common good, common house (τὸ λήϊτον), significant protective envelope common to the double embryo. [58] We note in passing that the Cabalists, by one of those puns which they are customary, have taught that the fermentation was to be done using a wooden vessel, or better, in a barrel cut in two, to which they applied the epithet of hollow oak. Latona, mythological princess, becomes, in the language of the adepts, the ton or the barrel, which explains why beginners come to identify with so much difficulty the secret vessel where our matter ferments.

---

58 The linguists want, moreover, that Λητω is close to Λαθειν, infinitive aorist second of Λανθανειν meaning to lie hidden, away from all eyes, be hidden or ignored, according to us, with the dark phase of which will soon issue.

At the end of the required time, we see rising to the surface, floating and moving constantly under the effect of boiling, a very thin film, as a meniscus, that the sages have named the Philosophical Island,[59] The first manifestation of thickening and coagulation. It is the famous island of Delos, in Greek Δῆλος, that is to say, apparent, clear, certain, which provides an unexpected refuge to Latona fleeing the persecution of Juno, and fills the heart of the artist, with an unmixed joy. This floating island, which Poseidon, with a stroke of his trident, brought out of the bottom of the sea, is also the saving ark of Noah carried on the waters of the Flood. *"Cum viderem quod aqua sensim crassior,"* says Hermes, *"duriorque fieri, inciperet, gaudebam; certo enim sciebam, ut inirem quod querebam.*[60]

Gradually, and under the continuous action of the internal fire, the film develops, thickens and expands to cover the entire surface of the melt. The moving island was then fixed, and this show gave the alchemist the assurance that the time of birthing of Latona had arrived. At that moment, the mystery returns. A heavy, dark, livid cloud, rising and exhaling from the warm and stabilized island, covers this land in darkness with darkness, envelops and conceals all things with its opacity, fills the philosophical sky with Cimmerian shadows (κιμμεϱικόν, mourning garment) and, in the great eclipse of the sun and the moon, conceals the supernatural birth of the hermetic twins, future parents of the stone.

The mosaic tradition reports that God, towards the end of the Flood, causes a warm wind to blow on the waters, which evaporates them and lowers their level. The summit of the mountains emerges from the immense liquid sheet, and the ark comes to land on Mount Ararat, Armenia. Noah opens the window of the ship and releases the crow, which is, for the alchemist, and in his tiny Genesis, the replica of the Cimmerian shadows and those dark clouds that accompany the occult elaboration of new beings and regenerated bodies.

By these concordances, and the material testimony of the work itself, the truth asserts itself victorious, in spite of the deniers, the skeptics, men of little faith, always ready to reject, in the domain of the illusion and the marvelous , the positive reality that they can not understand because it is not known and less taught.

Panel 6 (plate XXX) – A woman, kneeling at the foot of a tomb on which we read this strange word: *TALACIS*, affects the deepest despair. The banner that embellishes this figure bears the inscription:

. VICTA. JACET. VIRTVS.   VIRTUE IS VANQUISHED

Motto of André Chénier, says Louis Audiat, by way of explanation, and without taking into account the time elapsed between the Renaissance and the Revolution. It is not a question of the poet, but of the virtue of sulfur, or of the gold of the sages, which rests under the stone, waiting for the complete decomposition of its perishable body. For the sulphurous earth, dissolved in mercurial water, prepares, by the death of the compound, the liberation of this virtue, which is properly the soul or the fire of sulfur. And this virtue, momentarily imprisoned in the corporal envelope, or this immortal spirit, will float on the chaotic waters until the formation of the new body, as Moses teaches us in Genesis (chapter I, v. 2).).

---

59 In particular the Cosmopolitan (*Traité du Sel*, Salt Treaty, p. 78) and the author of *Songe Verd* (The Green Dream).

60 "When I saw this water gradually getting thicker, and beginning to harden, I was looking forward to it, because I certainly knew that I would find what I was looking for".

It is therefore the hieroglyph of mortification that we have before us, the same that is repeated in the engravings of the *Pretiosa Margarita*, novella, whose drama of the Great Work was illustrated by Pierre Bon de Lombardy. Many philosophers have adopted this mode of expression and veiled, under funeral or macabre subjects, the putrefaction specially applied to the second Work, that is, to the operation charged with decomposing and liquefying philosophical sulphur, resulting from the first labor, into a perfect Elixir. Basil Valentine shows us a skeleton standing on his own coffin, in one of his *Twelve Keys*, and depicts a burial scene in another. Flamel not only places the humanized symbols of the *Ars magna* at Cemetery of the Innocents, but he decorates his tumulus plaque, which can be seen exposed in the chapel of the Cluny Museum, with a corpse eaten away by worms with this inscription:

From the earth I come and to the earth I return

Senior Zadith encloses an emaciated agonist inside a transparent sphere. Henri de Linthaut draws, on a page of the manuscript of the Dawn, the inanimate body of a crowned king, lying on the mortuary slab, while his spirit, under the figure of an angel, rises to a lost lantern in the clouds. And ourselves, after these great masters, have exploited the same theme in the frontispiece of the *Mysteries of the Cathedrals*.

As for the woman who, on the tomb of our box, translates her regrets into disordered gestures, she depicts the metallic mother of sulphur; it is her who owns the singular word engraved on the stone that covers her child: *Taiacis*. This baroque term, probably born of the whim of our Adept, is, in reality, only a Latin phrase with words assembled, and written backwards so that it can be read starting at the end: *Sic ai at, alas!* So at least... (will he be reborn). Supreme hope at the bottom of the supreme pain. Jesus himself had to suffer in his flesh, die and remain in the tomb for three days, in order to redeem men, and then rise again in the glory of his human incarnation and the fulfilment of his divine mission.

Panel 7 (plate XXX) – Represented in full flight, a dove holds in its beak an olive branch. This subject is distinguished by the inscription:

. SI . TE. FATA. VOCANT   IF FATES CALLS YOU THERE

The emblem of the dove with the green branch is given to us by Moses in his description of the Universal Flood. It is said, indeed (Genesis, chapter VIII, v. 11), that Noah, having sent forth a dove, it returned in the evening by bringing back a green branch of olive. This is the sign par excellence of the true way and the regular operation of operations. For the labor of the Work being an abridgment and a reduction of the Creation, all the circumstances of the divine work must be reduced to that of the alchemist. Therefore, when the patriarch brings the crow out of the ark, we must understand that our work is about the first lasting color, that is, the color black, because the death of the compound, become effective, the materials putrefy and take a very dark blue color that its metallic reflections can compare to the feathers of the raven. Moreover, the biblical account states that this bird, retained by the corpses, does not return to the ark. However, the analogical reason why black is called crow is not based solely on an aspect identity; the philosophers have again given decomposing compost the expressive name of *blue body* (from which comes the old medieval curse), and the cabalists that of beautiful body, not because it is pleasant to see, but because it brings the first testimony of activity of philosophical materials. However, despite the sign of good omens that the authors agree to recognize in the appearance of the color black, we recommend to welcome these demonstrations with reserve, not attributing them more value than they have..

We know how easy it is to obtain it, even in foreign substances, provided that they are processed according to the rules of the art. This criterion is therefore insufficient, although it justifies this known axiom, that all dry matter dissolves and corrupts in moisture which is natural and homogeneous to it. That is why we warn the beginner and advise him, before giving himself to the transports of a joy without tomorrow, to wait prudently for the manifestation of the green color, symptom of the desiccation of the earth, of the absorption of the waters and of the vegetation of the new formed body.

So, brother, if heaven deigns to bless your labor and, according to the word of the Adept, if you make yourself vocal, you will first obtain the olive branch, symbol of peace and union of the elements, then the white dove that brought it to you. Only then can you be sure that you possess this wonderful light, gift of the Holy Spirit, which Jesus sent on the fiftieth day (Πεντηκοστή) to his beloved apostles. This is the material consecration of initiation baptism and divine revelation. "And as Jesus came out of the water, says St. Mark (ch. I, v. 10), John suddenly saw the heavens open and the Holy Spirit descend upon him in the body form of a dove".

Panel 8 (plate XXX) – Two forearms whose hands are joined, come out of a string of clouds. Their motto is:

. ACCIPE. DAQVE. FIDEM.   RECEIVE MY WORD AND GIVE ME YOURS

This reason is, in short, a translation of the sign used by the alchemists to express the element water. Clouds and arms compose a triangle with a summit directed downwards, the hieroglyph of water, opposed to the fire symbolized by a similar but returned triangle.

It is certain that we cannot understand our first mercurial water under this emblem of union, since the two hands held together in a pact of fidelity and attachment belong to two distinct individualities. We have said, and we repeat here, that initial mercury is a simple product, and the first agent to extract the sulphurous and igneous part of metals. However, if the separation of sulphur by this solvent allows it to retain a few portions of mercury, or allows it to absorb a certain amount of sulphur, although these combinations may be called philosophical mercury, it should not be expected that the stone will be produced using this single mixture. Experience shows that philosophical mercury, subjected to distillation, easily abandons its fixed body, leaving pure sulphur at the bottom of the retort. On the other hand, and despite the assurance of the authors who grant mercury the preponderance in the Work, we note that sulphur designates itself as the essential agent, since it is ultimately it that remains, exalted under the name of Elixir or multiplied under that of philosopher's stone, in the final product of the work. Thus mercury, whatever it may be, remains subject to sulphur, because it is the servant and slave, who, letting himself be absorbed, disappears and merges with his master. Therefore, since universal medicine is a true generation, which any generation cannot be achieved without the help of two factors, of similar species but of different sexes, we must recognize that philosophical mercury is powerless to produce stone, and this because it is alone. It is he, however, who holds the role of female in the work, but this one, say of Spanish and Philaletes, must be united with a second male, if we want to obtain the compound known as Rebis, the raw material of the Magisterium.

It is the mystery of the hidden word, or *verbum demissum*, which our Adept received from his predecessors, which he transmits to us under the veil of the symbol, and for the preservation of which he asks of us, that is, that is to say, the oath not to discover what he thought good to keep secret: *accipe daque fidem* (take my word and give me yours).

Panel 9 (plate XXX) – On rocky ground, two doves, unfortunately decapitated, are facing each other. They carry for epigraph the Latin adage:

. CONCORDIA. NVTRIT. AMOREM.   CONCORD NOURISHES LOVE

Eternal truth, whose application we find everywhere on earth, and that the Great Work confirms by the most striking example that it is possible to meet in the order of mineral things. The entire hermetic work is, in fact, only a perfect harmony, realized according to the natural tendencies of the inorganic bodies between them, of their chemical affinity and, if the word is not too excessive, of their mutual love.

The two birds that make up the subject of our bas-relief represent these famous Diana Doves, the object of so many researchers' despair, and the famous enigma that Philaletes imagined to cover the device with the double mercury of the sages. In proposing this obscure allegory to the sagacity of the aspirants, the great Adept did not dwell on the origin of these birds; he only teaches, in the most brief way, that "Diana's Doves are inseparably wrapped in the eternal embraces of Venus". However, the ancient alchemists placed under Diana's protection "with lunar horns" this first mercury, which we have often talked about as a universal solvent. His whiteness, his Argentinean brilliance also earned him the epithet of the Moon of the Philosophers and Mother of the Stone; it is in this sense that Hermes understands it when he says, when speaking of the Work: "The Sun is his father and the Moon his mother". Limojon de Saint-Didier, to help the investigator decipher the enigma, written in the *Entretien d'Eudoxe et de Pyrophile* (The Interview Between Eudoxus and Pyrophilus): "Finally, consider how Geber teaches to make the sublimations required of this art; for me, I can do no more than to make the same wish as another philosopher did: *Sidera Veneris, and corniculatæ Dianæ tibi propitia sunto.*[61]

We can therefore consider the Doves of Diana as two parts of mercury dissolving –the two points of the crescent moon– against one of Venus, which must keep her favorite doves closely embraced. The correspondence is confirmed by the double quality, volatile and aerial, of the initial mercury whose emblem has always been taken among the birds, and by the very material from which the mercury comes, rocky, chaotic, barren land on which the doves rest.

When, according to the law of Moses, the Holy Virgin fulfilled the seven days of purification (Exodus 13:12), Joseph accompanied her to the temple at Jerusalem to present the Child and offer the victim, according to the law of the Lord (Leviticus, XII, 6, 8), namely: a couple of turtledoves or two small doves. Thus appears, in the sacred text, the mystery of the Ornithogal, this famous milk of the birds –Ὀρνίθιον γάλα–, which the Greeks spoke of as something extraordinary and very rare. "To milk the milk of the birds" (Ὀρνίθιον γάλα ἀμέλγειν) was a proverb for them that was equivalent to succeeding, to knowing the favor of destiny and success in any enterprise. And we must agree that one must be the elect of Providence to discover the doves of Diana and to possess the ornithogal, hermetic synonym of Virgin Milk dear to Philaletes. Ὄρνις, in Greek, denotes not only the bird in general, but more specifically the cock and the hen, and it is perhaps from this that derives the term ὀρνίθιον γάλα, eggnog, obtained by mixing a yellow of egg in hot milk. We will not insist on these reports, because they would reveal the secret operation hidden under the expression of the doves of Diana. Let us say, however, that the plants called ornithogals are bulbous lilies, with beautiful white flowers, and we know that the lily is, par excellence, the emblematic flower of Mary.

---

61 "May the star of Venus and the horns of Diana be favorable to you".

IX

Sixth series (plate XXXI).

DAMPIERRE-SUR-BOUTONNE
Panels of the Upper Gallery – Sixth Series – Plate XXXI

Panel 1 – Piercing the clouds, a man's hand throws seven balls against a rock, and they bounce back towards him. This bas-relief is decorated with the inscription:

. CONCVSSVS. SVRGO.   STRUCK, I BOUNCE BACK

Image of the action and the reaction, as well as the hermetic axiom *Solve and coagula*, dissolve and coagulate.

A similar subject is noticed on one of the ceiling panels of the Chapel Lallemant, in Bourges; but the balls are replaced by chestnuts. Now, this fruit, to which its thorny pericarp has given the common name of hedgehog (in Greek ἐχῖνος, sea urchin, sea chestnut), is a rather exact figuration of the philosopher's stone as it is obtained by the short way. It appears, in fact, to consist of a sort of crystalline and translucent nucleus, almost spherical, of a color similar to that of the "rubis balai" (glitter wine color), enclosed in a capsule more or less thick, red, opaque, dry and covered with asperities, which, at the end of the work, is often cracked, sometimes even open, like the husks of nuts and chestnuts. So these are the fruits of the hermetic labor that the heavenly hand throws against the rock, emblem of our mercurial substance. Whenever the stone, fixed and perfect, is taken up by the mercury in order to dissolve it, to feed on it again, to increase in it not only in weight and in volume, but also in energy, it returns by coction to its original state, color, and appearance. It can be said that after touching the mercury it returns to its point of departure. It is these phases of fall and ascension, of solution and coagulation which characterize the successive multiplications which give to each rebirth of the stone a theoretical power tenfold of the preceding one. However, and although many authors do not envisage any limit to this exaltation, we think with other philosophers that it would be imprudent, at least as far as transmutation and medicine are concerned, to go beyond the seventh reiteration. This is the reason why Jean Lallemant and the Adept of Dampierre only figured seven balls or chestnuts on the grounds of which we speak.

Unlimited for speculative philosophers, multiplication is however limited in the practical domain. The more the stone progresses, the more penetrating and rapidly elaborated it becomes: it requires, at each degree of increase, only one eighth of the time required by the previous operation. Generally –and we consider here the long way–, it is rare that the fourth repetition requires more than two hours; the fifth is therefore completed in one and a half minutes, while twelve seconds would be sufficient to complete the sixth: the immediacy of such an operation would make it impractical. On the other hand, the ever-increasing use of weight and volume would mean that a large part of the production would have to be reserved because of the lack of a proportional quantity of mercury, which is always long and tedious to prepare. Finally, the stone multiplied at the fifth and sixth degrees would require, given its igneous power, a large mass of pure gold to direct it towards the metal –otherwise one would be exposed to losing it entirely. It is therefore preferable, in every respect, not to push too far the subtlety of an agent already endowed with considerable energy, unless one wants, leaving the order of metallic and medical possibilities, to possess this universal Mercury, brilliant and luminous in the darkness, in order to build its perpetual lamp. But the transition from the solid to the liquid state, which must be carried out in this place, being eminently dangerous, can only be attempted by a very learned master with a consummate skill.

From all the foregoing, we must conclude that the material impossibilities reported about transmutation tend to ruin the thesis of a growing and indefinite geometric progression, based on the number ten dear to pure theoreticians. Let us keep unthinking enthusiasm, and never allow ourselves to be circumvented by the specious arguments, the brilliant but hollow theories of prodigious lovers. Science and nature reserve us enough marvels to satisfy us, without us feeling the need to add to it still the vain fantasies of the imagination.

Panel 2 (plate XXXI) – It is a dead tree, with cut branches, bare roots, that presents us this bas-relief. It bears no inscription, but only two signs of alchemical notation engraved on a cartouche; one, schematic figure of the level, expresses Sulfur; the other, an equilateral triangle with an upper apex, designates the Fire.

The dried-out tree is a symbol of the ordinary metals reduced by their ores and melts, to which the high temperatures of the metallurgical ovens have made lose the activity which they possessed in their natural shelter. This is why philosophers call them dead and recognize them as unfit for the labor of the Great Work, until they are revived, or reincrudated according to the consecrated term, by that internal fire which never abandons them completely. Because the metals, fixed in the industrial form that we know them to have, still retain, in the depths of their substance, the soul which vulgar fire has tightened and condensed, but which it has not been able to destroy. And this soul, the wise have called it fire or sulfur, because it is truly the agent of all the mutations, of all the accidents observed in the metallic material, and that incombustible seed that nothing can ruin altogether, neither the violence of the strong acids, nor the ardor of the furnace. This great principle of immortality, charged by God himself to assure, to maintain the perpetuity of the species and to reform the perishable body, subsists and is found even in the ashes of the calcined metals, while these have suffered the disintegration of their parts and saw consumed their body envelope.

Philosophers therefore judged, not without reason, that the refractory qualities of sulfur, its resistance to fire, could belong only to fire or some spirit of an igneous nature. This is what led them to give it the name under which it is designated and that some artists believe come from its aspect, although it does not offer any relation with the common sulfur. In Greek, sulfur is called θεῖον, a word whose root is θεῖος, which means divine, marvelous, supernatural; τὸ θεῖον not only expresses divinity, but also the magical, extraordinary side of a thing. Now, the philosophical sulfur, considered as the god and the animator of the Great Work, reveals by its actions a formative energy comparable to that of the divine Spirit. Thus, and although it is necessary to attribute precedence to mercury,

Seek the sulfur in the dead trunk of the vulgar metals, and at the same time you will obtain this natural and metallic fire which is the main key of the alchemical labor. "This is," says Limojon de Saint-Didier, "the great mystery of art, since all the others depend on the intelligence of this one. I would be satisfied, adds the author, if it were permitted me to explain to you this unambiguous secret; but I cannot do what no philosopher has thought to be in his power. All you can reasonably expect from me is to tell you that natural fire is a potential fire, which does not burn your hands, but which makes its effectiveness seem as long as it is excited by the external fire".

Panel 3 (plate XXXI) – A hexagonal pyramid, made of riveted sheet metal, door, hanging on its walls, various emblems of chivalry and hermeticism, armor pieces and honorable pieces: targes, armet, arm-guard, gauntlets, crown and garlands. His epigraph is taken from a verse of Virgil (Aeneid , XI, 641):

. SIC. ITVR. AD. ASTRA.   THUS IT IS IMMORTALIZED

This pyramidal construction, whose shape is reminiscent of the hieroglyph adopted to designate fire, is none other than the Athanor, a word by which alchemists signal the philosophical furnace essential to the maturation of the Work. Two side doors are arranged and face each other; they close glass windows that allow observation of the phases of the work. Another, located at the base, gives access to the fire; finally, a small plate, near the top, serves as a damper and evacuation mouth to gases from combustion. Inside, if we refer to the very detailed descriptions of Philaletes, Le Tesson, Salmon and others, as well as the reproductions of Rupescissa, Sgobbis, Pierre Vicot, Huginus at Barma, etc., the Athanor is arranged to receive a bowl of earth or metal, called nest or arena, because the egg is incubated in the hot sand (Latin, *arena*, sand). As for the fuel used for heating, it seems rather variable, although many authors give preference to thermogenic lamps.

At least that's what the masters teach about their furnace. But Athanor, home of the mysterious fire, claims to have a less vulgar conception. Through this secret furnace, prison of an invisible flame, it seems to us more in conformity with the hermetic esotericism to hear the prepared substance –amalgam or rebis–, serving as an envelope and matrix for the central nucleus where these latent faculties sleep, which the common fire will soon make active. Matter alone being the vehicle of natural and secret fire, immortal agent of all our achievements, remains for us the only and true Athanor (from the Greek Ἀθάνατος, which is renewed and never dies). Philaletes tells us, about the secret fire, which the wise men cannot do without, since it is it that causes all the metamorphoses within the compound, that it is of metallic essence and of sulphurous origin. It is recognized as a mineral because it is born from the prime mercurial substance, the sole source of metals; sulphurous because this fire, in the extraction of metallic sulphur, has taken on the specific qualities of the "father of metals". It is therefore a double fire –the double igneous man of Basil Valentine–, which contains both the attractive, agglutinating and organizing properties of mercury, and the drying, coagulating and fixing properties of sulphur. If we have any hint of philosophy, we will easily understand that this double fire, animator of rebis, needing only the help of heat to pass from the potential to the present, and to make its power effective, cannot belong to the furnace, although it metaphorically represents our Athanor, that is to say the place of energy, of the principle of immortality enclosed in the philosophical compound. This double fire is the pivot of art and, according to Philaletes expression, "the first agent that makes the wheel turn and moves the axle"; it is therefore often referred to as the epithet *fire of the wheel*, because it seems to develop its action in a circular mode, the purpose of which is the conversion of the molecular building, a rotation symbolized in the Wheel of Fortune and in the Ouroboros.

Thus, the matter destroyed, mortified and then recomposed into a new body, thanks to the secret fire excited by that of the furnace, rises gradually with the help of multiplications, until the perfection of pure fire, veiled under the figure of the immortal Phoenix: *sic itur ad astra* (thus it is immortalized). In the same way the workman, faithful servant of nature, acquires, with sublime knowledge, the high title of knight, the esteem of his peers, the gratitude of his brethren and the honor, more enviable than all the worldly glory, to be among the disciples of Elijah.

Panel 4 (plate XXXI) – Closed with its narrow lid, its belly bounced but cracked, a vulgar pot of earth fills with its plebeian and cracked majesty, the surface of this panel. Its inscription affirms that the vase of which we see the image must open by itself and make manifest, by its destruction, the completion of what it contains:

. INTS . SOLA . FIENT . MANIFESTA . RVINA.   ONLY THE INSIDE MAKES THE RUIN MANIFEST

Among so many different figures, emblems with which it fraternizes, our subject seems all the more original as its symbolism relates to the dry way, also called Work of Saturn, as rarely translated into iconography as it is described in the texts. Based on the use of solid and crystallized materials, the short way (*ars brevis*) only requires the help of the crucible and the application of high temperatures. This truth, Henckel had interviewed when he remarks that "the artist Elias, quoted by Helvetius, claims that the preparation of the philosopher's stone begins and ends in four days time, and that he has indeed shown, this stone still adheres to the sides of the crucible; it seems to me, continues the author, that it would not be so absurd to question whether what the alchemists call great months, are not so many days –which would be a very narrow space of time–, and whether there is not a method in which the whole operation would consist only in keeping the materials for a long time in the greatest degree of fluidity, which we obtain by a violent fire, maintained by the action of the bellows; but this method cannot be performed in all laboratories, and perhaps not everyone would find it practicable".[62]

But, unlike the wet way, whose glass utensils allow easy control and observation, the dry way cannot illuminate the operator, at any time of the work. Also, although the time factor, reduced to a minimum, constitutes a serious advantage in the practice of *ars brevis*, on the other hand, the necessity of high temperatures presents the serious inconvenience of an absolute uncertainty as to the progress of the operation. Everything happens in the deepest mystery inside the carefully closed crucible, buried in the center of incandescent coals. It

---

62 J.-F. Henckel. *Traité de l'Appropriation* (Treatise on Appropriation), in *Pyritologie ou Histoire naturelle de la Pyrite* (Pyritology or Natural History of Pyrite). Paris, J.-T. Hérissant, 1760, p. 375, § 416.

is therefore important to be very experienced, to be well acquainted with the conduct and power of fire, since we cannot, from beginning to end, discover the slightest indication. All the characteristic reactions of the wet way being indicated in the classic authors, it is possible for the studious artist to acquire the precise reference points to authorize him to undertake his long and painful work. Here, on the contrary, it is devoid of any guide that the traveler, bold to the point of temerity, engages in this arid and burnt desert. No road drawn, no clue, no milestone; nothing but the apparent inertia of the earth, the rock, the sand. The brilliant kaleidoscope of the colored phases does not weaken its indecisive march; it is in blindness that he pursues his path, with no certainty other than that of his faith, with no hope but his confidence in the divine mercy.

However, at the end of his career, the investigator will see one sign, the only one, the one whose appearance indicates the success and confirms the perfection of sulphur by the total fixation of mercury; this sign consists in the spontaneous rupture of the vessel. Once time has expired, by discovering part of its wall laterally, when the experiment is successful, one or more lines of dazzling clarity are noticed, clearly visible on the less bright background of the envelope. These are the cracks that reveal the happy birth of the young king. Just as at the end of incubation the hen egg breaks under the stress of the chick, so the shell of our egg breaks as soon as the sulphur is completed. There is, between these effects, an obvious analogy, despite the diversity of the causes, because, in the Mineral Work, the failure of the crucible can only logically be attributed to a chemical action, unfortunately impossible to conceive or explain. It should be noted, however, that this well-known fact frequently occurs under the influence of certain combinations of lesser interest. For example, by abandoning new crucibles that have been used only once for melting metal glass, producing *hepar sulphuris* or diaphoretic antimony, and after cleaning them thoroughly, they are found cracked after a few days, without being able to discover the obscure reason for this late phenomenon. The considerable distance between their bellies shows that the fracture appears to occur by the thrust of an expansive force, acting from the centre to the periphery, at room temperature and long after use of the vessels.

Note finally the remarkable concordance that exists between the pattern of Dampierre and that of Bourges (Lallemant hotel, ceiling of the chapel). Among the hermetic panels of the latter, one also sees a earthen pot, inclined, whose opening, flared and very broad, is closed with a membrane of parchment tied on the edges. Its belly, pierced, lets beautiful crystals of different thicknesses escape. The indication of the crystalline form of sulfur, obtained by the dry route, is therefore very clear and confirms, by specifying it, the esotericism of our bas-relief.

Panel 5 (plate XXXI) – A celestial hand, whose arm is clad with iron, brandishes the sword and the spatula. On the phylactery we read these Latin words:

. PERCVTIAM. AND. SANABO.   I WILL HURT AND HEAL

Jesus said the same thing, "I will die and rise again". Esoteric thought of capital importance in the execution of the Magisterium. "This is the first key," says Limojon de Saint-Didier,[63] "who opens the dark prisons in which the sulfur is enclosed; it is the one who knows how to extract the seed from the body, and who forms the stone of the philosophers by the

---

63 *Le Triomphe hermétique. Lettre aux Vrays Disciples d'Hermès* (The Hermetic Triumph. Letter to the True Disciples of Hermes). Op cit., P. 127.

conjunction of the male with the female, the spirit with the body, the sulfur with the mercury. Hermes has clearly demonstrated the operation of this first key by these words: '*Cavernis metallorum occultus est, which lapis is venerabilis, colore splendidus, mens sublimis and mare patens*.'"[64]

The cabalistic device, under which our Adept concealed the technique that Limojon is trying to teach us, consists in the choice of the double instrument shown on our panel. The wounding sword, the spatula charged with applying the healing balm, is truly one and the same agent with the dual power to kill and resurrect, to mortify and regenerate, to destroy and to organize. Spatula, in Greek, is said σπάθη; however, this word also means saber, sword, and derives its origin from σπάω, to tear off, to extract, to extract. We therefore have here the exact indication of the hermetic meaning provided by the trowel and the sword. From then on, the investigator in possession of the solvent, the only factor capable of acting on the bodies, destroying them and extracting the seed, will only have to look for the metallic subject that seems most appropriate to him to fulfill his purpose. Thus, the dissolved, crushed, "torn to pieces" metal will abandon this fixed and pure grain, the spirit that it carries within it, a brilliant gem, adorned with a magnificent color, the first manifestation of the stone of the sages, the nascent Phoebus and the effective father of the great Elixir. In an allegorical dialogue between a monster folded up at the bottom of an obscure cave, provided with "seven horns full of water", and the wandering alchemist, pressing questions from this debonair sphinx, Jacques Tesson makes this fabulous representative of the seven vulgar metals speak: "You must hear," he said, "that I came down from the heavenly regions and I've fallen down here in these caverns of the earth, where I nourished myself for a while; but I desire nothing more than to return there; and the way to do this is for you to kill me and then to resurrect me, and from the instrument that you will kill me, you will resurrect me. For, as the white dove says, the one who killed me will bring me back to life".[65]

We might make an interesting remark about the means, or instrument, expressly represented by the steel armband with which the celestial arm is fitted, for no detail should be neglected in a study of this kind; but we think that it is proper not to say everything, and prefer to leave to anyone who will take the trouble to decipher this complementary hieroglyph. Alchemical science is not taught; each one must learn it himself, not in a speculative way, but with the help of persevering work, by multiplying attempts and attempts so as to always subject the productions of thought to the control of the experience. . The one who fears manual labor, the heat of the furnaces, the dust of coal, the danger of unknown reactions, and the insomnia of long wards, that one will never know anything.

Panel 6 (plate XXXI) – An ivy is figured wrapped around a dead tree trunk, all of whose branches have been cut off by a man's hand. The phylactery that completes this bas-relief bears the words:

. INIMICA. AMICITIA.   THE ENEMY FRIENDSHIP .

The anonymous author of the *l'Ancienne Guerre des Chevaliers* (Ancient War of the Knights) in a dialogue between stone, gold and mercury, makes gold say that the stone is a worm inflated with venom, and accuses it of being the enemy of men and metals. Nothing is more true; so much so that others reproach us for containing a terrible poison, whose only

---

64 "He (the sulfur) is hidden deep within the metals; it is he who is the venerable stone, of brilliant color, an elevated soul and a vast sea".

65 Jacques Tesson, *Le Lyon verd or l'Œuvre des Sages* (Green Lyon or the Work of the Wise). First treaty. Ms. quoted.

smell, they say, would be enough to cause death. However, it is this toxic mineral that is the basis of universal medicine, to which no human disease can resist, as incurable as it may be considered. But what gives it all its value and makes it infinitely precious in the eyes of the wise man is the admirable virtue it possesses of reviving reduced and molten metals, and of losing its poisonous properties by granting them its own activity. It therefore appears as the instrument of the resurrection and redemption of the metal bodies, which died under the violence of the reduction fire, which is why it bears in its coat of arms the sign of the Redeemer, the cross.

By what we have just said, the reader will have understood that the stone, i. e. our mineral subject, is represented on this motif by ivy, a perennial plant with a strong odor and a nauseating smell, while the metal represents the inert and mutilated tree. Because it is not a dry tree, simply devoid of foliage and reduced to its skeleton, that we see here: it would then express, for the hermetist, the sulphur in its igneous dryness; it is a trunk, voluntarily mutilated, that the saw has amputated from its master branches. The Greek verb πρίω also means to saw, cut with the saw and to grasp, squeeze, bind strongly. Our tree, being both sawn and grasped, we may think that the creator of these images wanted to indicate clearly the metal and the dissolving action exerted against it. Ivy, kissing the trunk as if to suffocate it, expresses well the dissolution by the prepared subject, full of vigor and vitality; but this dissolution, instead of being ardent, effervescent and fast, seems slow, difficult, always imperfect. This is because the metal, although completely attacked, is only partially solubilized; it is therefore recommended to frequently repeat the affusion of water on the body, to extract sulphur or seed "which makes all the energy of our stone". And metallic sulphur receives the life of its enemy itself, in reparation for its enmity and hatred. This operation, which the sages called reincrudation or return to the primitive state, has as its main purpose the acquisition of sulphur and its revival by the initial mercury. This return to the original material of the treated metal should therefore not be taken literally, since a large part of the body, made up of coarse, heterogeneous, sterile or mortified elements, is no longer susceptible to regeneration. In any case, it is enough for the artist to obtain this sulphur principle, separated from the open metal and made alive, thanks to the incisive power of our first mercury. With this new body, where friendship and harmony replace aversion –because the respective virtues and properties of the two opposing natures are confused in him–, he can hope to reach first the philosophical mercury, through the mediation of this essential agent, then the Elixir, object of his secret desires.

Panel 7 (plate XXXI) – Where Louis Audiat recognizes the figure of God the Father, we simply see that of a centaur, a banner, bearing the abbreviations of the Senate and the Roman people, half hiding. The whole decorates a standard whose shaft is securely stuck in the ground.

It is indeed a Roman sign, and we can conclude that the soil on which it floats is itself Roman. By the way, the letters:

S. P. Q. R.

the abbreviation for *Senatus Populusque Romanus* (The Roman Senate and People), usually accompany the eagles and form, with the cross, the arms of the Eternal City.

This sign, placed expressly to indicate a Roman land, gives us to think that the philosopher of Dampierre was not unaware of the particular symbolism of Basil Valentine, Senior Zadith, Mynsicht, etc. For these authors call Roman earth and Roman vitriol the terrestrial substance which furnishes our solvent, without which it would be impossible to reduce the metals into mercurial water, or, if one prefers, philosophical vitriol. Now, according to Valmont de Bomare, "the Roman vitriol, still called vitriol of the Adepts, is not the Copperas

Green vitriol (sulphate of iron), but a double vitriolic salt of iron and copper."[66] Chambon is of the same opinion and quotes as equivalent the vitriol of Salzburg, which is also a cupro-ferric sulphate. The Greeks called it Σῶρυ, and the Hellenic mineralogists describe it as a salt of strong and unpleasant smell, which, when crushed, became black by taking a spongy consistency and a greasy appearance.

In his *Testamentum*, Basil Valentine points out the excellent properties and rare virtues of vitriol; but the truth of his words will only be recognized if we know, beforehand, which body he speaks about. "Vitriol, he writes, is a notable and important mineral to which no one else in nature can be compared, because Vitriol becomes familiar with all metals more than all other things; it is very soon allied with them, since, of all metals, one can make a vitriol or crystal; because vitriol and crystal are only recognized for one and the same thing. That is why I did not want to lazily delay its merit, as the reason requires, since Vitriol is preferable to other minerals, and that it must be given first place after metals. For, although all metals and minerals are endowed with great virtues, this one nevertheless, namely Vitriol, is sufficient to draw from it and make the blessed stone, which no one else in the world could accomplish alone in imitation". Further on, our Adept returns to the same subject by specifying the dual nature of the Roman vitriol: "I say here on this subject, that you must strongly imprint this argument in your mind, that you carry your thoughts entirely on the metallic vitriol, and that you remember that I have entrusted to you this knowledge that we can, of Mars and Venus, make a magnificent vitriol in which the three principles meet, which often serve to give birth and produce our stone".

Let's note one more important remark from Henckel[67] about vitriol. "Of all the names that have been given to vitriol," says this author, "there is not one that has a connection with iron; it is always called chalcantum, chalcitis, cuperosa or cupri rosa , etc. And it is not only among the Greeks and the Latins that iron has been deprived of the part which belongs to it in vitriol; the same has been done in Germany, and to this day all vitriols in general, and especially those containing the most iron, are given the name of kupfer wasser, copper-colored water, or, which amounts to the same thing, that of copperas".

Panel 8 (plate XXXI) – The subject of this bas-relief is rather singular; there is a young gladiator, almost a child, striving to slash, with great sword strokes, a hive filled with honey cakes and whose lid he has removed. Two words make up the sign:

. MELITVS. GLADIVS.   THE HONEYED SWORD

This bizarre act of an impetuous youth carried away, giving battle to the bees like Don Quixote to his mills, is, basically, only the symbolic translation of our first work, original variant of the theme so well known and so often exploited hermetically, the striking of the rock. It is known that after their departure from Egypt, the children of Israel had to camp at Rephidim (Exodus, XVII, I, Numbers, XXXIII, 14), "where there was no water to drink for the people". On the advice of the Lord (Exodus, XVII, 6), Moses, struck the rock in Horeb three times with his rod, and a spring of living water flowed from the arid stone. Mythology also offers us some replicas of the same prodigy. Callimachus (*Hymn to Jupiter*, 31) says that after the goddess Rhea struck the Arcadian mountain with her scepter, it opened in two and the water escaped with abundance. Appolonius of Alexandria (*Argonauts*, 1146) relates the

---

66 Valmont de Bomare. *Minéralogie ou Nouvelle Exposition du Règne minéral* (Mineralogy or New Exposition of the Mineral Kingdom). Paris, Vincent, 1774.

67 J.-F. Henckel. *Pyritology*, ch VII, p. 184. Op. Cit.

miracle of Mount Dindyme and assures that the rock had never before given birth to any source. Pausanias attributes a similar fact to Atalanta, who, in order to quench her thirst, made a fountain spring by striking with her javelin a rock in the vicinity of Cyphantus, in Laconia.

In our bas-relief, the gladiator takes the place of the alchemist, depicted elsewhere as Hercules, the hero of the twelve symbolic works, or as a knight armed from head to toe, as can be seen on the gate of Notre-Dame de Paris. The youth of the character expresses this simplicity that must be observed throughout the book, imitating and closely following the example of nature. On the other hand, we must believe that if the Adept of Dampierre gives preference to the gladiator, it is to signify without doubt that the artist must work or fight alone against matter. The Greek word μονόμαχος, which means gladiator, is composed of μόνος, alone, and μάχομαι, fight. As for the hive, it owes the privilege of representing the stone to this cabalistic device that makes the hive drift from the rock by permutation of vowels. The philosophical subject, our first stone –in Greek πέτρα– is clearly visible under the image of the hive or rock, because πέτρα also means rock, a word used by the sages to designate the hermetic subject.

Moreover, our swordsman, by hitting the emblematic hive with double blows and randomly cutting its honey combs, makes it a shapeless, heterogeneous mass of wax, propiolis and honey, incoherent magma, a real jumble, to use the language of the gods, from which the honey flows to the point of coating its sword, substituted for the stick of Moses. This is the second chaos, the result of the primitive struggle, which we call cabalistic melodrama, because it contains honey (μέλι) –viscous and glutinous water of metals–, always ready to flow (μέλλω). The masters of art tell us that the whole work is a work of Hercules, and that we must begin by hitting the stone, rock or hive, which is our raw material, with the magic sword of secret fire, in order to determine the flow of this precious water that it contains in its womb. Because the subject of the wise is hardly anything more than frozen water, which is why it is called Pegasus (from Πηγάς, rock, ice, frozen water or hard, dry earth). And the fable tells us that Pegasus, among other actions, kicked out the Hippocrene fountain. Πήγασος, Pegasus, has as its root πηγή, source, so that the winged messenger of poets merges with the hermetic source, of which he possesses the essential characteristics: the mobility of living waters and the volatility of spirits.

As an emblem of the first matter, the hive is often found in decorations borrowing their elements from the science of Hermes. We saw it on the ceiling of Hotel Lallemant and among the panels of the alchemical stove in Winterthur. It still occupies one of the spaces of the Game of the Goose, labyrinth of the sacred art, and collection of the main hieroglyphs of the Great Work.

Panel 9 (plate XXXI) – The sun, piercing the clouds, directs its rays towards a pipit nest,[68] containing a small egg and placed on a grassy mound. The phylactery, which gives the bas-relief its meaning, bears the inscription:

. NEC. TE. NEC. SINE. TE.   NOT YOU, BUT NOTHING WITHOUT YOU

---

68 The Meadow pipit (*Anthus pratensis*) is a small bird next to larks. It nests in the grass. It was called Άνθος by the Greeks: but this word has another meaning of a clearly esoteric character. Άνθος also refers to the flower and the most perfect, the most distinguished part of a thing; it is also the efflorescence, foam or foam of solutions whose light parts rise and crystallize on the surface. This is enough to give a clear idea of the birth of the little bird whose only egg is to produce our Phoenix.

Allusion to the sun, father of the stone, following Hermes and the plurality of hermetic philosophers. The symbolic star, represented in its radiant splendor, takes the place of the metallic sun or sulphur, which many artists believed to be natural gold. A serious error, all the more excusable as all the authors perfectly understand the difference between the gold of the wise and the precious metal. Indeed, it is the sulphur of metals that masters speak about when they describe how to extract and prepare this first agent, which, moreover, bears no physical and chemical resemblance to vulgar gold. And it is also this sulphur, combined with mercury, that collaborates in the generation of our egg by giving it the vegetative capacity. This real father of the stone is therefore independent of it, since the stone comes from it, hence the first part of the axiom: *nec te*; and since it is impossible to obtain anything without the help of sulphur, the second proposal is justified: *nec sine te*. However, what we say about sulphur is true for mercury. So that the egg, a manifestation of the new metallic form emanating from the mercurial principle, if it owes its substance to mercury or hermetic Moon, draws its vitality and its possibility of development from the sulphur or sun of the wise.

In summary, it is philosophically correct to ensure that metals are composed of sulphur and mercury, as Bernard Trévisan teaches; that stone, although formed by the same principles, does not give birth to a metal; and that sulphur and mercury, considered in isolation, are the only relatives of stone, but cannot be confused with it. We would like to draw the reader's attention to the fact that the philosophical coction of rebis provides sulphur, and not an irreducible assembly of its components, and that this sulphur, by complete assimilation of mercury, has particular properties that tend to distance it from the metallic species. And it is on this constancy of effect that the multiplication and augmentation technique is based, because new sulphur is always likely to absorb a determined and proportional quantity of mercury.

X

Seventh series (plate XXXII).

Panel 1 – The tables of the hermetic law, on which we read a French sentence, but so singularly presented, that Mr. Louis Audiat did not know how to discover the meaning:

. EN . RIEN . GIST . TOVT .   IN NOTHING IS EVERYTHING

A primordial motto, which ancient philosophers delight in repeating, and by which they mean to signify the absence of value, the vulgarity, the extreme abundance of the basic material from which they derive all that is necessary for them. "You will find everything in everything that is nothing but a styptic or astringent virtue of metals and minerals," writes Basil Valentine in the book of the *Twelve Keys*.

Thus, true wisdom teaches us not to judge things according to their price, the pleasure received from them, the beauty of their appearance. It leads us to estimate in man his personal merit, not the outside or his condition, and in the bodies the spiritual quality that they hold hidden in them.

In the eyes of the wise man, iron, this pariah of human industry, is incomparably more noble than gold, and gold is more despicable than lead; for this bright light, this ardent, active and pure water that base metals, minerals and stones have preserved, is lacking only in gold. This sovereign to whom so many people pay tribute, for whom so many consciences debase themselves in the hope of obtaining its favours, has nothing rich and precious but clothing. A sumptuously adorned king, gold is nevertheless only an inert but magnificent

DAMPIERRE-SUR-BOUTONNE
Panels of the Upper Gallery – Seventh Series – Plate XXXII

body, a brilliant corpse with regard to copper, iron or lead. This usurper, whom an ignorant and greedy crowd raises to the rank of god, cannot even claim to belong to the old and powerful family of metals; stripped of his coat, he then reveals the baseness of his origins and appears to us as a simple metallic resin, dense, fixed and fusible, triple quality that makes him notoriously unfit for the realization of our purpose.

Thus we see how vain it would be to work on gold, for he who has nothing can obviously give nothing. It is therefore to the rough and vile stone that one must address oneself, without repugnance for its miserable appearance, its foul smell, its black color, its sordid rags. For it is precisely these unattractive characters that make it possible to recognize it, and have made it look from time immemorial as a primitive substance, resulting from the original chaos, and that God, during the creation and organization of the universe, would have reserved for his servants and his elect. Drawn from the Void, it bears the imprint and suffers the name: Nothing. But philosophers have discovered that in its elemental and disorderly nature, made of darkness and light, bad and good, gathered in the worst confusion, this Nothing contained all that they could desire.

Panel 2 (plate XXXII) – The capital letter H surmounted by a crown, which M. Louis Audiat presents as the emblazoned signature of the King of France Henry II, offers today only an inscription partially hammered, but which was formerly read:

. IN. TE. OMNIS. DOMINATA. RECVMBIT.   IN YOU RESTS ALL THE POWER

We have previously had the opportunity to say that the letter H, or at least the graphic character related to it, had been chosen by philosophers to designate the spirit, the universal soul of things, or that active and almighty principle that we recognize to be, in nature, in perpetual movement, in active vibration. It is on the form of the letter H that the builders of the Middle Ages built the facades of the cathedrals, glorifying temples of the divine spirit, magnificent interpreters of the aspirations of the human soul in its rise towards the Creator. This character corresponds to the eta (H), seventh letter of the Greek alphabet, initial of the solar verb, dwelling place of the spirit, star that gives light: Ἥλιος, sun. He is also the head of the prophet Elijah –in Greek Ἠλιάς solar–, who, the Scriptures say, ascended to heaven, like a pure spirit, in a chariot of light and fire. It is still the centre and heart of one of Christ's monograms: I H S, abbreviation of *Iesus Hominum Salvator*, Jesus the Savior of Men. This is also the sign used by medieval Freemasons to designate the two columns of Solomon's temple, at the foot of which the workers received their wages: Jachin and Boaz, columns of which the towers of the metropolitan churches are only the free, but bold and powerful translation. Finally, it is the indication of the first step of the scale of the wise, *scala philosophorum*, of the knowledge acquired by the hermetic agent, mysterious promoter of the transformations of mineral nature, and of the secret found of the lost Word. This agent was formerly designated, between the Adepts, under the epithet of magnet or attractive. The body charged with this magnet called itself Magnesia, and it was it, this body, which served as an intermediary between heaven and earth, feeding on astral influences, or celestial dynamism, which it transmitted to the passive substance, attracting them as a true magnet. In one of his allegorical accounts, De Cyrano Bergerac thus speaks of the magnesian spirit, of which he seems very well informed, both in terms of preparation and use.

"You have not forgotten, I think," wrote our author, "that my name is Helias, because I told you so before. You will therefore know that I was in your world and that I lived with Elyseus, a Hebrew like me, on the pleasant banks of the Jordan, where I lived a life sweet enough among the books, not to be lamented, even though it passed away. However, the more the lights of my mind grew, the more the knowledge of those I did not have grew. Never did our priests bring Adam back to me, only the memory of this perfect Philosophy he had possessed made me sigh. I despaired of being able to acquire it, when one day, after having sacrificed for the atonement of the weaknesses of my mortal being, I fell asleep, and the Angel of the Lord appeared to me in a dream; as soon as I was awakened, I did not fail to work on the things he had prescribed to me: I took some magnet about two feet square, which I put in a furnace; then, when it was well purged, precipitated and dissolved, I drew the attraction from it; I calcined all this Elixir and reduced it to the size of about a mediocre ball.

"After these preparations, I had a very light iron carriage built, and from there to a few months, all my machines having been completed, I entered my industrious chariot. You'll be asking me what's the point of all this stuff. Know that the Angel had told me in a dream that if I wanted to acquire perfect science as I wanted, I would go up to the world of the Moon, where I would find before the Paradise of Adam, the Tree of Knowledge, because as soon as I had taste its fruit, my soul would be enlightened by all the truths of which a creature is capable; that is the journey for which I had built my chariot. Finally, I climbed into it and, when I was firm and leaning firmly on the seat, I threw this magnet ball high into the air. Now, the iron machine, which I had intentionally forged more massive in the middle than at the ends, was removed immediately, and in perfect balance, as I arrived where the magnet had attracted me, and, as soon as I had jumped until then, my hand made it go back... In truth, it was a surprising sight, for the steel of this flying house, which I had polished with great care, reflected on all sides the light of the sun so bright and bright, that I myself thought I was being carried away in a chariot of fire... When I have since reflected on this miraculous rapture, I imagined that I could not have overcome, by the occult virtues of a simple natural body, the vigilance of the Seraphim that God ordered for the guard of this paradise. But because he likes to use second causes, I believed that he had inspired me this way to enter it, as he wanted to use Adam's ribs to make him a woman, even though he could form her from earth as well as he did".[69]

As for the crown, which completes the important sign we are studying, it is not the crown of King Henry II of France, but the royal crown of the chosen ones. It is the one that adorns the Redeemer's forehead on the crucifixes of the 11th, 12th and 13th centuries, especially in Amiens (Byzantine Christ called Saint-Sauve) and in Notre-Dame de Trèves (top of the gate). The knight of Revelation (ch. VI, v. 2), ridden on a white horse, emblem of purity, receives as distinctive attributes of his high virtues an arch and a crown, gifts of the Holy Spirit. Now, our crown –the initiates know what we hear about–, is precisely the domicile of choice of the spirit. It is a miserable substance, as we have said, barely materialized, but it contains it in abundance. And this is what the ancient philosophers fixed in their corona *radiata* (radiant crown), decorated with projecting rays, which was attributed only to gods or deified heroes. Thus we will explain that this matter, a vehicle of mineral light, is revealed, thanks to the radiant signature of the spirit, as the promised land reserved for the chosen ones of Sapience.

Panel 3 (plate XXXII) – It is an ancient and often exploited symbol that we find in this place: the dolphin twisted on the arm of a sea anchor. The Latin epigraph which serves him as a sign gives the reason:

. SIC. TRISTIS. AVRA. RESEDIT.   THUS THIS TERRIBLE STORM CALMS DOWN

We have had several opportunities to highlight the important role that fish play in alchemical theatre. Under the name of dolphin, *échénéis* or remora, it characterizes the wet and cold principle of the Work, which is our mercury, which coagulates little by little on contact and by the effect of sulphur, the agent of desiccation and fixity. The latter is represented here by the marine anchor, the stabilizing organ of the vessels, to which it provides a point of support and resistance against the effort of the waves. The long operation of progressive filling and final fixation of mercury offers a great analogy to sea crossings and the storms that envelop them. It is an agitated and stormy sea that presents in small scale, the constant and regular boiling of the hermetic compost. The bubbles burst on the surface and follow one another constantly; heavy vapors charge the atmosphere of the vase; the cloudy, opaque, livid clouds darken the walls, condense into droplets dripping on the effervescent mass. Everything contributes to the spectacle of a reducing storm. Raised on all sides, tossed by the winds, the ark nevertheless floats in the heavy rain. Asteria is about to form Delos, a hospitable and life-saving land for the children of Latona. The dolphin swims on the surface of the impetuous waves, and this agitation continues until the remora, the invisible host of the deep waters, finally stops, like a powerful anchor, the drifting ship. The calm is reborn, the air is purified, the water is erased, the vapors are absorbed. A film covers the entire surface, and, thickening and consolidating every day, marks the end of the flood, the landing stage of the ark, the birth of Diana and Apollo, the triumph of the earth over water, of dry over wet, and the time of the new Phoenix. In the general upheaval and the struggle of the elements, this permanent peace

---

69 From Cyrano Bergerac. *L'Autre Monde, ou Histoire comique des États et Empires de la Lune* (The Other World, or the comic history of the States and Empires of the Moon). Paris, Bauche, 1910, p. 38.

is acquired, the harmony resulting from the perfect balance of principles, symbolized by the fish fixed on the anchor: *sic tristis aura resedit.*

This phenomenon of mercury absorption and coagulation by a much lower proportion of sulphur seems to be the primary cause of the remora fable, a small fish to which the popular imagination and hermetic tradition attributed the ability to stop the largest ships in their tracks. Here is what the philosopher René François says about it, in an allegorical and instructive speech: "The emperor Caligula once became enraged, returning to Rome with a powerful naval army. All the superb ships, both armed and so well hoped for, were sailing satisfactorily; the pounding wind filled all the sails; the waves and the sky seemed to be in favour of Caligula, second in his designs, and as for the most beautiful, but, the commanding imperial galley stops abruptly, while the others are flying. The emperor is furious, the pilot blows louder his whistle and four hundred comitres and rowers at the oar, five per bench, sweat by pushing; the wind gets stronger, the sea gets stronger, the sea gets angry from this affront, everyone is full of this miracle, when the emperor imagines that some sea monster stops him on this place. So forceful dives rushed out to sea and, swimming between two waters, made the rounds around this floating castle; they were going to find a mean little fish, half a foot long, who had attached himself to the tiller, took his time to stop the gallery that was taming the universe. It seems that he wanted to make fun of the emperor of the human race, who is so proud of his crowds of armed men and his iron thunders that make him lord of the earth. "Here", it is said in his fish language, "a new Annibal at the gates of Rome, who has detained in a floating prison, Rome and its emperor; Rome the princess that will lead on earth the captive kings in her triumph, and I will lead the Prince of the Universe through the lands of the Ocean in marine triumph. Cesar will be king of men, and I will be the Cesar of Cesars; all the power of Rome is now my slave and can make all its last effort, for as long as I want, I will keep it in this royal jail. By attaching myself to this galleon, I will do more in an instant than they have done in eight hundred years, slaughtering the human race and people around the world. Poor emperor! How far from your tale you are, with all your one hundred and fifty million income, and three hundred million men in your pay: a mischievous little fish has made you back its slave! May the sea be rough, may the wind be unleashed, may the whole world become a galley slave and all the trees become oars, they will not take a step without my approval and my permission... Here is the true Archimedes of fish, because only he stops everyone; here is the animated magnet that captivates all the iron and weapons of the first monarchy in the world; I do not know who calls Rome the golden anchor of the human race, but this fish is the anchor of the anchors... Oh wonder of God! This piece of fish is a disgrace, not only to the Roman greatness, but to Aristotle who loses his credit, and to the philosophy that makes it bankrupt, because they have no reason to make an effort, that a mouth without teeth stops a ship pushed by the four elements, and stops it take in the midst of the most cruel storms. Pliny says that all nature is hidden as a sentinel, and housed in garrison in the smallest creatures; I believe him, and, as for me, I think that this little fish is the moving flag of nature and all its gendarmerie; it is it that aggravates and stops these galleys; it is it that clamps, with no other strap than a fish's snout, which cannot be clamped... Alas! Why do not lower the horns of our vain arrogance, with such holy consideration; for if God being played by a little sea skimmer, and the pirate of nature, he stops and hooks all our designs, which fly at full sail from one pole to the other, if he uses his omnipotence there, at what point will he reduce our affairs? If he does everything with nothing, and a fish, or rather a little nothing, swimming and acting like a fish, overwhelms all our hopes, alas! when he uses all his power and all the armies of his justice, hey! where will we be?".[70]

Panel 4 (plate XXXII) – Near the tree with golden fruit, a robust and stocky dragon exercises its vigilance at the entrance of the Hesperides garden. The particular phylactery on this subject bears, engraved, this inscription:

. AB. INSOMNI. NO . CVSTODITA. DRACONE.

APART FROM THE DRAGON WHO WATCHES, THINGS ARE NOT GUARDED

The myth of the dragon who watches over the famous orchard and the legendary Golden Fleece is well enough known to save us the trouble of reproducing it. It is sufficient to indicate that the dragon is chosen as a hieroglyphic representative of the raw mineral material with which the Work must begin. This means what is its importance, the care that must be taken in the study of external signs and qualities likely to allow their identification, to have the hermetic subject recognized and distinguished between the multiple minerals that nature makes available to us.

In charge of watching over the wonderful enclosure where philosophers will collect their treasures, the dragon is said never to slumber. His fiery eyes remain constantly open. He knows neither rest nor weariness and cannot overcome the insomnia that characterizes him and ensures his true raison d'être. This is expressed in the Greek name it bears. Δράκων has as its root δέρκομαι, to look, see, and, by extension, live, a word that is itself close to δερκευνής, which sleeps with its eyes open. The primitive language reveals to us, through the cloak of symbols, the idea of intense activity, of a perpetual and latent vitality enclosed in the mineral body. Mythologists call our dragon Ladon, a word whose assonance is close to Laton and which can be assimilated to the Greek Λήθω (Leto), a hidden, unknown, ignored being, like the matter of philosophers.

The general appearance, the recognized ugliness of the dragon, his ferocity, and his singular vital power correspond exactly with the external peculiarities, properties, and faculties of the subject. The special crystallization of the latter is clearly indicated by the scaly epidermis of this one. Similar are the colors, because the material is black, punctuated with red or yellow, like the dragon which is the image. As for the volatile quality of our mineral, we see it translated by the membranous wings of which the monster is provided. And because he vomits, it is said, when he is attacked, fire and smoke, and his body ends in a snake's tail, the poets, for these reasons, gave birth to him from Typhon and 'Echidna. The Greek Τυφάων, poetic term of Τυφῶν or Τυφώς –the Egyptian Typhoon–, means to fill with smoke, to light, to set alight. Ἔχιδνα is none other than the viper. Whence we may conclude that the dragon owes its warm, ardent, sulphurous nature to Typhon, while owing to its mother its cold and moist complexion, with the characteristic form of ophidians.

Now, if philosophers have always concealed the vulgar name of their subject under an infinity of epithets, on the other hand they have been very prolix with regard to its form, its virtues and, sometimes, its preparation. By mutual agreement, they affirm that the artist cannot hope to discover or produce anything outside the subject, because he is the only body capable, in all nature, of providing him with the indispensable elements. Excluding other

---

70 René François. *Essay des Merveilles de Nature et des plus nobles artifices* (Essay of the Wonders of Nature and the most noble artifices). Lyon, J. Huguetan, 1642, ch. XV, p. 125.

minerals and other metals, it retains the principles necessary for the development of the Great Work. By its monstrous but expressive figuration, this primitive subject clearly appears to us as the guardian and the sole dispenser of hermetic fruits. He is the depository, the watchful conservative, and our Adept speaks as a sage when he teaches that, apart from this solitary being, philosopher's things are not guarded, since we would look for them vainly elsewhere. Also, it is about this first body, a parcel of the original chaos and common mercury of the philosophers, that Geber shouts out: "Praise be to the Most High, who created our mercury and gave it a nature to which nothing resists; for without it the alchemists could do all their work would become useless".

"But," asks another Adept, "where is this aurific mercury, which resolves into salt and swelling, becomes the radical wet of the metals and their animated seed? He is imprisoned in a prison so strong that even nature can not draw him from it, if the industrious art does not facilitate its means".[71]

Panel 5 (Plate XXXII) – A swan, majestically placed on the calm water of a pond, has its neck crossed by an arrow. And it is his ultimate complaint that is reflected in the epigraph of this pleasantly executed little subject:

PROPRIIS. PEREO. PENNIS.   I DIE BY MY OWN FEATHERS

The bird provides one of the materials for the weapon that will be used to kill it; the tail of the arrow, ensuring its direction, making it precise, and the feathers of the swan, filling this office, thus contribute to its loss. This beautiful bird, whose wings are emblematic of volatility, and snowy whiteness the expression of purity, has the two essential qualities of the initial mercury or our dissolving water. We know that he must be overcome by sulphur, –from its substance and which he himself generated–, in order to obtain after his death this philosophical mercury, partly fixed and partly volatile, which subsequent maturation will raise to the degree of perfection of the great Elixir. All the authors teach that it is necessary to kill the living if one wishes to resurrect the dead; this is why the good artist will not hesitate to sacrifice the bird of Hermes, and to provoke the mutation of its mercurial properties into sulphurous qualities, since any transformation remains subject to prior decomposition and cannot be achieved without it.

Basil Valentine assures that "one must feed a white swan to the double-igneous man," and, he adds, "the roasted swan will be for the king's table." No philosopher, to our knowledge, has raised the veil that covers this mystery, and we wonder whether it is expedient to comment on such grave words. However, remembering the long years in which we have stationed ourselves in front of this door, we think it would be charitable to help the worker, who had reached that point, to cross the threshold. Let us stretch out a helping hand and discover, within the permitted limits, what the greatest masters have thought prudent to reserve.

It is obvious that Basil Valentine, by using the expression double igneous man, speaks about a second principle, resulting from a combination of two agents of hot and burning complexion, having, therefore, the nature of metallic sulphur. Hence it can be concluded that, under the simple denomination of sulphur, the Adepts, at a given time of work, conceive two combined bodies, of similar properties but of different specificity, taken conventionally

---

71 *La Lumière sortant par soy-mesme des Ténèbres* (The light coming forth from the Darkness), ch. II, song V, p. 16. Op. Cit.

for one. Having said that, what substances will be able to release these two products? Such a question has never been answered. However, if we consider that metals have their emblematic representatives represented by mythological deities, sometimes male, sometimes female; that they hold these particular assignments of experimentally recognized sulphurous qualities, symbolism and fable will likely throw some clarity on these obscure things.

Everyone knows that iron and lead are under the domination of Ares and Chronos, and that they receive the respective planetary influences of Mars and Saturn; tin and gold, subjected to Zeus and Apollo, espouse the vicissitudes of Jupiter and the Sun. But why do Aphrodite and Artemis dominate copper and silver, subjects of Venus and the Moon? Why is mercury indebted to the Olympus messenger, the god Hermes, for its complexion, even though it is sulphur-free and fulfils the functions reserved for chemical-hermetic women? Should we accept these relations as true, and is there not a deliberate, premeditated confusion in the distribution of metallic divinities and their astral correspondences? If we were asked about this point, we would answer without hesitation in the affirmative. Experience shows, for sure, that silver has a magnificent sulphur, as pure and bright as gold, but without having the fixity. Lead produces a poor product, almost even in color, but not very stable and highly impure. The sulphur in tin, clean and bright, is white and would cause the metal to be placed under the protection of a goddess rather than under the authority of a god. Iron, on the other hand, has a lot of fixed sulphur, a dark red, dull, unclean, so defective that, despite its refractory quality, one cannot really know what to use it for. And yet, except for gold, one would vainly seek, in other metals, a brighter, more penetrating and more manageable mercury. As for the sulphur of copper, Basil Valentine describes it very precisely in the first book of his Twelve Keys: "The lascivious Venus, he says, is well colored, and all her body is almost nothing more than a tincture and color similar to that of the Sun, which, because of its abundance, draws heavily on red. But because his body is leper and sick, the fixed tincture cannot remain there, and, the perishing body, the tincture perishes with him, unless it is accompanied by a fixed body, where he can establish his seat and his dwelling in a stable and permanent way".[72]

If it is well understood what the famous Adept wants to teach, and if we carefully examine the relations existing between the metallic sulphurs and their respective symbols, we shall find little difficulty in reestablishing the esoteric order according to the job. The enigma will be deciphered and the problem of double sulfur will be easily solved.

Panel 6 (plate XXXII) – Two horns of abundance intersect on the Mercury caduceus. Their epigraph is this Latin maxim:

. VIRTVTI. FORTUNA. COMES.   FORTUNE ACCOMPANIES VIRTUE

An axiom of exception, a questionable truth in its application to genuine merit, in which fortune so rarely rewards virtue, it is advisable to seek confirmation and rule from elsewhere. Now it is the secret virtue of the philosophical mercury, represented by the image of the caduceus, that the author of these symbols hears. The cornucopias reflect all the material wealth that the possession of mercury provides good artists. By their crossing in X, they indicate the spiritual quality of this noble and rare substance, whose energy shines like a pure fire, in the center of the body exactly sublimated.

---

72 *Les Douze Clefs de Philosophie* (The Twelve Keys of Philosophy). Text corrected on the Frankfurt edition; Éditions de Minuit, 1956, p. 86.

The caduceus, the attribute of the god Mercury, cannot give place to the least equivocation, both in terms of the secret meaning and the point of view of the symbolic value. Hermes, father of hermetic science, is at the same time considered as creator and creature, master of philosophy and matter of philosophers. His winged scepter bears the explanation of the enigma he proposes, and the revelation of the mystery covering the composite of the compound, a masterpiece of nature and art, under the vulgar epithet of mercury of the sages .

Originally, the caduceus was only a simple wand, a primitive scepter of a few sacred or fabulous characters belonging more to tradition than to history. Moses, Atalanta, Cybele, Hermes use this instrument, endowed with a kind of magical power, under similar conditions and generating equivalent results. The Greek ῥάβδος is, indeed, a rod, a stick, a javelin shaft, a stinger and the scepter of Hermes. This word derives from ῥάσσω, which means to strike, share, destroy. Moses strikes with his rod the arid rock that Atalanta, like Cybele, pierces with his javelin. Mercury separates and kills the two snakes engaged in a furious duel, throwing at them the stick of πτεροφόροι, i. e. couriers and messengers, qualified as wing bearers because they had, as a badge of their charge, wings to their bonnet. Hermes' winged petase therefore justifies its function as a messenger and mediator of the gods. The addition of snakes to the rod, completed by the hat (πέτασος) and the heels (ταρσοί), gave the caduceus its final shape, with the hieroglyphic expression of perfect mercury.

On the panel of Dampierre, the two serpents show dog heads, one of a dog, the other of a bitch, pictorial version of the two opposite principles, active and passive, fixed and volatile, put in contact with the mediator figured by the wand magic, which is our secret fire. Artephius calls these principles Dog of Corascene and Bitch of Armenia , and it is these same serpents that the Hercules child stifles in its cradle, the only agents whose assembly, the fight and the death, realized through the fire philosophical, give birth to the living and animated hermetic mercury. And as this double mercury has double volatility, the wings of the petasus, opposite to those of the heels on the caduceus, serve to express these two qualities together, in the clearest and most telling manner.

Panel 7 (Plate XXXII) – In this bas-relief, Cupid, the bow of one hand and the other an arrow, straddles the Chimera on a heap of dotted clouds. The phylactery that emphasizes this subject indicates that Eros is here the eternal master:

. ÆTERNVS. HIC. DOMINVS.   HERE IS THE ETERNAL MASTER

Nothing is more true, moreover, and other panels have taught us the same. Eros, mythical personification of concord and love, is, par excellence, the lord, the eternal master of the Work. He alone can make the agreement between enemies that an implacable hate constantly pushes to devour each other. He fills the peaceful office of the priest whom we see united –on an engraving of the Twelve Keys of Basil Valentine–, the hermetic king and queen. It is also he who shoots, in the same play, an arrow towards a woman holding a huge flask completely filled with nebulous water...

Mythology tells us that the Chimera carried three different heads on a lion's body finished in a snaketail: one was a lion's head, the other a goat's head and the third a dragon's head. Of the monster's constituent parts, two are predominant, the lion and the dragon, because they bring into the assembly, one the head and body, the other the head and tail. By analyzing the symbol in the order of successive acquisitions, the first place belongs to the dragon, which is always confused with the snake; we know that the Greeks called δράκων the dragon rather than the snake. This is our initial material, the very subject of art, considered in its first being and in the state in which nature provides it. The lion comes next, and even though it is the child of the subject of the sages and a deciduous metal, he greatly surpasses his own parents and quickly becomes more robust than his father. As the unworthy son of an old man and a very young woman, he testified from birth to an inconceivable aversion to his mother. Unsociable, fierce, aggressive, one cannot expect anything from this violent and cruel heir, if he is not reduced, thanks to a providential accident, to more calm and balance. Encouraged by his mother Aphrodite, Eros, already dissatisfied with the character, unleashed a bronze arrow and seriously injured him. Half paralyzed, he is then brought back to his mother, who, in order to restore this ungrateful son, nevertheless gives him his own blood, or even part of his flesh, and dies after having saved him. "The mother", says the Turba Philosophorum, "always feels more pity for the child than the child for the mother". From this close and prolonged contact of sulphur-lion and dissolver-dragon a new being is formed, regenerated in some way, with mixed qualities, symbolically represented by the goat, or, if we prefer, by the Chimera itself. The Greek word Χίμαιρα, Chimera, also means young goat (cabalistically X-μήτηρ). However, this young goat, which owes its existence and its brilliant qualities to the timely intervention of Eros, is none other than philosophical mercury, resulting from the alliance of sulphur and mercury principles, which has all the faculties required to become the famous golden fleece ram, our Elixir and our stone. And it is all the order of hermetic labor that the ancient Chimera discovers, and, as Philaletes says, it is also all our philosophy.

The reader will excuse us for using the allegory to better situate the important points of the practice, but we have no other means and continue the old literary tradition. And if we reserve, in the narrative, the essential part which belongs to the little Cupid –master of the Work and lord of the house–, it is only by obedience to the discipline of the Order, and not to be perjured to ourselves. For the rest, the perspicacious reader will find, voluntarily disseminated in the pages of this book, additional indications on the role of the mediator, of whom we should not speak any more in this place.

Panel 8 (Plate XXXII) – Here we find a pattern already met elsewhere and especially in Britain. It is an ermine, figured inside a small enclosure that limits a circular fence, special symbol of Queen Anne, wife of Charles VIII and Louis XII. It can be seen, next to Louis XII's emblematic porcupine, at the mantelpiece of the grand fireplace at the Hotel Lallemant in Bourges. His epigraph contains the same meaning and uses almost the same words as the famous motto of the order of Hermine: *Malo mori quam fædari*, I prefer death to blemish. This order of chivalry, founded first in 1381 by John V, Duke of Brittany, was to disappear in the 15th century. Afterwards restored by the King of Naples, Ferdinand I, in the year 1483, the order of Hermine, having lost all hermetic character, formed only an inconsistent association of patrician chivalry.

The inscription engraved on the phylactery of our box carries:

. MORI. POTIVS. QVAM. FEDARI.   RATHER DEATH THAN DEFILEMENT

Beautiful and noble maxim of Anne of Brittany; maxim of purity, applied to the small carnivore whose white fur is, it is said, the object of the hasty care of its elegant and supple owner. But, in the esotericism of sacred art, the ermine, image of philosophical mercury, signals the absolute sharpness of a sublimated product, which the addition of sulphur, or metallic fire, contributes to make even more brilliant.

In Greek, ermine is called ποντικός, a word derived from πόντος or πόντιος, the gulf, the abyss, the sea, the ocean; it is the Pontic water of the philosophers, our mercury, the sea purged again with its sulfur, sometimes simply the water of our sea, what must be read water of our mother, that is to say of the matter primitive and chaotic called the subject of the wise. The masters teach us that their second mercury, this Pontic water of which we speak, is a permanent water, which, unlike liquid bodies, "does not wet hands", and their source flowing into the hermetic sea. To obtain it, they say, it is advisable to strike the rock three times in order to extract the pure wave mixed with the coarse and solidified water, generally represented by boulders emerging from the ocean. The word πόντιος expresses especially all that dwells in the sea; it awakens in the mind that hidden fish that mercury has captured and retains in the meshes of its net, the one that the ancient custom of the Feast of Kings sometimes offers us in its form (sole, dolphin), sometimes under the aspect of the "bather" or the bean, hidden between the laminated slices of the traditional slab.[73] The pure and white ermine thus appears as an expressive emblem of the common mercury united to sulfur-fish in the substance of philosophical mercury.

As for the enclosure, it reveals to us what are these external signs which, according to the Adepts, constitute the best criterion of the secret product and provide the testimony of a canonical preparation and in conformity with natural laws. The braided palisade used as an ermine pen and, in fact, as an animated mercury envelope, would be sufficient to explain the design of the stigmas in question. But our goal being to define them unequivocally, we will say that the Greek word χαράκωμα, palisade, derived from χαράσσω, to trace, engrave, mark with an imprint, thus has an origin similar to that of the term χαρακτήρ, i. e. lineament engraved, distinctive shape, character. And the specific character of mercury is precisely to affect its surface with a network of intersecting lines, woven in the manner of wicker baskets (κάλαθος), frails, crates, two-handled baskets and open baskets. These geometric figures, all the more apparent and better engraved as the matter is purer, are an effect of the omnipotent will of the Spirit or Light. And this will gives the substance a cruciform external disposition (Χίασμα) and gives mercury its effective philosophical signature. This is why this envelope is compared to the meshes of the net used to catch the symbolic fish; to the Eucharistic basket worn on its back by the Ἰχθύς of the Roman Catacombs; to the manger of Jesus, the cradle of the Holy Spirit incarnated in the Savior of men; to the cist of Bacchus, which was said to contain an unknown mysterious object; to the cradle of Hercules as a child, suffocating the two snakes sent by Juno, and to that of Moses saved from the waters; to the cake of the kings, bearing the same characters; to the cake of Little Red Riding Hood, perhaps the most charming creation of these hermetic fables that are the the *Tales of Mother Goose*, etc.

But the significant imprint of animated mercury, a superficial mark of the work of the metallic spirit, can only be obtained after a series of operations, or purifications, long, ungrateful, and repulsive. Also, we must not neglect any pain, any effort and fear neither time nor fatigue, if we want to be assured of success. Whatever one does or attempts to do, the spirit will never remain stable in an unclean or insufficiently purified body. The motto, all spiritual, that accompanies our ermine proclaims it: *Rather death than defilement.* That the artist remembers one of the great works of Hercules, the cleaning of the stables of Augias; "All the waters of the flood must pass through our earth", say the wise. These are expressive images of the labor required for perfect purification, a simple, easy work, but so tedious that it

---

73 Cf. Fulcanelli. *Le Mystère des Cathédrales* (The Mystery of the Cathedrals). Paris, J. Schemit, 1926, p. 126.

has discouraged a number of alchemists more eager than industrious, more enthusiastic than persevering.

Panel 9 (Plate XXXII) – Four horns from which flames escape, with the motto:

.FRVSTRA.   IN VAIN

It is the lapidary translation of the four fires of our coction. The authors who have spoken about them describe them as so many different and proportionate degrees of the elementary fire acting, within the Athanor, on the philosophical rebis. At least this is the meaning suggested to beginners, and that they should be quick, without too much thought, to put it into practice.

Yet philosophers themselves certify that they never speak more obscurely than when they appear to express themselves precisely; therefore, their apparent clarity abuses those who let themselves be seduced by the literal sense, and do not seek to ensure whether or not it is consistent with observation, reason and the possibility of nature. That is why we must warn the artists who will try to create the Work according to this process, that is, by subjecting the philosophical amalgam to the increasing temperatures of the four regimes of fire, that they will unerringly be victims of their ignorance and frustrated by the expected result. First of all, they should seek to discover what the ancients meant by the pictorial expression of fire, and that of the four successive degrees of its intensity. For it is not the fire of kitchens, our fireplaces or blast furnaces. "In our Work," says Philaletes, "ordinary fire only serves to keep away the cold and the accidents it could cause". In another part of his treatise, the same author says positively that our coction is linear, that is, equal, constant, regular and uniform throughout the work. Almost all philosophers have taken the example of the coction fire or maturation, the incubation of the hen's egg, not in terms of the temperature to be adopted, but in terms of uniformity and permanence. Therefore, we strongly advise to consider first of all the relationship that the sages have established between fire and sulphur, in order to obtain this essential notion that the four degrees of one must unerringly correspond to the four degrees of the other, which is to say a lot in a few words. Finally, in his such a meticulous description of the coction, Philaletes does not fail to point out how far the real operation is from his metaphorical analysis, because instead of being direct, as is generally believed, it includes several phases or diets, simple repetitions of a single and same technique. In our opinion, these words represent the most sincere words said about the secret practice of the four degrees of fire. And, although the order and development of these works are reserved by philosophers and always enveloped in silence, the special character of the coction thus understood will nevertheless allow wise artists to find the simple and natural way to facilitate their execution.

Mr. Louis Audiat, whose rather spicy fantasies we noted during this study, has not been asked ancient science for a plausible explanation of this curious chamber. "The joke," he writes, "is also mixed up in our texts. Here is a thick malice in a short word: *Frustra*. And flaming horns! It is vain to watch the woman!".

We do not believe that the author, moved by compassion in the face of this "testimony" of the unfortunate Adept, wanted to show the slightest irreverence for the memory of his companion... But ignorance is blind and misfortune is bad counselor. Mr. Louis Audiat should have known this and refrained from generalizing...

XI

The eighth and final series includes only one panel devoted to the science of Hermes. It represents steep rocks whose wild silhouette stands in the middle of the waves. This lapidary picture bears the sign:

. DONEC. ERVNT. IGNES.   AS LONG AS THE FIRE LASTS

Allusion to the possibilities of action that the man owes to the igneous principle, spirit, soul or light of things, unique factor of all the material mutations. Of the four elements of ancient philosophy, only three appear here: the earth, represented by the rocks, the water by the sea wave, the air by the sky of the carved landscape. As for the fire, animator and modifier of the three others, it seems excluded from the subject only to better underline its preponderance, its power and its necessity, as well as the impossibility of any action on the substance, without the help of this spiritual force, capable of penetrating it, of moving it, of changing into actuality what it has potential.

As long as the fire lasts, life will radiate in the universe; the bodies, subject to the laws of evolution of which it is the essential agent, will accomplish the different cycles of their metamorphoses, until their final transformation into spirit, light or fire. As long as the fire lasts, the matter will continue its painful ascent to full purity, passing from the compact and solid form (earth) to the liquid form (water), then from the gaseous state (air) to the radiant state (fire). As long as fire will last, the man will be able to exercise his industrious activity on the things which surround him, and, thanks to the marvelous igneous instrument, to submit them to his own will, to bend them, to subjugate them to his utility. As long as the fire lasts, science will benefit from extensive opportunities in all areas of the physical plane and will expand the scope of its knowledge and achievements. As long as the fire lasts, man will be in direct contact with God, and the creature will know his Creator better ...

No subject of meditation appears to be more beneficial to the philosopher; no one asks more for the exercise of his thought. Fire envelops us and bathes us on all sides; it comes to us through the air, water, the earth itself, which are its preservatives and the various vehicles; we meet it in everything that approaches us; we feel it acting in us for the entire duration of our earthly existence. Our birth is the result of its incarnation; our life, the effect of its dynamism; our death, the consequence of its disappearance. Prometheus stole fire from heaven to animate the man he had, as well as God, formed from the earth's silt. Vulcan created Pandora, the first woman, whom Minerva endowed with movement by breathing in vital fire. A simple mortal, the sculptor Pygmalion, eager to marry his own work, begged Venus to enliven his statue of Galatea with celestial fire. To seek to discover the nature and essence of fire is to seek to discover God, whose real presence has always been revealed under the igneous appearance. The burning bush (Exodus, III, 2) and the burning of the Sinai when the decalogue was handed over (Exodus, XIX, 18) are two manifestations by which God appeared to Moses. And under the figure of a being of jasper and sardonyx in the color of flame, seated on an incandescent and shining throne, that Saint John describes the Master of the universe (Revelation, IV, 3, 5). "Our God is a devouring fire," writes St. Paul in his *Epistle to the Hebrews* (ch. XII, 29). It is therefore not without reason that all religions have considered fire as the clearest image and the most expressive emblem of divinity. "One of the oldest symbols, says Pluche, since it has become universal, is the fire that is perpetually maintained in the place of the assembly of peoples. Nothing could give them a more sensitive idea of the power, beauty, purity and eternity of the being they come to worship. This magnificent symbol has been in use throughout the East. The Persians regard it as the most perfect image of the divinity. Zoroaster did not introduce its use under Darius Histarpès, but he did raise the bar with new views on a practice established long before him. The Pryantheum of the Greeks were perpetual fires. The Vesta of the Etruscans, Sabines and Romans was nothing more. The same use has been found in Peru and other parts of America. Moses kept the practice of perpetual fire in the holy place, among the ceremonies he chose and prescribed in detail to the Israelites. And the same symbol so expressive, so noble and so little able to throw man into illusion, still exists today in all our temples".[74]

To pretend that fire comes from combustion is to point out a fact of current observation without providing any explanation. Most of the shortcomings of modern science derive from this indifference, whether intended or not, to an agent so important and so universally spread. What can one think of the strange obstinacy observed by certain scholars in ignoring the point of contact that it constitutes, the link it makes between Science and Religion? If heat is born of movement, as it is claimed, who, then, will we ask, generates and maintains the movement, producer of fire, if not fire itself? A vicious circle from which materialists and skeptics can never escape. For us, fire cannot be the result or the effect of combustion, but its true cause. It is by its release of the serious matter, who kept him shut up, that fire broke out, and that the phenomenon known as combustion appeared. And, whether this release is spontaneous or provoked, common sense obliges us to admit and maintain that combustion is the result of the igneous release and not the primary cause of fire.

Imponderable, elusive, always moving, fire possesses all the qualities we recognize in spirits; it is nonetheless material, since we experience its brightness when it shines, and that, even obscure, our sensibility detects its presence by radiant heat. Now, is not the spiritual quality of fire revealed to us in the flame? Why does it constantly rise, like a true spirit, despite our efforts to force it to lower itself to the ground? Is there not a formal manifestation of this will which, by freeing it from the material influence, removes it from the earth and brings it closer to its heavenly homeland? And what is the flame, if not the visible form, the very signature and the effigy of fire?

But what we must above all remember, as having priority in the science that interests us, is the high purifying virtue possessed by fire. Pure principle par excellence, physical manifestation of purity itself, it thus signals its spiritual origin and discovers its divine filiation. A rather singular observation, the Greek word πῦρ, which is used to designate fire, presents exactly the pronunciation of the pure French qualifier; also, the hermetic philosophers, by uniting the nominative with the genitive, created the term πῦρ-πυρός, the fire of fire, or phonetically, the pure of the pure, and regarded the Latin *purpura* and the word purple as the seal of perfection absolute in the own color of the philosopher's stone.

XII

Our study of the panels of Dampierre has been completed. We only need to mention a few decorative motifs that have no connection with the previous ones; they show symmetrical ornaments –ornaments, interlacing motifs, arabesques, with or without figures–,

---

74 Noël Pluche. *Histoire du Ciel* (History of the Heavens). Paris, widow Estienne, 1739. Tome I, p. 24.

whose construction indicates a later execution than that of the symbolic subjects. All are devoid of phylacteries and inscriptions. Finally, the bottom slabs of a small number of panels are still waiting for the sculptor's hand.

It is to be presumed that the author of the wonderful Grimoire, of which we have undertaken to decipher the pages and the signs, must, as a result of unknown circumstances, have interrupted a work which his successors could not pursue or complete, for want of understanding it. Be that as it may, the number, the variety, the esoteric importance of the subjects of this superb collection make of the high gallery of the castle of Dampierre an admirable collection, a true museum of alchemical emblems, and class our Adept among the unknown masters best informed of the mysteries of sacred art.

But before leaving this magisterial ensemble, we will allow ourselves to bring the subject closer to a curious stone picture that we see at the Palais Jacques-Cœur in Bourges, and which seems to us to be able to take the place of its conclusion and summary. This carved panel forms the tympanum of an open door on the court of honor and represents three exotic trees –palm tree, fig tree and date palm–, growing among herbaceous plants; a frame of flowers, leaves and twigs surrounds this bas-relief (plate XXXIII).

Bourges – Jacques-Cœur Palace – Tympanum
The Secret Agreement – Plate XXXIII

The palm tree and the date tree, trees of the same family, were known to the Greeks as Φοίνιξ (Latin *Phoenix*), which is our hermetic Phoenix; they represent the two magisteries and their result, the two white and red stones, which have only one and the same nature understood under the cabalistic name of Phoenix. As for the fig tree occupying the centre of the composition, it indicates the mineral substance from which the philosophers draw the elements of the miraculous rebirth of the Phoenix, and it is the entire work of this rebirth that constitutes what is known as the Great Work.

According to the Apocryphal Gospels, it was a fig tree or sycamore tree (Pharaoh's fig tree) that had the honour of sheltering the Holy Family when they fled to Egypt, nourishing them it with its fruits and quenching their thirst with the limpid and fresh water that Jesus the Child made flow from the roots.[75] Now, fig tree, in Greek, is said to be συκῆ, from σῦκον, fig, a word frequently used for κύσθος, root κύω, carry in its bosom, contain: it is the Virgin Mother who carries the Child, and the alchemical emblem of the passive, chaotic, aqueous and cold substance, matrix and vehicle of the incarnate spirit. Sozomene, author of the 4th century, affirms that the tree of Hermopolis, which bowed before the Child Jesus, is called *Persea* (*Hist. Eccl.*, lib. V, cap. XXI). It is the name of the Balanus (Balanites Ægyptiaca), a shrub from Egypt and Arabia, a kind of oak called the Greeks βάλανος, acorn, a word by which they also referred to the myrobolan, the fruit of the myrobolan tree. These various elements are perfectly related to the subject of the sages and the technique of *ars brevis*, which Jacques Coeur seems to have practiced.

Indeed, when the artist, witness of the combat in which the remora and the salamander are engaged, removes from the defeated igneous monster his two eyes, he must then apply himself to gather them in only one.

This mysterious operation, easy however for those who know how to use the corpse of the salamander, provides a small mass quite similar to the acorn of an oak tree, sometimes chestnut, depending on whether it is more or less covered with the rough matrix from which it is never completely free. This provides us with an explanation of the acorn and oak, which are almost always found in hermetic iconography; chestnuts, particular to the style of Jean Lallemant; the heart, the figs and the fig tree, of Jacques Coeur's fig tree; of the little bell, an accessory to the jester's rattle; of the pomegranates, pears and apples, frequent in the symbolic works of Dampierre and Coulonges, etc. On the other hand, if we take into account the magical and almost supernatural nature of this production, we will understand why some authors have referred to the hermetic fruit under the epithet of *myrobolan*, and why also this term has remained in the popular mind as synonymous with something wonderful, surprising or extremely rare.[76]

The priests of Egypt, directors of initiatory colleges, used to ask the layman, soliciting access to sublime knowledge, this seemingly absurd question: "Is halalidge and myrobalan grain sown in your country?". An interrogation which did not fail to embarrass the ignorant neophyte, but to which the informed investigator could answer. Halalidge seed and Myrobolan are identical to the fig, the date palm fruit, the phoenix egg which is our philosophical egg. It is it the one that reproduces the fabulous eagle of Hermes, with plumage dyed with all the colors of the Work, but among which red dominates, as its Greek name wants it: φοίνιξ, purple red. Cyrano Bergerac does not hesitate to talk about it, in the course of an allegorical narrative in which is mixed the language of birds which the great philosopher possessed admirably. "I begin to fall asleep in the shade," he said, "when I saw in the air a marvelous bird hovering over my head; he supported himself with a movement so light and imperceptible that I doubted several times whether it was not yet a little universe balanced by his own center. He descended, however, little by little, and finally came so close to me that my relieved eyes were full of his image. His tail appeared green, his stomach was enamelled, his

---

75 See *Évangile de l'Enfance* (Gospel of the Childhood), ch. XXIII, XXV, in *Apocryphes de Migne* (Apocrypha of Migne), t. I, p. 995.

76 Today the word *myrobolan*, is written *mirobolant* in French, but the etymology and pronunciation have not changed.

wings incarnate, and his purple head shone with a golden crown, the rays of which sprang from his eyes. It was a long time to fly in the clouds; and I stood so much to everything he became, that my soul having receded and shortened to the sole operation of seeing, it did not nearly reach that of hearing, to make me understand that the bird spoke as it sung. Thus, gradually out of my ecstasy, I distinctly noticed the syllables, the words, and the speech he uttered. Here, then, in the best way I can remember, are the terms he used to weave his song:

"You are a stranger, whistled the bird very agreeably, and born in a world of which I am a native. Now, this secret propensity of which we are moved for our compatriots, is the instinct which impels me to want you to know my life ...

"I can see that you are very eager about learning who I am. It is me that among you that is called Phoenix. In each world there is only one at a time, which lives there for a hundred years; for, at the end of a century, when on some mountain of Arabia he has laid a big egg amidst the coals of his pyre, from which he sorted the material of twigs of aloe, cinnamon, and incense, it takes off and raises its flight to the Sun, like the homeland where his heart has long aspired. He had made every effort beforehand for this journey; but the weight of his egg, whose hulls are so thick that it takes a century to incubate it, always delayed the undertaking.

"I doubt that you will find it difficult to conceive this miraculous production; that's why I want to explain it to you. The Phoenix is hermaphrodite; but between the hermaphrodites, it is yet another Phoenix quite extraordinary because ...[77]

"He remained a quarter of an hour without speaking, and then he added: I see that you suspect from falsehood what I have just learned; but if I do not tell the truth, may I never return to your Globe and may an eagle fall upon me".[78]

Another author expands further on the mytho-hermetic bird and points out some particularities that would be difficult to find elsewhere. "The Cesar of the Oyseaux", he says, "is the miracle of nature,[79] which wanted to show in here what it was doing, building itself a Phoenix by forming the Phoenix. For it has enriched it wonderfully, making it a head crowned by a royal plume and imperial head-plume, with a tuft of feathers and a crest so bright that it seems to carry the crescent of silver or a golden star in the head. The robe and the down are of a golden changing color that shows all the colors of the world; the big feathers are of incarnate and blue, gold, silver and flame; the collar is a quilt of all gems, and not a rainbow, but a phoenix bow. The tail is celestial in color with a golden splinter representing the stars. His tail feathers, and all his coat, is like a early spring, rich in all colors; it has two eyes in its head, brilliant and flamboyant, which seem two stars, golden legs and nails of scarlet; all its bodice and imposing bearing show that it has some feeling of glory, that it had held his rank and asserted its imperial majesty. Its food itself has I don't know what's real, because it consists only of incense tears and balsam chrism. Being in the cradle, says Lactantius, the heaven distilled nectar and ambrosia for it. It alone is a witness of all the ages of the world, and wanted to transform the golden souls of the century into silver, from silver into brass, and brass into iron. He is the only one whose company has never been lacking in heaven and the world, and he is the only one who plays with death and turns it into his wet nurse and his mother, giving birth to life. It has the privilege of time, of life and death, at the same time, because when it feels charged with years, saddened by a long old age and despondent for so

---

77 The author interrupts thus, suddenly, its revelation.

78 From Cyrano Bergerac. *L'Autre Monde. Histoire des Oiseaux* (The other world. History of Birds). Paris, Bauche, 1910.]

79 Hermetic expression dedicated to the philosopher's stone.

many years that it has seen one after another, it allows itself to be dragged by a desire and just aspiration to renew itself through a miraculous death. Then, it is a heap that has no name in this world, for it is not a nest or a cradle or place of birth, for there it leaves life. So it is not another inanimate phoenix, being nest and tomb, matrix and grave, the palace of life and death at the same time that, in favor of the Phoenix, they agree for this occasion. Now, however, whether it is now, on the trembling arms of a palm tree, he makes a pile of cinnamon and frankincense strands; on the incense of the breakage, on the breakage of the nard; then, with a pitiful eye, recommending himself to the Sun, its murderer and its father, perches or lies on this burning balm, to despoil himself from his burdensome years.[80]

"The Sun, favoring the just desires of this bird, lights the pyre, and, reducing everything to ashes, with a musky blast, brings him back to life. Then, poor Nature falls into a trance, and with horrible impetus, fearing to lose the honor of this great world, commands that everything remain still on Earth. The clouds would not dare to pour a drop of water on the ashes or on the earth; the winds, however rabid they may be, would not dare to run through the field; alone the Zephyr is master, and spring reigns while the ashes are inanimate, and Nature strives for everything to favor the return of her Phoenix. Oh great miracle of divine providence! Almost at the same time, this cold ash, not wanting to leave for a long time the poor Nature in mourning or to frighten her, I do not know how, warmed up by the fecundity from the rays of the Sun, it becomes a worm, then an egg and finally a bird ten times more beautiful than the other. You would say that all Nature has risen, because, in fact, as Pliny writes, the sky begins again its revolutions and its sweet music, and you would say properly that the four elements, without saying anything, sing the motet for four with their blossoming joy, in praise of Nature and in order to commemorate the repetition of the miracle of the birds and the world."[81] (see plate XXXIV, in the next page).

The panel with three sculpted trees of the Bourges palace carries a motto, like the panels of Dampierre. On the framing border decorated with flowering branches, the attentive observer discovers, indeed, isolated letters, very cleverly concealed. Their meeting is one of the favorite maxims of the great artist Jacques Cœur:

DE. MY . JOY. DIRE. MAKE . TAIRE.   OF MY JOY, TO SAY, TO DO, TO BE SILENT

However, the joy of the Adept lies in his occupation. The work, which makes this wonder of nature sensitive and familiar to him –which so many ignorant people call chimeric– constitutes his best distraction, his noblest enjoyment. In Greek, the word χαρά, joy, derived from χαίρω, to rejoice, to please, to please in, to please in, still means to love. The famous philosopher therefore clearly refers to the labor of the Work, his most precious task, whose many symbols, moreover, enhance the brilliance of the sumptuous dwelling. But what can we say, that confessing this unique joy, pure and complete satisfaction, intimate joy of success?

---

80 Here we find the symbolic palm of Delos, against which Latona had relied when she gave birth to Apollo, according to what Callimachus reports in the *Hymn to Delos*:
"To celebrate, Oh Delos! these lucky moments,
Pure gold shone to your foundations;
Gold covered your palm tree with a glittering leaf;
Gold colored your lake with a dazzling wave;
And, for a whole day, from its deep chasms,
Inopus vomited pure gold with large bubbles".
81 René François. *Essay des Merveilles de Nature et des plus nobles artifices* (Essay about the Wonders of Nature and the most noble artifices). Lyon, J. Huguetan, 1642, ch. V, p. 69.

Rouen – Mansion of Bourgtheroulde (16th Century)
The Phoenix on his Immortality – Plate XXXIV

As little as possible, if we do not want to perjure ourselves, to stir up the envy of some, the greed of others, the jealousy of all, and risk becoming the prey of the powerful. What then to do with the result, which the artist, according to the rules of our discipline, commits himself to use modestly? To use it unceasingly for the good, to consecrate its fruits to the exercise of charity, in accordance with philosophical precepts and Christian morality. What is there to keep quiet about? Absolutely everything that concerns the alchemical secret and concerns its implementation; for revelation, remaining the exclusive privilege of God, the disclosure of processes remains prohibited, not communicable in clear language, permitted only under the veil of the parable, the allegory, the image or the metaphor.

Jacques Coeur's motto, in spite of its brevity and innuendo, is in perfect harmony with the traditional teachings of eternal wisdom. No philosopher, truly worthy of the name, would refuse to subscribe to the rules of conduct which it expresses and which can be translated as follows:

About the Great Work say little, do a lot, always keep quiet .

The Bodyguards of François II, Duke of Brittany

I

When, towards the year 1502, Anne, duchess of Brittany and twice queen of France, formed the project of assembling, in a mausoleum worthy of the veneration which she carried to them, the bodies of her deceased parents, she entrusted the performance to a Breton artist, of great talent, but on whom we have little information, Michel Colombe. Anne was then twenty-five years old. His father, Duke Francis II, had died at Couëron fourteen years earlier, on September 9, 1488, only surviving his second wife, Marguerite de Foix, mother of Queen Anne, for sixteen months. She died, on May 15, 1487.

This mausoleum, begun in 1502, was not completed until 1507. The plan is the work of Jean Perréal. As for the sculptures, which make it one of the purest masterpieces of the Renaissance, they are by Michel Colombe, who was helped in this work by two of his pupils: Guillaume Regnauld, his nephew, and Jehan de Chartres, "His disciple and servant," though the latter's collaboration is not absolutely certain. A letter, written on the 4th of January, 1511, by Jean Perreal to the secretary of Marguerite de Bourgogne, on the occasion of the work which this princess was having done in the chapel of Brou, informs us that "Michel Colombe worked by the month and received twenty monthly escudos for five years". He was paid 1,200 ecus for the sculpture work, and the tomb cost a total of 560 pounds.[1]

According to the desire expressed by Marguerite de Bretagne and François II, to be buried in the Carmelite church of Nantes, Anne built the mausoleum, which took the name of Tomb of Carmelites, under which it is generally known and designated. It remained in place until the Revolution, at which time the Carmelite church was sold as a national property. It was secretly removed and kept by an art lover anxious to remove the masterpiece from revolutionary vandalism. The turmoil passed, it was rebuilt in 1819, in the cathedral Saint-Pierre, Nantes, where we can admire it today. The vaulted sepulcher, built under the

---

1   Cf. Abbot G. Durville, *Études sur le vieux Nantes* (Studies on old Nantes). tome II. Vannes, La-folye Frères, 1915.

ceremonial mausoleum, contained, during its opening on the order of the king, by Mellier, mayor of Nantes, on October 16 and 17, 1727, the three coffins of Francis II, of Marguerite de Bretagne, his first wife, deceased on September 25, 1449, and Marguerite de Foix, second wife of the duke and mother of Queen Anne. There was also a small box containing a reliquary "of decorated pure gold",[2] egg-shaped, surmounted by the royal crown, covered with inscriptions finely enamelled letters, and containing the heart of Anne of Brittany, whose body rests on the basilica Saint-Denis.

Among the descriptive relations which various authors have left of the tomb of the Carmelites, some of which are very detailed. We will choose, to give a glimpse of the work, of Brother Mathias de Saint-Jean, Carmelite of Nantes, who published it in the seventeenth century.

"But what seems to me to be the rarest and most admirable," says this writer, "is the Tomb raised in the choir of the Church of the Carmelites, which, as everyone admits, is one of the most beautiful and magnificent that can be seen, forcing me to make a special description of it for the satisfaction of the curious.

"The devotion that the former Dukes of Brittany had to the Blessed Virgin Mother of God, patron saint of the Order and of this Church of the P. P. Carmelites, and the affection they have for the Religious of this House, led them to choose the place of their Burial. And Queen Anne, by a unique testimony of her pity and affection for this place, wanted to have this beautiful Monument erected there in memory of her father François Second and his mother Marguerite de Foye.

"It is built in a square, eight feet wide by fourteen feet long: its material is all fine Italian marble, white and black, porphyry and alabaster. It is raised on the plane (ground) of the Church, six feet high. The two sides are adorned with six, a two-foot-high, niches, whose background is well worked porphyry, adorned around white marble pilasters, in all the right proportions and architectural rules, enriched with delicately worked moresques (arabesques): and all these twelve niches are filled with figures of the twelve Apostles, white marble, each with its different posture, and the instruments of its passion. The two ends of the building are adorned with such architecture, and each one is divided into two niches similar to the others. At the end towards the master Altar of the Church are placed in these niches the figures of Saint Francis of Assisi and Saint Margaret, patrons of the last Duke and Duchess who are buried there: and at the other end are similarly seen in niches the figures of S. Charlemagne and S. Louis, King of France. Below the so-called sixteen niches surrounding the Tomb, there are as many cavities, made in circles of fourteen inches in diameter, whose bottom is of white marble carved in the shape of a shell, and all are filled with figures of mourners with their funeral clothes, all in various postures, whose work is considered by few people, but it is admired by all those who hear it.

"This part is covered with a large table of black marble all in one piece, and which exceeds the solid body (the mass of the tomb) about eight inches, around in the form of

---

2　Canon G. Durville, from whose work we are borrowing these details, has kindly sent us an image of this curious piece, unfortunately empty of its content, which is part of the collections of the Th. Dobrée Museum in Nantes, of which he is the curator. "I am sending you", he writes, "a small photograph of this precious reliquary. I placed it for a moment in the very place where Queen Anne's heart was, in the thought that this circumstance would make you more interested in this little souvenir". We ask Canon Durville to kindly accept here the expression of our heartfelt thanks for his pious solicitude and delicate attention.

cornice, to serve as entablature and ornament to this tomb. On the top of this stone lie two large figures of white marble, eight feet long, one of which represents the Duke, and the other the Duchess with their ducal garments and crowns. Three figures of angels of white marble, of three feet each, hold cushions under the heads of these figures, which seem to soften under the weight, and the angels weep. At the feet of the figure of the Duke, there is a figure of Lyon lying naturally represented, which carries on its mane the coat of the arms of Brittany: and at the feet of the figure of the Duchess, there is the figure of a Greyhound, which also bears at the collar the arms of the house of Foïe that art animates wonderfully well.

"But what is most wonderful in this room are the four figures of the Cardinal Virtues, placed at the four corners of this sepulture, made of white marble, six feet high: they are so well carved, if well planted, and have so much connection to the natural, that the natives and the foreigners have not seen anything better, neither in the ancient Rome nor in the moderns of Italy, France, and Germany. The figure of Justice is placed on the right corner as you enter, carrying a raised sword in the right hand, and a book with a scale in the left, the crown in her head, dressed in cloth and fur which are the marks of the science, fairness, severity, and majesty that accompany this virtue.

"On the opposite left side, is the figure of Prudence, who has two faces opposite to each other in a same head: one of an old man with a long beard, the other of a young boy; in the right hand (left) she holds a convex mirror which she stares at, and on the other a compass, at her feet a snake, and these things are symbols of the consideration and wisdom with which this virtue proceeds in his actions.

"At the right angle, on the upper side, is the figure of Strength, dressed in a coat of mail (armor) and the helmet in the head; in her left hand she supports a tower, from whose crevices a snake (a dragon) emerges which she stifles with the right hand, which marks the vigor with which this virtue is used in the adversities of the world to prevent violence, or bear the weight.

"At the opposite corner is the figure of the Temperance clad in a long dress, sur-rounded by a cord: with the right hand, it supports the machine of a clock, and the other a flange brake, hieroglyphic of the regulation and the moderation that this virtue puts in human passions".[3]

The praises that Brother Mathias de Saint-Jean makes of these bodyguards of Francis II, represented by the cardinal Virtues of Michel Colombe, seem to us perfectly deserved.[4] "These four statues," says de Caumont, "are admirable for grace and simplicity. Their garments are rendered with rare perfection, and in each figure a striking individuality is observed, although all four are equally noble and beautiful".[5]

It is these statues, imbued with the purest symbolism, guardians of ancient tradition and science, that we will particularly study.

---

3   *Le Commerce honorable, etc., composé par un habitant de Nantes* (The Honorable Trade, etc., composed by a resident of Nantes). Nantes, Guillaume Le Monnier, 1646, p. 308-312.

4   Michel Colombe, born at Saint-Pol-de-Leon in 1460, was about forty-five years old when he executed them.

5   De Caumont, *Cours d'Antiquités Monuments* (Antique Monuments Course), 1841; Part 6, p. 445.

II

With the exception of Justice, the Cardinal Virtues are no longer represented with the singular attributes that give ancient figures their enigmatic and mysterious character. Under the pressure of more realistic designs, symbolism has been transformed. The artists, abandoning any idealization of thought, obey naturalism in preference; they tighten closely the expression of attributes and facilitate the identification of allegorical characters. But by perfecting their processes and moving closer to modern formulas, they have unconsciously struck a deadly blow to the traditional truth. For the ancient sciences, transmitted under the veil of various emblems, are part of the science of Diplomatics and have a double meaning, one that is apparent and comprehensible to all (exoteric), the other hidden and accessible only to the initiated (esoteric). By specifying the symbol, limited to its positive, normal and defined function; by individualizing it to the point of excluding any related or relative idea, it is stripped of this double meaning, of the second expression that makes it precisely the didactic value and the essential scope. The elders depicted Justice, Fortune and Love, blindfolded. Did they claim to express only the blindness of one, the blindness of others? Could we not discover, in the attribute of the eye band, a special reason for this artificial and undoubtedly necessary darkness? It would be enough to know that these figures, commonly subject to human vicissitudes, also belong to the scientific tradition, to easily recognize it. And one would even notice that the occult meaning is more clear than that obtained by direct analysis and superficial reading. When poets tell us that Saturn, father of the gods, devoured his children, we believe, with the Encyclopedia, that "such a metaphor serves to characterize an era, an institution, etc., whose circumstances or results become fatal to those who should have received only its benefits". But if we replace this general interpretation with the positive and scientific reason that constitutes the basis of legends and myths, the truth emerges immediately, bright and obvious. Hermeticism teaches that Saturn, symbolic representative of the first earth metal, generator of others, is also their only and natural dissolver; however, as any dissolved metal assimilates to the dissolver and loses its characteristics, it is exact and logical to claim that the dissolver "eats" the metal, and that thus the fabulous old man devours his offspring. We could give many examples of this duality of meaning expressed in traditional symbolism. That alone suffices to show that, together with the moral and Christian interpretation of the cardinal virtues, there exists a second teaching, secret, profane, ordinarily unknown, which belongs to the material domain of acquisitions, of ancestral knowledge. Thus we find, sealed in the form of the same emblems, the harmonious alliance of Science and Religion, so fruitful in wonderful results, but which the skepticism of our days refuses to recognize and conspires to always exclude.

"The theme of the Virtues", quite rightly remarks M. Paul Vitry, "was constituted in the thirteenth century in Gothic art. But, adds the author, while the series had remained rather variable among us as number, as order and as attributes, it had settled early in Italy, and was limited either to the three theological Virtues: Faith Hope, Charity, more often perhaps still to the four cardinal virtues: Prudence, Justice, Strength, Temperance. It had also been applied early to the ornamentation of funeral monuments.

"As for the way to characterize these Virtues, it seems to have been more or less settled with Orcagna and its Golden Tabernacle of San Michele, around the middle of the 14th century. Justice carries the sword and scales and will never change. The essential attribute of Prudence is the snake; sometimes one or more books are added, later a mirror. Almost from the beginning also, through an idea similar to that of Dante, who had given three eyes to his Prudence, the image makers gave two faces to this Virtue. Temperance sometimes puts its sword back into its sheath, but more often than not it holds two vases and seems to mix water and wine: it is the elementary symbol of sobriety. Finally, Strength has Samson's attributes; it is armed with the shield and the club; sometimes it has the skin of a lion on its head and a disc with the world in its hands; other times, finally, and this will be its final attribute, in Italy at least, it carries an entire or broken column...

"Without the rest of the great monuments, manuscripts, books, engravings were in charge of spreading the type of Italian Virtues and could even make it known to those who, like Colombe, had probably not made the trip to Italy. A series of Italian engravings from the late 15th century, known as the Italian Card Game, show us, amidst representations of different social conditions, Muses, ancient gods, liberal arts, etc.., a series of figures of the Virtues; they have exactly the attributes we have just described... We have here a very curious specimen of these documents that could be brought back by people such as Perréal, who had followed the expeditions, documents that could circulate in the workshops and provide themes while waiting for them to impose a new style.

"This symbolic language, moreover, had no difficulty in being understood in our country; it was entirely in keeping with the allegorical spirit of the 15th century. One only has to think, to realize it, of the Roman de la Rose and all the literature that came out of it. Miniaturists had illustrated these works extensively and, apart from these allegories of Nature, Deduction and False Semblance, French art certainly did not ignore the Virtues series, although it was not a theme as frequently used as in Italy".[6]

However, without absolutely denying, some Italian influence in the splendid figures of the Tomb of the Carmelites, Paul Vitry points out the new, essentially French character that Michel Colombe was going to give to the ultramontane elements reported by Jean Perreal. "Even admitting," continues the author, "that they borrowed the idea from the Italian tombs, Perreal and Colombe were not going to accept, without modification, this theme of the Cardinal Virtues. Indeed, "Temperance will carry in its hands a clock and a bit with its bridle instead of the two vases that the Italians had commonly given it. As for the Force, armed and helmeted, instead of its column, it will hold a tower, a sort of crenellated dungeon, from which it violently tears a struggling dragon. Neither in Rome, Florence, Milan, nor Como (the southern gate of the cathedral) do we know anything similar.

But while we can easily discern, in the cenotaph of Nantes, the respective parts belonging to masters Perréal and Colombe, it is more difficult to discover how far the personal influence, the founder's own will, could extend. Because we cannot believe that she was, for five years, disinterested in a work that was particularly close to her heart. Did Queen Anne, the gracious sovereign whom the people, in her naive affection, familiarly called "the good duchess in wooden shoes", know the esoteric scope of the guardians of the mausoleum raised in memory of her parents? We would be happy to resolve this issue in the affirmative. Her biographers assure us that she was highly educated, gifted with a keen intelligence and remarkable foresight. His library already seemed important for the time. "According to the only document, says Le Roux de Lincy, which I was able to discover relating to the entire library formed by Anne de Bretagne (Index des Comptes de Dépenses de 1498), there were handwritten and printed books in Latin, French, Italian, Greek and Hebrew. Eleven hundred

---

6   Paul Vitry. *Michel Colombe et la sculpture française de son temps* (Michel Colombe and the French sculpture of his time). Paris, E. Lévy, 1901, pp. 395 et seq.

and forty volumes, taken in Naples by Charles VIII, had been given to the Queen... Perhaps it will come as a surprise to see works in Greek and Hebrew in the Queen's collection; but it should not be forgotten that she had studied the two learned languages and that the character of her spirit was above all serious".[7] She was depicted to us seeking the conversation of diplomats, to whom she liked to respond in their own language, which would justify a very careful multilingual education and probably also the possession of the hermetic cabal, the gay knowledge or the double science. Did she meet the famous scientists of her time and, among them, contemporary alchemists? We lack information in this regard, although it seems difficult to explain why the large fireplace in the living room of the Lallemant Hotel bears the ermine of Anne of Brittany and the porcupine of Louis XII, if we do not want to see in it a testimony of their presence in the philosophical residence of Bourges. Anyway, his personal fortune was considerable. The pieces of silverware, gold ingots, precious gems formed the mass of an almost inexhaustible treasure. The abundance of such wealth made it particularly easy to exercise a generosity that quickly became popular. The columnists tell us that she willingly paid the poor minstrel who had distracted her for a few moments with a diamond. As for her livery, it offered the hermetic colors chosen by her: black, yellow and red, before the death of Charles VIII, and only the two extremes of the Work, black and red, since that time. Finally, she was the first queen of France who, breaking resolutely with the custom established until then, mourned her first husband in black, while custom forced the sovereigns to always wear it in white.

III

The first of the four statues that we are going to study is the one that offers us the various attributes responsible for clarifying the allegorical expression of Justice: the lion, the scales and the sword. But, besides the esoteric meaning, which is distinctly different from the moral sense which is assigned to these attributes, the figure of Michel Colombe presents other revealing signs of his occult personality. There is no detail, however small, that can be neglected in all such analysis, without having been seriously examined beforehand. Now, the ermine surcoat worn by Justice is lined with roses and pearls. Our Virtue has a forehead girded with a ducal crown, which may have led us to believe that it reproduced the features of Anne of Brittany; the pommel of the sword which she holds with her right hand is adorned with a radiant sun; finally, and this is what characterizes it in the first place, it appears here unveiled. The peplum which covered it entirely slipped on her body; retained by the projection of the arms, it comes to double the mantle in its lower part. The sword itself has left its sheath of brocade, which is now suspended at the tip of the iron (Plate XXXV).

As the very essence of justice and its purpose demand that it has nothing hidden, that the search for and the manifestation of the truth obliges it to show itself to all in the full light of equity, the veil, half withdrawn, must necessarily reveal the secret individuality of a second figure, deftly concealed in the form and attributes of the first. This second figure is none other than Philosophy.

---

7 Le Roux de Lincy, *Vie de la Reine Anne de Bretagne, femme des Rois de France Charles VIII et Louis XII* (Life of Queen Anne of Brittany, wife of the Kings of France Charles VIII and Louis XII). Paris, L. Curmer, 1860, t. II, p. 34.

Cathedral of Nantes – Tomb of Francis II
Justice (16the Century) – Plate XXXV

In Roman antiquity, a veil decorated with embroidery was called *peplum* (in Greek πέπλος or πέπλα), it was used to dress the statue of Minerva, daughter of Jupiter, the only goddess whose birth was wonderful. The fable, in fact, says that she came out fully armed from her father's brain, whose head, by order of the owner of Olympus, Vulcan had split. Hence its Greek name of Athena –Αθηνά, made up of ά, private, and τιθήνη, nurse, mother, meaning born without a mother. Personification of Wisdom, or Knowledge of Things. Minerva must be seen as divine and creative thought, materialized in all nature, latent in us and in all that surrounds us. But it is a woman's clothing, a woman's veil (κάλυμμα), that is at issue here, and this word gives us another reason for the symbolic epithet. Κάλυμμα, has just covered, wrapped, hidden, which formed κάλυξ, rosebud, flower, and also Καλυψώ, Greek name of the nymph Calypso, queen of the mythical island of Ogyria, which the Greeks called Ωγύγιος, a term close to Ωγυγία, which has the meaning of ancient and great. We thus find the mystical rose, flower of the Great Work, better known as the philosopher's stone. So it is easy to grasp the relationship between the expression of the veil and that of the roses and pearls adorning the fur overcoat, since this stone is still called the precious pearl (*Margarita pretiosa*). "Alciat," says Brother Noel, represents Justice in the guise of a virgin whose crown is gold and the white tunic, covered with a large purple drapery. His eyes are soft and his posture modest. She wears a rich jewel on her chest, symbol of her inestimable value, and puts her left foot on a square stone". One could not better describe the double nature of the Magisterium, its colors, the high value of this cubic stone, which carries the whole Philosophy, hidden, for the common man, under the traits of Justice.

Philosophy confers on those who embrace it a great power of investigation. It allows us to penetrate the intimate constitution of things, which it cuts off as with the sword, discovering the presence of the *spiritus mundi* of which the classical masters speak, which has its centre in the sun and draws its virtues and its movement from the radiation of the star. It also gives knowledge of the general laws, rules, rhythm and measures that nature observes in the elaboration, evolution and perfection of created things (the scales). Finally, it establishes the possibility of acquiring science on the basis of observation, meditation, faith and written teaching (the book). By the same attributes, this image of Philosophy informs us, secondly, about the essential points of the work of the Adepts, and proclaims the necessity of the manual work imposed on researchers wishing to acquire the positive notion, the indisputable proof of its reality. Without technical research, frequent testing and repeated experiments, we can only get lost in a science whose best treatises carefully hide physical principles, their application, materials and time. Whoever therefore dares to claim to be a philosopher and does not want to plough for fear of coal, fatigue or expense, this one must be regarded as the most vain of the ignorant or the most brazen of the imposters. "I can give this testimony," said Augustin Thierry, "who on my part will not be a suspect: there is something in the world that is better than material enjoyment, better than fortune, better than health itself, it is dedication to science". The activity of the wise is not measured by the results of speculative propaganda; it is controlled by the furnace, in the solitude and silence of the laboratory, not elsewhere; it is manifested without claim or verbiage, by the attentive study, the precise, persevering observation of reactions and phenomena. Whoever does otherwise will sooner or later verify Solomon's maxim (Prov., XXI, 25), saying that "the desire of the lazy will destroy him, because his hands refuse to work". The true scientist does not shrink from any effort; he does not fear suffering, because he knows what the price of science is, and only science provides him with the means "to hear the sentences and their interpretation, the words of the wise and their profound discourses" (Prov., I, 6).

Regarding the practical value of the attributes of Justice, which affect hermetic work, the student will find from experience that the energy of the universal spirit has its signature in the sword, and that the sword has its correspondence in the sun, as the animator and perpetual modifier of all bodily substances. It is the only agent of the successive metamorphoses of the original matter, subject and foundation of the Magisterium. It is through him that mercury is transformed into sulphur, sulphur into Elixir and Elixir into Medicine, then receiving the name of the Crown of the Sage, because this triple mutation confirms the truth of the secret teaching and consecrates the glory of its happy artisan. The possession of the fiery and multiplied sulphur, masked under the term philosopher's stone, is for the Adept what the triple crown is for the Pope and the crown for the monarch: the major emblem of sovereignty and wisdom.

We have already had, many times before, the opportunity to explain the meaning of the open book, characterized by the radical solution of the metallic body, which, having abandoned its impurities and given up its sulphur, is then called open. But here one remark is in order. Under the name of freedom and under the image of the book, adopted to qualify the material holding the solvent, the sages have pretended to designate the closed book, the general symbol of all crude bodies, minerals or metals, such as nature provides them to us or the human industry delivers them to the trade. Thus, the ores extracted from the deposit, the metals extracted from the melt, are expressed hermetically by a closed or sealed book. Similarly, these bodies, subjected to alchemical work, modified by the application of occult procedures, are translated into iconography using the open book. It is therefore necessary, in practice, to extract mercury from the closed book that is our primitive subject, in order to obtain it alive and open, if we want it in turn to open the metal and make the inert sulphur it contains lively. The opening of the first book prepares the opening of the second. For there are, hidden under the same emblem, two closed books (the crude subject and the metal) and two open books (mercury and sulphur), although these hieroglyphic books really are one, since the metal comes from the original material and the sulphur originates from mercury.

As for the scales, applied against the book, it would suffice to note that it reflects the necessity of the weight and the proportions to believe dispensed from speaking more about it. Now, this faithful image of the instrument used for weighing, and to which the chemists assign an honorable place in their laboratories, conceals, however, an arcane of great importance. This is the reason which obliges us to account for it and to indicate briefly what the scale conceals under the angular and symmetrical aspect of its form.

When philosophers consider the weight relationships of materials between them, they hear about one or the other part of a double esoteric knowledge: that of the weight of nature and that of the weights of art.[8] Unfortunately, the wise men, says Solomon, hide science; bound to remain within the narrow limits of their vow, and respectful of accepted discipline, they never clearly establish how these two secrets differ. We will try to go further than them and will say, in all sincerity, that the weights of art are applicable exclusively to distinct bodies, which can be weighed, while the weight of nature refers to the relative proportions of the components of a given body. So that, describing the reciprocal quantities of various materials, with a view to their regular and appropriate mixing, the authors really speak of the weights of art; on the contrary, if it is a question of quantitative values within a synthetic and radical combination –such as that of sulphur and mercury principles united in philosophical mercury–, it is the weight of nature that is then considered. And we will add, in order to remove any confusion in the reader's mind, that if the weights of art are known to the artist and rigorously determined by him, on the other hand the weight of nature is always ignored, even by the greatest masters. This is a mystery that belongs to God alone and whose intelligence remains inaccessible to man.

The Work begins and ends with the weights of art; thus the alchemist, preparing the way, encourages nature to begin and perfect this great work. But, between these extremes, the artist does not have to use the balance, the weight of nature intervening alone. To such an extent that the manufacture of common mercury, that of philosophical mercury, operations known as imbibitions, etc., are carried out without it being possible to know, even approximately, what are the quantities retained or decomposed, what is the assimilation coefficient of the base, as well as the proportion of spirits. This is what the Cosmopolitan implies when he says that mercury does not take more sulphur than it can absorb and retain. In other words, the proportion of assimilable matter, directly dependent on clean metallic energy, is always variable and cannot be evaluated. The whole work is therefore subject to the qualities, natural or acquired, of both the agent and the initial subject. However, even assuming the agent obtained with a maximum of virtue –which is rarely achieved–, the basic matter, as nature

---

8   Until the lover, for the third time having renewed the weights, Atalante granted the reward to her winner. (*Michaelis Maieri Atalante Fugiens*. Oppenheimii, 1618. Epigramma authoris.)

offers it to us, is far from being constantly equal and similar to itself. In this regard, we will say, often because we have checked its effect, that the authors' assertion based on certain external particularities, such as yellow spots, blooms, plaques or red dots, hardly deserves to be taken into consideration. Rather, the mining region could provide some indication of the desired quality, although several samples, taken from the mass of the same deposit, sometimes reveal significant differences between them.

Thus it will be explained, without recourse to abstract influences or to mystical interventions, that the philosopher's stone, in spite of regular work, conforms to the natural necessities, never leaves in the hands of the workman a body of equal power of transmutative energy in direct and constant relationship with the quantity of materials used.

IV

Here, in our opinion, is the masterpiece of Michel Colombe and the capital piece of the tomb of the Carmelites. "On its own," writes Leon Palustre, "this statue of Strength would suffice for the glory of a man, and one can not defend oneself from contemplating it with a lively and profound emotion.[9] The majesty of the attitude, the nobility of the expression, the grace of the gesture –which one would wish more vigorous–, are all characteristics that reveal a consummate mastery, an incomparable skill in craftsmanship.

With her head covered with a flat morion, with the lion's nose in his head, and her bust draped with the finely carved corselet, Strength supports a tower with her left hand and, with her right hand, tore it off –not a snake as most descriptions describe it–, a winged dragon, which it strangled by squeezing its neck. A large drapery with long fringes, the folds of which are on the forearms, forms a loop through which one of its ends passes. This drapery, which, in the spirit of the statuary, was to cover the emblematic Virtue, confirms what we said earlier. Like Justice, Strength appears to be revealed (plate XXXVI).

Daughter of Jupiter and Themis, sister of Justice and Temperance, the elders honored her as a deity, without however adorning her images with the singular attributes we see her presenting today. In Greek antiquity, the statues of Hercules, with the club of the hero and the skin of a lion of Nemea, personified both physical and moral strength. The Egyptians, on the other hand, represented her by a woman of powerful complexion, with two bull horns on her head and an elephant by her side. The modern ones express it in very different ways. Botticelli sees her as a robust woman, simply sitting on a throne; Rubens adds a shield with the figure of a lion, or follows her with a lion. Gravelot shows her crushing vipers, a lion skin thrown on her shoulders, her forehead surrounded by a laurel branch and holding a bundle of arrows, while at her feet are crowns and scepters. Anguier, in a bas-relief of Henri de Longueville's tomb (Louvre), uses a lion eating a boar to define Strength. Coysevox (balustrade of the marble courtyard, in Versailles) covered her with a lion skin and made her carry an oak branch with one hand, and the base with the other column. Finally, among the bas-reliefs that decorate the peristyle of the Saint-Sulpice church, Strength is depicted armed with the flaming sword and the shield of the Faith.

In all these figures and in many others, the enumeration of which would be tedious, we find no analogy, in terms of attributes, with those of Michel Colombe and the sculptors of

---

9   Leon Palustre. *Les Sculpteurs français de la Renaissance: Michel Colombe* (French sculptors of the Renaissance: Michel Colombe). *Gazette des Beaux-Arts* (Gazette of the Beaux-Arts), 2nd period, t. XXIX, May-June 1884.

Cathedral of Nantes – Tomb of Francis II
Strength – Plate XXXVI

his time. The beautiful statue of the tomb of the Carmelites is therefore of special value and becomes for us the best translation of esoteric symbolism.

One cannot reasonably deny that the tower, so important in the medieval fortification, contains a clearly defined meaning, although we have not been able to discover any part of its interpretation. As for the dragon, we know better his double expression; from the moral and religious point of view, it is the translation of the spirit of evil, demon, devil or Satan; for the philosopher and the alchemist, it has always been used to represent the raw, volatile and dissolving material, otherwise called common mercury. Hermetically, we can therefore consider the tower as the envelope, the refuge, the protective asylum, the mineralogists would say the gangue or the mining, the mercurial dragon. This is the meaning of the Greek word πύργος, tower, asylum, refuge. The interpretation would be even more complete if one likened to the artist the woman who extirpates the monster from his lair, and his mortal gesture to the goal he must propose in this painful and dangerous operation. Thus, at least, we could find a satisfactory and almost true explanation of the allegorical subject used to reveal the esoteric side of Strength. But we should suppose that we know the secret science to which these attributes refer. Now, our statue is itself responsible for informing us both of its symbolic significance and of the related branches of that all that is wisdom, represented by all the cardinal virtues. If the great initiate had been asked what his opinion was, he would certainly have answered, by the voice of Epistemon,[10] that tower of fortification or strong castle is as much to say as *tour de force;* and a *tour de force* demands "courage, wisdom, and power; courage because there is danger, wisdom, for knowledge is necessarily required; power, for whoever cannot do it, should not undertake it". On the other hand, the phonetic cabal, which makes the French word *tour* (tower) the equivalent of the attic τοῦϱος, completes the meaning of the gargantuan feat.[11]

Indeed, τοῦϱος is substituted and used for τὸ ὄϱος; τὸ (which, what), ὄϱος (goal, term, object that one proposes) thus marking the thing which it is necessary to reach, which is the proposed goal. Nothing, we see, could be better suited to the figurative expression of the stone of the philosophers, a dragon enclosed in his fortress, the extraction of which was always considered a tour de force. The image, moreover, is speaking; for if one finds it difficult to understand how the dragon, robust and voluminous, could withstand the compression exerted between the walls of his narrow prison, one does not understand more by what miracle he passes entirely through a simple crack in the masonry. Here again the version of the prodigy, the supernatural and the marvelous is recognizable.

Finally, let us point out that Strength still bears other imprints of the esotericism that it reflects. The braids of his hair, hieroglyphs of solar radiation, indicate that the Work, subject to the influence of the star, cannot be executed without the dynamic collaboration of the Sun. The braid, named in Greek σειϱά, is adopted to represent vibratory energy, because, among the ancient Hellenic peoples, the sun was called σείϱ. The scales imbedded on the corselet's gorget are those of the snake, another emblem of the mercurial subject and replica of the dragon, scaly too. Scales of fish, arranged in a semi-circle, decorate the abdomen and evoke the joining, to the human body, of a mermaid's tail. Now, the mermaid, fabulous monster and hermetic symbol, is used to characterize the union of nascent sulfur, which is our fish, and common mercury, called virgin, in philosophical mercury or salt of wisdom. The same meaning is furnished to us by the Twelfth Night cake, to which the Greeks gave the same name as to the moon: σελήνη; this word, formed of the roots σέλας, brightness, and ἕλη, sunlight, had been chosen by the initiates to show that the philosophical mercury gets its brilliance from the sulfur, just as the moon receives its sunlight. A similar reason attributed the name of σειϱήν, mermaid, to the mythical monster resulting from the assemblage of a woman and a fish; σειϱήν, contracted term of σείϱ, sun, and μήνη, moon, also indicates the lunar mercurial matter combined with the solar sulfurous substance. It is, therefore, a translation identical to that of the Twelfth Night cake, adorned with the sign of light and spirituality –the cross–, testimony of the real incarnation of the solar ray emanated from the universal Father in grave matter, matrix of all things, and *terra inanis et vacua* of the Scriptures.

---

10 The Greek word Ἐπιστήμων means scholar, who is instructed by, clever at; root ἐπίσταμαι, to know, to know, to examine, to think.

11 The capital work of Rabelais, entitled *Pantagruel,* is entirely devoted to the burlesque and cabalistic exhibition of alchemical secrets, whose pantagrelism embraces the whole and constitutes the scientific doctrine. Pantagruel is formed of an assembly of three Greek words: παντᾶ, put for πάντη, completely, absolutely; γύη, path; ἕλη, the sunlight. The gigantic hero of Rabelais thus expresses the perfect knowledge of the solar path, that is to say of the universal way.

V

"Wearing a matron headdress with a throat collar" –thus expressed Dubuisson-Aubenay in his *Itinéraire en Bretagne*, in 1636–, Michel Colombe's Temperance is provided with attributes similar to those assigned to it by Cochin. According to the latter, she is "dressed in simple dresses, a bridle bite in one hand, and in the other a pendulum clock". Other figures show it holding a bridle or cup. "Quite often," said Noël, "she seems to be leaning on an inverted vase, with a bit in her hand, or mixing wine with water.

The elephant, who is considered the most sober animal, is his symbol. Ripa gives two emblems: one, a woman with a turtle on her head, who holds a bridle and silver money; the other, of a woman in the action of tempering, with pincers, a red iron in a vase full of water".

With the left hand, our statue supports the crafted box of a small clock with weights, of the model used in XVIth century. We know that the dials of these devices had only one hand, as evidenced by this beautiful figure of the time. The clock, which is used to measure time, is taken for the hieroglyph of time itself and viewed, as well as the hourglass, as the main emblem of old Saturn (plate XXXVII).

**Cathedral of Nantes – Tomb of Francis II
Temperance (16th Century) – Plate XXXVII**

Some observers who were a little superficial thought they recognized a lantern in the clock, easily identifiable though, of Temperance. The error would hardly alter the deep meaning of the symbol, because the meaning of the lantern completes that of the clock. Indeed, if the lantern illuminates because it carries light, the clock appears as the dispenser of this light, which is not received all at once, but little by little, progressively, over the years and with the help of time. Experience, light, truth are philosophical synonyms; however, nothing, except age, can make it possible to acquire experience, light and truth. Thus, we see *Time*, the only master of wisdom, as an old man, and the philosophers in the senile and weary attitude of men who have long worked to obtain it. It is this need for time or experience that François Rabelais emphasizes in his Addition to the last chapter of *Pantagruel* fifth book, when he writes: "When then your philosophers, God guiding, accompanying to some clear lantern, will devote themselves to carefully research and investigate, as is the natural of humans (and of this quality are Herodotus and Homer called Alphestes, that is to say researchers and inventors)[12], they will find the faithful response made by the wise Thales to Amasis, king of the Egyptians, to be true, when he was asked which thing has more prudence, he answered: Time; because in time have been and in time will be all latent things invented; and this is the cause why the ancients called Saturn Time, Father of Truth, and Truth the daughter of Time. Infallibly they will also find that all the knowledge they and their predecessors have accumulated, for just they is only the smallest part of what it is, and which they don't know".

But the esoteric reach of Temperance lies entirely within the bridle which she holds with her right hand. It is with the bridle that the horse is steered; by means of this piece, the rider imposes on his horse the orientation he likes. One can also consider the bridle as the essential instrument, the mediator placed between the rider's will and the horse's progress towards the proposed objective. This means, the image of which has been chosen from among the constituent parts of the harness, is referred to in hermetic terms as cabala. So that the special expressions of the bridle, about restrain and steering, make it possible to identify and recognize, in a single symbolic form, Temperance and the Cabalistic Science.

With regard to this science, one remark is in order, and we believe it to be all the more justified since the unadvised student readily confuses the hermetic cabal with the system of allegorical interpretation that the Jews claim to have received by tradition, and which they call Kabbala. In fact, there is nothing in common between these two terms, except their pronunciation. The Hebrew kabbala only deals with the Bible; it is therefore strictly limited to sacred exegesis and hermeneutics. The hermetic cabala applies to books, texts and documents of the esoteric sciences of antiquity, the Middle Ages and modern times. While the Hebrew kabbala is only a process based on the decomposition and explanation of each word or letter, the hermetic cabala, on the contrary, is a true language. And, since the vast majority of didactic treatises of ancient sciences are written in cabala, or they use this language in their essential passages; since the great Art itself, according to Artephius own admission, is entirely cabalistic, the reader cannot grasp anything of it if he does not possess at least the first elements of the secret idiom. In the Hebrew kabbala, three meanings can be discovered in each sacred word; hence three different interpretations or kabbalas. The first, called Gematria, involves the analysis of the numeral or arithmetic value of the letters composing the word; the second, called Notarikon, establishes the meaning of each

---

12 In Greek, ἀλφηστήρ or ἀλφηστής, means inventor, industrious, from ἀλφή discovery, which gave the verb ἀλφάνω imagine, find by searching.

letter considered separately; the third, or Themurah (i. e. change, permutation), uses certain letter transpositions. This last system, which seems to have been the oldest, dates from the time when the Alexandrian school flourished, and was created by a few Jewish philosophers concerned to accommodate the speculations of Greek and Eastern philosophies with the text of the holy books. We would not otherwise be surprised if the authorship of this method could go back to the Jewish Philo, whose reputation was great at the beginning of our era, because he was the first philosopher cited as having tried to identify a true religion with philosophy. It is known that he tried to reconcile Plato's writings with the Hebrew texts, interpreting them allegorically, which is perfectly in line with the purpose of the Hebrew kabbala. In any case, according to the work of very serious authors, the Jewish system cannot be assigned a date very much earlier than the Christian era, even extending the starting point of this interpretation to the Greek version of the Septuagint (238 B.C.). However, the hermetic cabal was used, long before that time, by the Pythagoreans and disciples of Thales of Miletus (640-560 B.C.), founder of the Ionian school: Anaximander, Pherecyde of Syros, Anaximene of Miletus, Heraclitus of Ephesus, Anaxagoras of Clazomene, etc., in a word, by all Greek philosophers and scholars, as shown by the Leiden papyrus.

What is also generally not known is that the cabala contains and preserves most of the native language of the Pelasgians, a deformed but not destroyed language in primitive Greek; mother tongue of Western idioms, and particularly of French, whose pelasgic origin is incontestably proven; an admirable language, of which is enough to know a little to easily find, in the various European dialects, the real meaning deviated by the time and the migrations of peoples from the original language.

Unlike the Jewish kabbala, created from scratch to veil, without a doubt, what the sacred text had that was too clear, the hermetic cabala is a precious key, allowing those who possess it to open the doors of sanctuaries, of these closed books of traditional science, to extract their spirit, to grasp their secret meaning. Known to Jesus and his Apostles (it was unfortunately supposed to provoke St. Peter's first denial), the cabala was used in the Middle Ages by philosophers, scholars, literary scholars and diplomats. Knights of different orders and knights-errants, troubadours, trouveres, and minstrels, traveling student of the famous Salamanca School of Magic, which we call Venusbergs because they said they came from the mountain of Venus, discussed among themselves in the language of the gods, still called gay-science or gay knowledge, our hermetic cabala.[13] It bears, moreover, the name and spirit of Chivalry, whose mystical works have revealed its true character to us. The Latin *caballus* and the Greek καβάλλης both mean *workhorse*; however, our cabal really supports the considerable weight, the burden of ancient knowledge and medieval chivalry, heavy baggage of esoteric truths transmitted by it through the ages. It was the secret language of the *cabaliers*, riders or knights. Initiates and intellectuals of antiquity all knew about it. Both, in order to access the fullness of knowledge, rode metaphorically the mare (cavale), a spiritual vehicle whose typical image is the winged Pegasus of the Hellenic poets. He alone facilitated the access of the chosen ones to the unknown regions; he offered them the possibility of seeing and understanding everything, through space and time, ether and light... Pegasus, in Greek Πήγασος, takes his name from the word πηγή, source, because made Hipocrene's fountain sprout from the ground with one kick, it is said, but the truth is of another order.

---

13 These student travellers wore a yellow, wool or knitted silk net around their necks as a sign of recognition and affiliation, as evidenced by *Liber Vagaborum*, published around 1510, attributed to Thomas Murner or Sébastien Brant, and Schimpf und Ernst, dated 1519.

It is because the cabala provides the cause, gives the principle, reveals the source of the sciences, that its animal hieroglyph has received the special and characteristic name that it bears. To know the cabala is to speak the language of Pegasus, the language of the horse, of which whose effective value and esoteric power is expressly indicated by Swift in one of its Allegoric Trips.

The mysterious language of the philosophers and disciples of Hermes, the cabala dominates all the didactics of the Great Art, as the symbolism embraces all the iconography. Art and literature thus provide the hidden science with the support of their own resources and their faculties of expression. In fact, and despite their peculiar character, their distinct technique, cabala and symbolism take different paths to reach the same goal and to merge into the same teaching. These are the two master columns, erected on the corner stones of the philosophical foundations, which support the alchemical pediment of the temple of wisdom.

All idioms can give shelter to the traditional meaning of cabalistic words, because the cabala, devoid of texture and syntax, adapts easily to any language, without altering its special genius. It brings to the dialects the substance of its thought, with the original meaning of names and qualities. So that any language is always likely to convey it, to incorporate it and, consequently, to become cabalistic by the double meaning it takes this way..

Apart from its pure alchemical role, the cabala has served as a tool in the development of several literary masterpieces, which many dilettantes know how to appreciate, without however suspecting what treasures they conceal under the pleasure, the charm or the nobility of style. It is because the authors, whether they have Homer, Virgil, Ovid, Plato, Dante or Goethe, were all great initiates. They wrote their immortal works, not so much to leave to posterity the imperishable monuments of human genius, as to instruct it in the sublime knowledge of which they were the depositories, and which they ought to transmit in their integrity. Thus we must judge, apart from the masters already mentioned, the marvelous artisans of poems of chivalry, epic poems, etc., belonging to the cycle of the Round Table and Grail ; the works of François Rabelais and those of Cyrano Bergerac; the *Don Quixote,* by Miguel Cervantes; the *Gulliver's Travels,* by Swift; the *Dream of Polylphilus,* by Francisco Colonna; the *Tales of Mother Goose,* by Perrault; the Songs of the King of Navarre, by Thibault de Champagne; *The Devil as a Predicator,* a curious Spanish work of which we do not know the author, and many other works which, although less famous, are not inferior to them either in interest or in science.

We will limit here this exposition of the solar cabala, having not received a license to make a complete treaty of it, nor to teach what are its rules. It is enough for us to have pointed out the important place occupied by it in the study of the "secrets of nature" and the necessity for the beginner to find the key of it. But, in order to be useful to him as much as possible, we will give, by way of example, the plain language version of an original cabalistic text of Naxagoras. Let us hope that the son of science will discover the manner of interpreting sealed books, and take advantage of such obscure teaching. In his allegory, the Adept endeavored to describe the ancient and simple path, the only one formerly followed by the old alchemist masters.

The following pamphlet is inserted at the end of the Treaty of Naxagoras, entitled *Alchymia denudata.* We made this version after a French translation written on the original book written in German.

Eighteenth-century translation of the original German Naxagoras text.	Version, in plain language, of the Cabalistic text of Naxagoras.
Description	**Description**
Well detailed description of the Golden Sand found near Zwickau, in Misnie around Niederhihendorff, and other nearby places,	A detailed description of how to extract, to liberate the Spirit of the Gold, enclosed in the vile mineral matter, with the intention of building up the sacred Temple of Light* and to discover other analogous secrets,
by JNVEJE ac. 5 Pct. ALC. 1715.	by JNVEJE comprising five points Alchemy. 1715.
It will soon be two years since a man from these mines had, from a third person, a small excerpt of a manuscript in quarto, about one inch thick, which came from two other Italian travelers who they named themselves therein.	It will soon be two years ago that a worker, skilled in metallic art, obtained, by a third agent,** an extract of the four elements, manually obtained by assembling two mercuries of the same origin, which their excellence has qualified as Roman, and who have always been so named.
It had been a long time since this extract had been well examined by MNN, because the latter counted to do much by the divining rod. At last he managed to touch his hands with what he was looking for. Here is the excerpt from this manuscript.	By this extract, known from antiquity and well studied by the Moderns, great things can be done, provided that we have received the illumination of the Holy Ghost. It is then that one manages to touch with his hands what one seeks. Here is the manual technique for this extract.
I. A village, named Hartsmanngrünn, near Zwickau. Under the village, there are many good grains. The mine is in veins.	I. A scoria surfaces above the mixture, formed by the fire, of the pure parts of the vile mineral matter. Underneath the scoria is a granular friable water. It is the vein or the metallic matrix.
II. Kohl-Stein, near Zwickau. There is a good vein of marcasite and lead grits. Behind Gabel, there is a blacksmith named Morgen-Stern who knows where there is a good mine, and an underground tunnel, and where cracks have been practiced. Inside there are yellow freezes, and the metal is malleable.	II. Such is the Stone Kohl,† concretion of the pure parts of the manure or Vile mineral matter. Friable and granular vein, it is born from iron, tin and lead. It alone bears the imprint of the solar ray. It is the expert craftsman in the art of steel-work. The wise call it Morning Star. It knows what the artist is looking for. It is the underground path that leads to the yellow, malleable and pure gold. Hard road and cut of crevasses, and obstacles.

* This is the name of the stone philosopher's, our microcosm, compared to the temple of Jerusalem, figure of the universe or macrocosm.

** The secret fire.

† Still called Alcohol, Water of life of the wise: it is the stone of fire of Basil Valentine.

III. Going from Schneeberg to the castle called Wissembourg, there is a little water flowing towards the mountain; it falls in the Mulde, opposite this water, there is a pond near the river, and beyond this pond, there is a little water where we find a marcasite which may well to compensate for the trouble we have taken to go there.	III. Having this stone, called Mountain of the Plyers,* go up to the White Fortress. It is the living water, which falls from the disintegrated body, into an impalpable powder, under the effect of a natural grinding comparable to that of a grinding stone. This white and lively water is agglomerated in the center, in a crystalline stone, of a color similar to tin-plated iron, which can greatly compensate for the pain required by the operation.
IV. At Kauner-Zehl, on the mountain of Gott, two leagues from Schoneck, there is an excellent copper sand.	IV. This luminous and crystalline salt, the first being of the Divine Body, will be formed, in a second stage, in copper-colored glass. It's our copper or brass, and the green lion.
V. At Grals, in Voigtland, below Schlossberg, there is a garden with a rich gold mine, what I have recently noticed. Take good note.	V. This calcined sand, will give its dye to the golden bough. The young sprouting of the sun will be born in the land of fire. It is the burnt substance of the stone, the closed rock of the garden** where our golden fruit ripens, as I have recently ascertained. Take good note of this.
VI. Between Werda and Laugenberndorff there is a pond called Mansteich. Below this pond is an old fountain at the bottom of the meadow. In this fountain, we find gold grains that are very good.	VI. Between this product and the second, stronger and better, it is useful to return to the Pond of the Dead Light,† by the extract returned in its original material . You will find the living water, dilated, without consistency. What will come from it is the Ancient Fountain,‡ generator of vigor, capable of changing the vile metals into gold grains.
VII. In the wood of Werda, there is a ditch, called Langgrab. Going to the top of this ditch, we find, in the ditch itself, a pit. Entering this pit, for the length of an alder, towards the mountain, you will find a vein of gold the length of a span.	VII. In the Green Forest lies the strong, the robust and the best of all.# There is also the Pond of the Crayfish.†† Follow it: the substance will separate by itself. Leave the ditch: its source is at the bottom of a cave where the stone, enclosed in its mine, grows.
VIII. At Hundes-Hubel there is a pit where there are gold grains en masse. This pit is in the village, near a fountain where the people fetch water for drinking.	VIII. During the increase, as you repeat, you will see the fountain full of brilliant granulations of pure gold. It is in the scoria, or in the matrix, enclosing the fountain of dry water, generator of gold, which the metallic people avidly drink.

    *   Because of his signature. Tenaille, in Greek, is λαβίς, from λαμβάνω, take, get, collect, and also conceive, become pregnant.

       ** Garden of the Hesperides.

       †   Second putrefaction, characterized by the violet, indigo or black coloration.

       ‡   The Fountain of Youth, first Universal Medicine, then Powder of projection.

       #   Cf. Cosmopolitan. The king of art is hidden "in the green forest of the nymph Venus".

       †† Constellation of the Zodiac of the philosophers, sign of the increase of fire.

IX. After having made different trips to Zwickau, to the small town of Schlott, to Saume and Crouzoll, we stopped at Brethmullen, where that place used to be. In the road that used to lead to Weinburg, which was call Barenstein, facing or towards the mountain going to Barenstein, or from behind in front of the setting sun, to the fibula, which was there in another time, there is an old well into which it passes through a vein. It is strong and very rich in good gold from Hungary and sometimes, even in gold from Arabia. The vein signal is on four metal separators "Auff-seigers vier", and beside it is written "Auff-seigers eins". It is a real mother lode.	IX. After various tests on the vile matter, until the yellow color, or fixation of the body, then thence to the crowned sun, we had to wait until the matter had been completely cooked in the water, according to the method of olden days. This long coction, formerly followed, led to the Luminous Castle or Brilliant Fortress, which is that heavy, western stone which is attained, without exceeding it, our own way, ...* For the truth comes out of the ancient well of this powerful tincture, rich in gold seed, as pure as the gold of Hungary, and sometimes even as the gold of Arabia. The sign, formed of four rays, designates and seals the mineral reducer. It is the largest of all tinctures.

*   Graphic symbol of the philosophical Vitriol. The points of suspension appear in the original.

But in order to close, on a less austere note, this study of the secret language designated by the name of hermetic or solar cabal, we will show how far historical credulity can go, when a blind ignorance allows to attribute to certain characters which only belonged to allegory and legend. The historical facts we offer to the reader's meditation are those of a monarch of Roman antiquity. We will scarcely need to point out the peculiar peculiarities, nor to underline all the cabalistic relations, so much they are evident and expressive.

The famous Roman emperor Varius Avitus Bassianus, saluted by the soldiers –we do not really know why–, under the names of Marcus Aurelius Antoninus,[14] Was nicknamed –it is not known more–, Elagable or Heliogabal.[15] "Born in 204, says the Encyclopedia, died in Rome in 222, he was descended from a Syrian family,[16] dedicated to the worship of the Sun at Emese.[17] He himself was, at a very young age, the high priest of this god, who was worshipped in the form of a black stone[18] and under the name of Elagabale. He was claimed to be the son of Caracalla. His mother, Sæmias[19] frequented the court and was below slander. Be that as it may, the beauty of the young high priest seduced the legion of Emesa, who proclaimed him Augustus at the age of fourteen. Emperor Macrin marched against him, but was beaten and killed.

14 Cabalistically, the assembly of raw material, Olympic or divine gold, and mercury . The latter, in the allegorical tales, always bears the name of Antony, Antoninus, Antolin, etc., with the epithet of pilgrim, messenger or traveler.

15 The Horse of the Sun, the bearer of science, the Solar Cabal.

16 Συρία or σισύρα, coarse skin coated with his hair: the future fleece of gold.

17 Ἔμεσις, vomiting: this is the scoria of the previous text.

18 The Philosophers' Stone, raw material, subject of art drawn from the original chaos, black in colour, but *primum ens,* formed by nature, of the Philosopher's Stone

19 Some historians call it Semiamira –half wonderful. At once vile and precious, abject and sought after, it is the prostitute of the Work. The wisdom makes her say of herself *Nigra sum sed formosa,* I am black, but I am beautiful.

"Heliogabalus' reign was nothing more than the triumph of superstitions and oriental debauchery. There is not infamy or cruelty that this singular emperor, with his cheeks covered in wax and his dragging dress, has not invented. He had brought his black stone to Rome, and forced the Senate and all the people to worship him publicly. Having removed from Carthage, the statue of Cælestis, which represented the Moon, he celebrated with great pomp and circumstance its wedding with his black stone, which depicted the Sun. He created a women's senate, married four women in succession, including a vestal, and one day gathered in his palace all the prostitutes of Rome, to whom he addressed a speech on the duties of their state. The Praetorians massacred Heliogabalus and threw his body into the Tiber. He was eighteen years old and had ruled four of them".

If this is not history, it is at least a beautiful story, full of "pantagruelism". Without failing in its esoteric mission, it would undoubtedly have, under the alert pen, the warm and colorful style of Rabelais, enormously gaining in flavor, in picturesque and in truculence.

VI

Before being elevated to the dignity of Cardinal Virtue, Prudence was for a long time an allegorical divinity to which the ancients gave a head to two faces –a formula which our statue reproduces exactly and in the most happy manner. Its anterior face offers the physiognomy of a young woman with a very pure curve, and its posterior face is that of an old man whose features, full of nobility and gravity, is prolonged in the silky waves of a river beard. Replica of Janus, son of Apollo and the nymph Créuse, this admirable figure does not yield to the other three nor in majesty, nor in interest.

Standing up, she is represented with her shoulders covered with the ample coat of the philosopher, which opens widely on the embossed chevron bodice. A simple shawl protects his neck; shaped like a cap around the old face, it comes to tie itself on the front, thus clearing the neck, embellished with a necklace of pearls. The skirt, with broad folds, is maintained by a cord with acorn, of heavy aspect, but of monacal character. Her left hand embraces the foot of a convex mirror, in which she seems to feel some pleasure in seeing her image, while her right hand holds the branches of a compass with dry points apart. A serpent, whose body appears gathered on itself, expires at its feet (Plate XXXVIII).

For us, this noble figure is a moving and evocative personification of Nature, simple, fertile, multiple and varied under the harmonious exterior, the elegance and perfection of the forms with which it adorns its most humble productions. Its mirror, which is that of Truth, has always been considered by classical authors as the hieroglyph of universal matter, and particularly recognized among them for the sign of the proper substance of the Great Work. Subject of the Sages, Mirror of Art are hermetic synonyms that veil the real name of the secret mineral from the common man. It is in this mirror, the masters say, that man sees nature in the open. It is thanks to him that he can know the ancient truth in its traditional realism. Because nature never shows itself to the researcher, but only through this mirror that keeps its image reflected. And to expressly show that this is our microcosm and the little world of sapience, the sculptor has shaped the mirror into a convex flat lens, which has the property of reducing the shapes while maintaining their respective proportions. The indication of the hermetic subject, containing in its tiny volume all that the immense universe contains, thus appears deliberate, premeditated, imposed by an esoteric imperative necessity, and whose interpretation is not in doubt. So that by patiently studying this unique

Cathedral of Nantes – Tomb of Francis II
Prudence (16th Century) – Plate XXXVIII

and primitive substance, a chaotic plot and a reflection of the great world, the artist can acquire the elementary notions of an unknown science, enter an unexplored field, fertile in discoveries, abundant in revelations, full of wonders, and finally receive the priceless gift that God reserves for elite souls: the light of wisdom.

Thus, under the outer veil of Prudence, appears the mysterious image of the old alchemy, and are we, through the attributes of the first, initiated into the secrets of the second. Moreover, the practical symbolism of our science lies in the presentation of a formula with two terms, two essentially philosophical virtues: prudence and simplicity. Prudentia and Simplicitas was the favorite motto of masters Basil Valentine and Senior Zadith. One of the wood engravings in the Azothic Treaty represents, in fact, at the foot of the Atlas, supporting the cosmic sphere, a bust of Janus –Prudentia–, and a young child spelling the alphabet – Simplicitas. But, while simplicity belongs above all to nature, as the first and most important of its prerogatives, man, on the contrary, seems endowed with the qualities grouped under the global term of prudence: foresight, circumspection, intelligence, wisdom, experience, etc. And although all of them require, in order to achieve their perfection, the help and support of time, some being innate, others acquired, it would be possible to provide in this sense a probable reason for the double mask of Prudence.

Truth, less abstract, seems to be more related to the alchemical positivism of the attributes of our cardinal Virtue. It is generally recommended to combine "a healthy and vigorous old man with a young and beautiful virgin". In these chemical weddings, a metallic child must be born and receive the epithet of androgynous, because it derives both from the nature of sulphur, its father, and from that of mercury, its mother. But in this place lies a secret that we have not discovered among the best and most sincere authors. The operation, thus presented, seems simple and very natural. However, we were stopped for several years by the impossibility of obtaining anything. This is because philosophers have skillfully welded two successive works into one, all the more easily because they are similar operations, leading to parallel results. When the wise speak of their androgynous nature, they mean the artificially formed compound of sulphur and mercury, put in close contact, or, according to the accepted chemical expression, simply combined. This indicates the prior possession of sulphur and mercury previously isolated or extracted, and not of a body generated directly by nature, at the end of the conjunction of the old and the young virgin. In practical alchemy, what we know the least is the beginning. Therefore, this is the reason why we take every opportunity to speak from the beginning, preferably at the end of the Work. In this we follow Basile Valentine authorized advice, when he says that "he who has the material will always find a pot to cook it, and who has flour should not worry about being able to make bread". However, elementary logic leads us to seek out the progenitors of sulphur and mercury, if we wish to obtain, by their union, the philosophical androgynous, otherwise called Rebis. Compositum of composites, animated Mercury, etc., proper material of the Elixir. Of these chemical parents of sulphur and mercury principles, one always remains the same, and it is the virgin mother; as for the old man, once his role is completed, he must give way to the one who is younger than him. Thus, these two conjunctions will each generate a offshoot of a different sex: sulphur, of dry and igneous complexion, and mercury, of a "lymphatic and melancholic" temperament. This is what Philaletes and d'Espagnet want to teach by saying that "our virgin can be married twice without losing any of her virginity". Others express themselves in a more obscure way, and content themselves with ensuring that "the sun and the moon of the sky are not the stars of philosophers". This means that the artist will never find the parents of the stone, directly prepared in nature, and that he will have to form first the hermetic sun and moon, if he does not want to be frustrated with the precious fruit of their alliance. We think we have said enough on this subject. Few words are enough for the wise man, and those who have worked for a long time will be able to benefit from our advice. We write for everyone, but everyone may not be called upon to hear us, because we are refused to speak more openly.

Folded back on itself, head turned backwards in the spasms of agony, the snake, which we see at the foot of our statue, is considered to be one of the attributes of Prudence; it is said to be very cautious in nature. We do not dispute this; but we will agree that this reptile, represented dying, must be so for the necessity of symbolism, because its inertia does not allow it to exercise such a faculty. It is therefore reasonable to assume that the emblem has another meaning, very distinct from the one assigned to it. In hermeticism, its meaning is similar to that of the dragon, which the sages adopted as one of the representatives of mercury. Let us recall the crucified serpent of Flamel, that of Notre-Dame de Paris, those of the caduceus, the one on the meditation crucifixes (which come out of a human skull serving as a base for the divine cross), the serpent of Aesculapius, the Greek Ouroboros −*serpens qui caudam devoravit*−, responsible for translating the closed circuit of the small universe that is the Work, etc. Now, all these reptiles are dead or dying, from the Ouroboros which devours itself, to those of the caduceus, killed with a blow of a stick, passing through the tempter of Eve, to whom the woman's posterity will crush the head (Genesis, III, 15). All express the same idea, contain the same doctrine, obey the same tradition. And the snake, hieroglyphic of the primordial alchemical principle, can justify the assertion of the wise, who assure that everything they seek is contained in mercury. He is truly the driving force, the animator of the great work, because he begins it, maintains it, perfects it and completes it. It is the mystical circle whose sulphur, the embryo of mercury, marks the central point around which it rotates, thus tracing the graphic sign of the sun, father of light, spirit and gold, dispenser of all earthly goods.

But, while the dragon represents the scaly and volatile mercury, produced by the subject's superficial purification, the snake, without wings, remains the hieroglyph of the common, pure and cleansed mercury, extracted from the body of Magnesia or first matter. This is the reason why some allegorical statues of Prudence have as their attribute the snake fixed on a mirror. And this mirror, the signature of the raw mineral provided by nature, becomes luminous by reflecting the light, that is, by manifesting its vitality in the snake, or mercury, that it kept hidden under its coarse envelope. Thus, thanks to this primitive living and invigorating agent, it becomes possible to restore to life the sulphur of dead metals. As the operation is carried out, the mercury, dissolving the metal, seizes the sulphur, animates it and dies, giving it its own vitality. This is what masters want to teach when they order to kill the living to resurrect the dead, to corporify the spirits and to revive the corporifications. Possessing this living and active sulphur, qualified as philosophical, in order to mark its regeneration, it will suffice to unite it, in appropriate proportion, to the same living mercury, to obtain, by the interpenetration of these living principles, the philosophical or animated mercury, material of the philosopher's stone. If we have understood well what we have tried to translate above, and if we bring together what is said here, the first two doors of the Work will be easily opened.

In short, one who has a fairly extensive knowledge of the practice will notice that the main secret of the work lies in the artifice of dissolution. And as it is necessary to carry out many of these operations –different in purpose, similar in technique– there are so many secondary secrets which, strictly speaking, really form only one. All art is reduced to dissolution, everything depends on it and how to perform it. This is the *secretum secretorum*, the key of the magisterium hidden under the enigmatic *axiom solve et coagula*: dissolve (the body) and coagulate (the spirit). And this is done in a single operation comprising two dissolutions, one violent, dangerous, unknown, the other easy, convenient, of a common use in the laboratory.

Having described elsewhere the first of these dissolutions and given, in unveiled allegorical style, the indispensable details, we shall not return to it.[20]

But in order to specify its character, we will draw the attention of the laborious to what distinguishes it from chemical operations understood under the same term. This indication may not be useless.

We have said, and we repeat, that the object of philosophical dissolution is the obtaining of sulphur which, in the Magisterium, plays the role of a forming agent by coagulating the mercury associated with it, a property which it holds from its ardent, igneous and desiccant nature. "Everything that dries eagerly drinks its wet," says an old alchemical axiom. But this sulphur, during its first extraction, is never stripped of the metallic mercury with which it forms the central nucleus of the metal, called essence or seed. Hence it follows that sulphur, preserving the specific qualities of the dissolved body, is in reality only the purest and most subtle portion of this very body. Consequently, we are entitled to consider, with the plurality of masters, that philosophical dissolution achieves the absolute purification of

---

20 In order to illustrate these precious indications of the Master, we add the beautiful and so telling composition of the god's Precious Gift, "written by Georges Aurach and painted with his own hand, the year of Salvation of the redeemed humanity, 1415" (see plate XXXIX, in the next page).

GOD'S PRECIOUS GIFT (15th century Manuscript)
Second Drawing – Georges Aurach – Plate XXXIX

imperfect metals. However, there is no example, whether spagyric or chemical, of an operation likely to produce such a result. All purifications of metals treated by modern methods are used only to remove the least persistent surface impurities. And these, brought from the mine or led to the reduction of ore, are generally not very important. On the contrary, the alchemical process, dissociating and destroying the mass of heterogeneous materials fixed on the nucleus, consisting of very pure sulphur and mercury, ruins most of the body and makes it resistant to further reduction. For example, one kilogram of excellent Swedish iron, or electrolytic iron, provides a proportion of radical metal, of perfect homogeneity and purity, varying between 7.24 and 7.32 grams. This very bright body is endowed with a magnificent purple coloring, which is the color of pure iron, similar to that of iodine vapors in terms of brightness and intensity. It should be noted that the sulphur of the iron, isolated, being red incarnate, and its mercury colored in light blue, the purple coming from their combination reveals the metal in its entirety. Subjected to philosophical dissolution, silver leaves few impurities, compared to its volume, and gives a body of yellow color almost as beautiful as that of gold, of which it does not have the high density. Already, as we taught at the beginning of this book, the simple chemical dissolution of silver in azotic acid detaches a tiny fraction of pure, golden-colored silver from the metal, which is sufficient to prove the possibility of a more energetic action and the certainty of the result that can be expected.

No one can dispute the importance and preponderance of dissolution, both in chemistry and alchemy. It is at the forefront of laboratory operations, and it can be said that most chemical work is dependent on it. In alchemy, the entire Work contains only a series of various solutions. We cannot be surprised, therefore, by the response of the Spirit of Mercury to Brother Albert in the dialogue that Basil Valentine gives us in the book of the *Twelve Keys*. "How can I have this body?" asks Albert; and the Spirit replies: By dissolution. "Whatever the method used, wet or dry, it is absolutely essential. What is fusion, if not a solution of the metal in its clean water? Similarly, inquartation, as well as the production of metal alloys, are real chemical solutions of metals by each other. Mercury, which is liquid at ordinary temperature, is nothing more than a molten or dissolved metal. All distillations, extractions, purifications require a prior solution and are only carried out after its completion. What about the discount? Is it not also the result of two successive solutions, that of the body and that of the reducer? If a zinc slide is immersed in a first solution of gold trichloride, a second solution, that of zinc, immediately engages and the reduced gold precipitates into an amorphous powder. The cupellation also demonstrates the need for a first solution –that of the alloyed or impure precious metal, by lead, while a second, the fusion of the formed surface oxides, eliminates them and perfect the operation. As for the special, clearly alchemical manipulations –imbibition, digestion, maturation, circulation, putrefaction, etc.– they depend on an earlier solution and represent so many different effects from the same cause.

But what distinguishes the philosophical solution from all the others, and at the very least ensures it a real originality, is that the solvent does not assimilate to the basic metal offered to it; it only removes the molecules, by breaking its cohesion, seizes the particles of pure sulphur which they can retain and leaves the residue, formed by the majority of the body, inert, disintegrated, sterile and completely irreducible. Therefore, a metallic salt cannot be obtained with it, as it is done with chemical acids. Moreover, known since antiquity, the philosophical solvent has never been used except in alchemy, by manipulators who are experts in the practice of the special skill required for its use. It is the latter that the sages talk about when they say that the Work is made of a unique thing. Unlike chemists and spagyrists, who have a collection of various acids, alchemists have only one agent, which has received many different names, the latest of which is Alkahest. To take the composition of liquors, simple or complex, qualified as alkahests, would take us too far, because the chemists of the 17th and 18th centuries each had their own particular formula. Among the best artists who have long studied the mysterious solvent of Jean-Baptiste Van Helmont and Paracelsus, we will only mention: Thomson (*Epilogismi chimici*, Leiden, 1673); Welling (*Opera cabalistica*, Hamburg, 1735); Tackenius (*Hippocrates chimicus*, Venice, 1666); Digby (*Secreta medica*, Frankfurt, 1676); Starckey (*Pyrotechnia*, Rouen 1706); Vigani (*Medulla chemiæ*, Dantzig, 1682); Christian Langius (*Opera Omnia*, Frankfurt, 1688); Langelot (*Salamander*, vid. Tillemann, Hamburg, 1673); Helbigius (*Introïtus ad Physican inauditam*, Hamburg, 1680); Frédéric Hoffmann (*De acido et viscido*, Frankfurt, 1689) ; Baron Schrœder (*Pharmacopæa*, Lyon, 1649); Blanckard (*Theatrum chimicum*, Leipzig, 1700) ; Quercetanus (*Hermes medicinalis*, Paris, 1604) ; Beguin (*Elemens de Chymie*, Paris, 1615) ; J.-F. Henckel (*Flora Saturnisans, Paris*, 1760).

Pott, a student of Stahl, also points to a solvent which, judging by its properties, would suggest its alchemical reality if we had not been better informed of its true nature.

The way our chemist describes it; the care he takes to keep its composition secret; the desired generalization of qualities that he usually strives to specify more precisely, would tend to prove it. "We still have to talk about an oily, anonymous solvent that no chemist I know of has clearly mentioned. It is a clear, volatile, pure, oily, flammable liquor like the spirit of wine, acid like good vinegar, and which passes through the distillation in the form of nebulous flakes. This liquor, digested and cohobated on metals, especially after they have been calcined, dissolves almost all of them; it extracts a very red tincture from gold, and when it is removed from the surface of the gold, a resinous material remains, entirely soluble in the spirit of wine, which acquires, in this way, a beautiful red color. The residue is totally irreducible, and I am sure that the salt of the gold could be prepared from it. This solvent mixes indifferently with aqueous or fatty liquors; it converts corals into a sea green liquor that appears to be their first state. It is a liquor saturated with ammonia salt and fat at the same time, and to say what I think about it, it is the true menstruum of Weidenfeld, or the wine spirit of philosophers, since the white and red wines of Raymond Lulle are removed from the same material. This is what makes Henry Khunrath give, in his Lunar components, in his Amphitheatrum, the name of fire-water and water-fire, because it is certain that Juncken was deeply mistaken when he tried to persuade that it is in the spirit of wine that we must seek the anonymous solvent of which we speak. This solvent provides a urinary spirit of a singular nature, which seems in some points to differ entirely from ordinary urinary spirits; it still provides a kind of butter that has the consistency and whiteness of antimony butter; it is extremely bitter and of medium volatility; these two products are very appropriate, both of them, to extract metals. The preparation of our solvent, although obscure and hidden, is however very easy to do; I will be dispensed from saying more about this matter because, as I have known it for a very short time and have been working on it, I still have a large number of experiments to do to make sure of all its properties. Moreover, not to mention the book *De Secretis Adeptorum,* by Weidenfeld, Dickenson seems to have discovered this menstruum in his treatise entitled Chrysopoeia".[21]

Without contesting Pott's probity, nor questioning the veracity of his description, and even less the one Weidenfeld gives under cabalistic terms, there is no doubt that the solvent of which Pott speaks is not that of the sages. Indeed, the chemical nature of its reactions and the liquid state under which it occurs, testify to this overabundance. Those who are instructed in the qualities of the subject know that the universal solvent is a true mineral, of dry and fibrous appearance, of solid, hard consistency, of crystalline texture. It is therefore a salt, and not a liquid or a flowing mercury, but a stone or stony salt, hence its hermetic qualifiers of Saltpetre (*sal petri,* stone salt), wisdom salt or Alembroth salt, which some chemists believe is the product of the simultaneous sublimation of mercury deuterochloride and ammonium chloride. And this is enough to remove Pott's solvent, as being too far from the metallic nature to be advantageously used in the work of the Magisterium. Moreover, if our author had kept in mind the fundamental principle of art, he would have been careful not to assimilate his particular liqueur to the universal solvent. This principle means, in fact, that in metals, by metals, with metals, can metals be perfected. Anyone who deviates from this first truth will never discover anything useful for transmutation. Consequently, if metal, according to philosophical teaching and traditional doctrine, is to be dissolved first of all, it should only be done with the aid of a metal solvent, which will be appropriate and very close to it by nature. Only similars can act upon similars. However, the best agent, extracted from our Magnesia

---

21 J.-H. Pott. *Dissertation sur le Soufre des Métaux, soutenue à Halle, en 1716* (Dissertation on Metal Sulphur), supported in Halle, in 1716). Paris, Th. Hérissant, 1759, t. I, p. 61.

or subject, takes the form of a metallic body, charged with metallic spirits, although strictly speaking it is not a metal. This is what committed the Adepts, to better remove it from the greed of the ambitious, to give it all possible names of metals, minerals, petrifications and salts. Among these names, the most familiar is certainly that of Saturn, considered as the metallic Adam. Therefore, we cannot complete our instruction better than by giving the floor to the philosophers who have dealt specifically with this subject. Here is the translation of a very suggestive chapter by Daniel Mylius, devoted to the study of Saturn, and which reproduces the teachings of two famous Adepts: Isaac the Dutchman and Theophrastus Paracelsus.

"No philosopher versed in hermetic writings does not know how high Saturn is, so much so that he must be preferred to the common and natural gold, and he is called the true gold and the subject matter of the philosophers. We will transcribe on this point the approved testimony of the most remarkable philosophers.

"Isaac Dutchman says in his *Vegetable Work*: Know, my son, that the stone of the philosophers must be made by means of Saturn, and when it has been obtained in its perfect state, it makes the projection both in the human body –outside and inside–, and in metals. Also know that in all vegetative works, there is no greater secret than in Saturn, for we find the putrefaction of gold only in Saturn where it is hidden. Saturn contains in its interior the pure gold, which is acceptable to all philosophers, provided that all its superfluity, i. e. the faeces, is removed from it and then it is purged. The outside is brought in, the inside manifested on the outside, and that is its redness, and it is then the Pure Gold.

"Saturn, moreover, easily enters into solution and coagulates in the same way; it lends itself willing to the extraction of its mercury. It can be easily sublimated, to such an extent that it becomes the mercury of the sun. For Saturn contains within it the gold Mercury needs, and its mercury is as pure as that of gold. It is for these reasons that I say that Saturn is, for our Work, much better than gold; for if you want to extract mercury from gold, it will take you more than a year to pull this body out of the sun, while you can extract mercury from Saturn in twenty-seven days. Both metals are good, but you can say with even more certainty that Saturn is the stone that philosophers do not want to name and whose name has, until now, been hidden. Because if we knew his name, many would have found, who are running after his research, and this Art would have become common and vulgar. This work would become brief and inexpensive. Also, to avoid these inconveniences, philosophers have hidden the name with great care. Some have wrapped him in wonderful parables, saying that Saturn is the vessel to which nothing foreign should be added, except what comes from him; in such a way that there is no man, however poor he may be, who cannot go to this Work, since it does not require great expenses, and that it takes little work and few days to obtain the Moon and, shortly afterwards, the Sun. We therefore find in Saturn everything we need for the Work. In him is the perfect mercury; in him are all the colors of the world that can manifest themselves; in him is the true darkness, whiteness, redness, and in him too is the weight.

"I entrust you therefore that one can understand, consequently, that Saturn is our philosophical stone and that bronze, from where the mercury and our stone can be extracted, in a little time and without great expenses, by means of our brief art. And the stone that we receive is our bronze, and the sharp water that is in it is our stone. And this is the Stone and Water on which philosophers have written mountains of books.

"Theophrastus Paracelsus, in the *Fifth Canon of Saturn*, says:

"Saturn thus speaks of his nature: the six (metals) joined me and infused their spirits into my decayed body; they added to it what they did not want and attributed it to me. But my brothers are spiritual and penetrate my body, which is fire, so that I am consumed by fire. In such a way that they (the metals), except the two, Sun and Moon, are purged by my water. My mind is the water that softens all the frozen and sleeping bodies of my brothers. But my body conspires with the earth, so much so that what is attached to this earth is made similar to it and brought back into its body. And I know nothing in the world that can produce that as I can. Chemists must therefore abandon all other processes and focus on the resources that can be derived from me.

"The stone, which in me is cold, is my Water, by means of which one can coagulate the spirit of the seven metals and the essence of the seventh, the Sun or the Moon, and, with the grace of God, enjoy as long as after three weeks one can prepare Saturn's menstruum, which will immediately dissolve the pearls. If the spirits of Saturn are melted in solution, they immediately coagulate en masse and tear off the animated oil from the gold; then, by this means, all metals and gems can be dissolved in an instant, which the philosopher will reserve for him as much as he considers appropriate. But I want to remain as obscure on this point as I have been clear so far".[22]

To complete the study of Prudence and the symbolic attributes of our science, we still have to talk about the compass that the beautiful statue of Michel Colombe holds in his right hand. We will do so briefly. Already, the mirror has informed us about the subject of art; the double figure, about the necessary alliance of the subject with the chosen metal; the snake, about the fatal death and the glorious resurrection of the body resulting from this union. In turn, the compass will provide us with the necessary additional information, which are those of proportions. Without their knowledge, it would be impossible to conduct and perfect the Work in a normal, regular and precise manner. This is expressed in the compass, whose branches are used not only for the proportional measurement of distances between them and for their comparison, but also for the perfect geometric layout of the circumference, an image of the hermetic cycle and the accomplished Work. In another part of this book, we have explained what these terms of proportions or weight mean –a secret veiled in the form of a compass– and have shown that they contain a double notion, that of the weight of nature and that of the weights of art. We will not return to this and will simply say that the harmony resulting from the natural, and forever mysterious, proportions is reflected in this saying of Linthaut: The virtue of sulphur extends only to a certain proportion of a term. On the contrary, the relationships between the weights of art, remaining subject to the artist's will, are expressed by the aphorism of the Cosmopolitan: The weight of the body is singular and that of water us plural. But, since philosophers teach that sulphur is likely to absorb up to ten and twelve times its weight of mercury, we immediately see the need for additional operations, of which the authors are poorly concerned: imbibitions and repetitions. We will act in the same way and submit these practice details to the beginner's own wisdom, because they are of easy execution and secondary research.

---

22 Daniel Mylius. *Basilica Philosophica*. Francofurti, apud Lucam Jennis, 1618. Tenth Council. *Théorie de la pierre des philosophes* (Philosophers' Stone Theory), Volume III, Book I, p. 67.

VII

In the cathedral of Nantes, the twilight gradually decreases.

Shade invades the ogival vaults, fills the naves, bathes the petrified humanity of the majestic building. At our side, the columns, powerful and low, rise towards the entangled arches, the crosspieces, the pendants that the growing darkness is now stealing from our eyes. A bell ringing. An invisible priest recites the evening prayer half aloud, and the bell tower from above answers the prayer from below. Only the quiet flames of the candles bite the darkness of the sanctuary with golden splinters. Then, after the service, a sepulchral silence hangs over all these inert and cold things, witnesses of a distant past, full of mystery and the unknown...

The four stone guardians, in their fixed attitude, seem to emerge, imprecise and unclear, from the midst of this half-light. The silent sentinels of the ancient tradition, these symbolic women, watching, at the corners of the empty mausoleum, the rigid, marmoreal images of scattered bodies, buried no one knows where, move and lead one to think. Oh vanity of earthly things! Fragility of human wealth! What remains today of those whose glory you were to commemorate and whose greatness you were to remember? A cenotaph. Even less: a pretext for art, a support for science, a masterpiece devoid of utility and purpose, a simple historical memory, but whose philosophical scope and moral teaching far exceeds the sumptuous banality of its first assignment.

And, before these noble figures of cardinal Virtues, veiling the four knowledge of the eternal Sapience, the words of Solomon (Prov., III, 13 to 19) come naturally to mind:

"Happy is the man that findeth wisdom, and the man that getteth understanding. For the merchandise of it is better than the merchandise of silver, and the gain thereof than fine gold. She is more precious than rubies: and all the things thou canst desire are not to be compared unto her. Length of days is in her right hand; and in her left hand riches and honour. Her ways are ways of pleasantness, and all her paths are peace. She is a tree of life to them that lay hold upon her: and happy is every one that retaineth her. The LORD by wisdom hath founded the earth; by understanding hath he established the heavens".

The Sundial of the Holyrood Palace of Edinburgh

It is a small building of extreme singularity. In vain do we question our memories: we cannot find an image analogous to this original and so strongly characterized work. It is rather an erected crystal, a gem raised on a support, a real monument. And this gigantic sample of mining productions, would be more in place in a museum of mineralogy than in the middle of a park where the public is not allowed to enter.

Executed in 1633, by order of Charles I, by John Milne, his master mason, with the collaboration of John Bartoun, it consists essentially of a geometric block, carved in regular icosahedron, with the sides carved with hemispheres and rectilinear-walled cavities, which is supported by a pedestal erected on a pentagonal base formed by three overlapping platforms. This base alone, having suffered from bad weather, had to be restored. Such is the Sundial of the Holyrood Palace (see plate XL, in the next page).

Antiquity, which we can always consult fruitfully, has left us a certain number of sundials of various forms, found in the ruins of Castel Nuovo, Pompeii, Tusculum, etc. Others are known to us from descriptions of scientific writers, Vitruvius and Pliny in particular. For example, the so-called Hemicyclium dial, attributed to Bérose (circa 280 BC), included a semicircular surface "on which a style marked the hours, the days and even the months". The one called Scaphe consisted of a hollow block, provided in the center of a needle whose shadow projected on the walls. It is believed to have been manufactured by Aristarchus of Samos (3rd century BC), as well as the Discus dial, made of a round, horizontal table with slightly raised edges. Among the unknown forms, of which most of us have only known names, were the dials: Arachne, where the hours were, it is said, engraved at the end of a thin threads, which gave it the appearance of a spider (the invention would be due to Eudoxe of Cnid, around 330 BC); Plinthium, a horizontal disk traced on a square column basis, was made by Scopus of Syracuse; Pelecinon, also Patroclus's horizontal dial; Conum, conical system of Dionysidore of Amisus, etc.

None of these forms or relationships correspond to that of the curious Edinburgh building; none can serve as a prototype. And yet, its name, the one that justifies its reason to be, is doubly accurate. It is both a multiple sundial and a real hermetic clock. Thus this strange

EDINBURGH - THE HOLYROOD PALACE
The Sundial – 1633 – Plate XL

icosahedron represents for us a double gnomonic work. The Greek word γνώμων, which has been entirely transmitted to the Latin and French languages (Gnomon), has a different meaning from that of the hand that indicates, by the shadow projected on a plane, the path of the sun. Γνώμων also refers to the one who becomes aware, who learns; it defines the prudent, the sensible, the enlightened. This word has as its root γιγνώσκω, which is still written γινώσκω, a double orthographic form whose meaning is to know, to understand, to think, to resolve. From there comes Γνῶσις, knowledge, erudition, doctrine, hence our French word Gnosis, the doctrine of the Gnostics and the philosophy of the Magi. We know that Gnosis was the set of sacred knowledge whose secrecy was carefully kept by the Magi and which was, for the initiated alone, the object of esoteric teaching. But the Greek root from which γνώμων and γνῶσις come, also formed γνώμη, corresponding to our gnome word, with the meaning of spirit, intelligence. However, the gnomes, underground geniuses who guard mineral treasures, constantly watching over gold and silver mines and gemstone deposits, appear as symbolic representations, humanized figures of the vital metallic spirit and material activity. Tradition tells us that they are very ugly and of very small stature; on the other hand, their naturalness is gentle, their character beneficial, their trade extremely favorable. It is then easy to understand the hidden reason for the legendary stories where the friendship of a gnome opens wide the doors of earthly riches...

The Gnomonic icosahedron of Edinburgh is therefore, apart from its actual destination, a hidden translation of the Gnostic Work, or Great Work of the Philosophers. For us, this small monument is not simply and solely intended to indicate the daytime time, but also the march of the sun of the wise in the philosophical work. And this march is regulated by the icosahedron, which is this unknown crystal, the Salt of Sapience, spirit or incarnate fire, the familiar and helpful gnome, friend of good artists, who ensures man's access to the supreme knowledge of ancient Gnosis.

Was the knighthood strange at all to the building of this curious Sundial, or at least to its special decoration? We do not think so and believe that we find proof of this in the fact that, on many sides of the solid, the emblem of the thistle is repeated with significant emphasis. There are, in fact, six flower heads and two flowering stems of the species known as *serratula arvensis*. Can we not recognize, in the obvious preponderance of the symbol, with the particular badge of the Knights of the Order of the Thistle,[1] the affirmation of a secret meaning imposed on the work and countersigned by them?

Moreover, did Edinburgh have, next to this Royal Order whose hieroglyphic esotericism leaves no doubt, a hermetic initiation centre placed under its dependence? We cannot say for sure. However, about thirty years before the construction of the sundial, fourteen years after the "official" suppression of the Order, which had become a secret Brotherhood, we see the appearance, in the immediate vicinity of Edinburgh, of one of the most learned Adepts and the most fervent propagators of the alchemical truth, Seton, famous under the pseudonym of the Cosmopolitan. "In the summer of 1601, writes Louis Figuier, a Dutch pilot named Jacques Haussen was attacked by a storm in the North Sea and thrown on the coast of Scotland, not far from Edinburgh, a short distance from the village of Seton or Seatoun. The shipwrecked were rescued by a local resident who owned a house and some land on this shore; he managed to save many of these unfortunate people, welcomed the pilot with great humanity into his house, and gave him the means to return to Holland".[2]

---

1   The Order of the Thistle, created by James V, King of Scotland, in 1540, originally consisted of twelve knights, like all the fraternities derived from the Round Table. It was also called the Order of Saint Andrew, because a chapel in the cathedral dedicated to the apostle was specially dedicated to them; the decoration bore the effigy of the chapel; and finally the Order's feast day was celebrated on November 30, the feast of Saint Andrew. Suppressed in 1587, it continued to exist secretly and was restored in 1687.

2   Cf. Louis Figuier. *L'Alchimie et les Alchimistes* (Alchemy and Alchemists). Paris, Hachette et Cie, 1856.

This man was named Sethon or Sethonius Scotus.[3]

The Englishman Campden, in his *Britannia* , reports, indeed, near the place of the coast where the pilot Haussen wrecked, a dwelling that he names Sethon House, and tells us to be the residence of the Earl of Winton. It is therefore probable that our Adept belonged to this noble family of Scotland, which would provide a valuable argument for the hypothesis of possible relations between Sethon and the Knights of the Order of the Thistle. Perhaps our man would have been formed in the very place where we see him practice those works of mercy and high morals which characterize high souls and true philosophers. Be that as it may, this fact marks the beginning of a new existence, devoted to the hermetic apostolate, wandering, eventful, brilliant, sometimes full of vicissitudes, lived entirely abroad, and which martyrdom tragically crowned two years later (December 1603 or January 1604). It seems, therefore, that the Cosmopolitan, solely preoccupied with his mission, never returned to his country of origin and that he left it, in 1601, only after having acquired the perfect mastery of the art. It was these reasons, or rather these conjectures, that brought us to bring the Knights of the Thistle closer to the famous alchemist, invoking the hermetic testimony of the Sundial of Edinburgh.

In our opinion, the Scottish sundial is a modern replica, both more concise and more scholarly, of the ancient Tabula Smaragdina. It consisted of two columns of green marble, according to some, or an artificial emerald plate, according to others, on which the Solar Work was engraved in cabalistic terms. Tradition attributes it to the Father of philosophers, Hermes Trismegistus, who declares himself the author, although his personality, very obscure, does not allow us to know if man belongs to the fable or to history. Some claim that this testimony of sacred science, originally written in Greek, was discovered after the Biblical flood in a rocky cave in the Hebron Valley. This detail, lacking even authenticity, helps us to better understand the secret meaning of this famous Table, which may well have never existed other than in the subtle and mischievous imagination of the old masters. We are told that it is green –like the spring dew, called for this reason Emerald of the Philosophers–, first analogy with the saline matter of the sages; that it was written by Hermes, second analogy, since this matter bears the name of Mercury, Roman deity corresponding to the Hermes of the Greeks. Finally, the third analogy, this green mercury used for the three Works, is called triple, hence the epithet Trismegist (Τρισμέγιστος, three times large or sublime) added to the name of Hermes. The Emerald Table thus takes on the character of a speech delivered by the mercury of the sages on the way in which the Philosopher's Work is elaborated. It is not Hermes, the Egyptian Thoth, who speaks, but rather the Emerald of the philosophers or the Isiac Table itself.[4]

---

3   This name is found in different spellings depending on the authors. Seton or Sethon is also called Sitonius, Sidonius, Suthoneus, Suehtonius and Seethonius. All these names are accompanied by the epithet Scotus, which refers to a Scot by birth. As for the Sethon Palace, in the former Haddingtonshire Parish, annexed to Tranent in 1580, it was first destroyed by the English in 1544. Rebuilt, Marie Stuart and Darnley stopped there on March 11, 1566, the day after Rizzio's murder; the queen returned there, accompanied by Bothwell, in 1567, after Darnley's murder. James VI (James VI of Scotland) stayed there in April 1603, when he came to take possession of the Crown of England. At the funeral of the first Earl of Winton, he attended the parade of the procession, sitting on a park bench. In 1617, this same monarch spent his second night in Seton, after crossing the Twed. Charles I and his court were received there twice in 1633. Today, there are no remains of this palace, which was completely destroyed in 1790. Let us add that Seton's family received its charter of ownership of the Seton and Winton lands in the 12th century.

4   The text of the Emerald Table, well known to the disciples of Hermes, can be ignored by some readers. So here is the most accurate version of these famous words:

The idea behind the Edinburgh dial reflects a similar concern. However, in addition to limiting his teaching to the alchemical practice alone, it no longer matters, in its qualities and nature, that he expresses, but only its physical form or structure. It is a crystalline building whose chemical composition remains unknown. Its geometric configuration only makes it possible to recognize the mineralogical characteristics of saline bodies in general. He teaches us that mercury is a salt, which we already knew, and that this salt has its origin in the mineral world. This is what Claveus, the Cosmopolitan, Limojon de Saint-Didier, Basile Valentine, Huginus à Barma, Batsdorff, etc., insistently repeat when they teach that the salt of metals is the stone of philosophers.[5]

We can therefore reasonably consider this sundial as a monument erected to the philosophical Vitriol, the initial subject and first being of the philosopher's stone. However, all metals are only salts, as evidenced by their texture and the ease with which they form crystallized compounds; in fire, these salts melt in their crystallization water and take on the appearance of oil or mercury. Our Vitriol obeys the same law, and, as it leads to success the artist happy enough to discover and prepare it, it has received from our predecessors the name of Victory Oil. Others, considering its color, and deliberately playing on its assonance, called it Huile de verre (*vitri oleum*, oil of glass), which marks its vitreous aspect, its fluidity with fire and its green colouring (*viridis*). It is this clear color that has made it possible to give it all the epithets that steal its true nature from the profane. Arnaud de Villeneuve tells us that it has been endowed with the names of trees, leaves, grasses and everything that has a green colorings, "in order to deceive fools". Metallic compounds, which give green salts, have contributed significantly to the extension of this nomenclature. Moreover, philosophers, overthrowing the order, enjoyed designating green things with hermetic qualifiers, to remind us of the importance that this color takes on in alchemy. Mercury, for example, or small mercury, which has become our macquereau (mackerel), is still used to disguise the sender's personality on April's Fool Day It is a mystical fish, the object of mystification. It owes its name and reputation to its brilliant green

---

"It is true, without lies, certain and very true:

"What is below is like what is above, and what is above is like what is below; by these things miracles are performed of one thing. And as all things are and come from ONE, through the mediation of ONE, so all things are born of this unique thing by adaptation.

"The Sun is the father, and the Moon the mother. The wind carried him in his belly. The Earth is its nurse and its receptacle. The Father of all, the Theme of the universal world is here. Its strength or power remains whole, if it is converted into earth. You will separate the earth from the fire, the subtle from the thick, gently, with great industry. He ascends from the earth and descends from heaven, and receives the power of the higher things and the lower things. In this way you will have the glory of the world, and all darkness will flee from you.

"It is strength, strong with all strength, for it will overcome all subtle things and penetrate all solid things. Thus, the world was created. From this will come out admirable adaptations, from which the means is given here.

"That is why I was called Hermes Trismegistus, having the three parts of universal philosophy.

"What I said about the Solar Work is complete".

The Emerald Table reproduced on a rock, in Latin translation, is found in one of the beautiful plates illustrating the *Amphitheatrum Sapientiæ Æternæ*, by Kunrath (1610). Joannes Grasseus, under the pseudonym of Hortulanus, gave a Commentary on it in the 15th century, translated by J. Girard de Tournus, in the *Miroir* d'Alquimie (Alchemy Mirror). Paris, Sevestre, 1613.

5   Pull the salt from the metals, says the Cosmopolitan, without any corrosion or violence, and this salt will produce white and red stone for you. The whole secret is salt, from which our perfect Elixir is made".

coloring, cut with black bands, similar to that of the mercury of the wise. Bescherelle reports that in 1430, the mackerel was the only marine fish that reached Paris, where, according to an ancient custom, it was prepared with green currants.[6] Do we know why the cuttlefish were given the name they bear? Simply because they lay green eggs, grouped in bunches of grapes. Our green mercury, the agent of putrefaction and regeneration, has caused the cuttlefish to be called σηπία, in the original language; the root of this word is σήπω, which means putrefy, reduce to rot. Thanks to its green eggs, cuttlefish has a cabalistic name, just like the Saturnia of the pear tree (*Saturnia pyri*), a large butterfly with emerald eggs.

The Greek alchemists used, in their formulas, to translate the hermetic solvent by the indication of its color. They assembled, to realize their symbol, two consonants of the word ΧΛΩΡΟΣ, green, X and P juxtaposed. Now, this typical figure exactly reproduces the Greek monogram of Christ, taken from his name. Must we see, in this similarity, the effect of a mere coincidence, or that of a reasoned will? The philosophical mercury is born of a pure substance, Jesus is born of a mother without spot; the Son of Man and the child of Hermes both lead the lives of pilgrims; both die prematurely, as martyrs, one on the cross, the other in the crucible; they rise again in the same way, the one and the other, the third day ... These are curious correspondences, certainly, but we could not affirm that the Greek hermetists have known them or that they have used them.

On the other hand, would it be a bold move to the point of recklessness to relate to the esotericism of our science such a practice of the Christian Church, which took place on May 1? On that day, in many cities, the clergy went in procession –the Green Procession–, cutting down the shrubs and branches that were decorated in the churches, especially those that were placed under the name of Our Lady. These processions are now abandoned; only the use of *mais* (decorated trees), which comes from them, has been preserved and is still being used in our villages. Symbolists will easily discover the reason for these obscure rites if they remember that Maia was Hermes' mother. We also know that the dew of May, or Emerald of Philosophers, is green, and that the Adept Cyliani metaphorically declares this vehicle indispensable for work. Therefore, we do not mean to imply that we must collect, following the example of certain spagyrists and the characters of *Mutus Liber*, the night dew of Mary's month, by attributing to it qualities of which we know it to be lacking. The dew of the wise is a salt, not a water, but it is the proper coloring of this water that serves to designate our subject.

Among the ancient Hindus, the philosopher's material was figured by the goddess Mudevi (Μύδησις, humidity, decay, from μυδάω, decay). Born, it is said, of the Sea of Milk, it was depicted painted green, mounted on a donkey, and carrying a banner in the middle of which was a raven.

Hermetic too, no doubt, the origin of this Feast of the Green Wolf, popular rejoicing which the use has long been held in Jumièges, and which was celebrated on June 24, day of solar exaltation, in honor of Saint Austreberthe. A legend tells us that the saint was laundering the linen of the famous abbey, where a donkey carried it. One day, the wolf strangled the donkey. St. Austreberthe condemned the guilty party to the service of his victim, and the wolf did it well until his death. It is the memory of this legend that the festival perpetuated. However, we are not given the reason why the green color was attributed to the wolf. But we can say, in a very certain way, that it is by strangling and devouring the donkey that the wolf becomes green, and that is enough. The "hungry and kidnapping wolf" is the agent indicated by Basil Valentine in the first of his *Twelve Keys*. This wolf (λύκος) is at first grey and

---

6   Cabalistically: coarse green salt.

does not let suspect the ardent fire, the bright light that he holds hidden in his coarse body. His encounter with the donkey makes this light manifest: λύκος becomes λύκη, the first light of the morning, the dawn. The grey wolf has dyed itself green, and it is then our secret fire, the nascent Apollo, Λυκηγενής, the father of light.

Since we gather in this place everything that can help the investigator to discover the mysterious agent of the Great Work, we will give him again the Legend of the Green Candles. This one refers to the famous Black Virgin of Marseille, Out Lady of Confession, which is housed in the crypts of the old abbey of Saint-Victor. This legend contains, behind the allegorical veil, the description of the alchemist's work to extract, from the coarse mineral, the living and luminous spirit, the secret fire it contains, in the form of translucent crystal, green, fusible like wax, and which the wise men call their Vitriol.

Here is this naive and precious hermetic tradition:

A young girl from ancient Massilia, named Martha, a simple little worker, and long orphaned, had dedicated a special cult to the Black Virgin of the Crypt. She offered her all the flowers she was going to pick on the hillsides –thyme, sage, lavender, rosemary–, and never failed, for whatever time it took, to attend the daily mass.

On the eve of Candlemas, the feast of Purification, Martha was awakened in the middle of the night by a secret voice inviting her to go to the cloister to hear the morning service. Fearing that she had slept more than usual, she dressed in haste, went out, and, like the snow, spreading its mantle over the ground, reflected a certain light, the believed that dawn was near She quickly reached the threshold of the monastery, whose door was open. There, meeting a cleric, she asked him to say a mass in his name; but, without money, she slipped from her finger a modest gold ring –her only fortune– and placed it, as an offering, under an altar candlestick.

As soon as the Mass began, what a surprise for the young girl when she saw the white wax of the candles turn green, of a celestial green, unknown, diaphanous green and brighter than the most beautiful emeralds or the most rare malachites! She could not believe it or take her eyes off it...

When the *Ite missa est* finally came to snatch her from the ecstasy of the prodigy, when she found, outside, the sense of familiar realities, she realized that the night was not over: the first hour of the day was only ringing at the belfry of Saint-Victor.

Not knowing what to think of the adventure, she went back to her home, but returned early in the morning to the abbey. There was already a great gathering of people in the holy place. Anxious and troubled, she inquired; she was told that no mass had been said since the day before. Martha, at the risk of being mistaken for a visionary, then told in details the miracle she had just witnessed a few hours earlier, and the faithful, in droves, followed her to the cave. The orphan had told the truth; the ring was still in the same place, under the candlestick, and the candles still shone with their incomparable green glow on the altar...[7]

In his Notice on the Ancient Abbey of Saint-Victor de Marseille, Father Laurin talks about the custom, which the people still observe, of carrying green candles to the processions of the Black Virgin. These candles are blessed on February 2, Purification Day, commonly known as the Candlemas Day. The author adds that "the candles of the Candlemas must be green, without the reason being well known. Documents indicate that green candles were in use elsewhere, in the monastery of the Sisters of Saint-Sauveur in Marseille in 1479 and in the

7   Cf. the small versified piece entitled *La Légende des Cierges verts* (The Legend of Green Candles), by Hippolyte Matabon. Marseille, J. Cayer, 1889.

metropolis of Saint-Sauveur in Aix-en-Provence until 1620, while elsewhere this use was lost and preserved in Saint-Victor".

These are the essential points of the symbolism peculiar to the Sundial of Edinburgh, which we wished to point out.

In the special decoration of the emblematic icosahedron, the visitor powerful enough to be able to approach it –because without any relevant reason he will never obtain authorization–, will notice, in addition to the hieroglyphic thistles of the Order, the respective monograms of Charles I, beheaded in 1649, and his wife, Marie-Henriette de France. The letters C R (*Carolus Rex*) apply to the first; M R (*Maria Regina*) refer to the second. Their son, Charles II, born in 1630 –he was three years old when the monument was built– is characterized on the faces of the stone crystal by the initials C P (*Carolus Princeps*), each topped by a crown, as well as those of his father. In addition to the arms of England, Scotland and the harp of Ireland, he will also see five roses and five separate and independent fleurs-de-lis, emblems of wisdom and chivalry, highlighted by the plume, formed by three ostrich feathers, which once adorned the knights' helmets. Finally, other symbols, which we have analyzed during these studies, will complete the clarification of the hermetic character of the curious building: the crowned lion, holding a sword with one leg and a scepter with the other; the angel, represented with his wings spread; Saint George knocking down the dragon and Saint Andrew offering the instrument of his martyrdom –the cross in X; the two roses of Nicholas Flamel, bordering with the shell of Saint-Jacques and the three hearts of the famous alchemist of Bourges, great silversmith of Charles VII.

We will finish here our visits to the old Philosopher's dwellings.

Admittedly, it would be easy for us to multiply these studies, for the decorative examples of the hermetic symbolism applied to civil constructions are still numerous today; we have preferred to limit our teaching to the most typical and well-characterized problems.

But before taking leave of our reader, thanking him for his kind attention, we will take a last look at the whole secret science. And, just as the old man, willingly evoking his memories, dwells on the salient hours of the past, so we hope to discover, in this retrospective examination, the capital fact, the object of the essential preoccupations of the true son of Hermes.

This important point, where the elements and principles of the highest knowledge are concentrated, cannot be sought or encountered in life, since life is within us, it radiates around us, it is familiar to us and we only need to know how to observe to grasp its various manifestations. It is in death that we can recognize it, in this invisible domain of pure spirituality, where the soul, freed from its bonds, takes refuge at the end of its earthly journey; it is in the nothingness, this mysterious nothing that contains everything, absence where all presence reigns, that we must find the causes whose multiple effects life shows us.

Also, is it at the moment when body inertia declares itself, at the very hour when nature finishes its work, that the sage begins his own. Let us then look at the abyss, scrutinize its depth, search the darkness that fills it, and nothingness will instruct us. Birth teaches little, but death, from which life is born, can reveal everything to us. She alone holds the keys of the laboratory of nature; it alone delivers the spirit, imprisoned in the center of the material body. Shadow dispenser of the light, sanctuary of the truth, asylum inviolate of the wisdom, it hides and jealously hides its treasures to timid mortals, to the undecided, to the skeptics, to all those who do not know it or do not dare to confront it.

For the philosopher, death is simply the linchpin that joins the material plane to the divine plan. It is the earthly gateway to heaven, the link between nature and divinity; it is the chain connecting those who are still to those who are no longer. And, if human evolution, in its physical activity, can at will dispose of the past and the present, on the other hand it is to death only that belongs the future.

Consequently, far from inspiring the wise man with a feeling of horror or repulsion, does death, an instrument of salvation, seem desirable to him because it is useful and necessary. And if we are not allowed to shorten ourselves the time fixed by our own destiny, at least we have received the license of the Lord to provoke it in the grave matter, subject, according to God's orders, to the will of man.

This explains why philosophers insist so much on the absolute necessity of material death. It is through it that the spirit, imperishable and always acting, brews, screens, separates, cleanses and purifies the body. It is from it that he takes the opportunity to assemble the assembled parts, to build with them his new dwelling, to finally transmit to the regenerated form an energy that it did not possess.

Considered from the point of view of its chemical action on the substances of the three kingdoms, death is clearly characterized by the intimate, profound and radical dissolution of the bodies. This is why dissolution, called death by the old authors, is affirmed as the first and most important of the Work's operations, the one that the artist must strive to achieve before any other. Whoever discovers the artifice of true dissolution and sees the subsequent putrefaction accomplished, will have in his power the greatest secret of the world. He will also have a sure way to access the sublime knowledge. This is the important point, this pivot of art, following the very expression of Philaletes, that we wished to point out to men of good faith, to voluntary and disinterested researchers.

However, by the fact that they are destined for final dissolution, all beings must necessarily derive a similar benefit from it. Our globe itself cannot escape this inexorable law. It has its time scheduled, as we have ours. The duration of its evolution is ordered, paid in advance and strictly limited. Reason shows it, common sense tells us, analogy teaches it, Scripture certifies it: In the noise of a terrible storm, heaven and earth will pass away...

For a time, times and half a time,[8] Death will extend its domination over the ruins of the world, over the remains of annihilated civilizations. And our land, after the convulsions of a long agony, will return to the confused state of original chaos. But the Spirit of God will float on the waters. And all things will be covered with darkness and plunged into the deep silence of the tombs.

End of the original 1930 version of the *Dwellings of the Philosophers*.

---

8 *Daniel*, ch. VII, 25, and XII, 7 *Revelation*, ch. XII, 14.

FULCANELLI

THE MYSTERY
OF THE CATHEDRALS

AND THE ESOTERIC INTERPRETATION
OF THE HERMETIC SYMBOLS
OF THE GREAT WORK

TRANSLATED FAITHFULLY FROM THE 1926 EDITION.
ILLUSTRATED WITH THE ORIGINAL
DRAWINGS FROM JULIEN CHAMPAGNE

www.ingramcontent.com/pod-product-compliance
Lightning Source LLC
Chambersburg PA
CBHW071856090426
42811CB00004B/626